Contents

p4   Introduction

p6   Experiments   Chapter 1

p28   Different kinds of experiments   Chapter 2

p50   Non-experimental techniques   Chapter 3

p88   Quantitative and qualitative methods   Chapter 4

p100   Inferential statistics   Chapter 5

p126   Plan your own study   Chapter 6

p136   Specification tables

p150   Glossary

p157   References

INTRODUCING RESEARCH METHODS

My younger daughter was once sitting in my study, watching me as I wrote about psychology. It suddenly occurred to her to ask 'So what is it that psychologists do?'

My answer was 'They try to explain why people do the things they do'.

After some further thought she asked 'How do they do that?'

The answer is that, once they have an explanation, they have to test it using research studies. And that is what this book is all about.

What you need to know

Research methods concepts are tricky. In order to understand them you need **practice**.

In this book there are **questions** on each spread to make sure you understand the concepts.

Suggested *answers* for these questions can be found on our website www.oxfordschoolblogs.co.uk/psychcompanion/blog/

On each spread there are also ideas for **mini studies** to help increase your understanding.

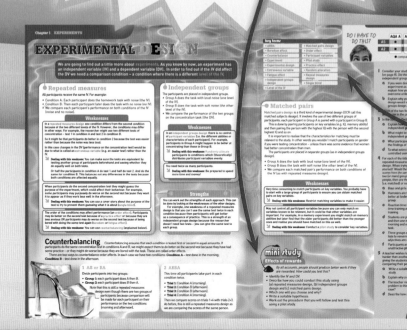

Key terms are defined in the glossary that starts on page 150.

Psychologists set up a situation where they can test cause-and-effect relationships.

Experiments

Psychologists ask people questions about their attitudes and what they think and feel.

Surveys: Questionnaires & interviews

Psychologists look at whether some aspects of human behaviour are linked.

Correlational analysis

Psychologists watch or listen to people.

Observations

Case studies

Psychologists study individuals or situations in detail.

Experiments

EXPERIMENTS

We introduce independent and dependent variables, and try out some experiments.

mini study Design your own study

PAGES 8–9

HYPOTHESES

A beginner's guide to writing a hypothesis.

mini study Assessing revision techniques

PAGES 10–11

ETHICS AND OTHER DESIGN ISSUES

We consider how to treat participants well, and also look at pilot studies and confederates.

mini study The Stroop effect

PAGES 12–13

EXPERIMENTAL DESIGN

Strategies to use to see if the independent variable did affect the dependent variable – repeated measures, independent groups or matched pairs.

mini study Effects of rewards

PAGES 14–15

SELECTION OF PARTICIPANTS

Techniques for getting a representative group of participants.

mini study How random is random?

PAGES 16–17

OPERATIONALISATION

More on writing hypotheses, to make them testable.

mini study Stress and friendship

PAGES 18–19

EXPERIMENTAL CONTROL

Keeping all variables constant, except the independent variable.

mini studies Testing some investigator effects

PAGES 20–21

DESCRIPTIVE STATISTICS

Ways to summarise your data – bar charts, medians and standard deviation.

mini study What month were you born?

PAGES 22–23

END OF CHAPTER TREATS

Multiple choice questions

Exam style questions 1 and 2

Model answers for exam style questions

PAGES 24–27

EXPERIMENTS

An **experiment** is a way of conducting research where:

One variable is made to change (by the experimenter)

[This is called the independent variable or IV]

The effects of the IV on another variable are observed or measured

[This is called the dependent variable or DV]

A variable is just a thing – something that can change. For example, noise is a variable – it can be soft or loud. Concentration is a variable – it can be high or low. Gender is a variable – it can be male or female.

Experiment 1

Does noise affect concentration?

The variable we are going to change (the **IV**) is noise. The two **levels of the IV** will be loud noise and soft noise.

The variable we are going to measure (the **DV**) is concentration.

Think for a moment about how you might do this.

You probably would decide to give people a task that assesses concentration. (One of my favourites on the internet is called 'mouse concentration game'.)

Divide your class in half into Group A and Group B.

Group A should have a radio playing very loudly while they do the task that assesses concentration. Record the time it took to complete the task.

Group B should do the same task in silence.

Which group performed the task more quickly?

Experiment 2
Drunken goldfish

Many early psychology experiments focused on learning in animals. The learning involved simple mazes where the animal is rewarded if it turns in the desired direction at the end of a maze shaped like a Y.

In one experiment goldfish were trained in a maze and afterwards placed in a water solution high in alcohol. Some of them keeled over.

When the goldfish were retested a week later those goldfish that had not been exposed to alcohol could remember the maze task perfectly but those who blacked out in the alcohol solution had no memory for the task. This demonstrates the severe effects of alcohol on learning (Ryback, 1969).

Don't try this experiment at home.

Experiment 3   Jazz bands

Can you get people to perform better simply by raising their expectations?

This was tested by telling musicians in one jazz band that they were playing a piece of music by a well-respected composer. Musicians in another jazz band were told that their piece of music was by a composer whose work had been negatively reviewed. The first band should play better.

However, there is a little problem with the design of this study. What if the first band played better because they actually *were* better? To overcome this problem the experiment could be designed so that both bands played two musical pieces: piece 1 and piece 2.

➤ Members of Band A were told that piece 1 was by the superior composer and piece 2 was by the inferior composer.

➤ Members of Band B were told that piece 1 was by the *inferior* composer and piece 2 was by the *superior* composer.

Weick *et al.* (1973) conducted this study and found that people did perform better if they thought they were playing well-respected work. Participants also remembered the piece better and liked it more.

People who take part in an experiment are called participants.

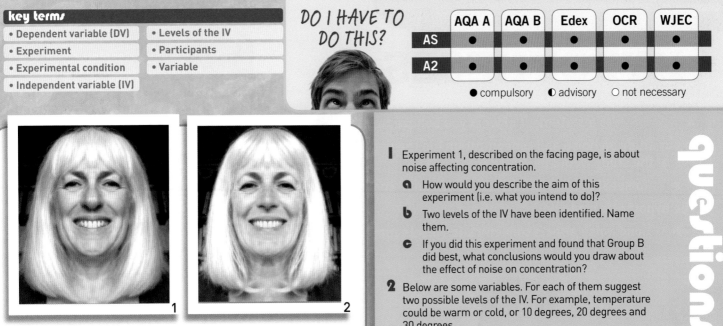
key terms
- Dependent variable (DV)
- Experiment
- Experimental condition
- Independent variable (IV)
- Levels of the IV
- Participants
- Variable

Experiment 4
The left side of the face

There are two photographs above. Which one would you rate as being more friendly?

One picture is a composite of the left side of my face and the other a composite of the right side of my face. (I don't really look like this!)

Some psychologists believe that the left side of your face (connected to the right side of your brain) should be better at displaying emotion. As it happens picture 1 is my left side.

You can do the same with a picture of your own face at www.symmeter.com/symfacer.htm

mini study
Design your own study

1. The place to start is with a research question. Here are a few suggestions:
   - *Are arts students more clever than science students?*
   - *Do blondes really have more fun than brunettes?*
   - *Can people detect water with a divining rod?*
   - *Or some other research question (that is legal and ethical).*

2. Work with a small group of other students and discuss the following questions:
   - What will the IV be?
   - What levels of the IV will you have? (These are called **experimental conditions**.)
   - What will you need to measure at the end? (This is the DV.)
   - How many participants will you need? Will everyone do both conditions? Or will you have two groups of participants (one for each condition)?
   - What will you expect to find?
   - What will the participants actually do?

3. When you have worked out what you will do, join with another group and explain your ideas to each other. The other group may ask useful questions that will help you to refine your ideas.

4. Conduct your study. You may be able to do this in class or each member of your group could go away and collect some data. Pool the data collected by your group and prepare a poster to present your results and conclusions.

1. Experiment 1, described on the facing page, is about noise affecting concentration.
   a. How would you describe the aim of this experiment (i.e. what you intend to do)?
   b. Two levels of the IV have been identified. Name them.
   c. If you did this experiment and found that Group B did best, what conclusions would you draw about the effect of noise on concentration?

2. Below are some variables. For each of them suggest two possible levels of the IV. For example, temperature could be warm or cold, or 10 degrees, 20 degrees and 30 degrees.
   a. Speed
   b. Jewellery
   c. Bananas
   d. Psychology students

3. You actually know all about experiments – you conduct them without thinking. For example, when you start a class with a new teacher you see how he or she responds to your behaviour – you might answer a question in class and make a joke on one occasion but no joke the next time to see if she likes jokes. You are experimenting with cause and effect.
   a. Identify the DV in this 'experiment'.
   b. There are two different IVs mentioned. Can you identify them?

4. Think about the goldfish experiment.
   a. What was the aim of this experiment?
   b. What was the IV?
   c. What were the two levels of the IV?
   d. What was the DV?

5. Look at the jazz band experiment.
   a. What was the aim of this experiment?
   b. What was the IV?
   c. What were the two levels of the IV?
   d. What was the DV?
   e. If participants did perform the piece by the superior composer better, what would you conclude from this study?
   f. How might you apply the results of this study to improving your own work?

6. Experiment 4 is about the left side of the face.
   a. What was the aim of this experiment?
   b. What was the IV?
   c. What were the two levels of the IV?
   d. What was the DV?
   e. If participants do select the right-hand photo more often, what would you conclude?
   f. Explain why it might be better to have several pairs of photos constructed in a similar way?

HYPOTHESES

A hypothesis is a statement of what you believe to be true.

In our study on noise and concentration (on the previous spread) the aim of the study would be:

➤ To see if loud noise affects participants' concentration.

The hypothesis could be:

➤ Loud noise affects concentration levels more than soft noise.

The following statements could also be hypotheses for the same experiment:

- Loud noise reduces concentration levels more than soft noise does.
- Loud noise has a different effect on concentration levels than soft noise.
- Noise affects concentration levels.
- Soft noise increases concentration levels whereas loud noise has the opposite effect.

Aim? Hypothesis? Help!

It is often difficult to understand the difference between research methods concepts, but your understanding will improve with experience.

- *The aim is a statement of what you are intending to investigate.*
- *The hypothesis states what you believe to be true, e.g. that noise affects concentration.*

The hypothesis should not be a prediction, e.g. 'I will find that noise affects concentration' or even 'Noise will affect concentration'. It is a statement of what you believe to be true: 'Noise has a negative effect on concentration'.

Why have directions?

Why do psychologists sometimes use a directional hypothesis instead of a non-directional one?

Often it makes sense to expect one condition to be better than the other. For example, when thinking of the noise and concentration experiment we might expect that loud noise would reduce concentration. Therefore, it makes sense to use a directional hypothesis.

Also, if you are repeating a study that was conducted before, it would make sense to follow what was previously found. So if a study found that people actually did better with the louder noise it would make sense to state this in the hypothesis.

Alternatively, it might make better sense to go for a non-directional hypothesis if there seems to be some doubt. For example, we might expect the results to go one way but one study found it went the other way. So we play safe and state no direction.

Psychologists use a directional hypothesis when past research (theory or study) suggests that the findings will go in a particular direction.

Psychologists use a non-directional hypothesis when past research is equivocal.

Different kinds of hypothesis:
Directional and non-directional hypotheses

A directional hypothesis states the kind of difference between two conditions or two groups of participants – higher or lower, faster or slower, better or worse and so on.

A non-directional hypothesis simply states that there is a difference between two conditions or two groups of participants.

Here are some examples:

Directional	Participants gain *higher* concentration scores when listening to soft noise than when listening to loud noise.
Non-directional	Concentration scores are *different* when the task is performed with a soft or a loud noise.
Directional	Participants who do homework with the TV on produce *lower* results than those who do homework with no TV on.
	Participants who do homework with the TV on produce *better* results than those who do homework with no TV on.
Non-directional	Participants who do homework with the TV on produce *different* results than those who do homework with no TV on.

One-tailed and two-tailed

Sometimes the terms 'one-tailed' and 'two-tailed' are used instead of 'directional' and 'non-directional'.

When you look at a one-tailed (directional) cat you know which way it is going.

But a two-tailed (non-directional) cat is going in both directions.

key terms

Aims

Alternative hypothesis

Conclusions

Directional hypothesis

Experimental conditions

Experimental hypothesis

- Hypothesis
- Non-directional hypothesis
- Null hypothesis
- One-tailed hypothesis
- Research hypothesis
- Two-tailed hypothesis

DO I HAVE TO DO THIS?

	AQA A	AQA B	Edex	OCR	WJEC
AS	●	●	●	●	●
A2	●	●	●	●	●

AQA A, AQA B and WJEC AS students do not need to cover the null hypothesis.

● compulsory ◐ advisory ○ not necessary

Different kinds of hypothesis

Experimental hypothesis

This is the hypothesis for an experiment.

Research hypothesis

This is the hypothesis written for any other kind of study.

Alternative hypothesis

This is just another term used for a hypothesis – it is used for statistical reasons that need not concern you now. It simply means it is the alternative to the null hypothesis.

Null hypothesis

Null hypothesis

In some circumstances (which you don't need to bother your head about) there is a need to state a null hypothesis.

The null hypothesis is not the opposite to the hypothesis. It is a statement of *no difference or no relationship*.

For example:
- There is no difference in the concentration levels of participants in the loud and soft noise conditions.
- There is no difference between drunken and sober goldfish in terms of their memory of the maze.
- There is no relationship between noise and concentration.

H_1

H_0

No, these are not chemical formulae. These are the abbreviations used for the alternative hypothesis (H_1) and the null hypothesis (H_0).

mini study

Assessing revision techniques

What is the best way to revise? Some people use visual images whereas others use words. Design a study to test this.

1. Work with a small group of other students and discuss the following questions:
   - What will the IV be?
   - What levels of the IV will you have? (These are the **experimental conditions**.)
   - What will you need to measure at the end? (This is the DV.)
   - How many participants will you need? Will everyone do both conditions? Or will you have two groups of participants?
   - What will you expect to find? State your hypothesis.
   - What will the participants actually do?
2. As before, show your design to some other people and make adjustments. Conduct your study and share your findings.
3. Draw **conclusions**. What have you learned about revision?

1 Read questions a–d below and identify which are aims and which is a hypothesis.

   a To see if blondes have more fun than brunettes.

   b Arts students are less clever than science students.

   c Whether alcohol causes goldfish to have poorer memories than no alcohol.

   d Positive expectations lead to differences in performance.

2 Write a hypothesis for the experiment on noise and concentration (on the previous spread).

   a Is your hypothesis directional or non-directional?

   b Try writing two more hypotheses, one directional and one non-directional.

   c Repeat this for the goldfish experiment on page 8.

   d Repeat this for the left side of the face experiment on page 9.

3 For each of the following, decide whether it is a directional or non-directional hypothesis.

   a Boys score differently on aggressiveness tests than girls.

   b Students who have a computer at home do better in exams than those who don't.

   c Participants remember the words that are early in a list better than the words that appear later.

   d Participants given a list of emotionally charged words recall fewer words than participants given a list of emotionally neutral words.

   e Hamsters are better pets than budgies.

   f Words presented in a phonemic form are recalled differently to those presented in a semantic form.

4 Now write your own. For each of the following experiments write a directional and a non-directional hypothesis.

   a A study to find out whether girls watch more television than boys.

   b A study to see whether teachers give higher marks on essays to more attractive students than to students who are less attractive.

   c A study to investigate whether lack of sleep affects schoolwork.

5 Explain the difference between an experimental hypothesis and a research hypothesis.

Questions on the null hypothesis.

6 Explain the difference between the alternative hypothesis and the null hypothesis. Use examples to help you.

7 Write a null hypothesis for each of the experiments described in question 4.

ETHICS *and other design issues*

Ethics relates to values of human behaviour, and the rightness or wrongness of our conduct. In your study of psychology so far, you may have considered whether certain studies showed sufficient ethical concern for the well-being and rights of the participants.

This is an important issue to consider when designing research. We will explore it in more detail later in the book but for now you need to have some awareness of ethical issues when designing and conducting your own research.

 This experiment may damage your health

Do not harm your participants

What constitutes 'harm'? Is it harmful for a person to experience mild discomfort or mild stress?

Brief your participants

Before you begin the study, you should ask participants if they are willing to take part.

How do they decide whether to take part or not? They need to have some information about what will be involved. For example, if you tell them that they will be receiving mild electric shocks, some potential participants may say 'no thanks'. But it wouldn't really be fair to give mild electric shocks without giving them the chance to say no.

So researchers must give participants information about any activities that might affect their decision to take part. This is called a **briefing** or asking for **informed consent**. (Note that it is not simply 'consent' but *informed* consent.)

Do not lie to your participants *(if possible)*

Is it acceptable to lie to participants about what an experiment is about? Is it acceptable to withhold information from participants about experimental aims? Such deception may be necessary so that participants' behaviour is not affected by knowing the aim of the experiment.

One way to deal with deception is to **debrief** participants afterwards. At the start of an experiment participants are briefed about what the task will involve. At the end they are debriefed.

Ethical This debriefing serves an ethical function. If any deception took place then participants should be told the true aims of the study and offered the opportunity to discuss any concerns they may have. They could be offered the opportunity to withdraw their data from the study.

Practical At the same time as debriefing takes place the experimenter could ask for further information about the research topic. For example, why the participant found one condition more difficult. This helps to make sense of the results.

Exam question: How would you conduct a pilot study?

Student answer: It is a small-scale trial run of a research study that involves looking at the procedures to see if they work.

Mark awarded zero.

What's wrong?

ANSWER *This answer concerns what a pilot study is, not how you would do it. A very common mistake made by students. Questions that begin with 'how' are different to 'what' questions.*

Pilot study

If you tried any of the experiments so far you probably were aware that there were problems with what you did. If you could repeat the study, you might do it differently.

Did you realise that there would be problems beforehand? Or did some of the difficulties only become apparent when you were doing the study? For example, some participants didn't understand what they had to do, or some participants talked to others throughout the task, or participants got bored.

If you didn't try these experiments, can you think what flaws in the design there might be?

The way to deal with this is to conduct a **pilot study** before the experiment proper. A pilot study is a small-scale trial run of a research design before doing the real thing.

It is done in order to find out if certain things don't work so you can correct them before spending time on the real thing.

Confederate

Sometimes the IV in an experiment involves the use of a person.

For example, you might want to find out if people respond differently to orders from someone wearing a suit or dressed in casual clothes. In this experiment the IV would be the clothing worn by a 'friend' of the experimenter. The experimenter would arrange for a person to give orders either dressed in a suit or dressed casually. This person is called a **confederate**.

Confederates are not always part of the IV, they may simply help guide the experiment.

Confederates are individuals in an experiment who are not real participants and have been instructed how to behave by the experimenter.

key terms
- Briefing
- Confederate
- Debrief
- Ethical issues
- Informed consent
- Pilot study

DO I HAVE TO DO THIS?

	AQA A	AQA B	Edex	OCR	WJEC
AS	●	●	●	●	●
A2	●	●	●	●	●

● compulsory   ◐ advisory   ○ not necessary

Example of a written debriefing

Thank you for taking part in our experiment. The true purpose of the study was to find out if it takes longer to identify the word colour when the word and colour are conflicting. This is called the Stroop effect.

1. Would you like to know the overall findings from the study? YES/NO

2. Did you feel distressed by any aspect of the study? YES/NO

3. What did you think the purpose of the study was? _____
   _____

4. Did you think that some of the lists were harder to read than others? YES/NO
   If so, which lists? _____

5. Do you think this might have affected your performance? YES/NO
   If so, how might it have affected your performance? _____
   _____
   _____

mini study
The Stroop effect

The is an all-time favourite study (Stroop, 1935). Before doing a full-scale project, first conduct a pilot study to check you understand what you need to do.

You will need:
- A stopwatch.
- A copy of the table of words on the right. This should be printed in colour and clear enough for participants to read. You can cut the table up so the five columns are on separate pieces of paper.
- It is also helpful to print the table out in black and white for the experimenter to use when checking the accuracy of each participant's performance.

Practice	List 1	List 2	List 3	List 4
brown	red	blue	green	brown
green	blue	green	purple	red
red	green	purple	blue	brown
purple	brown	red	green	purple
red	purple	brown	blue	green
brown	blue	red	brown	purple
green	red	blue	purple	brown
blue	brown	green	red	brown
red	green	brown	blue	red
blue	red	purple	green	purple
purple	purple	brown	blue	green
red	red	purple	red	brown
purple	blue	red	brown	green
green	brown	blue	purple	red
purple	purple	red	green	blue
red	red	green	brown	purple
green	green	blue	purple	red
red	purple	brown	red	green
purple	blue	purple	brown	red
green	purple	green	red	blue
purple	brown	purple	blue	green
blue	green	red	purple	brown
green	brown	green	brown	blue
brown	red	blue	green	purple
blue	green	red	purple	blue
purple	purple	brown	blue	red
blue	brown	blue	red	green
green	blue	green	brown	purple
brown	purple	brown	green	blue
purple	blue	purple	red	brown
stop	*stop*	*stop*	*stop*	*stop*

1 Consider the study on revision techniques on page 11.

a What are the aims of this study?

b If you told participants these aims, how do you think it would affect their behaviour during the study?

c How reasonable do you think it is to withhold this information about the aims of this study?

d What information about participation would you tell the participants in order to obtain their informed consent to take part?

e Identify at least **two** important things you would mention in the debriefing.

2 Consider the Stroop effect study.

a You decide to conduct a pilot study. What would you actually do in this pilot study?

b Outline **two** benefits of doing a pilot study for this research.

3 Research has found that people feel less nervous when taking a test if there is someone else in the room rather than if they are alone.

a This study would involve using a confederate. What would the confederate do?

b Identify at least **two** ethical issues that might arise in this study.

Instructions

1. Participants should read the practice list first with the experimenter so they can practise what they have to do. In order to do this:
   - Cover up lists 1–4.
   - Participants should state the word and not the colour the word is written in. For example, for the word 'blue' they should say 'blue'.
   - Participants should take great care to say the colour correctly and not race against the clock. Mistakes should be corrected.
   - The experimenter should check that the words are read correctly. In order to do this a non-colour version is easier to use.
   - Experimenter says 'start' to signal that the participant should begin reading the first list and at this time the experimenter should start the timer.
   - Participant says 'stop' at the end of the list, and the experimenter records how long it took to read the list.

2. Participants should now read the remaining lists. Each time they should cover up the remaining list and follow the same instructions as above.

EXPERIMENTAL DESIGN

We are going to find out a little more about experiments. As you know by now, an experiment has an independent variable (IV) and a dependent variable (DV). In order to find out if the IV did affect the DV we need a comparison condition – a condition where there is a different level of the IV.

Repeated measures

All participants receive the same IV. For example:

- Condition A: Each participant does the homework task with noise (the IV).
- Condition B: Then each participant later does the task with no noise (no IV).
- We compare each participant's performance on both conditions of the IV (noise and no noise).

Weaknesses

In a repeated measures design one condition differs from the second condition because of the two different levels of the IV. However, the conditions may differ in other ways. For example, the researcher might use two different tests of concentration – test 1 in condition A and test 2 in condition B.

So it might be that participants do better in condition 2 because the test was easier rather than because the noise was less loud.

In this case changes in the DV (performance on the concentration test) would be due to what is called an extraneous variable (e.g. an easier test) rather than the IV.

➘ **Dealing with this weakness:** You can make sure the tests are equivalent by testing another group of participants beforehand and seeing whether they do equally well on both tests.

➘ Or half the participants in condition A do test 1 and half do test 2. And do the same for condition B. This balances out any differences in the tests because both conditions are affected equally.

When participants do the second concentration test they might guess the purpose of the experiment, which could affect their behaviour. For example, some participants may purposely do worse on the second test because they want it to appear as if they work less well in the afternoon.

➘ **Dealing with this weakness:** You can use a cover story about the purpose of the test to try to prevent them guessing what it is about (single blind).

The order of the conditions may affect performance (an order effect). Participants may do better on the second test because of a practice effect or because they are less anxious OR participants may do worse on the second test because of being bored with doing the same test again (boredom or fatigue effect).

➘ **Dealing with this weakness:** You can use counterbalancing (explained below).

Independent groups

The participants are placed in independent groups.

- Group A does the task with loud noise (one level of the IV).
- Group B does the task with soft noise (the other level of the IV).
- We compare the performance of the two groups on the concentration task (the DV).

Weaknesses

In an independent groups design there is no control of participant variables (i.e. the different abilities or characteristics of each participant). For example, participants in Group A might happen to be better at concentrating than those in Group B.

➘ **Dealing with this weakness:** Randomly allocate participants to conditions which (theoretically) distributes participant variables evenly.

You need twice as many participants.

➘ **Dealing with this weakness:** Be prepared to spend more time and money!

Strengths

You can work out the strengths of each approach. This can be done by looking at the weaknesses of the other designs.

For example, one weakness of a repeated measures design is that you can't use the same test twice in each condition because then participants will get better as a consequence of practice. This is a strength of an independent groups design because the researcher doesn't need two tests – you can give the same test to each group.

Counterbalancing

Counterbalancing ensures that each condition is tested first or second in equal amounts. If participants do the same concentration test in conditions A and B, we might expect them to do better on the second test because they have had some practice – or they might do worse because they are bored with the task. These are called order effects.

There are two ways to counterbalance order effects. In each case we have two conditions: **Condition A** – test done in the morning; **Condition B** – test done in the afternoon.

1 AB or BA

Divide participants into two groups:

- **Group 1:** each participant does A then B.
- **Group 2:** each participant does B then A.

Note that this is still a repeated measures design even though there are two groups of participants because comparison will be made for each participant on their performance on the two conditions (morning and afternoon).

2 ABBA

This time all participants take part in each condition twice.

- **Trial 1:** Condition A (morning).
- **Trial 2:** Condition B (afternoon).
- **Trial 3:** Condition B (afternoon).
- **Trial 4:** Condition A (morning).

Then we compare scores on trials 1+4 with trials 2+3. As before, this is still a repeated measures design as we are comparing the scores of the same person.

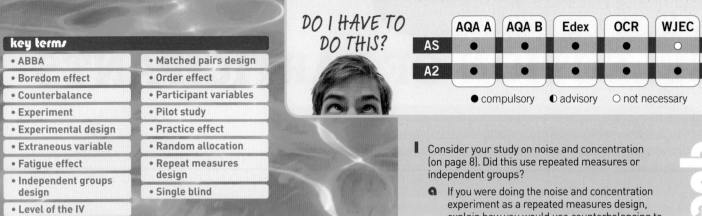

key terms

• ABBA	• Matched pairs design
• Boredom effect	• Order effect
• Counterbalance	• Participant variables
• Experiment	• Pilot study
• Experimental design	• Practice effect
• Extraneous variable	• Random allocation
• Fatigue effect	• Repeat measures design
• Independent groups design	• Single blind
• Level of the IV	

● Matched pairs

Matched pairs design is a third kind of experimental design (OCR call this matched subjects design). It involves the use of two different groups of participants; each participant in Group A is paired with a participant in Group B.

This is done by pairing participants on key variables (e.g. IQ, memory ability) and then pairing the person with the highest IQ with the person with the second highest IQ and so on.

It is important to realise that the characteristics for matching *must* be relevant to the study. In other words you wouldn't match participants on gender if you were testing concentration – unless there was some evidence that women had better concentration than men.

The participants are placed in separate groups (as in independent groups design).

- Group A does the task with loud noise (one level of the IV).
- Group B does the task with soft noise (the other level of the IV).
- We compare each matched pair's performance on both conditions of the IV (as with repeated measures design).

Weaknesses

Very time consuming to match participants on key variables. You probably have to start with a large group of participants to ensure you can obtain matched pairs on key variables.

➜ **Dealing with this weakness:** Restrict matching variables to make it easier.

May not control all participant variables because you can only match on variables known to be relevant, but it could be that other variables are important. For example, in a memory experiment you might match on memory abilities but later find that the older participants did better than the younger ones and realise you should have matched on this as well.

➜ **Dealing with this weakness:** Conduct a **pilot study** to consider key variables.

mini study
Effects of rewards

By all accounts, people should produce better work if they are rewarded. How could you test this?

- Identify the IV and DV.
- Describe how you could conduct this study using (a) repeated measures design, (b) independent groups design and (c) matched pairs design.
- Which one will you choose and why?
- Write a suitable hypothesis.
- Work out the procedure that you will follow and test this using a pilot study.

1 Consider your study on noise and concentration (on page 8). Did this use repeated measures or independent groups?

  a If you were doing the noise and concentration experiment as a repeated measures design, explain how you would use counterbalancing to overcome order effects.

  b Explain why you think that the repeated measures design would not be as good as the independent groups design.

2 Which of the two forms of counterbalancing (1 or 2) did we use in the jazz band experiment on page 8?

3 In the Stroop effect study (on the previous spread):

  a Explain how you could you do this as an independent groups design.

  b What might be the disadvantage of using an independent groups design for this experiment?

  c What participant variables might have affected the findings of the Stroop effect study?

  d To what extent were these participant variables controlled using the repeated measures design?

4 For each of the following experiments state whether it is repeated measures, independent groups or matched pairs design. When trying to decide it might help you if you ask yourself '*Would the findings be analysed by comparing the scores from the same person or by comparing the scores of two (or more) groups of people*'? If it is two or more groups of people, then are the people in the different groups related (i.e. matched) or not?

  a Boys and girls are compared on their IQ test scores.

  b Hamsters are tested to see if one genetic strain is better at finding food in a maze compared to another group.

  c Reaction time is tested before and after a reaction time training activity to see if test scores improve after training.

  d Students are put in pairs based on their GCSE grades, and then one member of the pair is tested in the morning and one tested in the afternoon on a memory task.

  e Three groups of participants are given different words lists to remember to see whether nouns, verbs or adjectives are easier to recall.

  f Participants are asked to give ratings for attractive and unattractive photographs.

5 A teacher wishes to find out whether one maths test is harder than another maths test. She plans to do this by giving the students in her maths class both tests and comparing their performance.

  a Write a suitable non-directional hypothesis for this study.

  b Explain why a non-directional hypothesis is appropriate.

  c The teacher realises that order effects may be a problem in this study. Explain why this might be the case?

  d Describe how she might deal with these order effects.

SELECTION OF PARTICIPANTS

In any study a researcher needs to select people to take part. The people that are selected are referred to as the sample. This sample is selected from a larger group, referred to as the target population.

A good sample should not be biased and thus should represent the target population. This means that later we can generalise the results of the study to people in the target population.

PEOPLE in the TARGET POPULATION

Generalise results from PARTICIPANTS in the study back to TARGET POPULATION

Select REPRESENTATIVE group of PARTICIPANTS to be the SAMPLE

How do you select a representative sample?

Psychologists have a range of **sampling techniques** – below and on the facing page.

Opportunity sample **aka** availability sample	Volunteer sample **aka** self-selected sample	Random sample	Systematic sample
Selecting people who are most easily available at the time of the study.	*Produced by asking for volunteers. The volunteers select themselves.*	*Every member of the target population has an equal chance of being selected.*	*Selecting every nth person, for example every 5th or 10th person.*
How? Select those most easily available, for example, ask people walking by you in the street.	How? For example, advertise in a newspaper or on a noticeboard.	How? Using a **random** technique, such as placing all names in a hat and drawing out the required number of names.	How? Use a predetermined system to select participants, such as selecting every 20th person from a phonebook.
+ Easiest method because you just use the first participants you can find, which means it is quicker than other methods.	**+** Access to a variety of participants (e.g. all the people who read a newspaper) which may make the sample more representative.	**+** Potentially unbiased because all members of the target population have an equal chance of selection – although some participants may decline to take part.	**+** Unbiased as participants are selected using an objective system.
– Inevitably biased because the sample is drawn from a part of the target population. For example, asking people in the street on a Monday morning where the target population is likely to exclude professional people (because they are at work) or people from rural areas.	**–** Sample is biased because participants are likely to be keener and therefore might be more helpful than most people or might be more inquisitive. This results in a **volunteer bias**.	**–** This form of sampling takes more time and effort than other methods because you need to obtain a list of all the members of your target population, identify the sample and then contact the people identified and ask if they will take part.	**–** Not truly unbiased/random unless you select a number using a random method, start with this person and then select every *nth* person.

Another strength of volunteer sampling is that it may be a good way to get a specialised group of participants. This is called purposive sampling (see page 89). For example, if you wanted to study the behaviour of medical students it would make sense to put an ad on the noticeboard of a medical school rather than standing around in a shopping centre hoping to find some.

key terms

- Availability sample
- Biased
- Generalisation
- Opportunity sample
- Purposive sample
- Quota sample
- Random
- Random sample
- Representative sample
- Sample
- Sampling techniques
- Self-selected sample
- Stratified sample
- Systematic sample
- Target population
- Volunteer bias
- Volunteer sample

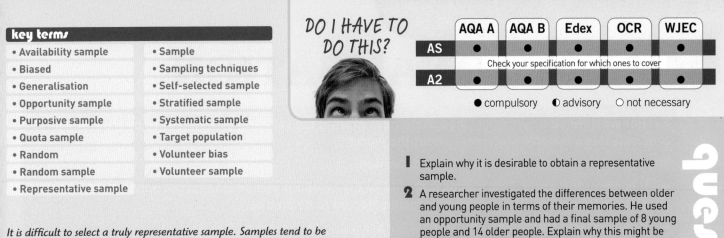

DO I HAVE TO DO THIS?

	AQA A	AQA B	Edex	OCR	WJEC
AS	●	●	●	●	●
	Check your specification for which ones to cover				
A2	●	●	●	●	●

● compulsory   ◑ advisory   ○ not necessary

It is difficult to select a truly representative sample. Samples tend to be biased in some way because some members of the target population are over- or under-represented in the sample.

The term bias refers to being unfair or prejudiced, for example 'Some English people are biased against Americans'.

Stratified sample	Quota sample

Participants are selected according to their frequency in the population.

How? Subgroups (or strata) within a population are identified (e.g. boys and girls, or age groups: 10–12 years, 13–15, etc). Participants are obtained from each of the strata in proportion to their occurrence in the target population.

Selection is done randomly.	Selection from the strata is done by another method, such as opportunity sampling.

+ Likely to be more representative than other sampling techniques because there is equal representation of subgroups.

− Although the sample represents subgroups, each quota taken may be biased in other ways, for example if you use opportunity sampling you only have access to certain sections of the target population.

mini study

How random is random?

Take 40 pieces of paper and write 20 boys' names and 20 girls' names on each slip. Put them in a hat and draw out 10 slips of paper. If the selection is representative you should get five boys and five girls.

Put the slips of paper back and draw 10 out again. Repeat this four times and then try drawing a larger sample, e.g. 20 slips of paper. Each time, record how many boys' and girls' names were drawn. You can record your results in the table below.

	Sample size 10				Sample size 20				Total
	1	2	3	4	5	6	7	8	
Boys									
Girls									

The point is that, in principle, random selection results in an unbiased and representative sample. Is this what you found? What happens if you try the same task with a random number table or using the random function on your calculator?

---

1 Explain why it is desirable to obtain a representative sample.

2 A researcher investigated the differences between older and young people in terms of their memories. He used an opportunity sample and had a final sample of 8 young people and 14 older people. Explain why this might be described as a biased sample.

3 Identify the sampling method in each of the studies below.

  a A university department undertook a study of mobile phone use in adolescents, using a questionnaire. The questionnaire was given to a group of students in a local comprehensive school, selected by placing all the students' names in a container and drawing out 50 names.

  b A group of psychology students interviewed shoppers in a local shopping centre about attitudes towards dieting.

  c A class of psychology students conducted a study on memory. They put a notice on the noticeboard in the sixth form common room asking for participants who have an hour to spare.

  d A researcher studied IQ in primary school children by selecting the first five names in each class register for every school he visited.

  e A polling company employed a panel of people to consult with regarding their opinions on political issues. They identified various subgroups in the population and then randomly selected members from each subgroup.

4 For each of the studies above, state **one** strength and **one** weakness of using that sampling method in that particular study.

5 Explain the difference between a random and a systematic sample.

6 A research study is conducted comparing the ability of boys and girls aged 5–12 to remember words. Their memories were tested giving them 30 words to remember.

  a Write a suitable directional hypothesis for this study.

  b Describe the target population.

  c Suggest a suitable sampling method and explain how you would do it.

  d Describe **one** strength of this method of selection.

  e What experimental design would be suitable?

  f Give **one** weakness of using this design in the context of this study.

7 A group of psychology students are interested to find out whether college students who like to climb mountains have more extravert personalities than other college students.

  a Describe the target population in this study.

  b Why might the researcher prefer to use a random sample instead of a volunteer sample?

  c How could the researcher obtain a random sample from this target population?

  d Describe how the researcher might select a volunteer sample.

  e Which sampling method is most likely to be biased?

OPERATIONALISATION

Earlier we defined a hypothesis as a statement of what the researcher believes to be true. More precisely it is a *testable* statement about the world.

There are two things to note about this definition:

► It is about the *world*. This means it should really be about people (the target population) and not about participants (the sample of people selected to be studied).

► It is a *testable* statement. This is what we are going to explain on this spread.

The process of science	For example
Psychologist observes human behaviour	When people feel nervous and scared they often like to have a friend with them, for example if you have to go to the doctor for an injection.
Psychologist provides an explanation for this behaviour	Stress may be reduced by having social support.
Psychologist produces a testable hypothesis in order to test whether the explanation is true	People have lower blood pressure when having an injection if a friend is present, than if no friend is present.
Psychologist conducts the study	

She looks stressed. But what do we mean by stressed? You could ask her. But what if you can't ask her? How else could we measure her stress?

What does 'testable' mean?

The aim of research is to test explanations. Before conducting a test (i.e. a study) we need to decide how to do this.

Consider the example on the left. We want to find out whether social support does reduce feelings of stress.

In order to find this out we need to decide what we will actually *do*. We have an IV and a DV and need to work out how to represent these.

➤ The **independent variable** (IV) is *social support*. How will we represent this? It could be just having another person present. Or several people. Or several acquaintances. Or close friends.

➤ The **dependent variable** (DV) is *feelings of stress*. How will we measure this? We could ask people to rate how stressed they are. We could measure their blood pressure (when people are stressed their blood pressure increases).

What we are doing is operationalising the variables. We are producing an operational definition for the independent and dependent variables, i.e. a definition we can work with.

Operationalisation means to define a variable by specifying a set of operations or behaviours that can be measured or manipulated.

Another example

Consider the Stroop effect experiment, described on page 13.

J. Ridley Stroop sought to investigate the effects of interference on performance speed (this was his research **aim**). In order to turn this aim into an experiment, he needed to operationalise the variables.

➤ The IV is *interference*. He operationalised this by creating a conflict between the colour word and the colour it was written in.

➤ The DV is *performance speed*, measured in terms of time taken to read the words on a list.

Thus the operationalised hypothesis is: people take longer to perform a task when word and colour conflict with each other than when they don't.

And some more examples

Research aim: to see if people work better in a silent or noisy environment.

➤ The IV is *noise* (two levels *silent or noisy*). This could be a classroom where everyone works in silence or where a radio is being played.

➤ The DV is *working better*. This could be operationalised as a higher score on a memory test.

Operationalised hypothesis: people obtain a higher score on a memory test when tested in quiet (no sounds) rather than noisy (radio playing) conditions.

Research aim: to see whether work makes people happy.

➤ The IV is *work*. Could be operationalised as an adult who has a full-time job (over 40 hours per week) or no job (claiming jobseekers allowance).

➤ The DV is *being happy*. This could be measured using a happiness questionnaire, so being happy would equate to a higher score on this questionnaire.

Operationalised hypothesis: adults obtain a higher score on a happiness questionnaire if they work full-time (over 40 hours per week) than if they don't work (received jobseekers allowance).

key terms

- Aim
- Dependent variable
- Hypothesis
- Independent variable
- Operationalisation
- Research prediction
- Science

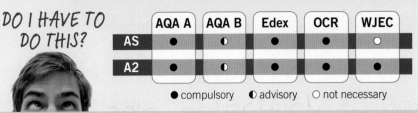

question 1.6

There is a distinction between a hypothesis and a research prediction – but, for the purposes of A level exams, a mixture of the two is generally acceptable as long as it is operationalised.

The hypothesis is about populations (people). It states our expectation about the world. It should be stated in the present tense and may be operationalised.

> ➤ People who work are happier than people who don't work.

The research prediction is about samples (participants). It predicts what we expect to find in a study. It is stated in the future tense and must be operationalised.

> ➤ Participants who work (over 40 hours a week) will be happier than those who don't work (receive job seekers allowance).

Ivy Devey

Do you get muddled about which is the IV and which is the DV in an experiment?

Think of Mrs Ivy Devey (on the right)

The IV comes first – the experimenter makes the conditions different.

Followed by the DV – this is what you measure at the end.

IV DV = Ivy Devey

mini study

Stress and friendship

Psychologists have found that people experience lower levels of stress if they have some social support.

- Identify and operationalise the IV and DV.
- Describe how you could conduct this study using (a) repeated measures design, (b) independent groups design and (c) matched pairs design.
- Which one will you choose and why?
- Write a suitable hypothesis for this study.
- Work out the procedure that you will follow and test this using a pilot study.

1 On the facing page we have explained what 'testable' means with an example of a study about stress and social support.

  a What operationalised IV and DV would you choose from the suggestions given?

  b Write an operationalised hypothesis for this study.

  c You could operationalise the IV by using a confederate who would stand beside the participant while doing a stressful task. Explain why this might not test your stated aims.

2 Suggest at least **two** ways that you could operationalise the following variables (in other words, suggest how you could define them so they could be identified or measured):

  a Doing something in the morning or afternoon.

  b Being drunk or not drunk.

  c A beautiful woman or a less attractive woman.

  d A young child or an older child.

  e Being hungry or not hungry.

3 A psychologist conducted a study to look at whether watching certain films made children more helpful (one film was about being helpful, the other was neutral). He advertised for participants in the local newspaper. A large number of children volunteered and a sample of 30 was selected for the actual experiment.

  a Identify the IV and DV in this experiment.

  b Describe how you would operationalise the DV.

  c State an operationalised hypothesis for this study.

  d State a suitable research prediction for this study.

  e Is your hypothesis directional or non-directional?

  f Select an experimental design for this study and state **one** strength of using this design in this study.

  g Describe **one** weakness of this experimental design and explain how this problem could be dealt with.

  h Describe the target population.

  i Suggest how the experimenter might select the sub-sample from all those who applied.

4 A psychology experiment aims to investigate how preschool children differ from those already at school in terms of their ability to remember symbols that look like letters.

  a If the experimenter wanted to obtain a random sample of each of the two age groups, how might this be done?

  b Explain the strength of using a random sample.

  c Describe the operationalised IV and DV.

  d Write a suitable directional and operationalised hypothesis.

  e Explain why you would use a directional rather than a non-directional hypothesis in this study.

  f The children were shown 20 different symbols. Why was it better to use 20 symbols rather than just 2 symbols?

  g Why might it be better to use 2 rather than 20 symbols?

EXPERIMENTAL CONTROL

There are IVs and DVs, and then there are EVs – extraneous variables.

On this spread the term *extraneous variable* is discussed. Some exam board use the term *confounding variable* instead. In fact, the two terms have slightly different meanings – for all but AQA B students there is no need to worry about this AQA B students can read more on page 34.

Consider the following **experiment**:

A class of psychology students conducted a study with the aim of finding out whether students could do their homework effectively while in front of the TV. The study involved two conditions – doing a test in silence and doing it with the TV on.

The IV was whether the TV was on or not.

The DV was the participants' score on the test.

We are investigating the effect of the IV on the DV:

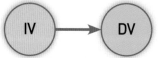

But what if there were other things that affected their score on the test?

It might be that the room was much colder when the TV group were being tested than when the silent group were tested.

This is called an extraneous variable (EV). Because room temperature was an additional variable that differed between the two groups

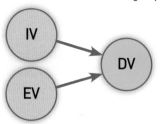

We might mistakenly conclude that performance on the test (DV) was worse because of the TV was on (IV). However, it really was because of the other variable, the temperature (EV).

Consequently, the **experimenter** might not have actually tested what he (or she) intended to test. Instead the influence of a different variable has been tested. If an experimenter fails to control such EVs then the results of the study might be meaningless. The experimenter might claim that the IV caused a change in the DV but in fact changes in the DV may actually be caused by something else – the EV(s).

Therefore, *control* is vital in experiments. An experimenter seeks to control as many *relevant* EVs as possible, i.e. those *extra* to the IV.

Different kinds of EV

Order effects

Order effects are an extraneous variable.

For example, if the TV and homework experiment is conducted using a repeated measures design, participants might do the test first with the TV on. Then they might do a similar test this time without the TV.

We compare their scores on the memory test (DV) and find the scores were better the second time.

The reason they might do better without the TV has nothing to do with TV distraction – it's because they were more practised at taking such tests.

Practice has become an alternative IV – it is an extraneous variable.

Participant variables

The participants in one group may be different to the participants in the other group in important ways.

For example, in the study on TV and homework, we had two groups of participants. One group watched TV while they did a test and the others didn't. It could be that one group happened to be more intelligent. 'Intelligence' or experience are participant variables – characteristics of the participants.

Personal characteristics, such as intelligence can become an alternative IV – they act as extraneous variables.

Situational variables

It might be that all the participants in the no TV condition did the test in the morning and all the participants in the TV on condition did the test in the afternoon.

For example, people are more alert in the morning and that is why they do better on the morning test. This is a situational variable.

Time of day has become an alternative IV – it is an extraneous variable.

Investigator effects

The behaviour of the investigator may affect participants and thus affect the DV.

For example, the investigator may act in a more positive way with one experimental group – perhaps because the investigator expects this group to do better. This is an investigator effect.

Acting in a less or more positive way has become an alternative IV – it is an extraneous variable.

Just to make this clear:

Control means making things change.

An experimenter controls the IV in the sense that they make it change – noisy or quiet, friend present or no friend present, reward or no reward.

Control also means keeping things constant.

An experimenter aims to keep everything else in the experimental environment constant.

You'll be pleased to know that we discuss these concepts again on pages 32–35, just to help you gain a deeper understanding.

- Confounding variable
- Control
- Counterbalancing
- Double blind
- Experiment
- Experimenter
- Extraneous variable
- Investigator
- Investigator effects
- Order effects
- Participant effects
- Participant variables
- Situational variables
- Standardised procedures
- Standardised instructions

DO I HAVE TO DO THIS?

	AQA A	AQA B	Edex	OCR	WJEC
AS	●	●	●	●	●
A2	●	●	●	◑	●

● compulsory ◑ advisory ○ not necessary

Some ways of dealing with extraneous variables

➤ *Order effects* can be controlled by using **counterbalancing** or using an independent groups design instead of repeated measures (see page 14).

➤ *Participant variables* can be controlled in a study with an independent groups design by randomly allocating participants to groups. This should ensure an even spread of important characteristics. Another way to control participant variables is to use a matched pairs design or repeated measures design.

➤ *Situational variables* can be controlled by using **standardised procedures** to ensure that all participants are tested under the same conditions. Standardised procedures are like a recipe – if different procedures are used the different outcomes may be due to the procedures and not the IV.

Standardised procedures include **standardised instructions**. This refers to the instructions that are given to participants at the beginning of a study. If some participants get different instructions this could affect their performance (an investigator effect).

➤ *Investigator effects* can also be dealt with using a **double blind** design. This is when both the participant and the person conducting the experiment don't know the aims of the experiment, therefore the **investigator** cannot affect the participants' performance.

How can the experimenter not know the aims of the study – he invented it so he has to know, doesn't he?

The answer is that the person actually conducting the study (experimenter) is often not the main researcher (investigator). So this person can be blind about the aims.

mini study

Testing some investigator effects

Conduct a simple experiment with two groups of participants. For example, just ask them to complete a maths test (the test shouldn't be too easy otherwise everyone will do well). Tell one group of participants that other people who took this test found it quite easy. Tell the second group of participants that people generally found the test quite difficult. Compare the two groups in terms of the score they get on the test.

- Identify the IV and DV in this study.
- Write a suitable hypothesis.
- Work out the procedure that you will follow and test this using a pilot study.
- Make any adjustments and try the real thing.
- Did you find any investigator effects?

1 Give an example of an extraneous variable described on this spread.

2 In each of the following studies, think of **one or more** possible extraneous variables that may affect the results of the study.

 a Two classes of primary school children are tested to see if older or younger children have better memories. One class contains older children. The other class contains younger children. The children are tested in their own classrooms by their own teacher.

 b Some students investigate whether men or women are more affected by alcohol. They give each participant a reaction time test and then give them two glasses of wine, followed by another reaction time test.

 c A teacher conducted the Stroop experiment (see page 13) with her class. Her older students had done the test before.

 d A psychological study tested the effects of vitamins on exam performance. Participants were told beforehand that the vitamins enhanced exam performance. One group of participants received a vitamin pill and the other group received a placebo (a pill looking the same as the vitamin pill but having no pharmacological properties). The exam performance of the two groups was measured.

3 For each of the extraneous variables you identified in question 3, decide whether it is an order effect, a participant variable, a situational variable or an investigator effect.

4 Mary Smith organises a project to enable her psychology class to have a go at using matched pairs design. The class is divided into two groups, one will receive word list A (nouns) and the other word list B (verbs). They will be tested on recall.

 a Suggest **two** participant variables that could be used to match classmates.

 b Explain why each of the variables you chose would be important to control in this study.

 c What are the two conditions in the experiment?

 d If Mary decided to use an independent measures design, suggest **one** way that participants could have been allocated to conditions.

 e Mary used words that were all of two syllables and of similar length. Give **one** reason why.

 f Mary decided to repeat the study using all the pupils in the school. She selected every 5th pupil in the register. Why is this not a random sample?

5 Explain the difference between a confounding variable and an extraneous variable.

DESCRIPTIVE STATISTICS

At the end of any study a researcher should have a lot of data, such as how long participants took to complete a task or what they scored on a test. The researcher needs to find a way to summarise this data from all the participants in order to draw conclusions. This is what various descriptive statistics do for us – they describe the data, and show us general patterns and trends.

A *conclusion* is a single sentence or a few sentences that succinctly describe the findings of a study.

For example:

- *The results showed a positive correlation between memory and GCSE scores.*
- *It appears that noise reduces the ability to concentrate.*

Strictly speaking, you should not go beyond the data with your conclusions – it is not appropriate to assume that the conclusions based on the participants in your study extend to all people. You can only draw an inference, such as this if you use **inferential statistics** *– these are covered in Chapter 5.*

EXAM BOARD ALERT

Only WJEC are strict about this – all other boards expect conclusions from descriptive statistics to be applied to the target population!

Measures of central tendency

Measures of central tendency inform us about central (or middle) values for a set of data. They are 'averages' – ways of calculating a typical value for a set of data.

An average can be calculated in different ways:

Mean

The **mean** is calculated by adding up all the numbers and dividing by the number of numbers.

Strengths

It makes use of the *values* of all the data. Note the use of the word 'values'. All measures of central tendency use all the data and use the values. But the mean is the only one that uses *all* the values when making the final calculation

Weaknesses

It can be unrepresentative of the numbers if there are extreme values.

For example:
2, 4, 5, 6, 9, 10, 12
mean = 6.86
2, 4, 5, 6, 9, 10, 29
mean = 9.42

Median

The **median** is the *middle* value in an *ordered* list.

Strengths

Not affected by extreme scores.

For example, in the data sets below left, the median in both cases would be 6.

Weaknesses

Not as 'sensitive' as the mean because not all values are reflected in the median.

Top tip – look to see if there are any extreme values in the data set given. If there are, then the median is best.

Mode

The **mode** is the value that is *most* common.

Strengths

Useful when the data are in categories.

For example, asking people to name their favourite colour. The mode would be the colour that received the most votes.

Weaknesses

Not a useful way of describing data when there are several modes. For example, if 12 people choose yellow and 12 people choose red and 12 people choose purple.

Typical exam question: 'Identify a suitable method of central tendency to use with the results from this study and explain why you would choose this method'.

Many students find it hard to remember the link between 'measures of central tendency' and 'mean, median, mode'. When asked in an exam to name a suitable measure of central tendency for a particular study, students often appear not to know that the answer must be mean, median or mode.

One way to help you remember connections is to produce memorable pictures. The flag on the left is an attempt to illustrate the idea of a central tendency and link this to the three appropriate terms. Try to develop your own memorable picture for this and other concepts – the more outrageous, the better!

Measures of dispersion

A set of data can also be described in terms of how dispersed or spread out the numbers are.

The easiest way to do this is to use the range.

Consider the data sets below:

3, 5, 8, 8, 9, 10, 12, 12, 13, 15
mean = 9.5   range = 12 (3 to 15)

1, 5, 8, 8, 9, 10, 12, 12, 13, 17
mean = 9.5   range = 16 (1 to 17)

The two sets of numbers have the same mean but a different range, so the range is helpful as a further method of describing the data. If we just used the mean, the data would appear to be the same.

The range is the difference between the highest and lowest number.

There is a more precise method of expressing dispersion, called the standard deviation. This is a measure of the spread of the data around the mean.

The standard deviation for the two sets of numbers above is 3.69 and 4.45 respectively. This can be worked out using a mathematical calculator.

	Strengths	Weaknesses
Range	It is easy to calculate. It provides you with direct information with little calculation.	Affected by extreme values. Doesn't take into account the number of observations in the data set.
Standard deviation	More precise measure of dispersion because all values taken into account.	Unduly affected by extreme values that increase the standard deviation and make it less representative of the data set.

You won't be asked to calculate the standard deviation in an exam.

key terms

- Bar chart
- Conclusion
- Descriptive statistics
- Graphs
- Histogram
- Inferential statistics
- Mean
- Measures of central tendency
- Measures of dispersion
- Median
- Mode
- Range
- Scattergram
- Standard deviation
- x axis
- y axis

DO I HAVE TO DO THIS?

	AQA A	AQA B	Edex	OCR	WJEC
AS	●	●	●	●	●
A2	●	●	○	●	●

AQA A no histogram / WJEC no standard deviation

● compulsory ◗ advisory ○ not necessary

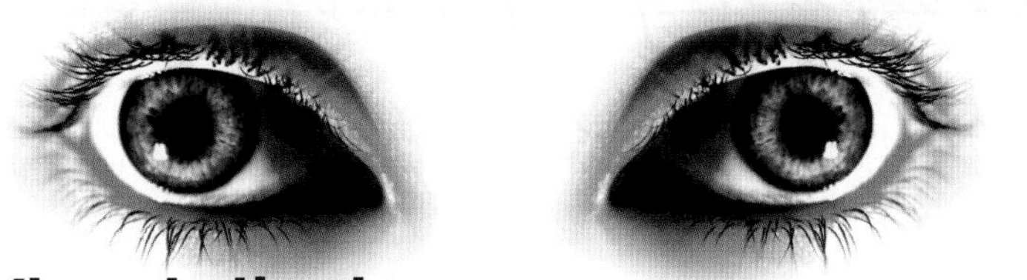

Visual display

A picture is worth a thousand words! **Graphs** provide a means of 'eyeballing' your data and seeing the results at a glance.

Tables – The numbers you collect are referred to as 'raw data' – numbers that haven't been treated in any way. These data can be set out in a table or summarised using types of averages and/or range.

Bar chart – The height of each bar represents the frequency of that item. The categories are placed on the horizontal (*x* axis) and frequency is on the vertical (*y* axis). Bar charts are suitable for words and numbers.

Histogram – Similar to a bar chart except that the area within the bars must be proportional to the frequencies represented. In practice this means that the vertical axis (frequency) must start at zero. In addition the horizontal axis must be continuous (therefore you can't draw a histogram with data in categories). Finally, there should be no gaps between the bars.

Scattergrams – A type of graph used when doing a correlational analysis (see page 64).

Examples of bar charts and histograms

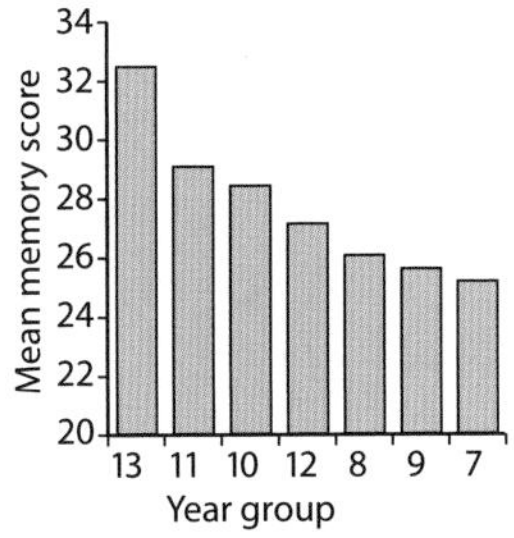

A bar chart showing the mean memory scores for each year group (maximum score is 40)

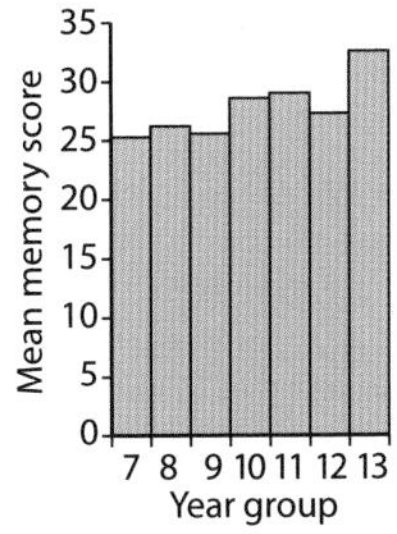

A histogram showing the same data as above

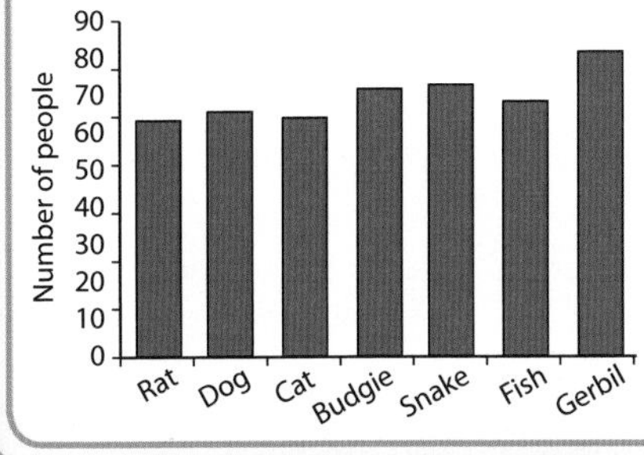

A bar chart showing students' favourite pets

1 For each of the following sets of data (data sets) (a) calculate the mean, (b) calculate the median, (c) calculate the mode, (d) state which of the three measures would be most suitable to use and why, (e) calculate the range.

Data set 1: 2, 3, 5, 6, 6, 8, 9, 12, 15, 21, 22

Data set 2: 2, 3, 8, 10, 11, 13, 13, 14, 14, 29

Data set 3: 2, 2, 4, 5, 5, 5, 7, 7, 8, 8, 8, 10

Data set 4: cat, cat, dog, budgie, snake, gerbil

2 Why is it better to know about the mean and range of a data set rather than just the mean?

3 Explain why it might be better to know the standard deviation of a data set rather than the range.

4 Standard deviation tells us on average how close each of the numbers is to the mean – it tells us how a set of numbers are distributed around the mean. Look at the following data sets. Which one do you think would have the smaller standard deviation?

Data set A: 2 2 3 4 5 9 11 14 18 20 21 22 25

Data set B: 2 5 8 9 9 10 11 12 14 15 16 20 25

5 There are three graphs on the left.
   a For each graph state what conclusion you could draw.
   b Explain **two** key differences between the bar chart and the histogram.

6 A psychologist has conducted an experiment to see how long it takes people to offer help when someone falls down. The results are shown below.

	Victim appears to be drunk	Victim has a cane
Mean response time	24.9 seconds	19.7 seconds
Range of scores	10–48	10–30
Standard deviation	11.7	6.8

State **one** conclusion that could be drawn from
   a The mean response times.
   b The range of each set of scores.
   c The standard deviations of each set of scores.

mini study
What month were you born?

It is thought that students born in September through to February do better than students born in March through to August because they are older. Devise a study to test this hypothesis.

- Put your findings in a table (or if you don't conduct the study invent a set of data).
- Represent your findings using descriptive statistics including drawing a suitable graph to represent your findings.
- Compare what you have done with others in your class and decide what works best.
- State **one** conclusion that could be drawn from your data.

MULTIPLE CHOICE QUESTIONS

1. The independent variable in a study is:
   a. The one that is excluded.
   b. The one that is manipulated by the experimenter.
   c. The one that is observed or measured.
   d. Not of interest to the experimenter.

2. A pilot study is:
   a. The first study conducted by a research team.
   b. A preliminary investigation.
   c. A small-scale trial run of a research design.
   d. A research project on efficient flying of airplanes.

3. Which of the following hypotheses is a non-directional hypothesis?
   a. Participants in the noise condition will do better on the memory test than those in the no noise condition.
   b. Participants who drink alcohol will have a slower reaction time than those who have no alcohol.
   c. Participants like words that are familiar better than those that are not familiar.
   d. Participants who expect to perform better perform differently to those given lower expectations.

4. One reason for using a directional hypothesis would be because:
   a. Past research suggests that participants will do better on one condition than another.
   b. Past research is equivocal about how participants will perform.
   c. There is no past research.
   d. The researcher wants to make a strong statement.

5. An extraneous variable is a variable that:
   a. Has been controlled by the experimenter.
   b. Is related to noise.
   c. May influence the dependent variable.
   d. The experimenter wants to find out more about.

6. A student plans to investigate the effects of practice on IQ test performance. Some participants are given two practice tests prior to the IQ test whereas others do no test beforehand. The dependent variable in this study is:
   a. The participants.
   b. The effects of practice.
   c. IQ test performance before the study.
   d. IQ test performance at the end of the study.

7. The study described in question 6 is:
   a. A repeated measures design.
   b. An independent groups design.
   c. A matched pairs design.
   d. A careful design.

8. In an independent groups design:
   a. There are two groups of participants.
   b. The analysis involves comparing measures from two groups of people.
   c. The analysis involves comparing two measures from the same person.
   d. Both a and b.

9. One advantage of doing a matched pairs design is:
   a. You need fewer participants than for repeated measures.
   b. You can control some participant variables.
   c. Order effects are not a problem.
   d. Both b and c.

10. The letters 'ABBA' refer to a research design:
   a. Created by a Swedish rock band.
   b. To control participant variables.
   c. To counterbalance for order effects.
   d. To control extraneous variables.

11. All sampling methods aim to be:
   a. Representative of the target population.
   b. Biased.
   c. Random.
   d. Difficult to conduct.

12. Selecting participants who just happen to be available is called:
   a. Opportunity sampling.
   b. Volunteer sampling.
   c. Random sampling.
   d. Quota sampling.

13. Which of the following could not be an extraneous variable in the study?
   a. An investigator effect.
   b. A confederate.
   c. An order effect.
   d. Lack of standardised procedures.

14. One way to improve the design of a study is to:
   a. Conduct a pilot study beforehand to see if some things don't work.
   b. Have lots of variables.
   c. Use a repeated measures design.
   d. Use a confederate.

15. Which of the following is a disadvantage of using a repeated measures design?
   a. It does not control participant variables.
   b. You have to use more participants than for independent groups design.
   c. There are more likely to be investigator effects than for independent groups design.
   d. There may be order effects.

16. In an experiment half of the participants do condition A first followed by condition B, the other participants do the conditions in the reverse order. This procedure is called:
   a. Countercontrol.
   b. Countercalling.
   c. Counterbalancing.
   d. Counteracting.

17. An individual who is instructed about how to behave by the researcher, often acting as the IV, is called:
   a. An extraneous variable.
   b. A dependent variable.
   c. The investigator.
   d. A confederate.

18. Which is the following is a random sample?
   a. Names drawn from a hat.
   b. Asking people if they would like to take part.
   c. Every 10th name in a register.
   d. Taking whoever happens to be there.

19. Which of the following is a measure of central tendency?
   a. Range.
   b. Bar chart.
   c. Mode.
   d. Interval.

20. Debriefing involves:
   a. Telling a participant the true aims of a study.
   b. Giving a participant a chance to discuss any psychological harm they may have experienced.
   c. Asking participants for feedback about the experiment.
   d. All of the above.

Answers on facing page

EXAM STYLE QUESTION 1

One area of psychological research concerns prejudice – people make biased judgements of another person's abilities based on race, age, gender and so on.

Many studies have looked at the effects of gender. For example, in one experiment participants were asked to mark students' essays. Those essays supposedly written by boys were given higher marks, on average, than girls' essays.

A group of psychology students decided to repeat this research to see if people today were still prejudiced about gender. The researchers selected four essays (essay A, essay B, essay C, essay D). Each essay had been given a mark of about 50% by their teacher.

The student participants were divided into two groups. For Group 1 essays A and B were given girls' names and essays C and D were given boys' names. For Group 2 this was reversed.

Participants were asked to give a mark to the essays out of 10, where 10 was excellent. The mean marks for boys' and girls' essays are shown in the graph below.

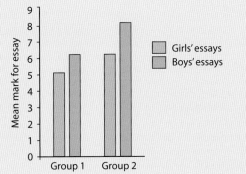

(a) (i) Write a suitable operationalised hypothesis for this study. (2 marks)

(ii) Identify whether your hypothesis is directional or non-directional and explain why you chose such a hypothesis. (1 mark + 2 marks)

(b) The student researchers decided to conduct a pilot study.

(i) Why would it be a good idea to conduct a pilot study? (2 marks)

(ii) Explain how the student researchers would conduct a pilot study. (2 marks)

(c) (i) Identify **one** method of selecting participants for this study. (1 mark)

(ii) Describe **one** strength and **one** weakness of using this method in this study. (2 marks + 2 marks)

(d) (i) Explain the term 'investigator effect'. (2 marks)

(ii) Suggest **one** investigator effect that may have been a problem in this study. (2 marks)

(iii) Explain how you could have dealt with this effect. (2 marks)

(e) Explain why the experiment was designed so that half the participants had girls' names for essays A and B and the other half had girls' names for essays C and D. (3 marks)

(f) (i) What measure of central tendency was used to describe the findings? (1 mark)

(ii) Explain **one** strength of this measure of central tendency. (2 marks)

(g) Describe **one** possible extraneous variable in this study and explain how this could be controlled. (2 marks + 2 marks)

(h) Describe **one** finding and **one** conclusion that can be drawn from the graph. (2 marks + 2 marks)

EXAM STYLE QUESTION 2

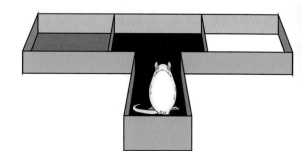

A classic experiment in psychology by Rosenthal and Fode (1963) looked at the effect of experimenter expectations on the performance of rats – the participants in this study were psychology students who were asked to train albino rats to learn to find food in a maze. The participants were instructed to run their rats ten times for each of five days on a T-maze. The rats had to learn to discriminate between one arm of the maze which was painted white, and the other which was painted dark grey. Running to the darker arm was always reinforced (i.e. food was placed there), while running to the white arm was never reinforced. The arms were interchangeable, and swapped round at random, so that the rats could not just learn to run in a given direction.

The participants (believing they were experimenters) were told that there were two groups of rats: one group were 'fast learners' (maze bright) having been bred for this characteristic, whilst the other group were 'slow learners' (maze dull). In fact there were no differences between the rats, they were all from the same litter and had been randomly assigned to the students.

The participants recorded success rates per rat per day, time taken for every correct response, and also some post-experimental data on their feelings about their rats and how they had interacted with them.

The findings of the study showed that the supposedly brighter rats actually made more correct responses and were quicker in their maze running. When the students were asked about their rats afterwards those with maze bright rats described them as smarter, more attractive and more likeable. The only explanation can be that the students' expectations affected the rats' performance.

(a) What was the aim of this research? (2 marks)

(b) (i) Identify the independent and dependent variables in this study. (2 marks)

(ii) Explain how the independent variable was operationalised. (2 marks)

(c) (i) Explain the meaning of the phrase rats were 'randomly assigned to students'. (2 marks)

(ii) Describe how the researchers could have randomly assigned the rats to students. (2 marks)

(iii) Why was it important to 'randomly assign' the rats to students? (2 marks)

(d) When the investigators produced the findings, they described the data using the median and standard deviation.

(i) What does the median tell us about data? (1 mark)

(ii) What does the standard deviation tell us about data? (2 marks)

(iii) Describe **one** strength of using the median. (2 marks)

(e) (i) The 'real' participants in the study were the students. Identify **one** suitable method of selecting these participants. (1 mark)

(ii) Explain how the investigators could have carried out this method of selection. (2 marks)

(f) (i) Identify **one** ethical issue that might arise in this study in relation to the student participants. (1 mark)

(ii) Explain how the investigators might have dealt with this issue. (2 marks)

(g) (i) What experimental design was used in this study? (1 mark)

(ii) Describe **one** strength and **one** weakness of using this experimental design in this study. (2 marks + 2 marks)

(iii) Identify an alternative experimental design that could have been used in this study. (1 mark)

(iv) Explain how you could conduct a study with the same aims using this alternative design. (3 marks)

Food was always placed in the darker arm of the T-maze, which was varied on each trial. The rats had to learn to run always to this side.

Examiner's tips for answering this question ⭐

(a) Don't be afraid to simply lift words from the text. If you write 'To study experimenter's expectations' this would receive only 1 mark as it lacks important details.

(b) (i) The briefest answer would be acceptable for a total of 2 marks.

(ii) This is an example of how your knowledge is tested in research methods questions. You are rarely asked to define a term (though there are sometimes questions like this). Most often you are required to *use* this knowledge. If you repeat the definition to yourself then you should be able to create an answer. A 1-mark answer might simply refer to rats being maze dull or maze bright. A definition of operationalisation would receive no marks.

(c) (i) This is another case of having to *use* your knowledge to work out the answer. If you understand the term 'random' and know how random allocations are done then you should be able to answer this question.

(ii) The focus this time is on 'how' you would do it.

(iii) Not an easy question but make sure that you say more than 'prevent bias'. Provide a bit more detail.

(d) (i) and (ii) and (iii) The number of marks available for each part should guide you to the length of answer required.

(iii) When providing a strength it helps to make a comparison between the mean and other measures of central tendency.

(e) (i) Any sampling method would be equally creditworthy, but maybe it is best to consider part (ii) to decide which one to use.

(ii) If you describe two methods only your first answer will be taken.

(f) (i) Debriefing often is not credited as an *issue*, so choose something else.

(ii) For 2 marks you would need to say more than 'I would debrief them'. You need to explain what this would involve.

(g) (i) This question is about experimental design. This is one of the questions that students always find difficult. When asked to name the experimental design, they don't appear to remember that the answer is one of the following: repeated measures, independent groups or matched pairs. To help you remember, think of

Expe**RIM**ental design
R = repeated measures
I = independent groups
M = matched pairs

(ii) You must relate your answer to this specific study.

(iii) Matched pairs might be a good choice because it gives you lots to write about for part (iv).

(iv) This last part is worth 3 marks so take care to provide sufficient details for the marks available. You can include any details related to design, such as how you would deal with order effects.

MODEL ANSWERS

A model answer is an answer that would get full marks. However, it isn't the only answer that would get full marks, it is simply one possible answer.

Exam style question 1

(a) (i) Write a suitable hypothesis for this study. (2 marks)
Essays that appear to be written by boys will get higher marks than essays written by girls.

(i) Identify whether your hypothesis is directional or non-directional and explain why you chose such a hypothesis. (1 mark + 2 marks)
The hypothesis is directional. I chose this because past research suggests that boys will do better.

(b) The student researchers decided to conduct a pilot study.

(i) Why would it be a good idea to conduct a pilot study? (2 marks)

A pilot study would enable you to check aspects of your research design so that you could put it right before doing the full-scale study.

(ii) Explain how the student researchers would conduct a pilot study. (2 marks)
They would get a small group of people, similar to the eventual participants, and then try out their design including the standardised instructions and other standardised procedures.

(c) (i) Identify one method of selecting participants for this study. (1 mark)

One method would be to use an opportunity sample.

(ii) Describe one strength and one weakness of using this method in this study. (2 marks + 2 marks)
One strength is that it is easy because you just use the first students you can find, like going to the sixth-form common room.
One weakness is that the sample is biased because it is just drawn from students at your college rather than people in general.

(d) (i) Explain the term 'investigator effect'. (2 marks)
An investigator effect is anything the investigator does that has an effect on the participant's performance other than what was intended.

(ii) Suggest one investigator effect that may have been a problem in this study. (2 marks)
A possible investigator effect would be that the investigator might unconsciously encourage the students to give better marks to the boys' essays.

(iii) Explain how you could have dealt with this effect. (2 marks)
You could make sure that the investigators do not talk to the participants so they don't have an opportunity to communicate their expectations.

(e) Explain why the experiment was designed so that half the participants had girls' names for essays A and B and the other half had girls' names for essays C and D. (3 marks)
This design would counterbalance any order effects. For example, if everyone had the same essays with girls' names then it might be that those essays were slightly worse and this would act as an extraneous variable.

(f) (i) What measure of central tendency was used to describe the findings? (1 mark)
The mean.

(ii) Explain one strength of this measure of central tendency. (2 marks)

The mean takes all the values of the scores into account in the final calculation so it clearly summarises all the data.

(g) Describe one possible extraneous variable in this study and explain how this could be controlled. (2 marks + 2 marks)
The boys might not take the task less seriously and therefore all their marks were about 5 and therefore no prejudice would show up. I could deal with this by explaining to the boys how important it was to mark the essays carefully.

(h) Describe one finding and one conclusion that can be taken from the graph. (2 marks + 2 marks)
The participants in both groups gave lower ratings to girls which suggests that people do have gender biases against women.

Exam style question 2

(a) What was the aim of this research? (2 marks)
The aim of the study was to find out if experimenter's expectations influence participant's behaviour.

(b) (i) Identify the independent and dependent variables in this study. (2 marks)

The IV is expectation and the DV is the number of correct responses.

(ii) Explain how the independent variable was operationalised. (2 marks)

The expectations were created by telling students that their rats were maze bright or maze dull.

(c) (i) Explain the meaning of the phrase rats were 'randomly assigned to students'. (2 marks)
This means that the rats were placed with each student using a random method so that each rat had an equal chance of being selected.

(ii) Describe how the researchers could have randomly assigned the rats to students. (2 marks)
This could be done by giving each rat a number and putting all the numbers in a hat. Then, for each student a number is picked out of the hat and that's the rat given to that student.

(iii) Why was it important to 'randomly assign' the rats to students? (2 marks)
This would prevent any bias because otherwise the best students might select certain rats.

(d) When the investigators produced the findings, they described the data using the mean and standard deviation.

(i) What does the median tell us about data? (1 mark)
It gives an average value for the scores, the middle value when all the scores are arranged in order.

(ii) What does the standard deviation tell us about data? (2 marks)
It tells us the average distance of each score from the mean.

(iii) Describe one strength using the median. (2 marks)
The median is less affected by extreme values than the mean.

(e) (i) The 'real' participants in the study were the students. Identify one suitable method of selecting these participants. (1 mark)
You could use a volunteer sample.

(ii) Explain how the investigators could have carried this method of selection. (2 marks)
They could put a notice up in the psychology department asking any students to come and take part in their study.

(f) (i) Identify one ethical issue that might arise in this study in relation to the student participants. (1 mark)
Deception.

(ii) Explain how the investigators might have dealt with this issue. (2 marks)
They would debrief the participants after the study and tell them the true aims of the study and see if they are feeling distressed in any way.

(g) (i) What experimental design was used in this study? (1 mark)
Independent groups.

(ii) Describe one strength and one weakness of using this experimental design in this study. (2 marks + 2 marks)
One strength: you avoid the problem that the students might have got better at training their rats if they did it with one maze bright and one maze dull rat.
One weakness: you can't control participant variables, such as some students being better with rats, which may act as an extraneous variable.

(iii) Identify an alternative experimental design that could have been used in this study. (1 mark)
Matched pairs.

(iv) Explain how you could conduct a study with the same aims using this alternative design. (3 marks)
I would decide on certain key participant variables, such as willingness to please, and assess the potential participants. Then I would pair them on these variables and randomly allocate them to one of the two groups.

2

Different kinds of experiments

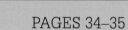

LAB AND FIELD EXPERIMENTS

PAGES 30–31

Continuing the story of experiments, starting with two main types of experiment.

mini study A field experiment on helping behaviour

VALIDITY – INTERNAL VALIDITY

PAGES 32–33

Our first look at the issue of validity – discussing participant effects and demand characteristics.

mini study Testing demand characteristics

MORE ABOUT INTERNAL VALIDITY

PAGES 34–35

Situational and participant variables (which are not the same as participant effects).

mini study The effect of expectations

VALIDITY – EXTERNAL VALIDITY

PAGES 36–37

Yet more issues related to validity, this time it's ecological validity and mundane realism.

mini study The testing effect

NATURAL EXPERIMENTS

PAGES 38–39

The third kind of experiment, where an experimenter makes use of an independent variable that has been varied by someone else!

mini study Music lessons can boost IQ

ETHICAL ISSUES

PAGES 40–41

First talked about in Chapter 1, now time for a more detailed consideration.

mini study Seeking presumptive consent

DEALING WITH ETHICAL ISSUES

PAGES 42–43

Including the code of ethics produced by the British Psychological Society.

mini study Ethical committee

EXPERIMENTAL AND CONTROL GROUPS

PAGES 44–45

Yet another kind of control.

mini studies The placebo effect and Testing the John Henry effect

END OF CHAPTER TREATS

PAGES 46–49

Multiple choice questions

Exam style questions 3 and 4

Model answers for exam style questions

LAB AND FIELD EXPERIMENTS

In Chapter 1 we considered experiments. We continue the story here. There are actually three main kinds of experiments: lab experiments, field experiments and natural experiments. The one thing they all have in common is they have independent and dependent variables.

We'll begin by looking at just two of these, lab and field experiments. You might think that is straightforward – a lab experiment is conducted in a lab and a field experiment is conducted in a field. But by now you should have realised that nothing in the land of research methods is quite that straightforward. The term 'field' just means outside of a lab. A field experiment could be conducted in a field but generally speaking it isn't in a field.

An experiment permits us to study cause and effect. It differs from non-experimental methods in that it involves the manipulation of one variable (the independent variable – IV), while trying to keep all other variables constant. If the IV is the only thing that is changed then it alone must be responsible for any alteration in the dependent variable (DV).

Many people think of a white sterile environment when they think of a lab. That may be true in some scientific subjects but not psychology. A lab is simply a restricted environment where it is possible to control extraneous variables.

> **Lab (laboratory) experiment** An experiment conducted in a special environment where **extraneous (confounding) variables** can be carefully controlled. Participants are aware that they are taking part in an experiment though they may not know the true aims of the study.

> **Field experiment** An experiment conducted in a more natural or everyday environment, i.e. in 'the field'. As with the lab experiment, the independent variable is still deliberately manipulated by the researcher. Participants are often not aware that they are participating in an experiment.

> **Field study** Any study which is conducted in an everyday environment. Note that not all studies conducted in a lab are experiments. There are controlled observations that are conducted in a laboratory (which we will look at in Chapter 4).

Lab versus field experiments

A Helping behaviour was investigated in a study on the New York subway. A **confederate** collapses on a subway train and investigators note whether help is offered. The confederate is either holding a black cane or carrying a paper bag with a bottle of alcohol and has a smell of alcohol (thus appears drunk). Piliavin *et al.* (1969) found that when the victim carried a cane 95% of bystanders helped within 10 seconds, if he appeared drunk help only came in 50% of the trials.

B Participants were asked to wait in a room before an experiment began. There was a radio playing either good or bad news and a stranger was present. Veitch and Griffitt (1976) found that when participants were asked to rate the stranger, the degree of liking was related to the kind of news they had been listening to. This shows that people like others who are associated with positive experiences.

C The participants were children aged between three and five years old. Each child was taken on their own to an experiment room where there were lots of toys including, in one corner, a five-foot inflatable Bobo doll and a mallet. The experimenter invited the 'model' to join them and then left the room for about ten minutes. Half of the children watched the model playing aggressively with a life-sized Bobo doll while the others watched the model play non-aggressively with the doll. Later they were given an opportunity to play with toys including the Bobo doll and were observed through a one-way mirror. The children who saw the aggressive behaviour were more likely to behave aggressively (Bandura *et al.*, 1961).

It may help you to understand the difference between lab and field experiments by looking at the examples below. Which of these do you think is a field experiment?

D A group of school pupils was given information about how their peers had performed on a maths task. They were either told that their peers had done well or done poorly on the test. The children were later given a maths test in class. Those who expected to do well did better than those led to expect to do poorly (Schunk, 1983).

E The Hawthorne Electric factory in Chicago asked researchers to study which factors led to increased worker productivity. The study found that increased lighting led to increased productivity – but then also found that *decreased* lighting led to increased activity (Roethlisberger and Dickson, 1939). The conclusion was that the participants knew they were being studied and this interest in their work was what explained their increased output, masking the real independent variable. This has been called the **Hawthorne effect**.

F Participants were tested in their teaching room and given nonsense trigrams (e.g. SXT) and then asked to count backwards until told to stop. Then participants were asked to recall the trigram. The counting interval was used to prevent the trigram being rehearsed. When the counting interval was three seconds participants could recall most trigrams; when it was 18 seconds they couldn't recall any trigrams (Peterson and Peterson, 1959).

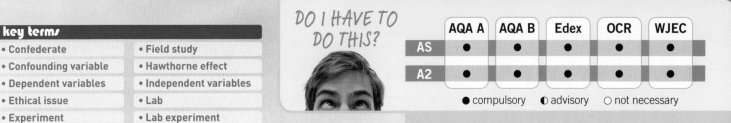

DO I HAVE TO DO THIS?

	AQA A	AQA B	Edex	OCR	WJEC
AS	●	●	●	●	●
A2	●	●	●	●	●

● compulsory ◑ advisory ○ not necessary

question 2.1

key terms

- Confederate
- Confounding variable
- Dependent variables
- Ethical issue
- Experiment
- Extraneous variables
- Field experiment
- Field study
- Hawthorne effect
- Independent variables
- Lab
- Lab experiment
- Mundane realism

What makes an experiment artificial?

There are various reasons why lab experiments tend to be more artificial or contrived than field experiments.

➤ Participants know they are being studied and this is likely to mean they don't behave 'normally' (naturally).

➤ The setting is not like everyday life. The term used to describe this is **mundane realism**. Lab experiments tend to be low in mundane realism. People behave more like they 'normally' do when a study is high in mundane realism, i.e. like everyday life.

➤ The IV or DV may be operationalised in such a way that it doesn't represent everyday life experiences, e.g. using lists of words to test how everyday memory works.

For all these reasons participants in a lab experiment are less likely to behave as they would in everyday life.

Field experiments have problems too

The same problems may also arise in field experiments, so that field experiments are not necessarily more like everyday life than lab experiments.

However, field experiments are *more* like everyday life and do tend to have higher mundane realism.

The trade-off for this increased mundane realism is that it is more difficult to control **extraneous variables**. This means that the results may be meaningless.

There is also a major **ethical issue** – if participants don't know they are being studied, is it right to manipulate and record their behaviour?

Mundane realism refers to how a study mirrors the everyday world. 'Mundane' means 'of the world', commonplace, ordinary.

mini study

A field experiment on helping behaviour

A number of studies have investigated the effects of appearance on behaviour, for example:

Leonard Bickman (1974) found that New York pedestrians were more likely to obey someone dressed as a guard than someone in a milkman's uniform or dressed casually. The confederates issued orders to passersby 'Pick up this bag for me', or 'This fellow is over-parked at the meter but doesn't have any change. Give him a dime', or 'Don't you know you have to stand on the other side of the pole?'

In this field experiment the IV is appearance and the DV is helping behaviour.

- Students should work in pairs. One member of the pair is the observer and the other is the confederate who wears one of two outfits: smartly dressed or casual.
- The task is to ask people if they would be prepared to stop and answer some questions for a school project. If the passerby says 'no', then thank them. If the passerby says 'yes' then explain that this was an experiment for your school work and all you wished to know was whether they were prepared to help or not.
- The observer should record:
  1. How many passersby said 'yes' or 'no' for each condition (smart or casual).
  2. Any other comments made by passersby.

⚠ **Warning:** This field experiment raises ethical issues. Check with your school/college before conducting it to see if they are happy with you stopping people in the street, and make sure to debrief participants carefully.

1 For each of the studies described on the facing page (A–F) answer the following questions:

 a Identify the IV and DV.

 b Was the task required of participants artificial?

 c Was the study conducted in a natural setting?

 d Was the setting high or low in mundane realism?

 e Did the participants know they were being studied?

 f Were the participants brought into a special (contrived) situation, or did the experimenter go to them?

 g What relevant variables might not have been controlled?

 h Do you think this was a lab or field experiment?

 i Describe **one** strength and **one** weakness of using this method in this context.

2 Consider the field experiment on helping behaviour described in the mini study below left. You can answer these questions even if you don't conduct the study.

 a What are the research aims of this experiment?

 b How do you know it is an experiment?

 c How do you know it is a field experiment?

 d Write a suitable hypothesis for this experiment.

 e What is a 'confederate'?

 f Which would be better – to use one confederate dressed in two different outfits or use two confederates, one dressed smartly and the other dressed casually? Explain your decision.

 g What method could you use to select your participants?

 h Give **one** strength and **one** weakness of using this method of selecting participants.

 i What is the experimental design in this study?

 j Describe **one** weakness of using this experimental design in this study.

 k Can you think of **one** ethical issue raised in this study (i.e. something that may harm participants)?

 l Name a suitable measure of central tendency to use with your data and explain why.

 m Present your data in a table like the one below. If you haven't conducted the study, invent some data.

	Smartly dressed	Casually dressed
Passerby said 'yes'		
Passerby said 'no'		

 n Draw a graph to illustrate your findings.

 o What do you conclude?

3 Consider how you could conduct a lab experiment on helping behaviour, using the same IV and DV.

 a What would be the strengths of this study compared with the field experiment version?

 b What would be the weaknesses?

VALIDITY – INTERNAL VALIDITY

Validity is probably THE MOST IMPORTANT CONCEPT in research methods. It concerns the question of whether any observed effect is a genuine one.

There is **validity**, and there is internal and external validity. We will begin with internal validity.

Internal validity is concerned with the following questions:

➤ Did the independent variable (IV) produce the change in the dependent variable (DV)?

➤ Or was the change in the DV caused by something else? In other words, by **extraneous (confounding) variables** (EV).

Losing sight of the wood for the trees

Sometimes we just get too focused on the little bits (the trees) and lose sight of the bigger picture (the forest). So step back for a minute.

Does it matter whether we classify a study as a lab experiment or a field experiment?

The answer is probably 'no'. What matters is the bigger picture:

- *Participant awareness.* Awareness factors are threats to **internal validity**.
- *Experimental control.* Lack of experimental control is a threat to **internal validity**.
- *Artificiality (low mundane realism)* is a threat to **external validity** (which we will look at on pages 36 and 37).

Participant effects

On page 20 we looked at things that may act as extraneous variables in experiments, including **participant variables**. Now we are concerned with something different – **participant effects**.

In both lab and field experiments participants may know their behaviour is being studied, but this is less likely in a field experiment. Why don't we want participants to be aware that they are participating in a study?

Think of the **Hawthorne effect** (see previous spread). The participants in the Hawthorne effect study showed improved productivity rates. This was the DV. The researchers initially assumed this change was due to increased lighting levels (the IV). Subsequently, they realised that there was an important EV, the fact that researchers were showing interest in what the workers were doing.

This shows that participants' behaviour is affected by the attention of a researcher.

Demand characteristics

People always seek cues about how to behave. Different situations demand different behaviours. Watching a football game at home you sit relatively quietly, but on a football ground you chant and jump up and down. These different situations 'demand' different behaviours.

In an experiment participants are often unsure about what to do. They actively look for clues that tell them what is expected of them. These clues are called **demand characteristics** – the totality of the cues that convey the experimental hypothesis to the participant.

For example

- A participant is given two memory tests, one in the morning and one in the afternoon. Participants might try to work out what is going on and guess that the experimenter is trying to see if people do better in the morning or afternoon. This might lead participants to try to perform the same each time because they have guessed the research aims.

- Participants are asked to fill in a questionnaire. The questions all appear to be about friendships. This leads participants to guess that the purpose of the study is to assess sociability and therefore participants emphasise their sociableness in their answers.

In all cases the result is that participants do not behave as they would usually. They have altered the behaviour as a consequence of the cues in the research situation. Thus demand characteristics may act as an extraneous (confounding) variable because they systematically affect the DV.

Participants want to offer a helping hand. If they know they are in an experiment they usually want to please the experimenter and be helpful, otherwise why are they there? This sometimes results in them being over-cooperative and behaving artificially.

Conversely, sometimes a participant deliberately behaves in a way to spoil an experiment.

Participant effects occur because of triggers in an experimental situation that may bias a participant's behaviour, e.g. because they know they are being studied or because of demand characteristics.

Internal validity is the degree to which the observed effect was due to the experimental manipulation rather than other factors, such as extraneous variables.

If internal validity is low then the results have little value.

Martin T. Orne invented the term demand characteristics.

'*The totality of cues that convey the experimental hypothesis to the [participant] become determinants of the [participant's] behaviour*' (Orne, 1962).

In one of Orne's studies participants had to sit in a room on their own for four hours. One group of participants were asked at the beginning of the study to sign a form releasing the experimenter from responsibility if anything happened to them during the experiment. They were also given a panic button to push if they felt overly stressed. The other group were given no information to arouse their expectations. The first group showed extreme signs of distress during isolation and this can only be explained in terms of the demand characteristics created (Orne and Scheibe, 1964).

Dealing with participant effects

Single blind design The participant doesn't know the true aims of the experiment or doesn't know that they are involved in an experiment.

Double blind design Both the participant *and* the person conducting the experiment are 'blind' to the aims. Therefore, the investigator cannot produce cues about what he/she expects.

Experimental realism If you make the experimental task sufficiently engaging then the participant pays attention to the task and not the fact that they are being observed.

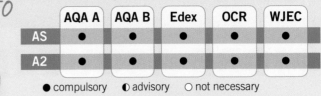
key terms

- Confounding variable
- Demand characteristics
- Double blind design
- Experimenter
- Experimental realism
- Experimenter bias
- Extraneous variables
- Hawthorne effect
- Internal validity (WJEC call this experimental validity)
- Investigator
- Investigator bias
- Investigator effects
- Operationalise
- Participant effects
- Participant variables
- Single blind design
- Standardised instructions
- Standardised procedures
- Validity

Experimenter bias

Experimenter bias (or investigator bias) is a kind of experimenter effect. It is the term used to specifically describe the effects of an experimenter's expectations on a participant's behaviour. A classic demonstration of this was in the experiment by Rosenthal and Fode described on page 26, which showed that even rats are affected by an experimenter's expectations.

Experimenter versus investigator

You might have noticed that sometimes we are talking about an **experimenter** and sometimes an **investigator**.

1. Not all psychology studies are experiments, so the term 'investigator' is more all-purpose.

2. In many experiments the person who designs the experiment is not the same as the minion who actually deals with the participants. To distinguish these roles we talk of investigators and experimenters. Officially it is the investigator who designs the study and the experimenter who conducts it, but there is some inconsistency in the way these terms are used!

Investigator effects

We discussed investigator effects on page 20.

Some people take a narrow view and define investigator effects only as the *direct* effects of an investigator/experimenter on the behaviour of participants.

Other people take a wider view and also include *indirect* effects of the investigator's behaviour on the final results. Thus, they include the following as investigator effects.

- *Investigator experimental design effect*. The investigator may **operationalise** the measurement of variables in such a way that the desired result is more likely.

- *Investigator loose procedure effect*. The investigator may not clearly specify the **standardised instructions** and/or **standardised procedures** which leaves room for the results to be influenced by the experimenter.

- *Investigator or experimenter fudging effect*. The investigator may invent extra data so that the findings fit the expectations, or the experimenter may do this to please the investigator.

- *Experimenter personal attributes effect*. For example, an experimenter who liked women but not men might treat male and female participants differently, and so produce a spurious gender effect in the data.

the bottom line

Investigator effects are any cues (other than the IV) from an investigator/experimenter that encourage certain behaviours in the participant that lead to the fulfillment of the investigator's expectations. Such cues act as extraneous/confounding variables.

1   Orne's panic button study (see facing page) is an example of demand characteristics. Outline the demand characteristics in this study.

2   Intons-Peterson's study (below) is also an example of demand characteristics. Outline the demand characteristics in this study.

3   In a research study participants' memory was tested in the morning and in the afternoon, to see if there was any difference in their ability to recall numbers.

   a   Give an example of **one** possible participant effect in this study.

   b   Describe how you might deal with this participant effect.

   c   Give an example of **one** possible experimenter/investigator effect in this study.

   d   Describe how you might deal with this investigator effect.

   e   Give an example of a possible demand characteristic in this study.

   f   Describe how you might deal with this problem.

4   A research study looked at whether first impressions matter. Participants were given a list of adjectives describing Mr Smith. One group had positive adjectives first, followed by negative adjectives. The other group had the adjectives in reverse order. They were all then asked to describe Mr Smith.

   Answer the questions a–f above for this study.

mini study

Testing demand characteristics

Margaret Intons-Peterson (1983) arranged for assistant experimenters (investigators) to run her study. Half of these investigators were led to believe that their participants would perform better on task A, and the others were led to believe that their participants would perform on task B. All participants did both tasks. The investigators were warned not to reveal these expectations to the participants and, in fact, were given a set of standardised instructions to read out.

Despite this, the participants' performances were affected by the investigator's expectations. The participants performed better in the condition in which their investigator expected them to perform better.

When videotapes of the experimental sessions were examined, it became apparent that the investigators were reading out the instructions for the condition where they expected better performance more slowly and clearly. This quite unintentional non-verbal cue turned out to be quite enough to affect the participants' performances.

➤ Design a study similar to this. The two tasks could be a simple cognitive task, for example task A might involve using imagery to remember a word list and task B might involve using repetition to remember a different word list.

➤ It is important to conduct a pilot study to check that people usually perform fairly equally on both tasks.

MORE ABOUT INTERNAL VALIDITY

We discussed extraneous (confounding) variables on pages 20 and 21, and promised that we would return to this topic. So here we are. You should ...

➤ Be aware of what we mean by an extraneous variable (EV) and a confounding variable.

➤ Be aware of examples of extraneous/confounding variables.

On this spread we are going to revisit the examples, emphasisng some key characteristics.

Extraneous and confounding variables

As noted earlier these two terms are used somewhat interchangeably. The only exam board that requires a knowledge of both is AQA B. WJEC use the term confounding and AQA A and OCR mention extraneous variables!

An extraneous variable is anything that has unwanted effects on the DV. Sometimes they are called 'nuisance variables' because they confuse everything.

A confounding variable is an extraneous variable that systematically varies with the IV. For example, if we wish to study the effects of watching TV while you study, we might test two groups of participants. Group 1 do a test while watching TV and Group 2 do the same test with no TV. But what if it happens that the TV group (Group 1) are tested in the morning while the no TV group (Group 2) are tested in the afternoon? Time of day may affect performance, so Group 1 do better because morning is when people are more alert. Time of day has varied systematically with the IV and acted as a confounding variable.

Extraneous variables is the general term, confounding variables are a specific type of extraneous variables.

So you can always use the term 'extraneous variable' but need to be more careful with the term 'confounding variable' because it has a more specific meaning.

Clever Hans *was an Arabian stallion owned by Wilhelm Von Osten. Hans demonstrated an astonishing ability to perform arithmetic calculations. Someone would ask a simple arithmetic question, for example 'What's 7 times 4?', and they would then start counting aloud. When they reached the answer to the arithmetic question the horse would start stamping its hooves. People were very impressed.*

However, rigorous testing showed that he was not in fact doing any adding, he was responding to subtle unconscious cues from his owner – Wilhelm was communicating expectations that acted as demand characteristics. The reason the horse did as expected was because of the cues, not his counting ability. Fulfilling expectations is the outcome of demand characteristics.

Situational variables

Situational variables are those features of a research situation that may influence participant's behaviour and thus act as EVs.

You'll see here that we have included order effects and investigator effects within this group – whereas on page 20 they were listed separately.

Time of day, temperature, noise

When we considered 'control' (page 20) we used the example of doing a test in the morning or afternoon. Any environmental variable, such as time of day, temperature or even noise levels at the time of testing, may act as an EV but only if it does affect performance on the behaviour tested, e.g. if the task is a cognitive task, time of day may be significant because people are more alert in the morning. However, if the task was concerned with obedience, time of day may not matter. If you think that noise is an EV, have a look at the experiment on page 135.

Order effects

One example of a situational variable is order effects, which were described on page 20. Improved participant performance may be due to practice (an EV) rather than the IV. Participant performance may also be worse because of boredom or fatigue rather than because of the IV.

Investigator effects

Investigator effects are any cues (other than the IV) from an investigator/experimenter that encourage certain behaviours in the participant, leading to a fulfillment of the investigator's expectations. Such cues act as an EV.

The way in which an investigator asks a question may lead a participant to give the answer the investigator 'wants' (similar to leading questions, see page 21). Alternatively, the way the investigator responds to a participant may encourage some participants more than others. For example, Rosenthal (1966) found that male investigators were more pleasant, friendly, honest, encouraging and relaxed when their participants were female than when they were male.

Demand characteristics

On the previous spread we listed demand characteristics under participant effects. It's debatable whether they belong there – or here. They are actually features of the experimental *situation* that elicit participant effects.

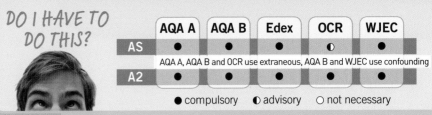

DO I HAVE TO DO THIS?

	AQA A	AQA B	Edex	OCR	WJEC
AS	●	●	●	◐	●

AQA A, AQA B and OCR use extraneous, AQA B and WJEC use confounding

	AQA A	AQA B	Edex	OCR	WJEC
A2	●	●	●	●	●

● compulsory ◐ advisory ○ not necessary

key terms

- Confounding variable
- Demand characteristics
- Extraneous variable
- Independent groups design
- Internal validity
- Investigator effects
- Leading questions
- Order effects
- Participant effects
- Participant variable
- Repeated measures design
- Situational variables

Participant variables

Any participant variable might act as an EV – but only if an independent groups **design** is used. When a repeated measures **design** is used participant variables are controlled.

Age, intelligence, motivation, experience

Participants in one condition may perform better because they have certain characteristics in common rather than because of the IV they receive. In the noise and memory experiment it might be that one group of participants were younger (and thus had better memories), or more intelligent, more highly motivated or more experienced at doing memory tests, and these would act as an EVs making the results meaningless.

Gender

Males and females are psychologically different in many ways because of the way they are socialised. For example, research suggests that women are more compliant than men because they are more oriented to interpersonal goals (Eagly, 1978). This means that if there are more women than men in one condition of an experiment this might mask the effects of the IV. However, it is important to realise that gender only acts as an EV in some circumstances. For example, we would not control gender in a memory experiment unless we had a reason to expect that it would matter.

Irrelevant participant variables

When considering participant variables as EVs we need only focus on those that are relevant to the task. Therefore, in the noise and memory task, a liking or disliking of spicy food would not be an EV (at least it would be hard to see why it would be).

Participant effects

Participant effects are different to participant variables. Participant effects might occur because participants actively seek cues about how to behave. See the previous spread for further discussion of participant effects.

mini study
The effect of expectations

There are many studies in psychology which have shown that a person's expectations affect what they see. One classic study was conducted by Leonard Carmichael et al. (1932). Participants were shown a set of drawings (central column) and then provided a verbal description (either the column on the left or on the right). When participants were later asked to redraw the image, the resulting object was typically affected by the verbal label that had been given.

➤ In order to conduct this study you need to devise a system to score participants' responses so you can tell whether or not their response was affected by the verbal label.

Consider the problems related to validity that may arise in each of the studies A–D listed below and answer the following questions.

1 Identify at least **two** issues concerning validity in this research (try to use all the different kinds of extraneous variables described on this spread).

2 Link each issue to the study by clearly explaining in what way this is an issue in the particular study.

3 Identify at least **one** method that could be used to deal with **one** of the issues of validity.

4 Link each method of dealing with the validity issue to the study by clearly explaining how the method would be used in the context of this particular study.

It might be useful to discuss your thoughts in small groups and then answer the questions yourself.

Study A
Participants' concentration was tested before and after lunch to see if having lunch made any difference to their ability to concentrate.

Study B
A psychology class conducted a study in their college on stress and blood pressure. Some students were tested after trying to complete an impossible puzzle (i.e. were stressed).

Study C
Men and women were compared in terms of helpfulness. A researcher approached male and female pedestrians asking them if they would be willing to help with his research. The researcher expected the women to be more helpful.

Study D
Carmichael et al.'s research described in the mini study below.

If you really want to be keen you could use the studies in Questions 2.5 (page 39) and 2.6 (page 41) and answer questions 1–4 above. By the time you have finished this you must have reached expert level on dealing with extraneous variables.

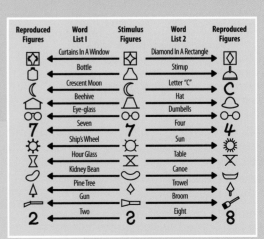

VALIDITY – EXTERNAL VALIDITY

Issues with the **validity** of an experiment can be internal or external.

A study that is low in internal validity is also low in external validity.

External validity concerns what goes on outside the experiment.

It is about generalising.

Internal validity concerns what goes on inside the experiment.

It is about control.

Internal validity is about what caused changes in the DV (was it the IV or was it something else? If it was something else any conclusions about the relationship between the IV and DV are not valid).

External validity is related to generalising – being able to apply or generalise the findings from an experiment to situations beyond the particular experiment.

Can we generalise to:

- different places or settings (called ecological validity)
- different people or populations (called population validity)
- different times (e.g. 1950s or 1990s) (historical validity).

External validity (ability to generalise) is enhanced through replication of a study. Imagine a study being conducted (study 1). Later, another researcher conducts study 2 which is an exact repeat of study 1. If the findings of study 2 are the same as study 1, this enhances the external validity of both studies because the results are not just a fluke.

Inevitably, studies in psychology involve a trade-off between control and generalisability. Greatest control exists in the lab. However, it is debatable to what extent findings from the lab can be generalised to other environments, and especially the less controllable environments in which everyday life is lived.

generalisability

control

Some psychologists argue that we can only discover things about behaviour if we uncover cause-and-effect relationships in highly controlled experiments. Others argue that field studies are the only real option for psychologists who are interested in how life is actually lived. The solution is to conduct both and use the results to build a picture of what is true about human behaviour.

It makes you think … mundane realism but no ecological valid

Milgram (1963)
Delivering painful shocks in a lab

Forty male participants were told that the study was investigating how punishment affects learning. There were two confederates: an experimenter and a 'learner'. The participant drew lots with the confederate and always ended up as the 'teacher'. He was told that he must administer increasingly strong electric shocks to the participant each time he got a question wrong.

Milgram found that 65% of the participants were fully obedient, i.e. continued to obey up to the maximum voltage of 450 volts.

Milgram repeated this study in many different situations:

- The location was moved to a run-down office (48% obedience).
- Teacher in same room as the learner (40% obedience).
- Teacher held learner's hand on shock plate (30% obedience).

These replications show that the initial conclusion was correct: situational factors affect obedience to unjust authority.

Hofling *et al.* (1966)
Nurses in the real world

This study was conducted in a US hospital. Nurses were telephoned by a 'Dr Smith' who asked the nurses to give 20mg of a drug called Astroten to a patient. This order contravened hospital regulations in a number of ways:

- Nurses were told not to accept instructions on the phone.
- Nor from an unknown doctor.
- Nor for a dose in excess of the safe amount (the dosage was twice that advised on the bottle).
- Especially for an unknown drug.

Nevertheless, 21 out of 22 (95%) nurses did as requested.

When the nurses involved in the study were interviewed afterwards they said, in their defense, that they had obeyed because that's what doctors expect nurses to do – they behaved as nurses do in everyday life.

Rank and Jacobsen (1977)
More nurses

In another study (this time in Australia) nurses in a hospital were also asked to carry out an irregular order. This time 16 out of 18 (89%) refused. There were important differences:

- The drug was familiar (*Valium*).
- The nurses could consult with peers.

Browning (1992)
An incident in the Second World War

In one encounter between German troops and civilians the commander, Major Trapp, had orders to shoot all the Jews in a small town – but Trapp told his men that if they didn't wish to obey orders he would assign them to other duties. Nevertheless most of the men did obey – despite the fact that the task involved many of the factors that Milgram had found led to reduced obedience (the task had face-to-face contact, there were some disobedient peers and there was absence of pressure from an authority figure).

key terms
- Ecological validity
- External validity
- Generalisability
- Historical validity
- Internal validity
- Mundane realism
- Population validity
- Replication
- Validity

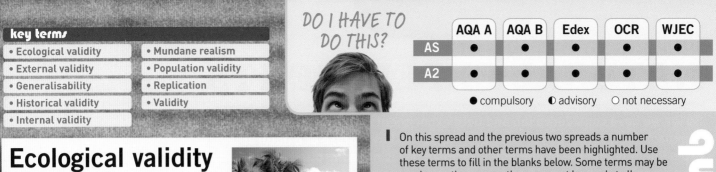

DO I HAVE TO DO THIS?

	AQA A	AQA B	Edex	OCR	WJEC
AS	●	●	●	●	●
A2	●	●	●	●	●

● compulsory   ◐ advisory   ○ not necessary

Ecological validity

Ecological validity is one form of external validity. It is the extent to which the results of a research study can be generalised from the set of environmental conditions created by the researcher to other environmental conditions – such as to everyday life or real life.

Many people think that ecological validity means 'the degree to which the behaviors observed and recorded in a study reflect the behaviours that actually occur in natural settings.'

This is not wrong but also not right.

1. Part of ecological validity concerns whether a research study mirrors real world or everyday experiences. This is **mundane realism** or 'representiveness'.

2. Another part of ecological validity concerns **generalisability** – the extent to which findings from one study (conducted in a unique setting) can be generalised to other settings (including the 'real world' or everyday experiences).

You might think that the study of nurses by Hofling *et al.* had high mundane realism and high ecological validity. *It had low mundane realism.* Even though it was conducted in a natural setting the tasks were quite artificial. Rank and Jacobsen's study used *more real-life tasks* – in this study the nurses dealt with a familiar drug and were allowed to consult with each other.

Hofling *et al.*'s study was conducted in a more natural setting than Milgram's but this *doesn't automatically mean that it had higher ecological validity.* Milgram's study concerned obedience of ordinary people to perceived authority (i.e. obeying an experimenter), so it wasn't really artificial at all. Whereas the doctor–nurse authority relationship is a special one and therefore it is not reasonable to generalise from this to all other kinds of obedience. It is part of a nurses' job to obey the orders of doctors, as the nurses in Hofling *et al.*'s study argued in their defence.

The replications by Milgram of his original study suggest that his findings *do* apply to other settings whereas the same is not true for the study by Hofling *et al.*, which was not replicated in another setting.

However, Browning's study challenges Milgram's conclusions because the findings were not replicated in this more 'real-world' setting.

The moral of the story: Don't assume that any study has ecological validity – search for confirming evidence. All research conducted in the real world is not automatically ecologically valid and all lab studies are not automatically ecologically *invalid*. Every study has some ecological validity – some are just more ecologically valid than others.

1 On this spread and the previous two spreads a number of key terms and other terms have been highlighted. Use these terms to fill in the blanks below. Some terms may be used more than once, others may not be used at all.

   a A repeated measures study where participants are able to guess the aim of the study. This might affect the _____ validity of the study.

   b A study that used an opportunity sample of people living in a city. This study would lack _____ validity.

   c Participants in a lab experiment know they are being studied. Their performance may improve because of the Hawthorne effect. This would affect the _____ validity of the study.

   d A study was replicated and the same findings were produced. This suggests that the study has _____ validity.

   e Participants want to please an experimenter and therefore respond to _____ _____.

   f Being able to apply the findings of a study to other settings is called _____ validity which is a kind of _____ validity.

   g A field experiment is conducted in a more everyday setting which may increase its _____ validity but decrease its _____ validity.

   h _____ _____ is the extent to which behaviours in a study mirror real life.

2 An area of research that has interested psychologists is massed versus distributed practice, i.e. whether learning is better if you practise something repeatedly in a short space of time (massed) or space your periods of practice (distributed). This topic has been studied in different settings.

   Study A *Participants were required to recall nonsense syllables on 12 occasions spread over 3 days or 12 days (Jost, 1897). Recall was higher over 12 days. This finding has been supported by subsequent research.*

   Study B *Post office workers had to learn to type postcodes either using massed or distributed practice (Baddeley and Longman, 1978). Distributed practice was again found to be superior.*

   Present arguments for why each of these studies could be viewed as having high and low ecological validity.

mini study
The testing effect

Memory research provides many useful ideas that might improve your approach to revision. Here's one of them.

Roediger and Karpicke (2006) conducted a study where two groups of students were given a passage to remember. Group A were told to read the passage four times over the period of one week. Group B were given the passage to read once and then told to try to recall as much as they could on three separate occasions. Both groups were tested after one week to see how much they remembered. Group B had the best recall.

Try repeating the study yourself.

➤ Identify potential extraneous variables.
➤ Consider how you will control these.

NATURAL EXPERIMENTS

So far we have considered lab and field experiments. There is a third kind of experiment, called a natural experiment. The key feature of a natural experiment is that the independent variable (IV) is not controlled by the experimenter. The IV would have varied even if the researcher had not been around - the researcher makes use of a naturally occurring event, treating the variations as an IV. The experimenter then measures the effect of this IV on a dependent variable (DV).

The reason for conducting a natural experiment is that there are some IVs that cannot be manipulated directly for practical or ethical reasons, as illustrated in the two examples below.

You may feel that a field experiment is a 'natural' experiment because we have said that field experiments are more natural than lab experiments (because they are conducted in environments more similar to everyday life).

The 'natural' in a natural experiment refers to the independent variable in the experiment not the environmental conditions – in a natural experiment you might measure the DV in a lab.

Examples of natural experiments

The effects of watching TV

A study was conducted on the island of St Helena, a tiny island in the South Atlantic (Charlton *et al.*, 2000). The reason for selecting this island was the residents received television broadcasts for the first time in 1995. This enabled researchers to study the effects of television on the behaviour of the island's residents. The IV in this study was life before and after exposure to television.

There would be practical difficulties in controlling this IV – you first of all would have to find a community where there is no television and then have to arrange to broadcast television to that community. It makes sense to find a situation where it varied naturally.

In this study there were a number of DVs, all of them measures of pro- and anti-social behaviour. Children on the island were assessed before television was broadcast and again afterwards. Charlton *et al.* found no changes after the introduction of television.

The effects of emotional deprivation

Psychologists are concerned about the effects of maltreatment on the development of children. For ethical reasons maltreatment is a variable that cannot be controlled by an experimenter – you couldn't treat one group of children badly to see what affect this has on their subsequent behaviour. In order to conduct research, psychologists make use of existing (natural) variables.

In one study the effects of emotional deprivation were demonstrated Widdowson (1951). The children in the study were residents of an orphanage with a particularly strict regime. The orphanage children were very small for their age. One possibility was that they weren't eating well enough so they were given dietary supplements. This had no effect. However, when a new supervisor arrived who gave them better emotional care they began to improve. It is likely that the hormones produced by stress affect growth, and the new supervisor reduced their stress.

In this study the IV was emotional care (strict regime versus new supervisor). This is something that could not ethically be changed. The DV was the children's growth.

Drawing conclusions from natural experiments

There are several reasons why researchers cannot draw cause-and-effect conclusions from natural experiments:

- Strictly speaking an experiment involves the deliberate changing of an IV by an experimenter. Therefore, natural experiments are not 'true experiments' because no one has *deliberately* changed the IV in order to observe the effect on the DV. This means that we cannot say for certain that the IV in a natural experiment has caused any change in the DV (but remember in a field or lab experiment poor design may also make causal conclusions unjustified).

- In a natural experiment participants are not randomly allocated to conditions. This means that there may be biases in the different groups of participants. For example, in the study on music and IQ (facing page) there are likely to be a number of differences between the music lesson and non-music lesson group aside from whether or not they took music lessons. For instance, the music lesson group may come from a more wealthy family and this is what determines their higher IQ. The wealth of the family would act as an extraneous variable.

- The sample studied may have unique characteristics. For example, in the St Helena study (left) the people were part of a particularly helpful and pro-social community, and this might explain why violence on TV didn't affect their behaviour as it has in other studies. The unique characteristics of the sample means that the findings can't be generalised to other groups of people.

Comparing lab, field and natural experiments

Lab experiment

To investigate causal relationships between an IV and DV under controlled conditions.

Strengths

Well-controlled.

Extraneous variables are minimised, thus higher internal validity.

Can be easily replicated, demonstrating external validity.

Weaknesses

Artificial, a contrived situation where participants may not behave naturally.

Investigator effects and participant effects may reduce internal validity.

Field experiment

To investigate causal relationships between an IV and DV in more everyday surroundings.

Strengths

Less artificial, usually higher mundane realism and higher ecological validity.

Avoids participant effects (if participants are not aware of study), and this may increase internal validity.

Weaknesses

Less control of extraneous variables, reduces internal validity.

More time consuming and thus more expensive.

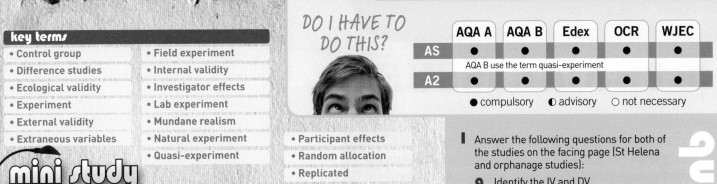

key terms

- Control group
- Difference studies
- Ecological validity
- Experiment
- External validity
- Extraneous variables

- Field experiment
- Internal validity
- Investigator effects
- Lab experiment
- Mundane realism
- Natural experiment
- Quasi-experiment

- Participant effects
- Random allocation
- Replicated

DO I HAVE TO DO THIS?

	AQA A	AQA B	Edex	OCR	WJEC
AS	●	●	●	●	●
AQA B use the term quasi-experiment					
A2	●	●	●	●	●

● compulsory ◑ advisory ○ not necessary

mini study

Music lessons can boost IQ

A recent study (Schellenberg, 2004) looked at the effects of music lessons on IQ. The participants (aged six years old) had their IQs tested before the study began. They were allocated to one of four groups: two groups had 36 weeks of extra-curricular music tuition, one had singing-based tuition, the other studied keyboard. A third group had extra drama lessons on top of normal school, and the last group (a control group*), simply attended school as usual. The children completed IQ and other tests at the end of the school year. Schellenberg found that the music groups' IQ performance increased significantly more than the drama and control groups.*

You can conduct similar research making use of existing data, and thus conduct a natural experiment.

- **IV** Divide your class into those who have received extra music lessons and those who have not. You must operationalise this IV, i.e. decide what constitutes 'having music lessons'. Would one week of lessons count?
- **DV** For each member of your class calculate a GCSE score. One way to do this is to assign a value to each grade, add all scores together and divide by the number of GSCE subjects. This gives you a final score for each student. You can use the table on the right to record your data.
- **Ethics** Individuals should record their data anonymously.
- **Analysis** Combine the data collected by your classmates. Calculate a mean score for all pupils with music lessons and all those without music lessons, and draw a graph to illustrate this data. What can you conclude?

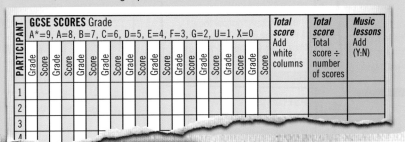

PARTICIPANT	GCSE SCORES Grade A*=9, A=8, B=7, C=6, D=5, E=4, F=3, G=2, U=1, X=0																		Total score Add white columns	Total score Total score ÷ number of scores	Music lessons Add (Y:N)
	Grade	Score	Grade	Score	Grade	Score	Grade	Score	Grade	Score	Grade	Score	Grade	Score	Grade	Score	Grade	Score			
1																					
2																					
3																					
4																					

Natural experiment

To investigate relationships between an IV and DV in situations where IV cannot be directly manipulated.

Strengths

Allows research where IV can't be manipulated for ethical or practical reasons.

Enables psychologists to study 'real' problems, such as the effects of a disaster on health (increased mundane realism and ecological validity).

Weaknesses

Cannot demonstrate causal relationships because IV not directly manipulated.

Less control of extraneous variables, therefore a threat to internal validity.

Can only be used where conditions vary naturally.

Participants may be aware of being studied, thus reducing internal validity.

Difference studies and quasi-experiments

What about a study where the IV is gender?

For example we might compare male and female behaviour on a task such as memory.

A person's gender has not been changed. It is simply something that exists, and therefore is not an IV.

The same principle applies to studies comparing old and young people, or introverts and extraverts, or Americans and British.

Such studies are simply difference studies.

Sometimes the term 'quasi-experiment' is used. 'Quasi' means 'almost', so a quasi-experiment is something that is almost an experiment but lacks certain key elements. Natural experiments are a kind of quasi-experiment but difference studies are not. In a quasi-experiment there is an IV.

1 Answer the following questions for both of the studies on the facing page (St Helena and orphanage studies):

a Identify the IV and DV.

b How do you think the IV was changed?

c Identify at least **one** potential threat to internal validity. [Hint: think of extraneous variables.]

d Identify at least **one** potential threat to external validity. [Hint: think of population validity.]

e What were the aims of this study?

f Write a suitable hypothesis for this experiment.

g Identify the target population.

h What was the experimental design?

2 Music lessons and IQ (see mini study) – the original study by Schellenberg was *not* a natural experiment. What kind of experiment was it? Explain the reasons for your answer.

3 Five studies are described below. Identify each study as a lab, field or natural experiment, and explain your decision.

Study A *Two primary schools use different reading schemes. A psychological study compares the reading scores at the end of the year to see which scheme was more effective.*

Study B *Children take part in a trial to compare the success of a new maths programme. The children are placed in one of two groups: the new maths programme or the traditional one, and taught in these groups for a term.*

Study C *The value of using computers rather than books is investigated by requiring children to learn word lists, either using a computer or with a book.*

Study D *The effect of advertisements on gender stereotypes is studied by showing children ads with women doing feminine tasks or doing neutral tasks and then asking them questions about gender stereotypes.*

Study E *A study investigated the anti-social effects of TV by seeing whether people who watch a lot of TV (over five hours a day) are more aggressive than those who don't.*

For each of the studies above (A–E) answer the following questions.

a Outline **one** strength of using the research method selected and explain why this strength would be particularly important for this particular study.

b Outline **one** weakness of using the research method selected and explain why this weakness would be particularly important for this particular study.

c Identify **one** problem related to internal or external validity in this research and describe how you could deal with this problem.

ETHICAL ISSUES

Participants want to protect their rights

Researchers want to conduct meaningful research.

Ethical issue

In Chapter 1 we considered ethics. There is considerably more to ethics than what was discussed there. We begin on this spread with a look at ethics and ethical issues. On the next spread we will look at how psychologists deal with ethical issues.

The topic of ethics concerns standards of behaviour that distinguish between right and wrong, good and bad, and justice and injustice. Some ethical standards are highly general and apply to all situations, such as being honest or being helpful to others. Other standards apply to specific situations, such as medical ethics or ethics when conducting research.

An ethical issue is a conflict between what the researcher wants and the rights of participants. They are conflicts about what is acceptable.

For example, an experimenter might want to study the effects of tattooing on self-esteem. But you can't tattoo someone without their permission. And even if you did have their permission there would have to be a very good reason for doing this study in order to justify the procedures used.

INFORMED CONSENT

Participants must be given comprehensive information concerning the nature and purpose of a study and their role in it.

Participant's view

Participants wish to know what they are letting themselves in for if they agree to take part in a study. It is necessary in order to be able to make an informed decision about whether to participate in a study.

Researcher's view

Providing comprehensive information may reduce the meaningfulness of the research because such information will reveal the study's aims and this could affect participants' subsequent behaviour.

For example, a researcher may want to see how obedient people are when given an order by someone in authority. If the researcher tells participants this at the outset of the study, participants might deliberately act more obediently.

DECEPTION

This occurs when a participant is not told the true aims of a study, or is deliberately misled in some way. Participants might be given some details about what they will be required to do in the study, but other information that might affect their behaviour will be withheld.

For example, they might be told that they will have to answer a questionnaire about certain social situations but not told that their obedience is being assessed.

Participant's view

This is an issue because it prevents participants being able to give truly informed consent as they don't have all the necessary information to make that decision.

Honesty is an important ethical principle.

Researcher's view

Some deception is relatively harmless and/or can be compensated for by adequate debriefing.

For example, in a memory experiment a participant might not be told that, at the end, they will be asked to rate faces for attractiveness instead of being tested for recall. Such a deception would not cause significant embarrassment or harm to the participants.

In addition, there is a difference between simply withholding information and actually telling participants a lie, such as telling them the study is about something completely different to the true aims.

RIGHT TO WITHDRAW

Participants have the right to know that they can freely decide not to continue participation in a study at any time. This ensures that they feel comfortable at all times.

Participants should also have the right to withdraw their data at the end of a study if they were unhappy about their participation in the study.

Participant's view

This is especially important if some information was withheld at the beginning of the study or if they didn't really understand what might be involved.

Participants may feel they shouldn't withdraw because it will spoil the study.

In some studies participants are paid or rewarded in some way (e.g. university credits) so they may not feel able to withdraw.

Researcher's view

The loss of participants may bias the study's findings because the participants who leave might be the more confident ones or the more intelligent ones.

PROTECTION FROM HARM

Harm includes any negative physical effects, such as physical injury or asking someone to smoke or drink alcohol, or any negative psychological effects, such as embarrassment or creating self-doubt.

Participant's view

Participants have no desire to be harmed! They would expect to be in the same state at the end of the study as they were at the beginning.

It is reasonable to expose individuals to risks equivalent to what would be experienced in their everyday lives.

Researcher's view

It may not be possible to estimate all possible negative effects before conducting a study.

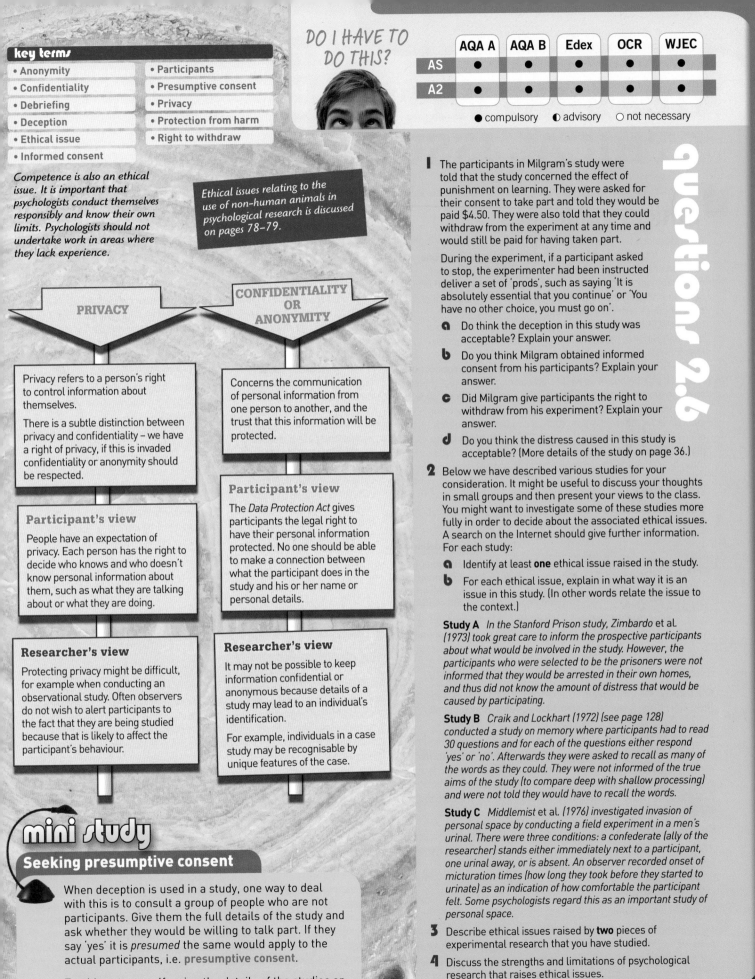

key terms
- Anonymity
- Confidentiality
- Debriefing
- Deception
- Ethical issue
- Informed consent
- Participants
- Presumptive consent
- Privacy
- Protection from harm
- Right to withdraw

DO I HAVE TO DO THIS?

Competence is also an ethical issue. It is important that psychologists conduct themselves responsibly and know their own limits. Psychologists should not undertake work in areas where they lack experience.

Ethical issues relating to the use of non-human animals in psychological research is discussed on pages 78–79.

PRIVACY

Privacy refers to a person's right to control information about themselves.

There is a subtle distinction between privacy and confidentiality – we have a right of privacy, if this is invaded confidentiality or anonymity should be respected.

Participant's view

People have an expectation of privacy. Each person has the right to decide who knows and who doesn't know personal information about them, such as what they are talking about or what they are doing.

Researcher's view

Protecting privacy might be difficult, for example when conducting an observational study. Often observers do not wish to alert participants to the fact that they are being studied because that is likely to affect the participant's behaviour.

CONFIDENTIALITY OR ANONYMITY

Concerns the communication of personal information from one person to another, and the trust that this information will be protected.

Participant's view

The *Data Protection Act* gives participants the legal right to have their personal information protected. No one should be able to make a connection between what the participant does in the study and his or her name or personal details.

Researcher's view

It may not be possible to keep information confidential or anonymous because details of a study may lead to an individual's identification.

For example, individuals in a case study may be recognisable by unique features of the case.

mini study

Seeking presumptive consent

When deception is used in a study, one way to deal with this is to consult a group of people who are not participants. Give them the full details of the study and ask whether they would be willing to talk part. If they say 'yes' it is *presumed* the same would apply to the actual participants, i.e. **presumptive consent**.

Try this out yourself, using the details of the studies on the right.

1 The participants in Milgram's study were told that the study concerned the effect of punishment on learning. They were asked for their consent to take part and told they would be paid $4.50. They were also told that they could withdraw from the experiment at any time and would still be paid for having taken part.

During the experiment, if a participant asked to stop, the experimenter had been instructed deliver a set of 'prods', such as saying 'It is absolutely essential that you continue' or 'You have no other choice, you must go on'.

a Do think the deception in this study was acceptable? Explain your answer.

b Do you think Milgram obtained informed consent from his participants? Explain your answer.

c Did Milgram give participants the right to withdraw from his experiment? Explain your answer.

d Do you think the distress caused in this study is acceptable? (More details of the study on page 36.)

2 Below we have described various studies for your consideration. It might be useful to discuss your thoughts in small groups and then present your views to the class. You might want to investigate some of these studies more fully in order to decide about the associated ethical issues. A search on the Internet should give further information. For each study:

a Identify at least **one** ethical issue raised in the study.

b For each ethical issue, explain in what way it is an issue in this study. (In other words relate the issue to the context.)

Study A *In the Stanford Prison study, Zimbardo et al. (1973) took great care to inform the prospective participants about what would be involved in the study. However, the participants who were selected to be the prisoners were not informed that they would be arrested in their own homes, and thus did not know the amount of distress that would be caused by participating.*

Study B *Craik and Lockhart (1972) (see page 128) conducted a study on memory where participants had to read 30 questions and for each of the questions either respond 'yes' or 'no'. Afterwards they were asked to recall as many of the words as they could. They were not informed of the true aims of the study (to compare deep with shallow processing) and were not told they would have to recall the words.*

Study C *Middlemist et al. (1976) investigated invasion of personal space by conducting a field experiment in a men's urinal. There were three conditions: a confederate (ally of the researcher) stands either immediately next to a participant, one urinal away, or is absent. An observer recorded onset of micturation times (how long they took before they started to urinate) as an indication of how comfortable the participant felt. Some psychologists regard this as an important study of personal space.*

3 Describe ethical issues raised by **two** pieces of experimental research that you have studied.

4 Discuss the strengths and limitations of psychological research that raises ethical issues.

DEALING WITH ETHICAL ISSUES

Ethical issues are dealt with in a number of ways. Three of them are considered below. Each of these are not separate, for example ethical guidelines are related to the cost-benefit approach.

On the facing page we also consider ways of dealing with specific ethical issues.

1 Ethical guidelines

All professions (such as solicitors, doctors, etc.) have a specialist organisation consisting of fellow professionals. One function of such an organisation is to monitor the behaviour of the professional group and maintain an ethical standard of behaviour among the membership through the publication of a code of ethics (ethical guidelines).

In the UK the *British Psychological Society* (BPS) monitors their behaviour of psychologists. In the US it is the *American Psychological Association* (APA).

The BPS produces documents that help guide the conduct of research psychologists as well as practising psychologists (such as those working with the mentally ill). There is a general *Code of Ethics and Conduct* for all psychologists as well as specific guidelines for different areas, such as conducting research online. The *Code of Human Research Ethics* (see below) tells psychologists what behaviours are not acceptable and tells them how to deal with common ethical dilemmas.

Weaknesses

Guidelines absolve the individual researcher of any responsibility. They close off discussions about what is right and wrong.

Issues versus guidelines

Ethical issues are not the same as ethical guidelines, although many of them are the same. For example, informed consent is both an issue and a guideline. An issue is a conflict, a guideline is a means of resolving this conflict.

Note that debriefing is not an issue but lack of debriefing is accepted by some exam boards as an ethical issue.

The BPS *Code of Human Research Ethics* (2010)

The table on the facing page is based on the BPS *Code of Human Research Ethics*. A few other points have been included below.

Scientific value

Research should be designed, reviewed and conducted in a way that ensures its quality, integrity and contribution to the development of knowledge and understanding. Research that is judged within a research community to be poorly designed ... can have the potential to cause harm.

On informing participants

It is recommended that at least one pilot test of the processes for informing and debriefing participants be carried out with a naïve person having a literacy level at the lower end of the range expected in the planned research sample.

Who can give consent

The consent of participants in research, whatever their age or competence, should always be sought, by means appropriate to their age and competence level. For children under 16 years of age and for other persons where capacity to consent may be impaired the additional consent of parents or those with legal responsibility for the individual should normally also be sought.

2 Ethical committees

All institutions where research takes place have an ethical committee (sometimes called an institutional review board, IRB) and the committee must approve any study before it begins.

They look at all possible ethical issues and at how the researchers plan to deal with these, weighing up the value of the research against the possible costs in ethical terms. In some cases the balance is seen to be reasonable, in other cases it is decided that the costs are simply too great or the research is simply not of sufficient value.

3 The cost-benefit approach

The main principle used, when dealing with ethical issues, is to balance the potential consequences of the research against the potential to produce meaningful findings that can be used to enhance human lives.

Weaknesses

Cost-benefit decisions are flawed because judgements are inevitably subjective.

In addition, the costs are not always apparent until after the study.

Finally, it is difficult to quantify costs and benefits. How much does personal distress cost? If the results of a study demonstrate that people are more likely to obey someone in uniform, how much is that benefit?

Special techniques
Debriefing

It is commonplace for participants to be debriefed after a research study. This gives the researcher an opportunity to assess the effects of the research procedures and offer some form of counselling if necessary. If deception has been involved in the study, the researcher will explain the true aims of the study and offer participants the right to withhold their data. The researcher may also use this as an opportunity to find out more from the participant in relation to the research.

Weaknesses You can't put the clock back. If a participant was distressed by taking part in the research study this is difficult to undo. Participants may say they didn't mind and enjoyed the experience as a form of self-reassurance.

Presumptive consent

There are situations where it is not possible to obtain informed consent (such as field experiments or where informed consent would invalidate the study). An alternative to gaining informed consent from participants is to gain informed consent from others. This can be done, for example, by asking a group of people whether they feel the study is acceptable. We then *presume* that the participants themselves would have felt the same, if they had been given the opportunity to say so.

Weaknesses The problem with presumptive consent is that what people say they would or wouldn't mind is different from actually experiencing it.

	AQA A	AQA B	Edex	OCR	WJEC
AS	●	◐	●	◐	◐
A2	●	◐	●	◐	◐

● compulsory　◐ advisory　○ not necessary

key terms

- Anonymity
- Ethical issues
- Code of ethics
- Confidentiality
- Debrief
- Deception
- Ethical committee
- Ethical guidelines
- Informed consent
- Presumptive consent
- Privacy
- Protection from harm
- Right to withdraw

Dealing with particular ethical issues

Informed consent

Participants are formally asked to indicate their agreement to participate. The researcher should inform the participants of all aspects of the research or intervention that might reasonably be expected to influence their willingness to participate.

Failure to include all details before obtaining informed consent means that additional safeguards are needed to protect the welfare and dignity of participants.

Weaknesses

If a participant knows such information this may invalidate the purpose of the study.

Even if researchers have sought and obtained informed consent, that does not guarantee that participants really do understand what they have let themselves in for.

Deception

The need for deception should be approved by an ethical committee, weighing up benefits (of the study) against costs (to participants).

Participants should be fully debriefed after the study and offered the opportunity to withhold their data.

Weaknesses

Debriefing can't turn the clock back – a participant may still feel embarrassed or have lowered self-esteem.

The right to withdraw

Participants should be informed at the beginning of a study that they have the right to withdraw.

Weaknesses

Participants may feel they shouldn't withdraw because it will spoil the study.

In many studies participation is a requirement of an undergraduate psychology course, so students wouldn't feel they could withdraw.

Protection from harm

Avoid any situation that may cause a participant to experience psychological (e.g. negative feelings) or physical damage.

Participants should not be exposed to risks greater than or additional to those encountered in their normal life styles.

Weaknesses

Researchers are not always able to accurately predict the risks of taking part in a study.

Confidentiality and anonymity

Researchers should not record the names of any participants. They should use numbers instead or use false names.

If confidentiality cannot be guaranteed, participants should be informed in advance.

Weaknesses

It is sometimes possible to work out who the participants were on the basis of the information that has been provided, for example the geographical location of a school. In practice, therefore, confidentiality/anonymity may not be possible.

Privacy

Do not observe anyone without their informed consent unless it is in a public place.

Participants may be asked to give their retrospective consent or withhold their data.

Weaknesses

There isn't universal agreement on what constitutes a public place.

Not everyone may feel this is acceptable, for example lovers on a park bench.

1 On the previous spread we considered ethical issues in four studies. For each study suggest how you would deal with the ethical issues you raised.

2 Four further studies are described below. For each study answer the following questions:

a Identify the IV and DV.

b How could you operationalise the DV?

c Identify **one** possible extraneous variable.

d In what way is this study high or low in external validity?

e What kind of experiment do you think this is? (Explain your answer.)

f Identify at least **two** possible ethical issues.

g Describe how you would deal with each ethical issue.

h Describe **one** limitation for each of your methods of dealing with the ethical issues.

Study A *In order to study the effects of sleep deprivation students are asked to limit their sleep to five hours for three nights and then sleep normally for the next three nights. Each day the students' cognitive abilities are assessed using a memory test.*

Study B *Participants volunteer to take part in a study. They are told the study is about public speaking but the real aim is to see how people respond to encouragement by others. Some participants speak in front of a group of people who smile at them, while others talk to a group who appear disinterested.*

Study C *A teacher decides to try a little experiment with her class of eight year olds. She gives half the class a test in the morning and half of them do the same test in the afternoon to see if time of day affects performance.*

mini study
Ethical committee

Divide your class into groups. Each group should devise a study that raises one of the ethical issues listed in the table on the left – but not a wild idea, something which might be just acceptable! Look through your psychology textbook for ideas.

Write a research proposal that identifies the ethical issues and how you intend to deal with them. You should also be clear about the aim of the research and why it is important.

Then present your proposal to an ethical committee consisting of some of your class members. An ethical committee should be composed of people who represent the different interests: university, psychology department, participants – so each class member on the committee should take one of these roles.

EXPERIMENTAL AND CONTROL GROUPS

The term control is used in several different ways when talking about experiments:

➤ **The experimenter controls the independent variable.**

➤ **The experimenter seeks to control extraneous variables.**

➤ **A control group acts as a baseline in some experiments.**

In an experiment there are often two levels of the independent variable (IV). For example, think back to our experiment on noise and concentration (page 8). The IV was noise, and the two levels were loud and soft noise. The soft noise condition acted as a comparison condition. Both loud and soft noises are **experimental conditions**.

The same experiment could have been conducted with noise and no noise. In this case the no noise condition is called a **control condition** because it is simply a baseline condition.

Here's another example: a researcher might want to investigate the effects that rewards have on performance. To do this, children are asked to collect rubbish from a playground and offered a chocolate bar as a reward. They collect several bags of rubbish.

We cannot conclude anything about the effects of the reward because all the children were told they would receive a reward. We need to have a control group so that we can make a comparison.

We need two groups: an **experimental group** (offered a reward) and a **control group** (offered no reward). This allows us to compare the effects of the reward (IV) on collecting rubbish (the dependent variable).

Or we could do a similar study using a **repeated measures design** instead of **independent groups design**. This time we need to have two conditions instead of two groups: an **experimental condition** (children offered a reward on one occasion) and a **control condition** (offered no reward on another occasion).

Control can mean keeping something constant (like keeping a ball spinning in one place) or can mean changing it in a desired way (such as directing the basketball into a hoop).

Problems with internal validity

If we have an experimental group and a control group, it is possible that the experimental group will perform differently for reasons other than the IV (experimental treatment).

Consider a study on the effectiveness of a new teaching programme. One class is taught using the new programme (experimental group) and compared with another class taught using the 'old' programme (control group).

➤ The classes may have a different teacher.

➤ The experimental group might improve simply because the teaching programme is new (and the students enjoy the novelty) not better.

➤ The control group might try extra hard to show that the old way is just as good or better than the new approach. This is called the **John Henry effect** (see facing page).

Paying homage to formal terms*

Learning about research methods is a bit like learning a foreign language. You have to learn to use a whole new vocabulary and you have to learn the meaning of this vocabulary. The problem with the vocabulary is that the meaning of the terms is not always black and white. You have to learn to look for the 'general drift' and not be fazed when you find that there are slightly different meanings as your understanding increases.

Don't get too tied up with the words themselves, they are just a vehicle for understanding.

*An excellent phrase 'invented' by Hugh Coolican (2004) to explain this problem.

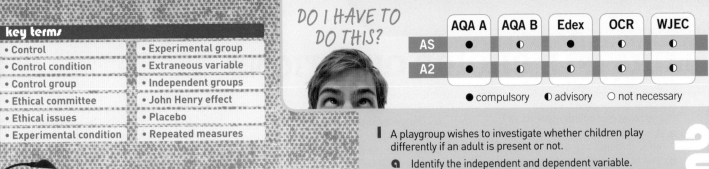

key terms

- Control
- Control condition
- Control group
- Ethical committee
- Ethical issues
- Experimental condition
- Experimental group
- Extraneous variable
- Independent groups
- John Henry effect
- Placebo
- Repeated measures

mini study
The placebo effect

In some studies the control condition involves the use of a placebo – a substance that has no active ingredient. For example, if a researcher wishes to find out whether a particular drug is effective for treating depression he/she would design a study where one group of depressed patients (the experimental group) receives the drug and a second group (the control group) does not receive the drug.

However, there is a problem. Research has shown that people get better if they just think they are getting a drug. In order to control for this both groups of participants are given a pill but one group is receiving a placebo – a drug that has no physiological effects but still creates expectations.

Investigating the placebo effect with real drugs is obviously beyond what would be acceptable for a student study, so here's a suggested alternative. Caffeine affects most people by raising their pulse rate and blood pressure.

- Divide your participants into two groups. Both groups will be given a strong cup of coffee. For one group (the placebo group) this will be a decaffeinated coffee. The other group will receive caffeinated coffee.
- Afterwards measure pulse rate and, if you can, blood pressure.
- All participants should be informed of the physiological effects of caffeine and told that they will either be in the caffeine or no-caffeine group. They will be informed afterwards about the group they were in. Anyone who knows they are sensitive to caffeine should decline to take part.

Before conducting this study.
- Consider possible extraneous variables.
- Consider ethical issues in this study and how you will deal with them. You might convene an ethical committee to decide whether your research design is ethically acceptable.

1 A playgroup wishes to investigate whether children play differently if an adult is present or not.

a Identify the independent and dependent variable.

b Write a suitable non-directional hypothesis for this study.

c Describe how you might design a study to investigate this using an independent groups design.

d What kind of experiment is this?

e Explain **one** strength and **one** weakness of this kind of experiment in the context of this study.

f In this study identify the experimental group and the control group.

g Identify **one or more** ethical issues and suggest how you would deal with these.

h To what extent would the findings of your study have representativeness?

i To what extent would the findings of your study have generalisability?

j How could you conduct a study with the same aims using a repeated measures design?

k Identify the experimental and control conditions in this new study.

l Describe **one** strength and **one** weakness of using a repeated measures design in this study.

2 A research study is investigating a new drug for treating depression. There are three conditions in the experiment: (1) the drug, (2) a placebo, (3) nothing. In this case the control condition is having no drug.

Answer questions a–l above.

CLASS ACTIVITY What is validity all about?

Using what you have learned in this chapter create something to represent the various aspects of validity. It could be a PowerPoint presentation, a mobile, a poster for your classroom, a leaflet, a cartoon strip, a poem, a rap song – anything that is entertaining AND forces you to process the material (processing leads to deeper understanding and more enduring memories).

a Explain how you might conduct this study.

b Explain why this design is preferable to the design in the mini study on the left.

c How many levels of the IV are there in this study?

mini study
Testing the John Henry effect

Here's a challenge for you. How could you design a study that would test the John Henry effect?

Your hypothesis would be 'People who think they are demonstrating an old method of performing a task try harder than people who think they are demonstrating a new method'.

- Identify the IV and DV.
- Consider how to operationalise each of these.

John Henry is an American legend. He worked on building the railroads, drilling holes by hitting thick steel spikes into rocks. There was no one who could match him, though many tried.

One day someone tried to sell a steam-powered drill to the railroad company, claiming that it could out-drill any man. So they set up a contest between John Henry and the new drill. After 35 minutes of maniacal hammering, John Henry had drilled two seven-foot holes whereas the man with the steam drill had only drilled one nine-foot hole.

MULTIPLE CHOICE QUESTIONS

1. Which of the following is not a characteristic of a field experiment?
   a. It is conducted in a natural environment.
   b. The IV is directly manipulated by the experimenter.
   c. Extraneous variables can be well controlled.
   d. Participants are often not aware that they are being studied.

2. Which of the following is *not* a characteristic of a lab experiment?
   a. It is conducted in a natural environment.
   b. The IV is directly manipulated by the experimenter.
   c. Extraneous variables can be well controlled.
   d. Participants are often aware that they are being studied.

3. Mundane realism refers to:
   a. Using video film to capture participants' behaviour.
   b. A study being boring and therefore not holding participant's interest.
   c. The extent to which a study mirrors the real world.
   d. A Spanish football team.

4. Variables in an experiment are operationalised, which means they are:
   a. Understandable to participants.
   b. Used in a medical experiment.
   c. Described in a way that can be easily measured or manipulated.
   d. Turned into numbers.

5. Lab experiments are sometimes artificial because:
   a. Participants know they are being studied and this may affect their behaviour.
   b. The setting may lack mundane realism.
   c. The IV may be operationalised in such a way that it doesn't represent real-life experiences.
   d. All of the above.

6. Internal validity is concerned with:
   a. The generalisability of research findings.
   b. The consistency of measurement.
   c. Whether an observed effect can be attributed to the IV.
   d. Whether the findings are what the experimenter expected.

7. External validity refers to:
   a. The generalisability of research findings.
   b. Whether the findings are what the experimenter expected.
   c. Whether an observed effect can be attributed to the IV.
   d. All of the above.

8. Which of the following is *not* a kind of external validity?
   a. Ecological validity.
   b. Mundane validity.
   c. Population validity.
   d. Historical validity.

9. Demand characteristics are:
   a. Features of an experiment that cannot be controlled.
   b. Threats to external validity.
   c. Problem behaviours.
   d. Cues in a study which help a participant work out the research hypothesis.

10. Which of the following would *not* be a threat to internal validity?
    a. Experimenter bias.
    b. Participant reactivity.
    c. Social desirability bias.
    d. Single blind design.

11. The person who designs an experiment is called the:
    a. Investigator.
    b. Experimenter.
    c. Participant.
    d. Designer.

12. The narrow definition of an investigator effect is any effect the investigator has on:
    a. An investigation.
    b. Participant's behaviour.
    c. Extraneous variables.
    d. All of the above.

13. Ecological validity concerns:
    a. Representativeness.
    b. Generalisability.
    c. Representativeness and reliability.
    d. Representativeness and generalisability.

14. Which of the following is the best definition for ecological validity?
    a. Ecological validity is the degree to which behaviour in the laboratory reflects real life.
    b. Ecological validity is the extent to which findings can be generalised from the lab to the real world.

c. Ecological validity is the extent to which findings can be generalised from the research setting to other settings.
    d. Ecological validity is the degree to which findings can be generalised from one group of people to the target population.

15. If the participants in a study are only men, then we might think the study had low:
    a. Population validity.
    b. Ecological validity.
    c. External validity.
    d. Both a and c.

16. In a natural experiment:
    a. The IV is controlled by an experimenter.
    b. The IV varies naturally.
    c. The DV is controlled by an experimenter.
    d. The DV varies naturally.

17. Natural experiments are not 'true' experiments because:
    a. Participants are not randomly allocated to conditions.
    b. The sample studied may have unique characteristics.
    c. The IV is not directly manipulated by the experimenter.
    d. All of the above.

18. Studies that compare the behaviour of males and females (gender studies) are:
    a. Difference studies.
    b. Natural experiments.
    c. Quasi-experiments.
    d. Both a and c.

19. Debriefing is:
    a. An ethical issue.
    b. An ethical guideline.
    c. An ethical issue and an ethical guideline.
    d. A folder for research notes.

20. If informed consent is not possible, then an alternative would be to:
    a. Give participants the right to withdraw.
    b. Debrief participants.
    c. Obtain presumptive consent.
    d. All of the above.

Answers on facing page

EXAM STYLE QUESTION 3

A recent study (Schutheiss, 2004) looked at whether one can explain people's responses to films in terms of hormones. Hormones are chemical substances produced in the body in response to certain situations. Different hormones have different effects. Female hormones are related to relaxation while male hormones are related to aggression. Men and women have both male and female hormones (strange but true).

The research question was whether hormones could explain why people feel more lovey-dovey after watching a romantic film and more aggressive after watching an exciting film.

In this study there were three groups of participants. One group viewed a romantic scene from *The Bridges of Madison County*, the second group watched an exciting scene form *The Godfather, Part II* and the third group watched a documentary on the Amazon rainforest. The films were shown in a cinema.

Each participant had their hormone levels tested before and immediately after viewing the 45-minute film clip.

The study found that both men and women experienced raised levels of female hormones when watching the romantic film. In the group watching the exciting scene the men had raised levels of male hormones whereas these hormones were lowered in the women. The third group, watching the Amazon rainforest, showed no significant changes in hormone levels.

(a) (i) What was the experimental design in this study? (1 mark)

(ii) Describe **one** strength of using this design. (2 marks)

(b) (i) Identify a suitable sampling method for this study. (1 mark)

(ii) Explain how you would carry this out. (2 marks)

(c) (i) Explain why this study could be considered to be a field experiment. (2 marks)

(ii) Describe **one** strength and **one** weakness of doing a field experiment. (2 marks + 2 marks)

(d) (i) Explain what is meant by demand characteristics. (2 marks)

(ii) Imagine that the researcher measured the dependent variable by asking participants to rate their feelings. Describe **one** way that demand characteristics would be a problem in such a study.

(e) Identify **one** ethical issue and say how you would deal with it. (3 marks)

(f) Explain why the third group watched a documentary on the Amazon Rainforest. (2 marks)

(g) (i) Explain what is meant by external validity. (1 mark)

(ii) Describe **one** reason why this study might lack external validity. (2 marks)

(h)(i) Describe **one or more** conclusions that could be drawn from this study. (3 marks)

(ii) Identify a suitable graph that could be used to show the findings from this study. (1 mark)

(iii) What labels would you put on the *x* and *y* (horizontal and vertical) axis of this graph? (2 marks)

Examiner's tips for answering this question

(a) (i) Remember the **RIM** tip from the end of Chapter 1 – candidates always find it difficult to work out what answers are possible – but remember, if you learn the three alternatives and guess, you have a 33% chance of getting it right!

A little clue to help you further – in the final analysis were comparisons between individuals or groups?

(ii) For 2 marks you need to provide some elaboration of your answer and might do this by making reference to the study, though contextualisation is not required.

If (a) (i) is wrong, then you won't get any marks for (a) (ii).

(b) (i) The question does say 'suitable', so you should bear this in mind – how is the researcher *likely* to obtain his sample?

(ii) For 2 marks your answer does not need to be very detailed but just saying '*I would advertise*' would be worth 1 mark.

Remember the emphasis is on 'how' you would do it.

(c) (i) It is arguable as to whether this study is a field experiment, but you are only asked to say why it might be considered to be one. Don't write a novel! There are only 2 marks available, but equally don't write only a few words. A 1-mark answer might merely mention that field experiments are in a natural environment.

(ii) In questions like this there is no requirement to set your answer in the context of the study – but you can do this as a way of providing the extra detail required. Don't forget to make comparisons (e.g. '*Field experiments are better than lab experiments in terms of…*' rather than just saying they are better).

(d) (i) This is one of the rare occasions that you are simply asked to define one of the key terms, more often you are required to apply your knowledge of the terms to answer questions.

(ii) In this part you do have to apply your knowledge to this study. This requires you to think on your feet. You would get a mark for saying anything that suggests you have tried to apply the concept appropriately, i.e. found something in the study that would elicit certain behaviour from the participants – aside from the IV – but you can't just repeat the definition again.

(e) Sometimes there are two parts to the question, as here. Many students forget the first part – to identify their ethical issue. Take care to answer both parts clearly and provide sufficient details about how you would deal with the ethical issue – for example, don't just say 'I would debrief them'.

(f) Here again is an example of having to apply your knowledge. The question uses the term 'explain' which means that just saying a '*control condition*' would not count as a sufficient answer because that just says what it is rather than explaining *why* you need a control condition.

(g) (i) Another straightforward definition, but just 1 mark.

(ii) Remember that if you are asked to provide 'one' of anything then only your first answer will be marked. It is acceptable to describe any of the types of external validity: population, ecological or even historical – even though this might not affect responses to a film, it *could* affect them.

(h) (i) You have the option, if you wish, of describing more than one conclusion in order to provide 3 marks worth of material. Don't be afraid to state the obvious but remember that conclusions are not the same as findings. You can state the findings and then say '*This suggests that …*'.

(ii) This is another question where you have a limited choice of answers: the answer must be a bar chart or histogram.

(iii) It might help to sketch the graph.

EXAM STYLE QUESTION 4

You may feel happy to accept 1 instead of 2 marks for research methods questions – but bear in mind that there are usually about 6 marks between one grade and the next. So every mark counts.

A local hospital decides to have mixed wards rather than separate wards for men and women. Before introducing this new scheme to all wards the hospital management decide to compare the effects of mixed versus separate wards on patient well-being. They offer participants the choice of whether they are in mixed or single-sexed wards.

The hospital employs a psychologist to conduct a study into the effects of mixed versus single-sex wards on the health and happiness of the patients. Health outcomes could be determined by looking at whether patients recover more quickly in one type of ward than another, and also at whether they have better signs of health (for example, lower blood pressure).

(a) (i) Identify the independent variable and the dependent variable in this study. (2 marks)

(ii) Suggest **two** ways that you could operationalise the dependent variable. (2 marks + 2 marks)

(b) (i) Write a suitable non-directional hypothesis for this study. (2 marks)

(ii) Explain why you would use a non-directional hypothesis instead of a directional hypothesis. (2 marks)

(c) (i) Explain why this study could be considered to be a natural experiment. (2 marks)

(ii) Describe **one** strength and **one** weakness of conducting a natural experiment. (2 marks + 2 marks)

(d) (i). How could the relationship between the researcher and participants have affected the validity of this study? (2 marks)

(ii) How could you deal with the problem identified in (i)? (2 marks)

(e) (i) Identify the experimental design used in this study. (1 marks)

(ii) Describe **one** weakness of this design in the context of this study. (2 marks)

(iii) Explain **one** way of dealing with this weakness. (2 marks)

(f) Explain why a pilot study might have been useful in this experiment. (2 marks)

(g) Describe **one** possible extraneous variable in this study and explain how you would deal with it. (3 marks)

Examiner's tips for answering this question

(a) (i) Brief detail is enough for 'identify'.

(ii) This is testing your understanding of 'operationalisation'. How would you make the dependent variable into something you could test or measure in some way? There are hints in the question.

(b) (i) If you produce a directional hypothesis you would score zero marks for both parts of this question. You would only get 1 mark for writing *'Patients on mixed wards will have different health outcomes'*.

(ii) An example of a 1-mark answer would be *'There is no previous research'*.

(c) (i) The same advice applies here as stated earlier – there is no need to write a long answer when only 2 marks worth is required. Just identify one or two features of a natural experiment that are present in this study. You might explain why it is an experiment, and why it is a natural experiment.

(c) (ii), (e) (ii), (e) (iii) and (g) These questions all have one thing in common – they require only 'one' thing. If you provide more than one, only the first answer will be marked even if a subsequent answer is more detailed. Check your answers and cross out anything that is not relevant or you don't want marked – this advice only applies to research methods questions, not to other parts of the exam.

(c) (ii) So often candidates just say *'It is more like real life'* or *'It is more difficult'*. Such statements need some further explanation.

(d) (i) There are lots of possible answers – you can write about participant effects or investigator effects. Make sure you write enough for 3 marks.

(ii) This answer must be clearly linked to (i) – when you get to part (ii) you may decide to change your answer to part (i) because it doesn't provide you with a very good answer to part (ii). But don't write two answers as only the first will be marked.

(e) (i) RIM.

(ii) An answer that is not contextualised would only get 1 mark, such as saying *'There is no control for participant variables – participants in one group may differ from those in the other group which might explain why they do better'*.

(iii) Don't just identify a way to deal with the problem but *explain* how you would do this.

(f) Make sure you answer the question. Don't explain what a pilot study is, or how you would do it – the question is about 'why'.

(g) Take care to answer both parts clearly and provide sufficient detail for three marks. Don't just give a 'knee-jerk' answer saying 'noise'. Think of a likely extraneous variable – noise wouldn't really be an extraneous variable in this study – unless you could explain why. An extraneous variable must vary systematically with the IV.

MODEL ANSWERS

A model answer is an answer that would get full marks. However, it isn't the only answer that would get full marks, it is simply one possible answer.

Exam style question 3

(a)(i) What was the experimental design in this study? (1 mark)
Independent groups.

(ii) Describe one strength of using this design. (2 marks)
One strength is that you won't suffer from order effects, such as guessing what the study was about if each participant had to watch all three films.

(b) (i) Identify a suitable sampling method for this study. (1 mark)
Volunteer sampling.

(ii) Explain how you would carry this out. (2 marks)
You would advertise in certain places, like a newspaper, asking for people who would be willing to take part in a psychology experiment.

(c) (i) Explain why this study could be considered to be a field experiment. (2 marks)
The study involves the use of real-life materials (a film) and takes place in a natural environment.

(ii) Describe one strength and one weakness of doing a field experiment. (2 marks + 2 marks)
One strength is that participants behave more like they would usually and this means that you can generalise to everyday life better. One weakness is that it is more difficult to control extraneous variables, such as noise.

(d) (i) Explain what is meant by demand characteristics. (2 marks)
They are cues in a research situation that lead participants to work out what the researcher expects to find.

(ii) Imagine that the researcher measured the dependent variable by asking participants to rate their feelings. Describe one way that demand characteristics would be a problem in such a study'.(2 marks)
It might be that some participants realised that the film was supposed to have an effect on them and therefore gave the answers expected.

(e) Identify one ethical issue and say how you would deal with it. (3 marks)
One issue would be psychological harm if a participant didn't want to watch The Godfather because it would distress them.
You could deal with it by asking participants for their informed consent before the experiment began which would involve telling them everything they would be required to do, including the kind of film they might have to watch.

(f) Explain why the third group watched a documentary on the Amazon rainforest. (2 marks)
This was a control condition to ensure that the effects were due to the different kinds of film.

(g) (i) Explain what is meant by external validity. (2 marks)
External validity is the extent to which you are able to generalise the findings of a study to other people, other settings and other historical times.

(ii) Describe one reason why this study might lack external validity. (2 marks)
The sample of participants might be unrepresentative of the wider population and thus the study would lack population validity.

(h) (i) Describe one or more conclusions that could be drawn from this study. (3 marks)
The findings suggest that hormones lead to the responses we recognise when watching certain sorts of films. This is true for romantic films but it seems that only men are affected by exciting films which could explain why women find such films boring.

(ii) Identify a suitable graph that could be used to show the findings from this study. (1 mark)
Bar chart.

(iii) What labels would you put on the x and y (horizontal and vertical) axis of this graph? (2 marks)
The x axis would be labeled 'Romantic film, exciting film and Amazon rain forest'. The y axis would be labeled with increase in levels of hormones.

Exam style question 4

(a) (i) Identify the independent variable and the dependent variable in this study. (2 marks)
The IV is type of ward and the DV is the effect on health and happiness.

(ii) Suggest two ways that you could operationalise the dependent variable. (2 marks + 2 marks)
One way is to compare recovery rates. Another way is to measure blood pressure.

(b) (i) Write a suitable non-directional hypothesis for this study. (2 marks)
Patients on mixed wards will have different recovery rates to those on single-sex wards.

(ii) Explain why you would use a non-directional hypothesis instead of a directional hypothesis. (2 marks)
It may be that there is no previous research on this topic so it is difficult to predict a direction.

(c) (i) Explain why this study could be considered to be a natural experiment. (2 marks)
There was an IV and DV, and the IV was not directly manipulated by the experimenter.

(ii) Describe one strength and one weakness of conducting a natural experiment. (2 marks + 2 marks)
Strength: can investigate things where it would be difficult to manipulate the IV directly, for example assigning patients to mixed or single-sex wards might be objectionable.
Weakness: can't claim to show a causal relationship because the IV is not directly manipulated.

(d) (i) How could the relationship between the researcher and participants have affected the validity of this study? (2 marks)
If the participants knew about the aims of the study then they might improve in the single-sex wards because they wanted to show that they were just as good as mixed-sex wards.

(ii) How could you deal with the problem identified in i.? (2 marks)
You could deceive the participants about the true aims of the study. You could tell them that the study was about a new kind of hospital bed.

(e) (i) Identify the experimental design used in this study. (1 marks)
Independent groups.

(ii) Describe one weakness of this design in the context of this study. (2 marks)
One weakness is that there is no control for participant variables – it could be that the patients in one group were healthier at the outset which is why they got better faster.

(iii) Explain one way of dealing with this weakness. (2 marks)
You could use a matched participants design and exclude all participants who were not matched.

(f) Explain why a pilot study might have been useful in this experiment. (2 marks)
You might find that the measures of heath and happiness didn't provide useful data or data that didn't find differences between the two groups. So you'd have to identify a different measure.

(g) Describe one possible extraneous variable in this study and explain how you would deal with it. (3 marks)
One possible extraneous variable would be that people who opt for the mixed-sex wards have a more outgoing personality which would affect the DV. You could deal with this by assessing personality and matching participants.

3

Non-experimental techniques

NON-EXPERIMENTAL METHODS AND SCIENCE PAGES 52–53

Experiments are not the only way to conduct scientific research. Also looking at the question 'What is science?'

mini study **The Forer effect**

QUESTIONNAIRES PAGES 54–55

If you want to know about participants' behaviour, why not ask them?

mini study **Design and use your own questionnaire**

INTERVIEWS PAGES 56–57

Situational and participant variables (which are not the same as participant effects).

mini study **What are your morals?**

RETURN TO VALIDITY PAGES 58–59

Oh yes! Interviews, questionnaires and psychological tests raise ther own issues.

mini study **Design your own psychological test – testing memory**

RELIABILITY PAGES 60–61

And here's another key concept for you, considering consistency or, if you prefer, dependability.

mini study **Split half method and test–retest method**

A COMPARISON OF QUESTIONNAIRES AND INTERVIEWS PAGES 62–63

Strengths and weaknesses of self-report. Plus a thought for you – are you fed up with all these technical terms?

mini study **Was Freud right?**

CORRELATION PAGES 64–65

Are age and beauty positively correlated?

mini study **Playing with scattergrams and correlation coefficients**

OBSERVATION PAGES 66–67

Experiments, self-report and now observation – watch or listen to your participants.

mini study **Unstructured observation**

DESIGNING OBSERVATIONAL STUDIES PAGES 68–69

Conducting an observation is not as simple as sitting and watching your participant – there's more than meets the eye.

mini study **Making systematic observations**

OBSERVATIONS: RELIABILITY AND VALIDITY PAGES 70–71

The particular issues for observational research.

mini study **Making your own coding system**

CONTENT ANALYSIS PAGES 72–73

What it says on the tin – the analysis of the content of something, indirect observation really.

mini study **Analysis of lonely hearts ads**

CASE STUDIES PAGES 74–75

Intriguing records about individual people, groups or events. We all love case studies.

mini study **A case study of you**

THERE ARE MANY OTHER METHODS PAGES 76–77

Role play, meta-analysis, longitudinal and snapshot studies, and more.

THE USE OF NON-HUMAN ANIMALS IN PSYCHOLOGICAL RESEARCH PAGES 78–79

All those cute cuddly puppy dogs – are not what this is about.

mini study **Bateson's cube**

END OF CHAPTER TREATS PAGES 80–81

Multiple choice questions

Exam style questions 5 and 6

Model answers for exam style questions

NON-EXPERIMENTAL METHODS AND SCIENCE

The first two chapters of this book were concerned with experimental techniques. There is more to scientific research than the use of experiments. On this spread we introduce a number of non-experimental techniques used in psychological research, and generally consider science and the scientific method.

Self-report and observational techniques are used in all sorts of studies. For example, a researcher might want to investigate whether people who go to single-sex schools are happier than those who go to mixed schools. In this experiment the dependent variable will be the participants' attitudes about the school they go to and this dependent variable would be measured using a questionnaire or an interview.

If you want to find out why people do the things they do, perhaps the most obvious thing to do is to ask them about their behaviour. This is called the **self-report method**, which includes **questionnaires** and **interviews**. Such techniques provide a lot of interesting information but may not be accurate – we are not always the best witnesses of ourselves because we forget what we did, or we want to give a good impression of ourselves, or because sometimes we just don't know why we do things.

So the next most obvious method is to watch and listen to what people do and say. This is called **observation**. Psychologists have developed systematic ways to watch and record what they see and hear.

There are a number of other non-experimental techniques as well, which we will explore in this chapter.

Conducting experiments is not the only way to conduct scientific research. Non-experimental methods can be equally scientific if they follow the principles of **science**.

The word science comes from the Latin word for 'knowledge'. Science is essentially a systematic approach to creating knowledge. The fact that it is systematic means we can rely on it in order to predict and control the world (e.g. build dams, create vaccines, treat schizophrenia). The method used to gain scientific knowledge is the scientific method.

1. Science is empirical

Empirical data is information gained through direct observation or experiment rather than by reasoned argument or beliefs. Scientific research aims to collect facts.

Why is this useful?

People can make claims about the truth of a theory or the benefits of a treatment but the only way we know such things to be true is through empirical evidence.

2. Science is objective

An important aspect of empirical data is that they should be objective, i.e. not affected by the expectations of the researcher. Systematic collection of measurable data is at the heart of the scientific method.

Why is this useful?

Without objectivity we have no way of being certain that data collected is 'real' or **valid**.

3. Science is controlled

In an experiment we assume that any changes in the dependent variable are due to changes in the independent variable – but this may not be true if **extraneous variables** have also affected the dependent variable.

Why is this useful?

Lack of control makes it difficult to interpret the results of a study because extraneous variables mean we cannot be certain that X caused Y.

An empirical test

The picture on the left is of a burger from a well-known fast food outlet. Or at least this is what you are led to expect you will get. What about the reality? You may think you know something but unless you test this empirically you cannot know if it is true. On the right is the empirical evidence of what the burgers are really like. 'Empirical' refers to information gained through direct objective experience. Science uses empirical methods to separate unfounded beliefs from real truths.

[Thanks to Professor Sergio della Sala for this tasty and memorable example of empiricism.]

key terms

- Deductive
- Empirical data
- Extraneous variables
- Forer effect
- Inductive
- Interview
- Objective
- Observation
- Questionnaire
- Replication
- Science
- Scientific method
- Self-report method
- Valid

DO I HAVE TO DO THIS?

	AQA A	AQA B	Edex	OCR	WJEC
AS	◑	●	◑	◑	◑
A2	●	◑	◑	◑	●

● compulsory ◑ advisory ○ not necessary

Not everything is an experiment

People rather casually use the word 'experiment' when they are referring to an investigation that does not involve both independent and dependent variables. Such studies are <u>not</u> experiments.

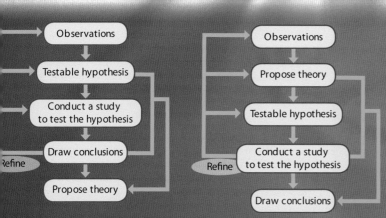

The scientific method can be *inductive* (on the left) or *deductive* (on the right). Induction is a bottom-up process – starting from the particular and ending with the general theory. Deduction is a top-down process – starting from the general (the theory) and generating particular hypotheses that can be tested.

In both cases the process involves repeating the processes over and over again to refine knowledge.

4. Scientific research can be replicated

Scientists record their methods and standardise them carefully so the same procedures can be followed in the future, i.e. **replicated**.

Why is this useful?

Repeating a study is the most important way to demonstrate the validity of any observation or experiment. If the outcome is the same this affirms the truth of the original results.

5. Scientists construct theories (explanations)

Theory construction is based on the **scientific method**. Consider Milgram's research.

➤ He started with the observation that Germans in the Second World War appeared to be exceptionally obedient (a dispositional hypothesis).

➤ In order to test this belief he conducted his well-known study (see page 36).

➤ He found in fact that even ordinary Americans were highly obedient.

➤ He concluded that situational rather than dispositional factors were a better explanation of why people obey.

➤ He further tested his explanation.

It might be appropriate to use the questions below for a group discussion.

1 If you can, identify **one or more** studies that have used observational techniques, questionnaires and/or interviews.

2 Five key features of science are listed on this spread. For each one try to think of your own examples.

3 In key feature number 5 we have used Milgram's study. However, we haven't provided a testable hypothesis. His study was not an experiment (there was no IV or DV). Try to write a testable hypothesis for Milgram's original study.

mini study
The Forer effect

This effect is named after Bertram R. Forer who, in 1949, asked his students to fill in a personality questionnaire. Afterwards he produced a unique personality analysis for each student based on their questionnaire answers – one example is shown in the light green box below.

He then asked each of the students to rate their personality analysis on a scale of 0 (very poor) to 5 (excellent) in terms of how much it related to themselves. Most of the students were very impressed and rated the statements as being true about them – the average was 4.26.

He then revealed that each student had in fact been given the same analysis. He had copied the statements from a newspaper astrology column!

Try to test the **Forer effect** (also known as the *Barnum effect*). You might, for example, give participants an online personality test and then say you have generated the profile below about them. Ask them to rate it for accuracy about them.

1. You have a great need for other people to like and admire you.
2. You have a tendency to be critical of yourself.
3. You have a great deal of unused capacity which you have not turned to your advantage.
4. While you have some personality weaknesses, you are generally able to compensate for them.
5. Your sexual adjustment has presented problems for you.
6. Disciplined and self-controlled outside, you tend to be worrisome and insecure inside.
7. At times you have serious doubts as to whether you have made the right decision or done the right thing.
8. You prefer a certain amount of change and variety and become dissatisfied when hemmed in by restrictions and limitations.
9. You pride yourself as an independent thinker and do not accept others' statements without satisfactory proof.
10. You have found it unwise to be too frank in revealing yourself to others.
11. At times you are extroverted, affable, sociable, while at other times you are introverted, wary, reserved.
12. Some of your aspirations tend to be pretty unrealistic.
13. Security is one of your major goals in life.

QUESTIONNAIRES

Questionnaires and interviews are referred to as self-report methods – because the person reports their own behaviour.

There are two ways you can ask questions – in person or in writing. In other words by conducting an interview or using a questionnaire. In both cases the researcher collects information by asking questions.

Both interviews and questionnaires have one advantage:

> You can access what people think – using observation as a method means the researcher relies on 'guessing' what people think and feel on the basis of how they behave. With an interview or questionnaire you can just ask people – whether they can and do give you valid answers is another matter.

There is one special advantage of using questionnaires:

> Once you have designed your questionnaire, you can then give it out to a large number of people relatively easily. This means you may collect a large amount of data.

Writing good questions

When writing questions there are three guiding principles:

1. **Clarity** Questions need to be written so that the reader (respondent) understands what is being asked. One way to do this is to **operationalise** certain terms. There should be no ambiguity.

   What does ambiguity mean? Something that is ambiguous has at least two possible meanings. For example 'Did you see the girl with the telescope?' could mean 'Did you see the girl when you were using the telescope' or it could mean 'Did you see the girl who was using a telescope'.

2. **Bias** Any bias in a question might lead the respondent to be more likely to give a particular answer (as in a **leading question**, see illustration on left). The major problem is **social desirability bias**. Respondents prefer to give answers that make them look more attractive, nicer, more geneorous, etc rather than being totally truthful.

3. **Analysis** Questions should be designed with analysis in mind. Once a researcher has collected all the data, the answers need to be summarised so that conclusions can be drawn. There are two broad categories of questions and two associated forms of analysis.

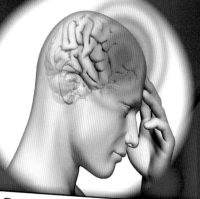

A leading question <u>leads</u> a person to give one answer rather than another. For example, if I ask you 'Do you get headaches frequently' and then asked about how many you get every week, what would you say?

When researchers asked people this question they found the average answer was 2.2 headaches per week. But when they asked a slightly different question 'Do you get headaches <u>occasionally</u>?' instead of saying 'frequently' people estimated an average of just 0.7 headaches. The way the question was asked affected the answer given, i.e. it was a leading question.

Closed questions
have a limited range of answers, see examples below.

(+) Produce quantitative data which are easier to analyse.

(–) Respondents may be forced to select answers that don't represent their real thoughts or behaviour.

Open questions
have a potentially infinite set of answers. For example, if you ask 'What kind of job do you do?' or 'What makes you feel stressed at work?' you may get 50 different answers from 50 people.

(+) Can provide unexpected answers and rich detail, thus allowing researchers to gain new insights.

(–) Likely to produce qualitative data which are more difficult to summarise because there is likely to be such a wide range of responses. In any research study we are looking for patterns so we can draw conclusions about the behaviour being studied. If you have lots of different answers it is more difficult to summarise the data and detect clear patterns.

Sometimes people define qualitative data as being about what people think and feel, but the closed questions on the left (producing quantitative data) also concern what people think and feel.

Examples of open questions

1 What factors contribute to making work stressful?

2 How do you feel when stressed?

Examples of closed questions

1 Which of the following makes you feel stressed? (You may tick as many answers as you like.)

☐ Noise at work   ☐ Lack of work
☐ Too much to do ☐ Workmates
☐ No job satisfaction

2 How many hours a week do you work?

☐ 0 hours ☐ Between 1 and 10 hours
☐ Between 11 and 20 hours
☐ More than 20 hours

3 *Likert scale*

Work is stressful?
☐ Strongly agree   ☐ Agree
☐ Not sure
☐ Disagree   ☐ Strongly disagree

4 *Rating scale*

How much stress do you feel? (Circle the number that best describes how you feel.)
At work:
 A lot of stress 5 4 3 2 1 No stress at all
At home:
 A lot of stress 5 4 3 2 1 No stress at all
Travelling to work:
 A lot of stress 5 4 3 2 1 No stress at all

5 *Forced choice* question

A The worst social sin is to be rude
B The worst social sin is to be a bore

key terms

- Closed questions
- Forced choice questions
- Interview
- Leading questions
- Likert scale
- Open questions
- Operationalise
- Piloting

- Qualitative data
- Quantitative data
- Questionnaire
- Rating scale
- Research method
- Research technique
- Social desirability bias
- Validity

DO I HAVE TO DO THIS?

	AQA A	AQA B	Edex	OCR	WJEC
AS	●	●	●	●	●
A2	●	●	●	●	●

● compulsory ◖ advisory ○ not necessary

Designing good questionnaires

A good questionnaire should contain good questions (obviously). Some other things to consider when designing a good questionnaire:

- *Filler questions.* It may help to include some irrelevant questions to mislead the respondent from the main purpose of the survey.
- *Sequence for the questions.* It is best to start with easy ones, saving difficult questions or questions that might make someone feel anxious or defensive until the respondent has relaxed.
- *Sampling technique,* i.e. how to select respondents. We described sampling techniques on pages 16–17.
- *Piloting.* The questions can be tested on a small group of people. This means you can refine the questions in response to any difficulties encountered.

Quantitative and qualitative data

Questionnaires may collect **quantitative data** – numerical information about your age, how many hours you work in a week, how highly you rate different TV programmes and so on.

Quantitative data are numbers that represents how much or how long, or how many, etc. there are of something, i.e. behaviour is measured in numbers or quantities.

Or questionnaires may collect **qualitative data** – data that express the 'quality' of things. This includes descriptions, words, meanings, pictures and so on.

Qualitative data can't be counted or quantified though it can be turned into quantitative data by placing the data in categories.

We discuss quantitative and qualitative data in more detail in Chapter 4.

A questionnaire or interview can be a research method or a research technique. For example, the aims of a study may be to find out about smoking habits in young people. The researcher would design a questionnaire to collect data about what people do and why. In this case the questionnaire is the research method.

On the other hand, the aims of a study might be to see if children who are exposed to an anti-smoking educational programme have different attitudes towards smoking than children not exposed to such a programme. The researcher would use a questionnaire to collect data about attitudes, but the analysis would involve a comparison between the two groups of children. This is an experimental study using a questionnaire as a research technique to assess the DV.

question 3.2

1 A psychology student designed a questionnaire about attitudes to eating. Below are some questions from this questionnaire:

> 1 Do you diet? (Circle your answer.)
> Always   Sometimes   Never
> 2 Do you think that dieting is a bad idea?
> 3 Explain your answer to (2)

For each question:

a State whether it is an open or closed question.

b State whether the question would produce quantitative or qualitative data.

c Give **one** criticism of the question.

d Suggest how you could improve the question in order to deal with your criticism.

e Suggest **one** strength of the question.

2 You have been asked to write a questionnaire about peoples' attitudes about ghosts and other paranormal phenomena.

a Write **one** closed question that would collect quantitative data.

b Write **one** open question that would collect qualitative data.

c Write **one** example of a leading question for this questionnaire.

d Explain how social desirability bias might affect the validity of the responses to your questionnaire.

e Describe **one** strength of using questionnaires to collect data in this study.

f Describe **one** weakness of using questionnaires to collect data in this study.

3 Explain the difference between qualitative and quantitative data.

mini study

Design and use your own questionnaire

Select a suitable topic, for example 'Methods of exam revision', 'Places people go for a good night out', 'Why people choose to study psychology' or 'How emotional are you?'. You could alternatively choose a topic related to your studies, such as a questionnaire on obedience in everyday situations.

Steps in questionnaire design

- Write the questions. (Keep the questionnaire short, somewhere between five and ten questions. Include a mixture of open and closed questions.)
- Construct the questionnaire.
- Consider ethical issues and how to deal with them.
- Write standarised instructions.
- Pilot the questionnaire.
- Decide on a sampling technique

Use the questionnaire

- Collect data.
- Analyse the data. Just select a few questions for analysis. For quantitative data you can use a bar chart. For qualitative data you can identify some trends in the answers and summarise these.
- Write a report of your investigation including a section describing the procedures and results.

INTERVIEWS

A semi-structured or unstructured interview has less structure than a structured interview! New questions are developed as you go along, similar to the way your GP might interview you. He or she starts with some predetermined questions but further questions are developed as a response to your answers. For that reason the unstructured or semi-structured approach is called the clinical interview.

People can be asked to describe their thoughts and feelings in writing (a questionnaire) or the questions can by given by an interviewer (face to face or on the telephone or via computer).

An interview can be structured or unstructured.

➤ **In a structured interview all the questions are decided in advance.**

➤ **In a semi-structured or unstructured interview, some or all of the questions are developed during the course of the interview.**

Many of the same issues apply to interviews as we have already discussed for questions on the previous spread, such as the use of **open** and **closed questions**, and **social desirability bias** and issues with **leading questions**. But there are also some special strengths and limitations.

Strengths

- For some people questionnaires are difficult, such as children or people who find writing difficult. Therefore, interviews are a better form of data collection.

- Another strength of using interviewing rather than questionnaires is that an experienced interviewer can elicit more extensive information through the use of gentle questioning techniques.

- Using a semi-structured or unstructured interview, the interviewer can develop further questions based on the interviewee's answers. This again increases the amount of information that can be gathered.

- Furthermore, an interviewer can deal with any ambiguous questions or uncertainty about questions by giving further explanation to the interviewee.

Weaknesses

- The way an interviewer asks a question may bias the answers given (called interviewer bias). For example, an interviewer might emphasise certain words and thus communicate expectations to the interviewee. Or an interviewer may unconsciously lead respondents to provide certain answers by verbal or visual cues.

- A further problem with interviewing is that people may feel less comfortable about revealing personal information than when writing answers to a questionnaire.

Examples of interviews in psychological research

Most people are law abiding citizens. They know the difference between good and bad. But how do we learn what is good behaviour and what is bad behaviour? The American psychologist Lawrence Kohlberg suggested that the way people think about right and wrong is a consequence of maturing – as a child gets older the way they think becomes more sophisticated and this affects their ability to think about moral decisions and ultimately affects their moral behaviour.

To investigate this Kohlberg (1978) used imaginary situations (moral dilemmas) such as the example on the right. After considering the dilemma participants were interviewed about their attitudes. For example, they were asked:

- Should Heinz steal the drug?

- Why or why not?

- [If subject originally favoured stealing, ask:] If Heinz doesn't love his wife, should he steal the drug for her?

- [If subject originally favoured not stealing, ask:] Does it make a difference whether or not he loves his wife?

- Why or why not?

- Suppose the person dying is not his wife but a stranger. Should Heinz steal the drug for the stranger?

- Why or why not?

In Europe, a woman was near death from a special type of cancer. There was one drug that the doctors thought might save her. It was a form of radium that a druggist in the same town had recently discovered. The drug was expensive to make but the druggist was charging 10 times what the drug cost him to make. He paid $400 for the radium and charged $4000 for a small dose of it. The sick woman's husband, Heinz, went to everyone he knew to borrow the money, but he could only get together about $2000, which is half of what it cost. He told the druggist that his wife was dying and asked him to sell it cheaper or let him pay later. But the druggist said "No. I discovered the drug and I'm going to make money from it". Heinz got desperate and broke into the man's store to steal the drug for his wife.

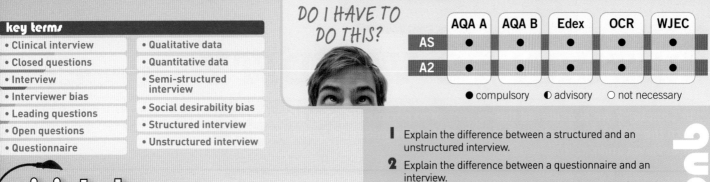

key terms

- Clinical interview
- Closed questions
- Interview
- Interviewer bias
- Leading questions
- Open questions
- Questionnaire
- Qualitative data
- Quantitative data
- Semi-structured interview
- Social desirability bias
- Structured interview
- Unstructured interview

mini study

What are your morals?

Try out the moral interviews below with a partner in your class. Take turns being the interviewer and interviewee as you try out both kinds of interview (Kohlberg's and Gilligan's).

If you want some more of Kohlberg's dilemmas have a look at www.haverford.edu/psych/ddavis/p109g/kohlberg.dilemmas.html

Discuss

- The differences in the information obtained.
- Which questions worked best and why?
- How truthful your interviewees were and why?

Analysis

Consider how you would interpret the results of your interviews.

The questions that produce **quantitative data** can be represented using bar charts whereas questions that produce **qualitative data** will need to be analysed in different ways. Read about how Gilligan and Attanucci analysed their qualitative data and consider how you might do something similar with your data.

Once you have identified categories (such as justice or care) you can then count how many of each you find. In Gilligan and Attanucci's research they wished to compare men and women, predicting that women would be more likely to show a care focus whereas men would show a justice focus.

1 Explain the difference between a structured and an unstructured interview.

2 Explain the difference between a questionnaire and an interview.

3 Would you describe Kohlberg's interviews as structured or unstructured? Or are they semi-structured (somewhere in between)? Explain your answer.

4 Would you describe Gilligan's interviews as structured or unstructured or semi-structured? Explain your answer.

5 In the questions used by Kohlberg and Gilligan find an example of a closed question and an open question, and a question that would produce quantitative data and a question that would produce qualitative data.

6 A psychologist intends to do research about attitudes towards dieting.

a Why would it be preferable to conduct an interview rather than a questionnaire?

b Why might it be better to conduct a questionnaire than an interview?

7 How can 'leading questions' be a problem in interviews and questionnaires?

8 Explain what interviewer bias is.

9 Explain why 'social desirability bias' is a problem in interviews.

10 Suggest how an interviewer might be able to avoid social desirability bias.

11 Explain how social desirability bias might affect the validity of a study using a self-report technique (i.e. questionnaire or interview).

12 Identify **two** (or more) ethical issues that might be important when conducting an interview and suggest how such issues might be dealt with.

Carol Gilligan criticised Kohlberg's research because it was based on imaginary situations. People might think differently when considering their own moral dilemmas. Therefore, Gilligan and Attanucci (1988) used a different approach. Participants were asked a set of questions about their own moral conflicts and decisions. For example, they were asked:

- Have you ever been in a situation of moral conflict where you had to make a decision but weren't sure what was the right thing to do?
- Could you describe the situation?
- What were the conflicts for you in that situation?
- What did you do?
- Do you think it was the right thing to do?
- How do you know?

Each participant was interviewed individually for approximately two hours, including general questioning about morality and identity as well as the specific questions listed above.

The interviewers were briefed to ask other questions to encourage the participants to elaborate and clarify their responses. For example, saying 'Is there anything else you want to add'.

Interviewers also asked participants to explain the meaning of key terms that they used, such as 'responsibility', 'fair' and 'obligation'.

Analysis

Gilligan and Attanucci tape-recorded the interviews and later transcribed them (i.e. produced a printed version). The dilemmas were analysed using the 'Lyons procedure', a system requiring intensive training.

Basically the process involves three people coding the answers. Each coder has to read the responses from each participant. First of all the coder looks at what the participant had said in discussing their moral problem. This discussion is then broken down into 'considerations', where a consideration is one argument or considered view.

Next, each 'consideration' has to be classified. For example, the following paragraph from Gilligan and Attanucci described one student's dilemma about whether to inform on someone who had violated an alcohol rule. The brackets identify each 'consideration':

[The conflict was that by all rights she should have been turned into the honour board for violation of the alcohol policy.] [I liked her very much.] [She was extremely embarrassed and upset. She was contrite, she wished she had never done it. She had all the proper levels of contriteness and guilt] and [I was supposed to turn her in and didn't.]

Gilligan and Attanucci classed each consideration as either justice (right or wrong) or care (people's feelings). The example above is largely justice.

RETURN TO VALIDITY

In Chapter 2 we considered the validity of experiments. Now we need to turn the spotlight to self-report and related techniques – questionnaires, interviews and psychological tests.

Questionnaire fallacy
The erroneous belief that a questionnaire actually produces a true picture of what people do and think.

Psychological tests

A psychological test is a task or set of tasks that measures some aspect of human behaviour. For example:

- *IQ tests* measure intelligence.
- *Personality tests* assess your personality type.
- *Mood scales* measure your emotional state.
- *Attitude scales* report on people's feelings and opinions.
- *Aptitude scales* measure what you're good at, such as artistic or numerical ability.

Such tests can involve almost any activity, although most commonly they involve filling in a questionnaire.

EXAMPLE TEST OF MENTAL ABILITIES

1. The same word can be added to the end of GRASS and the beginning of SCAPE to form two other English words. What is the word?

2. Sally likes 225 but not 224; she likes 900 but not 800; she likes 144 but not 145. Which does she like – 1600 or 1700?

3. Fill in the missing number: 0,1,1,2,3,5,8,13,–,34,55

4. If you count from 1 to 100, how many 7s will you pass on the way?

5. What is the following word when it is unscrambled? H C P R A A T E U

6. Which of the following objects is least like the others? Poem   Novel   Painting   Statue   Flower

7. Four years ago, Jane was twice as old as Sam. Four years on from now, Sam will be 3/4 of Jane's age. How old is Jane now?

© Dr Abbie F. Salny, provided courtesy of Mensa International, from http://www.mensa.org/workout

Answers
1. Land   2. 1600 (a square number)   3. 21   4. 20   5. Parachute   6. Flower (not human made)   7. 12

Validity
Social desirability bias

The answers obtained on any questionnaire may be affected by social desirability bias, which is essentially a form of participant effect (see page 32). Participants wish to present themselves in the best possible way and therefore may not give answers that truly represent what they think or feel. Instead, they behave in the most socially acceptable way for the purposes of a research study.

Interviewer bias

Interviewer bias refers to the way an interviewer's behaviour may affect or bias the answers an interviewee gives. For example, when doing a psychological test face to face with an interviewer, the interviewer may subtly and unconsciously tilt his head to encourage the correct answer to a test item.

Leading questions

If questions are poorly designed they produce answers that are meaningless. For example, if a question contains a suggestion of the expected answer (a leading question) then the answers provided wouldn't truly represent a participant's thoughts and feelings. The same applies to ambiguous questions. In other words, a poorly designed set of questions will lower the validity of the data collected.

Content validity

One way to think about validity is in terms of the question 'Has the researcher measured what he intended to measure?' For example, if a researcher aimed to measure intelligence then the questions used should be related to intelligence rather than any other characteristic. Seems obvious – but sometimes questionnaires and psychological tests and experiments are actually measuring something else.

If a questionnaire or interview or test is not measuring the intended content then any score or data will be meaningless, and the measure is said to lack content validity.

How aggressive are you?

For each scenario below rate your reaction.   1 = I don't feel angry at all   3 = I feel a little angry   5 = I feel furious

1. On your way home from work you stop at the shopping mall to pick up some dinner. As you walk past a restaurant you catch a glimpse of your partner with another woman/man. They are kissing publicly and very passionately. Up until this moment you believed your relationship was stable, loving and committed – this is your soul mate, or so you thought. How angry does that make you feel?

2. You overhear a friend badmouthing you. How angry does that make you feel?

3. Your friend persuades you to hire her/his cousin for a moving job. The guy turns out to be pretty clumsy – he even manages to drop a box labelled 'fragile', shattering your valuable wine glasses into hundreds of pieces. How angry does that make you feel?

4. At a karaoke night with friends, your partner pokes fun at your singing in front of your friends. You thought your voice was pretty good, but it looks like your so-called better half thinks you deserve two thumbs down. How angry does that make you feel?

5. You and a friend decide to catch a weekend matinée. You're getting drawn into the story but the guy behind you keeps bumping the back of your seat whenever he changes position...and he seems to be getting more restless as the movie progresses. How angry does that make you feel?

From http://tinyurl.com/ycrt2oy

Ceiling and floor effects

Test scores may not be accurate becau of a ceiling effect. If all the questions on a test are easy then everyone will do well, i.e. hit the ceiling. The reverse may sometimes be true, where all the questions are too hard and everyone does poorly, i.e. hits the floor.

DO I HAVE TO DO THIS?

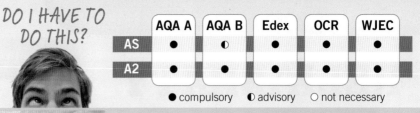

key terms

- Ceiling effect
- Concurrent validity
- Construct validity
- Content validity
- Face validity
- Floor effect
- Interview
- Interviewer bias
- Leading question
- Lie scale
- Participant effect
- Predictive validity
- Psychological test
- Questionnaire fallacy
- Social desirability bias
- Validity

Assessing validity

Lie scale

One way to assess whether people are telling the truth is to include a few questions that act as 'truth detectors' to test truthfulness. For example, asking 'Are you always happy?' The truthful answer is 'no' but a person who wishes to present themselves in a positive light may be tempted to answer 'yes'. Respondents who lie on a high proportion of lie scale items may not be giving truthful answers on the rest of the questionnaire.

Face validity

Face validity concerns the issue of whether a self-report measure looks like it is measuring what the researcher intended to measure. For example, whether the questions are obviously related to the topic. Face validity only requires intuitive measurement.

Concurrent validity

Concurrent validity can be established by comparing performance on a new self-report measure with a previously validated one on the same topic. To do this participants are given both measures at the same time and then their scores are compared. If the new measure produces a similar outcome as the older one then this demonstrates the concurrent validity of the new measure.

Predictive validity

We would expect that a person who does well on an intelligence test should go on to gain high grades in their A level exams. In other words their intelligence should predict success on other related measures. Therefore, we can check this out as a means of assessing the predictive validity of a measurement.

Construct validity

Construct validity is assessed by looking at the underlying construct(s) of a test or questionnaire. Consider, for example a questionnaire on aggression. The validity could be assessed by considering various theoretical views about aggression and the extent to which they have been represented by the questionnaire.

Improving validity

In terms of internal validity, if measures of validity are low then the items on the questionnaire/interview/test need to be revised, for example to produce a better match between scores on the new test and an established one.

1 In each of the following studies describe **two** features of the study that might affect the validity of the study and suggest how the validity might be improved.

a A psychologist conducts interviews with students about their attitudes towards exams.

b A psychologist conducts a study to see if students do more homework in the winter or spring term. To do this he asks students to keep a diary of how much time they spend on homework each week.

2 A research team receive funding to assess the effectiveness of a new drug. They intend to give one group of participants a placebo (a substance that has no physiological effect) and the other group will receive the actual drug. Effectiveness will be assessed by comparing the severity of the patients' symptoms before and after the study to see if there has been any improvement.

a This study is an experiment. Explain why it is an experiment and explain what kind of experiment it is.

b Write a hypothesis for this experiment.

c Describe how you could collect information about the patients' symptoms.

d Discuss **two or more** issues of validity that might arise in this study.

e Suggest how the researcher might deal with these issues.

3 On the facing page there is a test of intelligence.

a To what extent do you feel this test measures the construct of 'intelligence' (i.e. to what extent does this test measure what it claims to measure)?

b If you don't feel all the questions measure intelligence, what do you think they are measuring?

c Describe **two or more** methods you could use to assess the validity of this test.

4 Also on the facing page is a test of aggressiveness.

a To what extent do you feel this test is likely to measure how aggressive a person is? What might the test be measuring instead?

b Why might it be desirable to use a lie scale in this test?

c Give an example of an item that could be used to create a lie scale for this aggressiveness test.

d Describe **one** other method you could use to assess the validity of this test.

mini study

Design your own psychological test – testing memory

One area of psychological research is memory and context – people remember information better if they are tested in the same room as where they originally learned the information.

For example, Abernethy (1940) arranged for a group of students to be tested before a certain course began. They were then tested each week. Some students were tested in their teaching room by their usual instructor, or by a different instructor. Others were tested in a different room either by their usual instructor or by a different one. Those tested by the same instructor in the same room performed best on their tests. Presumably familiar things (room and instructor) acted as memory cues.

In order to repeat this study you need a valid means of measuring memory.

- Devise a suitable test of memory.
- Consider various issues discussed on this page such as ceiling effects and content validity.
- Find another memory test on the internet and consider the concurrent validity of the test you devised.
- Pilot your measurement scale to see if it works.

RELIABILITY

If you use a ruler to measure the height of a chair and then found the next day that the measurement was different, you would probably think the chair must have changed because you would expect the ruler to be reliable (consistent). If the fluctuation was due to some change in the ruler it would be pretty useless as a measuring instrument – not dependable, consistent or reliable.

Any tool used to measure something must be reliable. For example, a psychological test assessing personality or an interview about drinking habits should produce the same results every time it is used *unless the object being measured has changed*.

If the 'tool' is measuring the same thing it should produce the same result on every occasion. If the result is different then we need to be sure that it is the thing (chair or personality or drinking habits) that has changed or is different, and not our measuring tool.

Measurement of intelligence

It has been suggested that the circumference of a person's head could be used as a measure of intelligence. This is likely to be a fairly RELIABLE measure of intelligence because adult head size is consistent from one year to the next.

You may even feel this is a VALID measure of intelligence. Afterall, if you have a bigger brain then you might have more intelligence. However, research doesn't bear this out. Intelligence is not rela ted to brain or head size. This means this measure of intelligence lacks VALIDITY.

External reliability is a measure of the extent to which one measure of an object (e.g. a chair) varies from another measure of the same object. One ruler should give the same measure even if there is a month between measurements.

If the same interview was conducted one day and then conducted a week later, the outcome should be the same – otherwise the interview is not reliable.

Two interviewers should also produce the same outcome. This is called **inter-interviewer reliability**. This can be assessed by comparing the results from both interviewers with the same interviewees.

Internal reliability is a measure of the extent to which something is consistent within itself. For example, all the questions on a psychological test should be measuring the same thing.

Assessing reliability

Internal reliability
Split half method

Split half reliability can be calculated by comparing two halves of a test, questionnaire or interview. This can be done by randomly selecting half the test items and placing them on Form A and placing the other items on Form B.

Therefore, you end up with 2 forms of the same test. Each form should yield the same score if the items on the test were consistent.

The two scores can be compared by calculating a correlation coefficient (see page 64).

Improving low internal reliability

Select the test items that produce the greatest similarity. You can do this by removing certain items and seeing if there is a stronger correlation with the remaining items.

External reliability
Test–retest method

The **test–retest method** involves giving the same test or questionnaire or interview to the same person on two separate occasions to see if the same results are obtained. If the test or questionnaire or interview is given at two different times with no 'treatment' in between it should yield the same results. If the results are not similar then the test/questionnaire/interview has low reliability.

The interval between test and retest must be long enough so that the participant can't remember their previous answers but not too long because then their thoughts or feelings or even abilities may have changed and we would expect their score to be different.

The two scores can again be compared by calculating a correlation coefficient.

Note that, in the case of an interview, then the same people must be interviewed by the same interviewer.

Improving low external reliability

A number of factors may cause poor reliability over time. For example, a poorly trained interviewer may not be consistent in the way they are asking questions and this may lead to different answers. Therefore the interviewer needs better training.

Or it might be that the test items or questions are ambiguous and therefore participants are not consistent in the answers they give. Therefore the questions should be examined again.

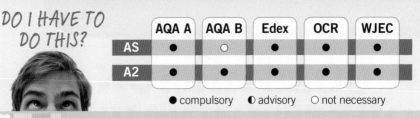

key terms

- External reliability
- Internal reliability
- Inter-interviewer reliability
- Reliability
- Split half reliability
- Test–retest method

DO I HAVE TO DO THIS?

	AQA A	AQA B	Edex	OCR	WJEC
AS	●	○	●	●	●
A2	●	●	●	●	●

● compulsory   ◐ advisory   ○ not necessary

mini study

Split half method and test–retest method

Two psychological tests are shown below. You can try out the two methods of assessing reliability.

Split-half method: Construct two smaller versions of this scale to see if it is internally reliable. Get everyone in your class to do the test and then calculate their score for Form A and Form B. Use the Excel method described on page 65 to calculate the correlation. Is it positive? Is it significant?

Test-retest method: Do the same questionnaire again (after a few days). Compare the second score for each person with their first score. Use the Excel method to calculate the correlation. Is it positive? Is it significant?

1 In a study on self-esteem, the researcher constructs a scale to measure a person's self esteem. The scale consists of 30 questions.

a How could the researcher assess the reliability of the self-esteem scale?

b Why would it matter if the reliability of the scale was low?

c How could the researcher improve the reliability of the scale?

d How could the researcher assess the validity of the self-esteem scale?

e How could the researcher improve the validity of the scale?

2 Consider the Dieting Beliefs Scale (below).

a Do you think it is measuring what it intends to measure? How could you determine whether it is or is not?

b If this scale lacked reliability, do you think this would affect the validity of the scale? Explain your answer.

The Rosenberg Self-Esteem Scale (Rosenberg, 1989)

Self-esteem refers to the opinion you have of yourself and your value as a person. The test below is one of the best known measures of self-esteem.

To assess self-esteem, tick one column for each statement.

		Strongly agree	Agree	Disagree	Strongly disagree
1	I feel that I'm a person of worth, at least on an equal plane with others.				
2	I feel that I have a number of good qualities.				
3	All in all, I am inclined to feel that I am a failure.				
4	I am able to do things as well as most other people.				
5	I feel I do not have much to be proud of.				
6	I have a positive attitude towards myself.				
7	On the whole, I am satisfied with myself.				
8	I wish I could have more respect for myself.				
9	I certainly feel useless at times.				
10	At times I think I am no good at all.				

To score the items, assign a value to each item as follows:

Items 1,2,4,6,7: strongly agree=3, agree=2, disagree=1, strongly disagree=0.
Items 3,5,8,9,10: strongly agree=0, agree=1, disagree=2, strongly disagree=3.

Dieting Beliefs Scale (Stotland and Zuroff, 1990)

This is a measure of weight locus of control, i.e. the extent to which an individual feels in control of their weight.

Indicate how well each statement describes your beliefs. After each statement place a number from 1 *(not at all descriptive of my beliefs)* to 6 *(very descriptive of my beliefs)*.

1.	By restricting what one eats, one can lose weight.	
2.	When people gain weight, it is because of something they have done or not done.	
3.	A thin body is largely a result of genetics.	
4.	No matter how much effort one puts into dieting, one's weight tends to stay about the same.	
5.	One's weight is, to a great extent, controlled by fate.	
6.	There is so much fattening food around that losing weight is almost impossible.	
7.	Most people can only diet successfully when other people push them to do it.	
8.	Having a slim and fit body has very little to do with luck.	
9.	People who are overweight lack the willpower necessary to control their weight.	
10.	Each of us directly is responsible for our weight.	
11.	Losing weight is simply a matter of wanting to do it and applying yourself.	
12.	People who are more than a couple of pounds overweight need professional help to lose weight.	
13.	By increasing the amount one exercises, one can lose weight.	
14.	Most people are at their present weight because that is the weight level that is natural for them.	
15.	Unsuccessful dieting is due to lack of effort.	
16.	In order to lose weight, people must get a lot of encouragement from others.	

To score items, reverse score numbers 3, 4, 5, 6, 7, 12, 14, 16,

For more psychological tests for students to use see www.yorku.ca/rokada/psyctest/

A COMPARISON OF QUESTIONNAIRES AND INTERVIEWS

Now that you understand the validity and reliability of self-report methods (questionnaires and interviews), you can appreciate the relative strengths and weaknesses of each. This spread reviews those strengths and weaknesses.

Questionnaires

Respondents record their own answers.

Strengths

- Can be easily repeated so that data can be collected from large numbers of people relatively cheaply and quickly (once the questionnaire has been designed).
- Questionnaires do not require specialist administrators.
- Respondents may feel more willing to reveal personal/confidential information than in an interview.

Weaknesses

- Answers may not be truthful, for example because of leading questions and social desirability bias. Though leading questions are likely to be less of a problem in questionnaires than in unstructured interviews.
- The sample may be biased because only certain kinds of people fill in questionnaires – literate individuals who are willing to spend time filling them in.
- Response set – a tendency for respondents to answer all questions in the same way, regardless of context. This would bias their answers.

Structured interview

Questions predetermined.

Strengths

- Can be easily repeated.
- Requires less skill than unstructured interviews.
- Easier to analyse than unstructured interviews because answers are given to the same set of questions.

Weaknesses

- The interviewer's expectations may influence the answers the interviewee gives (interviewer bias). This may especially be true because people don't always know what they think. They may also want to present themselves in a 'good light' and therefore give 'socially desirable' answers (social desirability bias).
- Interviews may not be comparable because different interviewers ask questions in a different way (low inter-interviewer reliability). Reliability may also be affected by the same interviewer behaving differently on different occasions.
- In comparison with unstructured interviews, the data collected in a structured interview will be restricted by the predetermined set of questions.

Unstructured or semi-structured interviews

Interviewer develops questions in response to respondents' answers to elicit more detailed answers or follow a particular line of questioning.

Strengths

- Generally more detailed information can be obtained from each respondent than in a structured interview.
- Can access information that may not be revealed by predetermined questions.

Weaknesses

- More affected by interviewer bias than structured interviews.
- Even more likely to be affected by leading questions than questionnaires.
- Requires well-trained interviewers, which makes it more expensive to produce reliable interviews.
- The answers from unstructured interviews are less easy to analyse than a structured interview because they are unpredictable.

★ Special tip

When an exam question asks 'Give **one** strength of a questionnaire', students often write something like *'The strength of a questionnaire is that you can collect lots of data'*. The problem with this is that it is not clear what 'lots of data' means. Compared to what? You can collect lots of data in an experiment or an interview.

➤ You need to provide clear detail (what is 'lots of data'? Why is there 'lots of data'?).
➤ You need to offer a comparison (compared to what? E.g. compared to an interview).

A good answer would say *'The strength of a questionnaire is that you can collect data from more people than you would if using the interview method, which results in lots more data'*.

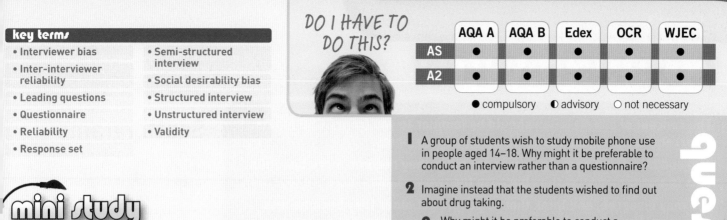

key terms

- Interviewer bias
- Inter-interviewer reliability
- Leading questions
- Questionnaire
- Reliability
- Response set
- Semi-structured interview
- Social desirability bias
- Structured interview
- Unstructured interview
- Validity

DO I HAVE TO DO THIS?

	AQA A	AQA B	Edex	OCR	WJEC
AS	●	●	●	●	●
A2	●	●	●	●	●

● compulsory ◑ advisory ○ not necessary

mini study

Was Freud right?

Freud proposed that early life experiences create our adult personalities. He suggested that frustration or over-indulgence during key developmental stages lead to predictable personality traits as indicated in the table below.

	Frustration or harsh treatment	Over-indulgence
Oral stage (age 0–1½ years)	Oral aggressive character characterised by aggressiveness, domination, pessimism, envy and suspicion.	Oral receptive character is optimistic, gullible, over-dependent on others, trusting and full of admiration for others.
Anal stage (age 1½–3 years)	Anal retentive character is neat, stingy, precise, orderly and obstinate.	Anal expulsive character is generous, messy, disorganised, careless and defiant.

1. Develop a questionnaire that will assess whether a person is an oral or anal personality. You can look on the internet for some examples to inspire you (search 'Freud personality test').
2. Various studies have found associations between personality types and certain behaviours. For example, Richard Wiseman found that anal retentive types are more likely to take out small amounts of money from a cash machine. In order to investigate this you need to add questions about other habits, such as cash withdrawals (Jarvis and Chandler, 2001).
3. Use a correlational analysis (see next spread) to determine whether you have found a relationship.

1 A group of students wish to study mobile phone use in people aged 14–18. Why might it be preferable to conduct an interview rather than a questionnaire?

2 Imagine instead that the students wished to find out about drug taking.

  a Why might it be preferable to conduct a questionnaire rather than an interview?

  b Why might it be preferable to use an unstructured interview rather than a structured interview?

  c Why might a structured interview be better than an unstructured interview?

3 A headteacher plans to study students' Facebook use and relate this to their exam performance.

  a Briefly describe how he might do this study.

  b How could he assess 'exam performance?

  c Outline **one** strength and **one** weakness of using a self-report technique in the research.

  d Identify **one** issue of reliability in this research and describe how you would deal with this issue of reliability.

  e Identify **one** issue of validity in this research and describe how you would deal with this issue of validity.

  f Identify **one** ethical issue that might arise in this research and describe how you would deal with this ethical issue.

4 Read the question posed in the box below on 'Homage to formal terms'.

  a Identify **two** strengths of collecting data using a smartphone app.

  b Identify **two** weaknesses of collecting data using a smartphone app.

  c Would you classify this self-report method as a questionnaire or a structured interview?

Paying homage to formal terms*

This issue is something we first introduced on page 44 – getting too tied up with the technical terms.

Consider the following:

Imagine that a psychologist decided to collect data using a smartphone app where questions were read out to you and you were required to give your answers verbally so they were recorded. Is this a questionnaire or an unstructured interview?

Answer – it doesn't really matter which it is. What matters is the underlying issues. The technique described wouldn't exclude people who can't write, a feature of an interview, but it would mean people might feel more willing to reveal personal information, a strength of a questionnaire.

Moral of this story – don't get too tied up with the labels we use for research methods concepts, just get to grips with the implications.

* This was a phrase introduced on page 44.

CORRELATION

A correlation is not (strictly speaking) a research method. It is a method of analysing research data.

The concept of a correlation should be familiar to you from GCSE maths. A correlation is a relationship between two variables.

Age and beauty co-vary. As people get older they become more beautiful. This is a positive correlation because the two variables increase together.

You may disagree, and think that as people get older they become less attractive. You think age and beauty are correlated but it is a negative correlation. As one variable increases the other one decreases.

Or you may simply feel that there is no relationship between age and beauty. This is called a zero correlation.

Scattergrams

A correlation can be illustrated using a scattergram (also called scattergraph). For each individual we obtain a score for each co-variable – in our case the co-variables are age and beauty.

The co-variables determine the *x* and *y* position of each dot. In other words, for one co-variable you locate its position on the *x* axis (horizontal) and for the other co-variable you locate its position on the *y* axis (vertical).

The top scattergram illustrates a positive correlation. The middle scattergram shows a negative correlation. The bottom scattergram is a zero correlation.

The correlation coefficient for each graph is: (1) +.76 (2) –.76 (3) –.006.

The plus or minus sign shows whether it is a positive or negative correlation. The coefficient (number) tells us how closely the co-variables are related. –.76 is just as closely correlated as +.76.

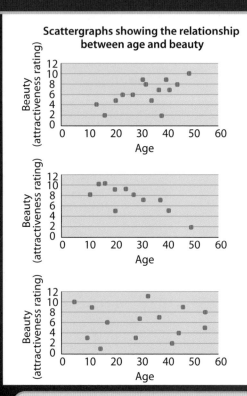

Scattergraphs showing the relationship between age and beauty

Correlation coefficient

The scatter of the dots indicates the degree of correlation between the co-variables. If the dots are closely grouped together roughly forming a line from the bottom left to the top right this indicates a positive correlation. If the dots form a line from bottom right to top left this indicates a negative correlation. If the dots form no pattern this indicates a zero correlation.

The closeness of this correlation is described using a correlation coefficient.

➤ A correlation coefficient is a number.

➤ A correlation coefficient has a maximum value of 1.0 (+1.0 is a perfect positive correlation and –1.0 is a perfect negative correlation).

Some correlation coefficients are written as –.76, whereas others are +.76. The plus or minus sign shows whether it is a positive or negative correlation.

The coefficient (number) tells us how closely the co-variables are related, –.76 is just as closely correlated as +.76, it's just that –.76 means that as one variable increases the other decreases (negative correlation), and +.52 means that both variables increase together (positive correlation).

A statistical test is used to calculate the correlation coefficient. These tests are discussed in Chapter 5.

A correlational hypothesis

In Chapter 1 we looked at hypotheses – but the hypotheses we wrote were for experimental studies. In a study using a correlational analysis there is no independent or dependent variable.

When conducting a study using a correlational analysis you need to produce a correlational hypothesis that states the expected relationship between *co-variables*.

For example, 'Age and beauty are positively correlated'.

Linear and curvilinear

The correlations we have considered on this spread are all linear correlations, i.e. perfect positive or negative correlations are arranged in straight lines.

However there is a different kind of correlation – a curvilinear correlation. The relationship is not linear, but curved. Nevertheless, there is still a predictable relationship. For example, anxiety and performance do not have a linear relationship. Performance on many tasks (such as completing a crossword puzzle or running a race) is lowered when anxiety is too high or too low; it is best when anxiety is moderate – as illustrated in the graph on the right.

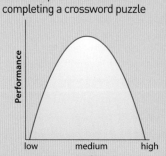

This is called the Yerkes-Dodson effect

Significance is a term that refers to the meaningfulness of a result. The issue is whether a correlation of .20 is large enough for us to conclude we have found a real pattern, or whether it is really closer to zero correlation. In Chapter 5 we will look in more detail at the concept of significance – but, for now, you need some sense about the size of a 'big enough' correlation coefficient to conclude whether the data are correlated.

The table on the right gives an approximate idea of the values needed. The more pairs of scores you have, the smaller the coefficient can be. To be significant the correlation coefficient should be larger than the number in the table.

Significance table	
N =	
4	1.000
8	0.643
12	0.503
16	0.429
20	0.380

A coefficient of either –.45 or +.45 would be significant if there were 16 pairs of data, but not if there were 12 pairs.

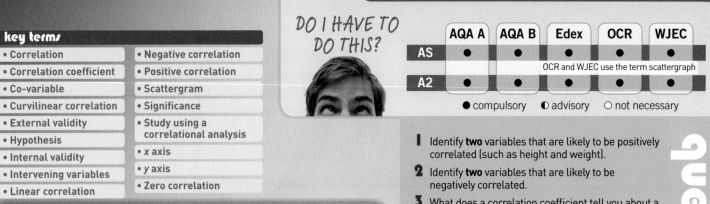

DO I HAVE TO DO THIS?

	AQA A	AQA B	Edex	OCR	WJEC
AS	●	●	●	●	●
A2	●	●	●	●	●

OCR and WJEC use the term scattergraph

● compulsory　◐ advisory　○ not necessary

key terms

- Correlation
- Correlation coefficient
- Co-variable
- Curvilinear correlation
- External validity
- Hypothesis
- Internal validity
- Intervening variables
- Linear correlation
- Negative correlation
- Positive correlation
- Scattergram
- Significance
- Study using a correlational analysis
- x axis
- y axis
- Zero correlation

Strengths

- Can be used when it would be unethical or impractical to manipulate variables and can make use of existing data.
- If a correlation is significant then further investigation is justified. If correlation is not significant then you can rule out a simple linear causal relationship.
- As with experiments, the procedures can be repeated again which means that the findings can be confirmed.

Weaknesses

- Cannot demonstrate cause-and-effect relationships.
- People often misinterpret correlations and assume that a causal relationship has been demonstrated. Such erroneous conclusions may lead to serious public misunderstandings, such as headlines that announce that day care is bad for children suggest that day care (or separation from your mother) *causes* difficulties for children.
- There may be intervening variables that can explain why the co-variables being studied are linked. For instance, in the day care example above one intervening variable might be that working mothers are more stressed and it is this intervening variable that causes the difficulty rather than going to day care.
- As with experiments, studies using a correlational analysis may lack internal/external validity. For example, the method used to measure IQ may lack validity or the sample used may lack generalisability.

mini study

Playing with scattergrams and correlation coefficients

You can get a clearer idea of scattergrams and correlation coefficients by entering some data and seeing what the scattergram looks like.

1. Prepare a set of data. You could use the ice-cream data on the right or collect your own data on age and beauty.
2. Using Excel (the Microsoft Office application) you can enter and alter pairs of numbers to see how this affects a scattergram and correlation coefficient. *The EXCEL method*
   - On an Excel sheet enter your data in two columns.
   - To see a scattergram click and drag your cursor from the top left to the bottom right of the two columns. From the toolbar menu select 'chart' and select 'XY scatter'.
   - To obtain the correlation coefficient, place the cursor in an empty box and type '=correl('. Then select (with your cursor) one column of your data and type a comma in the box and then select your other column of data and finish with a closing bracket. The formula should look something like: =correl(a6:a13,b6:b13). When you press return the correlation coefficient should appear in this box.
   - Alter one of the values and see how this affects the scattergram and correlation coefficient.
   - Try to produce a scattergram with the following correlation coefficients: −.10, +.10, −.90, +.90.

question 3.7

1. Identify **two** variables that are likely to be positively correlated (such as height and weight).

2. Identify **two** variables that are likely to be negatively correlated.

3. What does a correlation coefficient tell you about a set of data?

4. Give **one** example of a positive correlation coefficient and **one** example of a negative correlation coefficient.

5. Explain what the following correlation coefficients mean:
   +1.00　−1.00　.00　−.60　+.40　+.10

6. Consider the number +.39.
   a. Identify the magnitude and sign of this number.
   b. Sketch a scattergram to approximately illustrate this correlation.
   c. If you conducted a study with 20 participants, would a correlation of +.39 be significant?

7. A study investigates whether there is a negative correlation between age and liking for spicy foods. Participants are asked to rate their liking for spicy foods on a scale of 1 to 10 where 10 means they liked it a lot and 1 not at all.
   a. What is meant by the term 'negative correlation' in this context?
   b. Why might you expect to find a negative correlation between these variables?
   c. Describe **one** strength and **one** weakness of conducting a correlational analysis in this research.
   d. Describe **one** issue of reliability in this research and describe how you could deal with this issue of reliability.
   e. Discuss **one** ethical issue that might arise in this research.

8. Guiseppe Gelato always liked statistics at school and now that he has his own ice-cream business he keeps various records. The table below shows his data.

All data rounded to 1000s

	Jan	Feb	Mar	Apr	May	Jun	Jul	Aug	Sep	Oct	Nov	Dec
Ice cream sales	10	8	7	21	32	56	130	141	84	32	11	6
Aggressive crimes	21	32	29	35	44	55	111	129	99	36	22	25

   a. Sketch a scattergram of Guiseppe's data.
   b. What can you conclude from the data and the scattergram?
   c. With reference to your conclusion in part b, what intervening variable might better explain the relationship between ice cream and aggression?
   d. Describe how you would design a study to show Guiseppe that ice cream does (or does not) cause aggressive behaviour. (You need to operationalise your variables and decide on a research design.)
   e. Describe **one** issue of validity in this research and describe how you could deal with this issue of validity.

OBSERVATION

At the beginning of this chapter we identified two non-experimental research methods used by psychologists – self-report methods and observation. It is now time to understand how observation is used in research.

Naturalistic observation and natural experiment

Both involve naturally occurring variables that have not been manipulated by the researcher, however in a natural experiment there is an independent variable (IV) and its effect is observed on a dependent variable (DV) so that we can draw tentative causal conclusions. In a naturalistic observation there is no IV.

Naturalistic observations

In a naturalistic observation everything has been left as it normally is.

The environment is unstructured, i.e. uncontrolled.

For example:

➤ Watching animals in their 'normal' or natural environment.

➤ Listening to children talking in their classroom.

Controlled observations

In controlled observations some variables are controlled by the researcher.

The environment or behaviour is controlled (i.e. structured) to some extent. Participants might know they are being studied and/or the study might be conducted in a laboratory in order to control variables in the environment.

For example:

➤ Watching gorillas in a zoo where they have been provided with specific play items.

➤ Listening to children who have been asked to talk about their families.

You might think that making observations is easy but if you try the mini study on the facing page, you will realise it is difficult.

1. It is difficult to work out what to record and what not to record.
2. It is difficult to record everything that is happening even if you do select what to record and what not to record.

Observational research, like all research, aims to be objective and rigorous. For this reason it is necessary to use observational techniques to enable *systematic* observations to be made.

Some exam boards use the terms slightly differently. Edexcel describe controlled observations as structured observations – so for Edexcel the term 'structured observation' refers both to the environment and the method of collecting data.

Unstructured observational techniques

In unstructured observations the researcher records all relevant behaviour but has no system. This technique may be used because the behaviour to be studied is largely unpredictable.

One problem with this is that the behaviours recorded will often be those which are most visible or eye-catching to the observer but these may not necessarily be the most important or relevant behaviours.

Structured observational techniques

In structured (or systematic) observations, the researcher uses various 'systems' to organise observations.

▪ *Research aims* Decide on an area to study (this may apply to unstructured observations as well).

▪ *Observational systems* How to record the behaviour you are interested in. For example, the use of behavioural categories or coding systems. These systems are explained on the next spread.

▪ *Sampling procedures* Who you are observing and when. These procedures are also explained on the next spread.

Method and technique

All research involves making observations. In some research the overall method is observational where the emphasis is on observing a relatively unconstrained segment of a person's freely chosen behaviour. In other research observation might just be used as a way to measure one of the variables.

To summarise!

		Method of data collection	
		Structure	**No structure**
Environment or behaviour	**Structure**	Controlled observation with structured observational techniques	Controlled observation with unstructured observational techniques
	No structure	Naturalistic observation with structured observational techniques	Naturalistic observation with unstructured observational techniques

key terms

- Controlled observation
- Lab
- Naturalistic observation
- Observation
- One-way mirror
- Structured observation
- Unstructured observation

DO I HAVE TO DO THIS?

	AQA A	AQA B	Edex	OCR	WJEC
AS	●	●	●	●	●
A2	●	●	●	●	●

● compulsory   ◑ advisory   ○ not necessary

An example of a naturalistic observation

Do little boys criticise each other if they behave like girls? Do little boys 'reward' each other for sex-appropriate play? Is the same true for little girls?

One study observed boys and girls aged between three and five years during their free-play periods at nursery school. The researchers classified activities as male, female or neutral and recorded how playmates responded. Praise and imitation constituted some of the positive responses. Criticism and stopping play were some of the negative responses. The researchers found that children generally reinforced peers for sex-appropriate play and were quick to criticise sex-inappropriate play (Lamb and Roopnarine, 1979).

An example of a controlled observation

The same research as described on the left could have been conducted by controlling some of the variables. For example, the researchers might have set up a special playroom in their **lab** with certain types of toys available (male, female and neutral). They could have observed the children through a **one-way mirror** so the children would be unaware of being observed.

An example of an experiment with structured observational techniques

In the 'Bobo doll study' described on page 30 (Bandura *et al.*, 1961) the children's aggressiveness was observed at the end of the experiment to see if those exposed to the aggressive model behaved more aggressively. At the end of the experiment each child was taken to a r oom that contained some aggressive toys (e.g. a mallet and a dart gun), some non-aggressive toys (e.g. dolls and farm animals) and a three-foot Bobo doll.

The experimenter stayed with the child while he/she played for 20 minutes, during which time the child was observed through a one-way mirror. The observers recorded what the child was doing every five seconds, for example noting:

- Imitation of physical aggression – any specific acts that were imitated.

- Imitative verbal aggression – any phrases that were imitated, such as 'POW'.

- Imitative non-aggressive verbal responses – such as 'He keeps coming back for more'.

- Non-imitative physical and verbal aggression – aggressive acts directed at toys other than Bobo, for example saying things not said by the model, or were not demonstrated by the model playing with the gun.

mini study

Unstructured observation

Work with a partner and take turns to observe each other. One of you will be Person A and the other will be Person B.

Person A should have a difficult task to do (e.g. answering some of the exam questions in this book). Person B observes Person A, doing this for 5 minutes

Then Person B should have a boring task to do (e.g. copying out the exam question). Person A observes Person B, doing this for 5 minutes

- The person doing the observing should note down any aspect of their partner's behaviour.

- Can you draw any conclusions from your observations?

- Was it easy or difficult to record all your partner's behaviours?

- How could you improve your record keeping?

1. Answer the following questions about the observational mini study below.

   a. Suggest a suitable hypothesis for the study.

   b. If you did the activity, summarise your observations. You might use a graph or other descriptive statistics to help you.

   c. What uncontrolled factors might affect your findings? (These relate to validity.)

   d. Suggest how you might be able to deal with **one or more** of these factors.

   e. In this study is observation the method or the technique?

   f. Are the observations controlled or naturalistic?

   g. If you did conduct the observation, can you suggest **one or more** difficulties that you encountered?

2. With reference to the study by Lamb and Roopnarine (an example of a naturalistic observation), suggest **one** strength and **one** weakness of studying children in this way.

3. With reference to the example of a controlled observation, suggest **one** strength and **one** weakness of studying children using controlled methods.

4. With reference to the study by Bandura *et al.* (an example of an experiment with structured observational techniques), answer the following questions.

   a. Identify the independent and dependent variables in this study.

   b. Explain how these variables have been operationalised.

   c. Explain how the observational environment has been controlled.

   d. Suggest **one** strength and **one** weakness of studying children using controlled methods.

   e. Explain how the method of collecting data has been structured.

   f. Suggest **one** strength and **one** weakness of studying children using structured observational techniques.

5. A group of students decided to study student behaviour in the school library.

   a. How could you conduct this as a naturalistic observation using unstructured techniques?

   b. How could you conduct this as a controlled observation using unstructured techniques?

   c. If you did use structured techniques, what behaviours would you look at? List five particular things that students do when they are studying, for example daydreaming.

   d. Suggest **one or more** hypotheses that you might investigate.

   e. How could you observe the students so that they were not aware that they were being observed?

   f. Discuss **one** ethical issue that might arise in this research.

   g. In this study is observation a method or a technique?

DESIGNING OBSERVATIONAL STUDIES

The key issue for observational research is the design of structured observations, which includes developing a method for recording data as well as a method for sampling data.

Recording data

When we watch somebody perform a particular action we see a continuous stream of action rather than a series of separate behavioural components. In order to make a reliable and objective record of what we observe we need to break this stream of behaviour into different categories. What is needed is **operationalisation** – dividing the behaviour being studied into a set of component behaviours. For example, when observing infant behaviour we can divide this into component behaviours such as smiling, crying, sleeping, etc. or when observing facial expression we can create a list of different expressions as shown below right.

> This set of component behaviours is called a list of **behavioural categories** or a **behaviour checklist**.

> Sometimes each behaviour is given a code to make recording easier and then the method is called a **coding system**.

> A further method is to provide a list of behaviours or characteristics and ask observers to rate each one using a **rating scale**.

Behavioural categories should:
> Be clearly operationalised and objective. The observer should not have to make inferences about the behaviour, for example having a category such as 'being happy' and having to say 'he's smiling and therefore must be happy'. All categories should be directly observable.
> Cover all possible component behaviours and avoid a 'waste basket' category.
> Be mutually exclusive, meaning that you should not have to mark two categories at one time.

Sampling procedures

In an **unstructured observation** data are recorded continuously – every instance of the behaviour seen or heard by the observer is recorded in as much detail as possible. This is possible to do if the behaviours the researcher is interested in do not occur very often.

In many situations, however, continuous observation is not possible because there would be too much data to record. Therefore, there must be a systematic (structured) method of sampling observations.

> **Event sampling** Counting the number of times a certain behaviour (event) occurs in a target individual or individuals. For example, counting how many times a person smiles in a ten minute period.

> **Time sampling** Recording behaviours in a given time frame. For example, noting what a target individual is doing every 30 seconds. The researcher may tick items in a checklist.

Observing faces

Google the Facial Action Coding System to find out more.

Paul Ekman and others developed the Facial Action Coding System (FACS) for observing facial expressions (Ekman and Friesen, 1978). This can be used to investigate, for example, what expressions are shown on a person's face when they are lying.

Observing bears in a zoo

*Robert Jordan and Gordon Burghardt (1986) undertook a study of black bears in a zoo in order to determine whether the presence of observers altered the animals' behaviour. They did this to establish whether **naturalistic observations** of animals was in fact 'naturalistic' – if the animals' behaviour was affected by the presence of observers then it wasn't so natural afterall.*

In this study they selected two bear enclosures in parks in the USA, one at Dollywood, Tennessee (less observed by people) and the other at Tremont, Pennsylvania. They found a much higher activity level at Tremont where the bears had more human contact.

The researchers spent one hour each day making recordings over a two-and-a-half-year period. Observations were recorded every 30 seconds (time sampling) using a behaviour checklist/coding system similar to the one below.

Behaviour checklist and coding system for recording postures and locations of captive black bears

Activity level 1: Reclining postures
 Lying on back (P6)
 Lying on front (P7)
 Lying on side (P8)
 Lying/sitting in a tree (P28)

Activity level 2: Sitting or standing
 Standing on all fours (P3)
 Standing on two feet (P29)
 Sitting erect or semi-erect (P4)

Activity level 3: Bipedal standing and slow locomotion
 Standing on two feet while touching an object (P1)
 Walking on all fours (P11)
 Rolling over (P18)

Activity level 4: Vigorous activity
 Running (P19)
 Ascending (e.g. trees) (P24)
 Descending (e.g. trees) (P27)
 Running a short distance and then walking (P32)
 Jumping (all legs off ground) (P35)

Code	Description	Code	Description
1.	Inner Brow Raiser	26.	Jaw Drop
2.	Outer Brow Raiser	27.	Mouth Stretch
4.	Brow Lowerer	28.	Lip Suck
5.	Upper Lid Raiser	41.	Lid Droop
6.	Cheek Raiser	42.	Slit
7.	Lid Tightener	43.	Eyes Closed
9.	Nose Wrinkler	44.	Squint
10.	Upper Lip Raiser	45.	Blink
11.	Nasolabial Deepener	46.	Wink
12.	Lip Corner Puller	51.	Head Turn Left
13.	Cheek Puffer	52.	Head Turn Right
14.	Dimpler	53.	Head Up
15.	Lip Corner Depressor	54.	Head Down
16.	Lower Lip Depressor	55.	Head Tilt Left
17.	Chin Raiser	56.	Head Tilt Right
18.	Lip Puckerer	57.	Head Forward
20.	Lip Stretcher	58.	Head Back
22.	Lip Funneler	61.	Eyes Turn Left
23.	Lip Tightener	62.	Eyes Turn Right
24.	Lip Pressor	63.	Eyes Up
25.	Lips Part	64.	Eyes Down

key terms

- Behavioural categories
- Behaviour checklist
- Coding system
- Covert observation
- Event sampling
- Naturalistic observation
- Non-participant observation

- Operationalisation
- Overt observation
- Participant observation
- Privacy
- Rating scale
- Sampling
- Time sampling
- Unstructured observations

DO I HAVE TO DO THIS?

	AQA A	AQA B	Edex	OCR	WJEC
AS	●	●	●	●	○
A2	●	●	●	●	○

● compulsory ◐ advisory ○ not necessary

Some other things about observations

Participant and non-participant

In some observations the observer is also a participant in the behaviour being observed (participant observation) which is likely to affect objectivity (see example on right). More often the observer is not a participant (non-participant observation).

Overt and covert

If a participant is aware of being observed (overt observation) they may alter their behaviour so validity is reduced. This can be overcome by making observations without a participant's knowledge (covert observation), such as using one-way mirrors. This may raise ethical issues regarding invasion of privacy.

Direct and indirect

In many studies, observations are made of data that has already been collected, for example observing advertisements on TV to see whether gender bias exists, or observing newspaper advertisements or children's books. These are indirect observations and one method of dealing with them is called content analysis (see page 72).

An example of a participant observation

In the 1950s the social psychologist Leon Festinger read a newspaper report about a religious cult that claimed to be receiving messages from outer space predicting that the end of the world would take place on a certain date in the form of a great flood. The cult members were going to be rescued by a flying saucer so they all gathered with their leader. Festinger was intrigued to know how the cult members would respond when they found their beliefs were unfounded. In order to observe this at first hand, Festinger and some co-workers posed as converts to the cause and were present on the eve of destruction. When it was apparent that there would be no flood, the group leader said that their prayer had saved the city. Some members didn't believe this and left the cult whereas others took this as proof of the cult's validity (Festinger et al., 1956).

mini study

Making systematic observations

You could organise a trip to the zoo to observe the behaviour of animals there, using the behaviour checklist on the facing page or developing one of your own. Don't forget the importance of piloting your checklist first and ensuring that everyone is using it reliably (inter-observer reliability – discussed on the next page).

Alternatively, you might observe students in a common room or cafeteria, using the behaviour checklist below. This is adapted from one used by Fick (1993) in a study looking at the effects of a dog on the nature and frequency of social interactions in nursing home residents.

- *Non-attentive behaviour* Participant is not engaged in group activity.
- *Attentive listening* Participant maintains eye contact with other group members.
- *Verbal interaction with another person* Participant initiates or responds verbally to another person.
- *Non-verbal interaction with another person* Participant touches, gestures, smiles, nods, etc to another person.

1. Decide on your research aims, for example you could compare social interactions in the morning and afternoon, or between boys and girls, or between different environments (class versus cafeteria).
2. State your hypothesis.
3. Draw up a grid to record your observations.
4. Decide on a sampling procedure.

1 Explain the difference between a behaviour checklist and coding system.

2 For each of the following observations state which sampling procedure would be most appropriate and explain how you would do it.

  a Recording instances of aggressive behaviour in children playing in a school playground.

  b Vocalisations (words, sounds) made by young children.

  c Compliance to controlled pedestrian crossings by pedestrians.

  d Litter dropping in a public park.

  e Behaviour of dog owners when walking their dogs.

3 What distinguishes a successful teacher from an unsuccessful one? A group of students decide to observe various teachers while they are teaching to see what differences there are.

  a Identify **two** ways in which you could operationalise 'successful teacher behaviour'.

  b Describe **one** way to minimise the intrusive nature of the observations.

  c How could data be recorded in this observational study?

  d Suggest **one** strength and **one** weakness of conducting an observational study in this context.

  e Describe **two** ways of ensuring that this study would be carried out in an ethically acceptable manner.

4 Sitting in a dentist's waiting room is an anxious experience. Can this be reduced by playing soft, calming music? An observational study was designed involving a number of different dental practices. Some were classed as 'relaxing' because they played soft music and had calming décor. Others were classed as 'normal' because they were just a typical waiting room with hard chairs and magazines. In each waiting room observations were made of how anxious each patient was. These observations were recorded by the dental receptionist so that the participants were not aware that they were being observed. The observations were used to produce an anxiety score.

  a Write an appropriate directional hypothesis for this study.

  b What experimental design has been used in this study?

  c Give **one** strength and **one** weakness of this experimental design.

  d The researcher used an opportunity sample for this study. Describe **one** strength and **one** weakness of this sampling method in the context of this study.

  e List at least **six** behavioural categories that could be used in this study when observing participants' behaviour.

  f What sampling method might the receptionist use when recording the data?

  g Design a form for the receptionist to use when recording behaviour.

OBSERVATIONS: RELIABILITY AND VALIDITY

We need to evaluate the observational techniques we have described. Part of that involves looking at issues of reliability and validity specific to observations.

Reliability

Observations should be reliable, as with all methods of collecting data. We need to feel confident that if the observations were repeated with the same participants the data would be the same (i.e. consistent).

One way to check reliability is to compare the observations made by two observers. If they are reliable they should produce the same record. The extent to which two (or more) observers agree is called **inter-rater reliability** or **inter-observer reliability**.

This is calculated by dividing the total agreements by the total number of observations. A result of +.80 or more suggests good inter-observer reliability.

Dealing with low reliability

Observers should be trained in the use a **coding system/behaviour checklist**. They should practise using it and discussing their observations.

Validity

Internal validity

Observations will not be valid (nor reliable) if the coding system/behaviour checklist is flawed. For example, some observations may belong in more than one category, or some behaviours may not be codeable. The result is that the data collected does not truly represent what was observed.

The validity of observations is also affected by **observer bias** – what someone observes is influenced by their expectations. This reduces the objectivity of observations.

External validity

Observational studies are likely to have greater **ecological validity** than some other kinds of research because they involve more natural behaviours (but remember the discussion on page 36 – naturalness doesn't always mean greater ecological validity).

Population validity may be a problem if, for example, children are only observed in middle-class homes.

Dealing with low internal and external validity

Conducting observations in varied settings with varied participants (improves external validity).

Dealing with low reliability (improves internal validity – assuming that the coding system is valid in the first place).

Using more than one observer to reduce observer bias and averaging data across observers (balances out any biases).

Training observers

The Behavioural Observation unit (BEO) at the University of Bern trains people in the use of observational techniques (BEO, 2004). They have a nursery school at the unit where children can be observed through a one-way mirror. The data collected has been used for various studies, such as comparing twins. The unit has devised a coding system called KaSo 12 which is shown on the right.

Assessing reliability

The graphs on the right show observations made of two children in the nursery class using KaSo 12. Each time three observers were used (blue, red and purple line). The figures represent the relative duration of a specific behaviour category expressed as a percentage of the total time.

No social participation
1. Occupied alone participation
2. Hanging around alone
3. Alone – onlooker
4. Alone – unclear

Social participation
5. Parallel behaviour 1
6. Parallel behaviour 2
7. Loosely associated but interactive
8. Role play – identifiable
9. Social particpation unclear

Not identifiable
10. Child not in view, generally unclear

coding system KaSo12

⭐ **Exam advice**

On the facing page are some strengths and weaknesses of observational research. In exams you are likely to be asked to outline just *one* strength (or just *one* weakness). So why do you need to remember more than one?

The answer is that you may be asked for one strength of a particular observational study and therefore must present a suitable one. This means that you really need to know a number of strengths/weaknesses so that you can select a criticism that is appropriate to the question scenario.

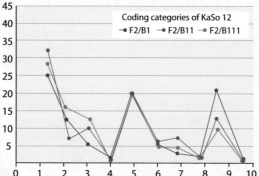

Child 1: mean correlation of the 3 profiles: r = 0.86

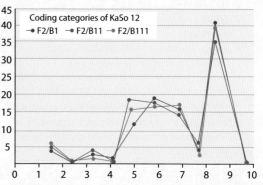

Child 2: showing a markedly different distribution of behaviour patterns but an even closer correlation: r = 0.93

key terms

- Behaviour checklist
- Coding system
- Deception
- Ecological validity
- Ethical committee
- External validity
- Extraneous variables
- Informed consent
- Inter-observer reliability
- Inter-rater reliability
- Internal validity
- Investigator effects
- Naturalistic observation
- Observer bias
- One-way mirror
- Population validity
- Privacy
- Reliability

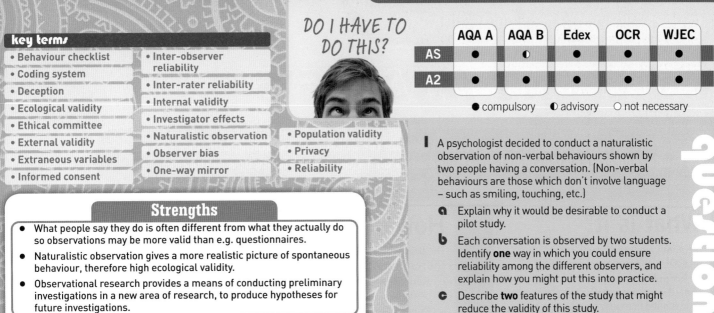

DO I HAVE TO DO THIS?

	AQA A	AQA B	Edex	OCR	WJEC
AS	●	◐	●	●	●
A2	●	●	●	●	●

● compulsory   ◐ advisory   ○ not necessary

Strengths

- What people say they do is often different from what they actually do so observations may be more valid than e.g. questionnaires.
- Naturalistic observation gives a more realistic picture of spontaneous behaviour, therefore high ecological validity.
- Observational research provides a means of conducting preliminary investigations in a new area of research, to produce hypotheses for future investigations.

Weaknesses

- In naturalistic observation there is little control of extraneous variables which may mean that something unknown to the observer may account for the behaviour observed.
- The observer may 'see' what he/she expects to see. This is called observer bias. This bias may mean that different observers 'see' different things, which leads to low inter-observer reliability.
- If participants don't know they are being observed there are ethical problems, such as deception and invasion of privacy. If participants do know they are being observed they may alter their behaviour.
- If participants know they are being observed they may change their behaviour (see investigator effects on page 34).

Ethical issues

In a naturalistic observation participants may be observed without their informed consent. However this is not always the case and some observations may be regarded as an invasion of privacy.

The use of one-way mirrors involves deception (lack of informed consent).

Dealing with ethical issues

- *Informed consent* should be sought where possible, for example in the observations of nursery children by the BEO (see left), parental permission was obtained for all children attending the nursery.
- *Invasion of privacy* Ethical guidelines generally advise that it is acceptable to observe people in public places (places where people expect to be seen by others). Participant confidentiality/anonymity should be protected.
- Ethical committees can be used to approve observational designs.

mini study

Making your own coding system

A number of studies have looked at how males and females are represented in children's books. For example, Peter Crabb and Dawn Bielawski (1994) examined American preschool books and found that female characters were more likely to be pictured using household objects whereas males were more likely to be using production objects (e.g. things related to agriculture, construction, transportation – i.e. work outside of the home).

Develop your own coding system to record the way males and females are represented in children's books. Start by looking at some children's books and the activities that men and women, boys and girls are engaged in.

Once you have developed a coding system, you could investigate the hypothesis that children's books support gender stereotypes.

1 A psychologist decided to conduct a naturalistic observation of non-verbal behaviours shown by two people having a conversation. (Non-verbal behaviours are those which don't involve language – such as smiling, touching, etc.)

a Explain why it would be desirable to conduct a pilot study.

b Each conversation is observed by two students. Identify **one** way in which you could ensure reliability among the different observers, and explain how you might put this into practice.

c Describe **two** features of the study that might reduce the validity of this study.

d Explain how you could deal with these two features that might reduce validity.

e Draw a suitable table for recording observations, showing some of the possible categories.

f Describe **one** way of ensuring that this study would be carried out in an ethically acceptable manner.

g Evaluate your method of dealing with ethics (i.e. did it actually deal with the ethical problem).

2 On the facing page are two graphs showing the observations of two children by three observers.

a Do you think that the graphs indicate an acceptable level of inter-observer reliability? Explain your answer.

b Outline **one** strength and **one** weakness of conducting an observation of children using KaSo12.

3 Imagine that you wished to investigate interpersonal deception to see if it was possible to use facial expressions to tell whether someone is lying or not.

a Describe how you would design a study using observational techniques to investigate this. Record at least **six** design decisions, and describe each one carefully.

b Would you describe your study as a naturalistic observation, a controlled observation or a natural, field or lab experiment? Explain why.

c What would be the relative advantages of doing this study as a naturalistic observation or doing it as a lab experiment?

4 Some psychology students plan to conduct on observational study on the effects of different dress styles – to see if men look more at girls dressed casually or smartly.

a Identify **two** (or more) ways you could operationalise 'being dressed casually' and 'being dressed smartly'.

b Identify **one** way in which you could ensure reliability among the different observers and explain how to do this.

c Describe what sampling technique you might use for making the observations.

d Explain **one** feature of the study that might affect the validity of the data being collected.

e What is the research method used in this study? Explain your answer.

CONTENT ANALYSIS

Observations can be made directly of what people (or animals) are doing, but they can also be made indirectly by looking at advertisements on TV or the contents of a magazine.

What is it?

A content analysis is what it says – the analysis of the content of something.

For example, a researcher might study the way men and women are represented in magazine advertisements and attempt to describe this content in some systematic way so that conclusions could be drawn. Content analysis is a form of indirect observation, indirect because you are not observing people directly but observing them through the artefacts they produce. These artefacts can be in TV programmes, books, songs, paintings, etc.

How do you do it?

The process involved in conducting a content analysis is similar to any observational study. The researcher has to make design decisions about:

- *Sampling method* – What material to sample and how frequently, for example using **time** or **event sampling**. Other considerations include deciding which TV channels or books to include, how many programmes, what length of time.
- *Method of recording data* – For example, using **behavioural categories** or a **coding system**.
- *Method of representing data* – The data can be recorded in each category in two different ways. Consider the example of performing a content analysis on the contents of magazines. First you identify the behavioural categories, such as articles about celebrities, articles about romantic relationships, quizzes and so on. Next you look through magazines and record data either by counting instances (**quantitative analysis**) or by describing examples in each category (**qualitative analysis**).

As with observations, if there is a team of researchers it is important to ensure that they are applying criteria in the same way by calculating **inter-observer reliability**.

Example of a QUANTITATIVE content analysis

Anthony Manstead and Caroline McCulloch (1981) were interested in the way men and women are portrayed in TV ads. They observed 170 ads over a one-week period, ignoring those that contained only children and animals. In each ad they focussed on the central adult figure and recorded frequencies in a table like the one below. For each ad there might be no ticks, one tick or a number of ticks.

	Male	Female
Credibility basis of central character		
Product user	☐	☐
Product authority	☐	☐
Role central character		
Dependent role	☐	☐
Independent role	☐	☐
Arguement spoken by central character		
Factual	☐	☐
Opinion	☐	☐
Product type used by central character		
Food/drink	☐	☐
Alcohol	☐	☐
Body	☐	☐
Household	☐	☐

Example of a QUALITATIVE content analysis

Katja Joronen and Päivi Åstedt-Kurki (2005) studied the role of the family in adolescents' peer and school experiences. They conducted **semi-structured interviews** with 19 adolescents aged 12–16, using questions such as 'What does your family know about your peers?' and 'How is your family involved in your school activities?' These interviews produced 234 pages of notes that were analysed using a qualitative content analysis.

1. All answers to the same question were placed together. Each statement was compressed into a brief statement.

2. These statements were compared with each other and categorised so that statements with similar content were placed together and a category (or theme) identified.

3. The categories were grouped into larger units producing eight main categories, for example:

   - Enablement, e.g. 'Yeah, ever since my childhood we've always had lots of kids over visiting' (girl, 15 years).
   - Support, e.g. 'They (family members) help if I have a test by asking questions' (boy, 13 years).

One of the conclusions drawn from this study is that schools should pay more attention to the multiple relationships that determine an adolescent's behaviour.

key terms

- Behavioural categories
- Coding system
- Content analysis
- Ecological validity
- Event sampling
- Inter-observer reliability
- Observation
- Observer bias
- Qualitative analysis
- Quantitative analysis
- Replicated
- Semi-structured interview
- Time sampling

DO I HAVE TO DO THIS?

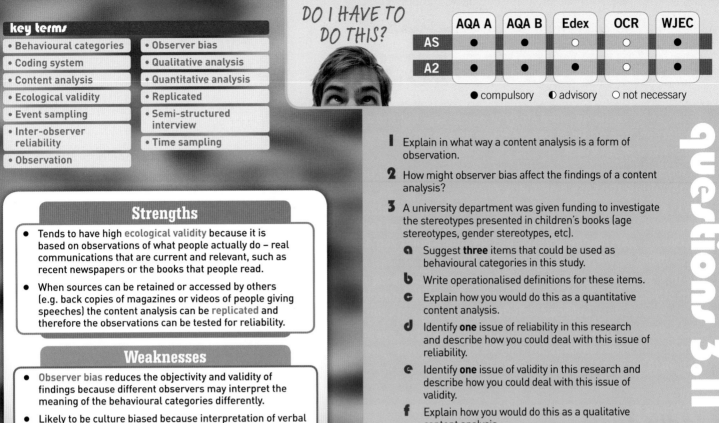

	AQA A	AQA B	Edex	OCR	WJEC
AS	●	●	○	○	●
A2	●	●	●	○	●

● compulsory   ◐ advisory   ○ not necessary

Strengths

- Tends to have high ecological validity because it is based on observations of what people actually do – real communications that are current and relevant, such as recent newspapers or the books that people read.

- When sources can be retained or accessed by others (e.g. back copies of magazines or videos of people giving speeches) the content analysis can be replicated and therefore the observations can be tested for reliability.

Weaknesses

- Observer bias reduces the objectivity and validity of findings because different observers may interpret the meaning of the behavioural categories differently.

- Likely to be culture biased because interpretation of verbal or written content will be affected by the language and culture of the observer and behavioural categories used.

mini study

Analysis of lonely hearts ads

Evolutionary psychologists propose that men and women seek different things in a partner because of the basic differences between eggs and sperm. Women produce relatively few eggs and each is at a high physiological cost. In addition, women have to spend time after giving birth feeding a child. Therefore, a woman will enhance her reproductive success by finding a male partner who has 'resources' (such as being wealthy or having property).

Men produce millions of sperm and so could potentially father millions of children. Their reproductive success will be maximised by finding a fertile partner. One way to ensure this is to find a young partner (younger women are more fertile). Signs of youthfulness include glossy abundant hair, slim waist and symmetrical face (which are all ingredients of physical attractiveness).

This led Robin Dunbar to predict that men and women would seek different things in a partner and also advertise different things. In lonely hearts ads women should seek resources and advertise attractiveness and men should do the opposite.

David Waynforth and Robin Dunbar (1995) analysed nearly 900 ads from 400 American newspapers and found support for this.

1. Explain in what way a content analysis is a form of observation.

2. How might observer bias affect the findings of a content analysis?

3. A university department was given funding to investigate the stereotypes presented in children's books (age stereotypes, gender stereotypes, etc).

   a. Suggest **three** items that could be used as behavioural categories in this study.

   b. Write operationalised definitions for these items.

   c. Explain how you would do this as a quantitative content analysis.

   d. Identify **one** issue of reliability in this research and describe how you could deal with this issue of reliability.

   e. Identify **one** issue of validity in this research and describe how you could deal with this issue of validity.

   f. Explain how you would do this as a qualitative content analysis.

4. A psychology student is interested in the effects of historical periods on the way people express themselves in songs. She decides to compare songs of the 1950s with those of the 1970s to consider the differences in the lyrics before and after the social revolution of the 1960s.

   a. Develop a suitable coding system to analyse the content of songs. The categories you select should be relevant to the issue of historical periods.

   b. Consider how you might use this content analysis to compare songs from the two different periods.

   c. Explain how you could measure the dependent variable using a content analysis.

   d. Develop a suitable coding system for your content analysis.

5. One study (Solley and Haigh, 1957) found that children draw more complex pictures of Santa before Christmas than afterwards.

   a. Develop a suitable coding system to analyse the content of the pictures. The categories you select should be relevant to the issue of classifying different drawings of Santa.

   b. Consider how you might use this content analysis to compare the drawings of Santa.

To replicate this study you might:

1. Look through lonely hearts ads and write down the sorts of things men and women advertise and seek.
2. Use this to decide on a list of behavioural categories to use when doing your content analysis.
3. Use your behaviour checklist to record the contents of male ads. For each male ad tick every category that has been included.
4. Then do the same for female ads.
5. Finally, place these into one of four categories: (1) seek resources, (2) advertise resources, (3) seek attractiveness, (4) advertise resources.
6. Represent your findings in a bar chart and draw conclusions.

You can read more about Dunbar's research at http://www.bbc.co.uk/science/humanbody/mind/articles/emotions/lonelyhearts.shtml

CASE STUDIES

A **case study** is the detailed study of one case – but the case could be one person, one group of people (such as a family or a football team or a school) or an event.

A case study may be conducted within a short space of time (one day) or may follow the case over many years.

The key feature of a case study is that a lot of information is collected about the case and this is likely to involve a variety of techniques – interviews, psychological tests, observations and even experiments to test what an individual can or can't do.

The information might be collected from the case being studied or from other people involved, such as family and friends. It is likely to be **qualitative data** but may include **quantitative data** too.

A case study may be about unusual individual(s) or events, such as a person with brain damage, or may be about 'normal' people or events, such as the life in the day of a typical teenager.

Events

Psychologists have studied the psychological effects of many important events, such as the collapse of the World Trade Towers in September 2001 or the causes of the London riots in August 2011.

Mob behaviour, London riots 2011

Psychologists have always been interested in mob behaviour so this case provided an opportunity to re-examine some of the explanations for the apparently unruly behaviour of 'mobs'. One such study was produced by Steve Reicher and Cifford Stott (2011), where they argue that mob behaviour is not unruly. 'They don't simply go wild but actually tend to target particular shops and particular types of people. The patterns of what they attack and don't attack reveals something about the way they see the world and their grievances about the world' (Furlong, 2011).

Rioters set fire to shops during the 2011 London riots.

Individuals

You will probably study a number of classic case studies, such as:

- *Genie*, locked in her room for much of her early life (see Rymer,1994 for a detailed account).
- *David Reimer*, the boy raised as a girl (see Colapinto, 2000).
- *Henry Molaison* (HM), whose hippocampus was removed to reduce epileptic seizures, resulting in an inability to form new memories (see Hilts, 1995), and another case study concerning memory; Clive Wearing whose memory was damaged by an infection (see his wife's account, Wearing, 2005).
- Freud's study of *Little Hans* to illustrate principles of psychoanalysis (Freud, 1909). Not to be confused with Watson's study of *Little Albert* which is not a case study because it was not a detailed record of the individual, just a record of several classical conditioning trials (Watson and Rayner, 1920).

The case of a teenage addict

Griffiths (1993) sought to gain a greater understanding of fruit machine addiction through the in-depth study of one individual. Data was collected through interviews with 'David' aged 18 and his mother. Initially David's parents put his problems down to adolescence. Once when his mother followed him discreetly, she saw that he went into an amusement arcade. It seemed he was just occupied with 'harmless fun'. Then his mother and sister began to find money missing. The more rows David had with his parents, the more he shut himself away.

Why did he continue? 'I always got the feeling of being 'high' or 'stoned' … Although winning money was the first thing that attracted me to playing fruit machines, this gradually converted to light, sounds and excitement.' Such information offers different insights into behaviour than just looking at quantitative data about addiction.

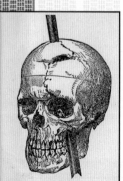

The case of Phineas Gage

In 1848 Phineas was working on the construction of the American railway. An explosion of dynamite drove a tamping iron right through his skull (see artists impression on left). He survived and was able to function fairly normally, showing that people can live despite the loss of large amounts of brain matter. However, the accident did affect Phineas' personality. Before the accident he was hard-working, responsible and popular, whereas afterwards he became restless and indecisive and swore a lot. His friends said he was no longer the same man.

This case was important in the development of brain surgery to remove tumours because it showed that parts of the brain could be removed without having a fatal effect.

Groups of people

The study of obedience *includes the behaviour of cult groups, such as the People's Temple Full Gospel Church led by the charismatic Reverend Jim Jones. He convinced members of his congregation to give him all of their money and property, he came to see himself as a god, and demanded that everyone else see him as one too. If people refused, they were publicly humiliated and even beaten.*

The US government began to have serious questions about the conduct of the church, so Jones moved it to South America, where he created Jonestown. However, he became more paranoid and eventually ordered his 900 followers, including children, to commit suicide by drinking a combination of poison mixed with Kool-Aid.

Many reality TV programmes *are case studies of a group of people. For example, in the 1970s a TV series was filmed of the lives of one family, the Wilkins from Reading. Although we should remember that, strictly speaking, these are not psychological studies and we should always be cautious about generalising from such 'anecdotal' material. For example, in the case of reality TV programmes, the material presented to us has been selected for impact and might not fairly represent the people studied.*

People are fascinated by such case studies. Is it because of the rich detail, that provides interesting insights into human behaviour?

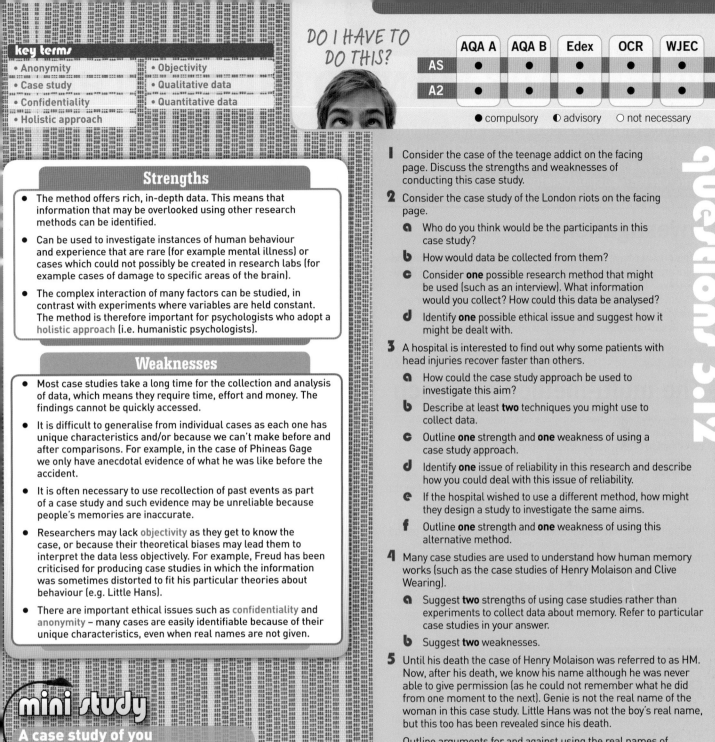

key terms

- Anonymity
- Case study
- Confidentiality
- Holistic approach
- Objectivity
- Qualitative data
- Quantitative data

Strengths

- The method offers rich, in-depth data. This means that information that may be overlooked using other research methods can be identified.

- Can be used to investigate instances of human behaviour and experience that are rare (for example mental illness) or cases which could not possibly be created in research labs (for example cases of damage to specific areas of the brain).

- The complex interaction of many factors can be studied, in contrast with experiments where variables are held constant. The method is therefore important for psychologists who adopt a holistic approach (i.e. humanistic psychologists).

Weaknesses

- Most case studies take a long time for the collection and analysis of data, which means they require time, effort and money. The findings cannot be quickly accessed.

- It is difficult to generalise from individual cases as each one has unique characteristics and/or because we can't make before and after comparisons. For example, in the case of Phineas Gage we only have anecdotal evidence of what he was like before the accident.

- It is often necessary to use recollection of past events as part of a case study and such evidence may be unreliable because people's memories are inaccurate.

- Researchers may lack objectivity as they get to know the case, or because their theoretical biases may lead them to interpret the data less objectively. For example, Freud has been criticised for producing case studies in which the information was sometimes distorted to fit his particular theories about behaviour (e.g. Little Hans).

- There are important ethical issues such as confidentiality and anonymity – many cases are easily identifiable because of their unique characteristics, even when real names are not given.

mini study

A case study of you

Conduct a case study of yourself.

- What background information about yourself might you include as part of this case study?
- Record a typical day in your life. Decide on which data you will collect and how. You might, for example, set a timer every 15 minutes and write down what you are doing and thinking at that moment.
- Collect information from other people about you. You might inteview other people about what they think about you, or you could design a questionnaire.
- Take some online psychological tests.

Conduct your observations.

- Afterwards consider how to present your findings.
- Compare your findings with case studies conducted by other people about their daily lives.

1 Consider the case of the teenage addict on the facing page. Discuss the strengths and weaknesses of conducting this case study.

2 Consider the case study of the London riots on the facing page.
  a Who do you think would be the participants in this case study?
  b How would data be collected from them?
  c Consider **one** possible research method that might be used (such as an interview). What information would you collect? How could this data be analysed?
  d Identify **one** possible ethical issue and suggest how it might be dealt with.

3 A hospital is interested to find out why some patients with head injuries recover faster than others.
  a How could the case study approach be used to investigate this aim?
  b Describe at least **two** techniques you might use to collect data.
  c Outline **one** strength and **one** weakness of using a case study approach.
  d Identify **one** issue of reliability in this research and describe how you could deal with this issue of reliability.
  e If the hospital wished to use a different method, how might they design a study to investigate the same aims.
  f Outline **one** strength and **one** weakness of using this alternative method.

4 Many case studies are used to understand how human memory works (such as the case studies of Henry Molaison and Clive Wearing).
  a Suggest **two** strengths of using case studies rather than experiments to collect data about memory. Refer to particular case studies in your answer.
  b Suggest **two** weaknesses.

5 Until his death the case of Henry Molaison was referred to as HM. Now, after his death, we know his name although he was never able to give permission (as he could not remember what he did from one moment to the next). Genie is not the real name of the woman in this case study. Little Hans was not the boy's real name, but this too has been revealed since his death.

  Outline arguments for and against using the real names of individuals in case studies.

6 Two famous studies are those of Little Hans and Little Albert. Explain why Little Hans is a case study while Little Albert probably isn't (there are no hard and fast rules!).

7 Note that many of these case studies concern individuals in unusual circumstances, often involving brain damage or some other kind of damage (physical or psychological). Explain why.

8 Many TV programmes or newspaper articles focus on one individual or on one group of people or one event. Why would psychologists be reluctant to regard these as case studies?

THERE ARE MANY OTHER METHODS

So far the main research methods and techniques used in Psychology have been covered, but there are others. In order to fully appreciate and evaluate the research studies you read, it helps to know about these other methods/techniques – some of which are discussed briefly on this spread.

Investigations

In this book we have looked at a range of different research methods. There are some occasions when a study doesn't fit into any of these categories. The study on page 53, on the Forer effect, is just that – it's not an experiment (no IV and DV), it's not a case study nor an observation. It does use a questionnaire as a technique to collect data. In such instances a study is just an *investigation*.

The multi-method approach

In reality very few studies simply use one method. Many studies reported in this book use the multi-method approach – a combination of all sorts of different techniques and methods to investigate the target behaviour.

For example, Milgram (1963) conducted a controlled observation in a lab. But he also extensively interviewed his participants after the study to find out their views on why they did or didn't obey.

Schaffer and Emerson (1964) conducted a study of infant attachment. This was a longitudinal study taking place over a period of about a year. The babies and their mothers were observed in their own homes at regular intervals. So the study was basically a non-experimental study, using **naturalistic observation**. The mothers were also interviewed so qualitative data was collected. Furthermore, there was an experimental element, when mothers were asked to record infants' responses (a DV) to seven everyday situations (an IV).

Role play

In some investigations participants are required to take on a certain role and then their behaviour can be observed as if it were everyday life. For example, they might be asked to imagine that they are lying, or to pretend that they are a prison guard or prisoner as in Zimbardo's Stanford prison study (see page 41) . **Role play** is a form of a controlled observation.

Strength

- This enables researchers to study behaviour which might otherwise be impractical or unethical to observe. For example Zimbardo used role play so he could see whether ordinary men would start behaving like prison guards/prisoners just because they were given those roles.

Weakness

- The question is whether people really do act as they would in everyday life. In Zimbardo's study the participants acting as guards may have been following what they *thought* was guard-like behaviour, as seen in films. If they were real-life guards they may have acted more in accordance with personal principles rather than according to social norms.

Cross-cultural studies

In **cross-cultural studies** psychologists compare behaviours in different cultures. This is a way of seeing whether cultural practices affect behaviour. It is a kind of natural experiment where the IV is, for example, child-rearing techniques in different cultures and the DV is some behaviour, such as attachment. This enables researchers to see if attachment differences are due to different culturally determined differences in child-rearing techniques.

Strength

- This technique does enable psychologists to see whether some behaviours are universal, i.e. not affected by cultural differences.

Weaknesses

- **Observer bias** can be a problem because researchers have expectations about how they anticipate other cultural groups will behave and this may affect their measurements. The use of indigenous (local) researchers can help overcome this.
- There may also be communication difficulties, which again can be overcome by using indigenous researchers.
- Researchers may use tests or procedures that have been developed in the US and are not valid in the other culture. This may make the individuals in the other culture appear 'abnormal' or inferior. The term used to describe this is an **imposed etic** – when a technique or psychological test is used in (i.e. imposed upon) one culture even though it was designed for use in another culture.
- The group of participants selected for study may not be representative of that culture and yet we make generalisations about the whole culture – or even the whole country.

Meta-analysis

A **meta-analysis** is a technique used in a number of research studies. A researcher or team of researchers combines the result of several studies that have addressed similar aims/hypotheses. Because the IVs in these studies tend to be measured in different ways, the researcher(s) use **effect size** as the DV in order to assess overall trends. We use effect sizes in our everyday lives, for example a weight loss programme may boast that it leads to an average weight loss of 30 pounds. This is the size of the effect.

Strength

- Analysing the results from a group of studies rather than from just one study can allow more reliable conclusions to be drawn. Often studies produce rather contradictory results (e.g. some studies may find no effect, some studies a small effect while others find a larger effect). A meta-analysis allows us to reach an overall conclusion.

Weakness

- The research designs in the different studies sampled may vary considerably which means that the studies are not truly comparable and thus the conclusions from the meta-analysis are not always valid.

key terms

- Attrition
- Case study
- Cohort effects
- Cross-cultural study
- Cross-sectional study
- Effect size
- Imposed etic
- Longitudinal study
- Meta-analysis
- Naturalistic observation
- Observations
- Observer bias
- Participant variables
- Role play
- Snapshot study

Longitudinal and cross-sectional studies

A **longitudinal study** (or design) is a study conducted over a long period of time in order to observe long-term effects, for example the difference between people of different ages.

An alternative way to study the effects of age is to conduct a **cross-sectional study** (or design). One group of participants of a young age are compared to another, older group of participants at the same point in time (e.g. in 2008) with a view to investigating the influence of age on the behaviour in question. This method is sometimes called a **snapshot study** because a snapshot is taken at a particular moment in time.

Cross-sectional studies and snapshot studies may look at other things rather than the effects of age. For example, a cross-sectional study might look at the behaviours of different professional groups (teachers, doctors, solicitors, etc.), i.e. different sections of society.

You can study the effects of aging on behaviours, such as intelligence by testing and interviewing the same person repeatedly as they get older (longitudinal). The alternative way to study the effects of ageing is test/interview separate groups of people representing the different ages we are interested in (cross-sectional). However, remember that longitudinal and cross-sectional designs are not only concerned with the effects of age.

Strengths

- Longitudinal studies control for **participant variables**.
- Cross-sectional studies have the advantage of being relatively quick.

Weaknesses

- In a longitudinal study **attrition** is a problem. Some of the participants inevitably drop out over the course of a study. The difficulty is that the ones who drop out are more likely to have particular characteristics (e.g. be the ones who are less motivated or more unhappy or who have done less well), which leaves a biased sample or a sample that is too small.

- In a longitudinal study participants are likely to become aware of the research aims and their behaviour may be affected (as in a repeated measures design).

- Another problem is that such studies take a long time to complete, and therefore are difficult to finance.

- In a cross-sectional study the groups of participants may differ in more ways than the behaviour being researched. For example, if a researcher is comparing teachers, doctors and solicitors these groups differ in terms of profession but might also differ because teachers have less money. In other words, differences between groups are due to participant variables rather than the independent variable (like an independent groups design).

Cohort effects occur because a group (or cohort) of people who are all the same age share certain experiences, such as children born just before the World War I had poor diets in infancy due to rationing.

- In a longitudinal study findings that consider only one cohort may not be generalisable because of the unique characteristics of the cohort.

- In a cross-sectional study, for example, the IQs of 20 somethings might be compared with 80 somethings, finding that the IQ of the latter group was much lower. This suggests that IQ declines with age. However, it might be that the 80 somethings had lower IQs when they were 20 something (due to e.g. poorer diet). This is a cohort effect.

1 Buss (1989) explored what males and females looked for in a marriage partner. For example, participants were asked to rate characteristics on a four-point rating scale from 3 (indispensable) to 0 (unimportant). These characteristics included good earning capacity, physical attractiveness, being religious and having an exciting personality. The study involved over 10,000 people from 37 different cultures. The research data was collected in most cases by native residents of each country. Research collaborators were unaware of the central hypotheses of the investigation.

  a Describe **two** potential weaknesses in this study and explain how they were or might be dealt with.

  b Describe **one** strength of this study.

2 Samuel and Bryant (1984) tested children's cognitive abilities. About 250 children were involved and divided into four age groups: 5, 6, 7 and 8 years old. The aim was to find out whether older children would perform better on a particular task (the ability to conserve quantity).

  a Explain why this is a natural experiment.

  b Explain why this is a cross-sectional design.

  c Describe **one** strength and **one** weakness of this design in this study.

  d How could the same study be conducted using a longitudinal design?

3 Köhnken et al. (1999) conducted a meta-analysis of 53 studies comparing the effectiveness of the cognitive compared with standard interviewing techniques used by police when interviewing eyewitnesses. They found an effect size of 34%, favouring the cognitive interview.

  a Explain what the findings of this study mean.

  b Describe **one** strength and **one** weakness of using this technique to analyse data.

4 Schultz et al. (1980) assessed the intelligence of 100 young and 100 older people (average age was about 20 years and 64 years respectively). They found declines in certain kinds of intelligence and spontaneous flexibility with age, but they found that some older participants were the best of all.

  a What is the independent variable in this study?

  b Does this study use a longitudinal or cross-sectional design?

  c Explain how the cohort effect might account for differences between the two groups.

5 Hodges and Tizard (1979) conducted a study of infants placed in a home for adoption. Some of these infants were eventually adopted whereas others returned to the natural homes. The children were assessed at the ages of 8 and 16 to see how their early experiences affected their social and cognitive development. Self-report methods were used to collect data from children, parents, teachers and matched controls.

  a Explain why this is a natural experiment.

  b Does this study use a longitudinal or cross-sectional design?

  c How might a cohort effect be a problem here?

  d Describe **one** strength and **one** weakness of using this design in this study.

THE USE OF NON-HUMAN ANIMALS

When considering the use of non-human animals (NHA) in psychological research there are two issues to consider:

The scientific value of such research – how much *can* the study of NHA tell us about human behaviour and experience.

The ethical issues – weighing up the conflict between the wider benefits for society and the potential harm to NHA.

This is not research on cosmetics, i.e. it is not trivial.

This is not medical research, i.e. it is not life-saving. Although psychologists do use drugs to treat mental disorders which includes preventing suicide.

Not all NHA research involves physical interventions, although psychological treatments may be equally damaging.

Some of the studies that you may be familiar with would not be allowed to take place today because of more stringent constraints.

Pictures of NHA research often evoke strong emotions, but you must focus on the logical arguments.

Remember that not all research with animals involves labs or experiments. Dian Fossey spent many years observing and recording the behaviour of gorillas in their natural habitat, increasing our understanding of the social lives of these animals.

If you wish to read more about animal research, the BBC website presents some excellent information – see http://www.bbc.co.uk/ethics/animals/

The scientific arguments

NHA may be studied simply because they are fascinating to study in their own right and such research may ultimately benefit NHA. For example, studies of NHA facing extinction may increase their survival. The main value of using NHA in psychological research is to conduct procedures that would not be possible with humans.

There are some justifications for this:

- Human beings and NHA have sufficient of their physiology and evolutionary past in common to justify conclusions drawn from the one being applied to the other. NHA studies have investigated connections between stress and disease, and helped understanding of drug abuse and physical dependence.
- The behaviour of NHA is simpler because it is less influenced by cognitive factors. Behaviourists believe that behavioural building blocks are the same in NHA and humans. We can therefore gain insights into human behaviour from the study of NHA.
- Researchers can have greater control and objectivity. For example, NHA don't to respond to **demand characteristics**.
- The NHA species used in laboratories have shorter natural lifespans than humans so developmental processes may be easier to observe.

However:

- Physiology and behaviour may be *similar* but not the same. For example, NHA may not be good models for human circadian rhythms if they are nocturnal or hibernate.
- It may be meaningless to compare human and NHA behaviour because of the influences of emotion, social context and cognition on human behaviour.
- The stress that animals endure in labs can affect their behaviour, making the results meaningless.

The ethical arguments

1. Pain and distress

Do NHA experience pain? One study (Sneddon *et al.*, 2003) injected rainbow trout with bee venom and found that the fish started rocking from side to side, indicating distress and pain. However, just responding to a noxious stimuli may not mean NHA *feel* pain, i.e. have self-awareness.

Do NHA have feelings (i.e. are they sentient beings)? They do form lasting relationships and they do demonstrate psychological capacities, such as self-awareness. For example, Epstein *et al.* (1981) attached paper dots to pigeon's feathers and found they could remove them by looking in the mirror. However, is this truly self-awareness or just self-recognition? Either way, recent European law (Treaty of Lisbon, 2009) has declared that all animals are sentient.

We might also remember that some human beings (e.g. those with brain damage) lack sentience. This suggests that lack of sentience does not provide moral justification for the use of animals.

2. Speciesism

Peter Singer (1990) argues that discrimination on the basis of membership of a species (**speciesism**) is no different to racial or gender discrimination (racism or sexism). However, Jeffrey Gray (1991) argues that we have a special duty of care to humans, and therefore speciesism is not equivalent to, for example, racism.

Gray asks, 'If you see two creatures fighting and you have a gun, who would you shoot if (1) it was your son and a stranger, (2) both are strangers, (3) it was your son and a lion, (4) it was a stranger and a lion?' He predicted that most people would save the humans rather than the lion.

Singer's response is that there is a difference between questions about life and questions about inflicting pain. He also points out that human behaviour is not always determined by principles of natural selection (the duty of care to your own species). For example, we can and do overcome our natural instincts of aggression in some situations.

3. Rights

Singer's view is a **utilitarian** one, i.e. whatever produces the greater good for the greater number of individuals is ethically acceptable. This means that, if animal research can alleviate pain and suffering, it is justifiable. Tom Regan (1984), on the other hand, argues that there are no circumstances under which animal research is acceptable (an **absolutist** position). Regan claims that animals have a right to be treated with respect and should never be used in research.

The 'animal rights' argument can be challenged by examining the concept of rights – having rights is dependent on having responsibilities in society, i.e. as citizens. It can therefore be said that as animals do not have any responsibilities, they do not have any rights.

It may be better to distinguish between rights and obligations. Obligations are owed by humans to animals (e.g. acting humanely, being aware of animals sentience).

What existing constraints?

Laws

In the UK the *Animals (Scientific Procedures) Act* (1986) requires that animal research only takes place at licensed laboratories with licensed researchers on licensed projects.

- Potential results are important enough to justify the use of animals. When considering costs versus benefits, investigators must consider whether the knowledge to be gained from any investigation justifies harm or distress to animal participants.
- The research cannot be done using NHA methods.
- The minimum number of animals will be used.
- Any discomfort or suffering is kept to a minimum by appropriate use of anaesthetics or pain killers.

The act relates only to vertebrate animals and only to those more than halfway through their gestation period. One invertebrate species (the octopus) was added in 1993. Primates, cats, dogs and horses have additional protection.

Guidelines

Professional organisations such as the *British Psychological Society* (BPS) produce guidelines, for example:

- *Confinement, restraint, stress and harm* – these should be minimised to reduce trauma to the animal.
- *Species* – use of different species should be considered with regards to pain and discomfort and procedures.
- *Numbers of animals* used in lab studies – the smallest number possible should be used by optimising design.
- *Caging and social environment* – should be appropriate to needs of the species to avoid distress caused by overcrowding or isolation.
- *Deprivation* (of food and water) – should be considered in the light of needs of the species and the individual.
- *Wild animals* – disturbance should be minimised and endangered species should only be used in conservation research.

Alternatives to NHA research

Recently the House of Lords (2002) pledged commitment to the three Rs: *reduction, refinement, replacement* – using alternatives, such as human research or computer simulation. A national group, *The National Centre for the Replacement, Refinement and Reduction Animals* (NC3Rs), has been set up to encourage, research and support the use of the 3Rs through research and education.

Do these constraints work?

Joan Dunayer (2002) argues that animal legislation simply sets standards for the imprisonment, enslavement, hurting and killing of animals.

Further questions are raised by a recent analysis of research by NC3Rs (Kilkenny *et al.*, 2009). A review was made of 271 US and UK studies that had used non-human animals (not all psychological studies). Only 59% of these studies mentioned the number of animals that were used, many of them reported different numbers of animals in the methods and results sections of the report, and many studies were poorly designed. The NC3Rs analysis concluded that there are a number of issues that need to be addressed in NHA research, including using more careful design as required by the 3Rs and providing more accurate scientific reporting.

1 Give **one** reason why NHA are good models for human behaviour, and **one** reason why they aren't.

2 Explain if sentience could be used as a criteria in deciding whether it is ethically acceptable to use NHA in psychological research.

3 Explain the concept of speciesism.

4 Do you support the utilitarian or the absolutist position regarding the ethics of using NHA in psychological research? Explain your answer.

5 The use of animals in psychological research is monitored and restricted by both legislation and professional guidelines.
- **a** Outline the legislation that restricts the use of NHA.
- **b** Outline the guidelines that restrict the use of NHA.
- **c** Explain how the 3Rs may help in reducing the use of animals in psychological research.
- **d** Do you feel these constraints are sufficient? Explain your answer.

6 British law also requires that any new drug (e.g. anti-depressants) must be tested on at least two different species of live mammal. One must be a large non-rodent. Does this make NHA research acceptable? Explain your answer.

mini study

Bateson's cube

Patrick Bateson (1986) suggested that decisions about the rights and wrongs of NHA research could be resolved by considering costs versus benefits. He proposed three main criteria:

- The degree of animal suffering.
- The quality/importance of the research.
- The likelihood of benefit.

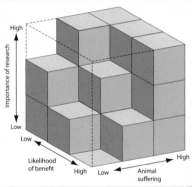

Select at least **four** NHA studies (including at least **one** lab experiment).

Using a five-point scale, rate each study on each of Bateson's three criteria:

(1) Suffering: 5 = high 1 = low
(2) Quality/importance: 5 = high 1 = low
(3) Likelihood of benefit: 5 = low   1 = high

Add up all three scores – the lower the score the more acceptable the research.

- - - - - - - - - - - - - -

Collect results from your classmates and produce a report.

MULTIPLE CHOICE QUESTIONS

1. Data that are stored in a numerical form so it can be counted are called:
   a. Qualitative data
   b. Quantitative data
   c. Questionnaire data
   d. Both a and c.

2. Closed questions tend to produce:
   a. Qualitative data
   b. Quantitative data
   c. Questionable data
   d. Both a and c.

3. Respondents often answer questions in a way that makes them look good rather than being truthful. This is called:
   a. A response set.
   b. A leading question.
   c. Social desirability bias.
   d. The Hawthorne effect.

4. One advantage of an interview in comparison with a questionnaire is that:
   a. The interviewer can adapt questions as she goes along.
   b. People may feel more comfortable about revealing personal information.
   c. Interviews can be delivered by less skilled personnel.
   d. Social desirability bias is less of a problem.

5. A leading question is a question which:
   a. Contains the answer in the question.
   b. Is the most important question on a questionnaire.
   c. Suggests what answer is desired.
   d. Tends to confuse respondents.

6. In a correlation you have:
   a. An IV and a DV.
   b. Co-variables.
   c. Factors.
   d. Both a and b.

7. A negative correlation is when:
   a. Two variables increase together.
   b. As one variable increases the other decreases.
   c. There is a weak correlation between two variables.
   d. There is a strong correlation between two variables.

8. A correlation coefficient of +.65 indicates:
   a. No correlation.
   b. A weak positive correlation.
   c. A moderate positive correlation.
   d. A strong positive correlation.

9. Which of the following could not be a correlation coefficient?
   a. 0
   b. +.79
   c. +1.28
   d. −.30

10. A scattergram (scattergraph) is:
    a. A descriptive statistic.
    b. A graph that illustrates a correlation.
    c. A collection of dots where each dot represents a pair of scores.
    d. All of the above.

11. One way to assess internal reliability is:
    a. Replication.
    b. Test–retest method.
    c. Split-half method.
    d. Ask a friend.

12. The key feature of a naturalistic observation is that:
    a. No set categories are used to record behaviour.
    b. Behaviour is observed.
    c. There is an independent variable.
    d. Everything has been left as it normally is.

13. A coding system is a method used in observational research for:
    a. Sampling behaviours.
    b. Making systematic observations.
    c. Determining validity.
    d. All of the above.

14. Event sampling involves:
    a. Noting what a target individual is doing every 30 seconds.
    b. Keeping a count of each time a target behaviour occurs.
    c. Making notes on all behaviours that occur.
    d. Noting what everyone is doing at a point in time.

15. When observations are made from data in a newspaper, this is called:
    a. Direct observation.
    b. Indirect observation.
    c. Content analysis.
    d. Both b and c.

16. The reliability of observations may be affected by:
    a. Lack of agreement between several observers when observing the same thing.
    b. Lack of agreement between observations made by one observer on several occasions.
    c. Lack of agreement between several observers when observing different things.
    d. Both a and b.

17. Which of the following ethical issues is *not* likely to be a problem in a naturalistic observation?
    a. Informed consent.
    b. Privacy.
    c. Confidentiality.
    d. Protection from psychological harm.

18. Role play is a kind of:
    a. Naturalistic observation.
    b. Controlled observation.
    c. Field experiment.
    d. Natural experiment.

19. A case study may concern:
    a. A single individual.
    b. An institution.
    c. An event.
    d. All of the above.

20. Longitudinal design is like:
    a. A repeated measures design.
    b. An independent groups design.
    c. Matched pairs design.
    d. Counterbalancing.

Answers on facing page

EXAM STYLE QUESTION 5

Sigmund Freud proposed that children go through various stages of development, and in each stage energy is focused on an area of the body. During the first stage of development the focus is on the mouth (the stage is called the oral stage). Freud suggested that either too much pleasure or too much frustration at this stage would lead a person to develop an oral personality.

One way to test this is to see whether adults with a focus on their mouths also have oral personalities. In one study, mouth focus was assessed by observing the number of mouth movements a participant made in a 20-minute period.

Oral personality was assessed in an interview, which provided a score for oral personality for each participant. The oral personality scores for 15 participants were: 3, 4, 5, 6, 6, 7, 7, 9, 10, 13, 15, 16, 17, 19, 20 (a highly oral personality would score 20).

The findings from the study are shown in the graph below. The correlation coefficient is +.74.

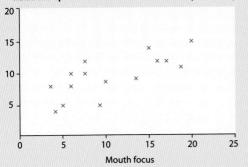

Relationship between mouth focus and oral personality

(a) (i) One co-variable in this study was 'mouth focus'. How was 'mouth focus' operationalised? (2 marks)

(ii) Identify the second co-variable in this study. (1 mark)

(b) (i) Identify the kind of graph that has been used to illustrate the findings of this investigation. (1 mark)

(ii) Write a suitable label for the y axis (vertical axis) of the graph. (1 mark)

(c) (i) What is meant by the term 'correlation coefficient'? (2 marks)

(ii) Using the information from the graph and/or correlation coefficient, describe the relationship between the co-variables. (3 marks)

(iii) Give **one** strength of an investigation using a correlational analysis. (2 marks)

(d) A newspaper article reports these findings claiming that 'mouth focus causes an oral personality'.

(i) Explain why this is not a valid conclusion. (2 marks)

(ii) Suggest a more suitable conclusion for this study. (2 marks)

(e) The researcher wished to summarise the findings using a measure of central tendency.

(i) Identify a suitable measure of central tendency for the scores for oral personality. (1 mark)

(ii) Explain why this would be a suitable measure of central tendency. (2 marks)

(f) Explain how the researcher could assess the reliability of the interview that was used. (2 marks)

(g) Explain how the researcher could assess the validity of the interview. (2 marks)

(h) The researcher decided to interview participants instead of using a questionnaire. Give **one** strength and **one** weakness of using an interview rather than a questionnaire. (2 marks + 2 marks)

(j) Give an example of a question that might have been used that would provide qualitative data. (2 marks)

(k) Identify **one** ethical issue that might arise in this study and explain how you would deal with it. (3 marks)

Examiner's tips for answering this question

(a) (i) This is an example of the kind of question where you are *not* asked to describe the meaning of a term (in this case, operationalisation) but are required to demonstrate your understanding by applying the definition to this example.

You would get just 1 mark for saying 'counting the number of mouth movements'.

(ii) For 1 mark a brief answer would be acceptable.

(b) These should be easy marks.

(c) (i) It is rare to get a question that simply requires a definition but there are a few. There is no requirement to contextualise your answer but you can do this if you think it is a means of providing extra detail. Just saying 'It is a number' wouldn't be sufficient for 2 marks.

(ii) Think carefully about how to get 3 marks worth of detail into your answer. Simply saying a 'positive correlation' would only score 1 mark.

(iii) There is no requirement to contextualise your answer but again this may be a helpful way to provide extra detail. Don't forget that you won't get 2 marks and you might not even get 1 mark if you provide a statement that could apply to all research methods, such as saying 'it shows you the relationship between two variables'.

(d) (i) If you just say 'You can't have cause-and-effect' this answer would only get 1 mark.

(ii) A helpful way to ensure that you provide a conclusion and not a finding is to start your answer with 'The findings suggest that ...'.

(e) (ii) Your answer should be based on the data given in the stimulus material, i.e. contextualised.

(f) and (g) In both of these questions you must focus on how you would do it not what is meant by the terms reliability or validity. You must also avoid writing about why you would do it. And finally, you must focus on the interview rather than the measure of mouth focus.

(h) Don't just trot out any strength and weakness of an interview.

(j) This provides an opportunity to demonstrate that you understand what is meant by qualitative data.

(k) Remember that debriefing may not be credited as an ethical issue but could be mentioned as a way of dealing with an ethical issue.

Answers for MCQs from page 80

1b 2b 3c
4a 5c 6b
7b 8d 9c
10d 11c 12d
13b 14b 15c
16d 17d 18b
19d 20a

pages 80 | 81

EXAM STYLE QUESTION 6

A group of psychology students were interested in non-verbal behaviour and decided to conduct a naturalistic observation of people's behaviour when chatting up the opposite sex, i.e. 'flirting behaviour'.

They decided to observe the body signals of women when they were talking to a man. To do this each member of the class had the task of locating a target couple in a suitable public place (such as a pub or club) and observing the woman's behaviour for ten minutes.

(a) Describe **two** strengths of a naturalistic observation. (2 marks + 2 marks)

(b) Identify the method used to select participants in this study. (1 mark)

(c) Identify **two** methods of operationalising 'flirting behaviour'. (1 mark + 1 mark)

(d) Explain how you would collect the data for this study. (3 marks)

(e) (i) What is meant by reliability? (2 marks)

(ii) Identify **one** way in which you could ensure reliability among the different observers, and explain how you might put this into practice. (3 marks)

(f) (i) Describe **one** way in which you could minimise the intrusive nature of your observations. (2 marks)

(ii) Explain why it would be important to prevent participants knowing they were being observed. (2 marks)

(g) Explain **two** features of the study that might affect the validity of the data being collected. (2 marks + 2 marks)

(h) (i) Identify **one** way the students ensured that this study would be carried out in an ethically acceptable manner. (1 mark)

(ii) Describe **one** weakness with this approach. (2 marks)

(iii) Name **one** other ethical issue that might arise in this study and explain how you would deal with this. (3 marks)

(j) Explain the difference between a naturalistic observation and an experiment. (3 marks)

MODEL ANSWERS

A model answer is an answer that would get full marks. However, it isn't the only answer that would get full marks, it is simply one possible answer.

Exam style question 5

(a) (i) One co-variable in this study was 'mouth focus'. How was 'mouth focus' operationalised? (2 marks)
By counting the number of mouth movements in a 20-minute period.

(ii) Identify the second co-variable in this study. (1 mark)
Oral personality.

(b) (i) Identify the kind of graph that has been used to illustrate the findings of this investigation. (1 mark)
Scattergram.

(ii) Write a suitable label for the y axis (vertical axis) of the graph. (1 mark)
Score for oral personality.

(c) (i) What is meant by the term 'correlation coefficient'? (2 marks)
It is a measure of the extent to which two variables are related, given as a number between +1 and −1.

(ii) Using the information from the graph and/or correlation coefficient, describe the relationship between the co-variables. (3 marks)
They both tell us that there is a reasonably strong positive correlation, as oral personality increases the mouth focus score increases.

(iii) Give one strength of an investigation using a correlational analysis. (2 marks)
It means that research can examine the relationship between variables without having to manipulate one of them, which might be unethical or impractical.

(d) (i) Explain why this is not a valid conclusion. (2 marks)
You can't claim a causal relationship if you have done a correlational study, so you can't say that early experience causes an oral personality.

(ii) Suggest a more suitable conclusion for this study. (2 marks)
The findings suggest that people who are focused on their mouth also have an oral personality.

(e) (i) Identify a suitable measure of central tendency for the scores for oral personality. (1 mark)
The mean.

(ii) Explain why this would be a suitable measure of central tendency. (2 marks)
It takes the values of all the data into account in the final calculation, which is not true for the median.

(f) Explain how the researcher could assess the reliability of the interview that was used. (2 marks)
The researcher could repeat the interview again a week later using the same participants to see if the same score was produced.

(g) Explain how the researcher could assess the validity of the interview. (2 marks)
Validity could be assessed by seeing if the score obtained on the interview was positively correlated with the score obtained on another measure of oral personality.

(h) Give one strength and one weakness of using an interview rather than a questionnaire. (2 marks + 2 marks)
One strength is that the interviewer could explain some of the questions.
One weakness is that the interviewees might be more reluctant to give personal information.

(j) Give an example of a question that might have been used that would provide qualitative data. (2 marks)
'Describe the feelings you get when you suck on a pencil.'

(k) Identify one ethical issue that might arise in this study and explain how you would deal with it. (3 marks)
One ethical issue is informed consent, which is not mentioned. Participants should be offered the chance to give their informed consent before taking part by being told what the study will involve.

Exam style question 6

(a) Describe two strengths of a naturalistic observation. (2 marks + 2 marks)
One strength is that you can study things in a more natural setting where people behave as they would in real life.
A second strength is that people often don't behave as they think they do, so observing them gives a more realistic picture.

(b) Identify the method used to select participants in this study. (1 mark)
Opportunity sample.

(c) Identify two methods of operationalising 'flirting behaviour'. (1 mark + 1 mark)
Lowering eyes, body facing towards the man.

(d) Explain how you would collect the data for this study. (3 marks)
One sampling method would be event sampling. The students would draw up a list of behaviours and keep a count of each time they saw each behaviour over the set time period. The list would be on paper.

(e) (i) What is meant by reliability? (2 marks)
Reliability refers to the consistency of measurements, within a set of measurements (internal) or between them (external).

(ii) Identify one way in which you could ensure reliability among the different observers, and explain how you might put this into practice. (3 marks)
You could calculate the extent of inter-observer reliability, which you would do by collecting the observations from two or more observers who had used the same coding system and correlating their answers. If the inter-observer reliability was less than 80% you would need to train the observers or improve your coding system.

(f) (i) Describe one way in which you could minimise the intrusive nature of your observations. (2 marks)
You could work out a coding system with numbers so you just note down a number for every observation so that it could be done easily.

(f) (ii) Explain why it would be important to prevent participants knowing they were being observed. (2 marks)
If they knew they were being observed they might change their behaviour and might be, for example, less flirty.

(g) Explain two features of the study that might affect the validity of the data being collected. (2 marks + 2 marks)
1. If participants knew they were being observed they wouldn't behave naturally.
2. If the observers couldn't properly see the people they were observing they might not make an accurate record of what was happening.

(h) (i) Identify one way the students ensured that this study would be carried out in an ethically acceptable manner. (1 mark)
They chose to conduct the observations in a public place which means they weren't invading privacy.

(ii) Describe one weakness with to this approach. (2 marks)
Even though it is a public place people may not think it is acceptable for a psychology student to note down their behaviour.

(iii) Name one other ethical issue that might arise in this study and explain how you would deal with this. (3 marks)
Informed consent could also be a problem. This could be dealt with by debriefing participants after making the observations and asking them if they would like to withhold their data.

(j) Explain the difference between a naturalistic observation and an experiment. (3 marks)
In a naturalistic observation you are not investigating a causal relationship so the effects of the IV are not observed on the DV, whereas they are in an experiment. Also in a naturalistic observation everything is left as it normally is whereas this is not true in experiments where some control is exerted even in a natural experiment.

4

Quantitative and qualitative methods

QUANT AND QUAL APPROACHES

PAGES 86–87

Understanding why qualitative approaches are increasingly common in psychological research.

mini study Looking for your own examples

QUALITATIVE RESEARCH DESIGN PAGES

PAGES 88–89

Looking at some basic principles of designing research studies to collect qualitative data.

mini study Designing your own qualitative research study

QUALITATIVE ANALYSIS

PAGES 90–91

The next step in qualitative research – analysing the data you have collected. This can be done quantitatively or qualitatively.

mini study Doing your own qualitative analysis

QUALITATIVE RESEARCH: RELIABILITY AND VALIDITY

PAGES 92–93

Like any good research, qualitative research seeks to demonstrate consistency and authenticity – reliability and validity.

mini study Qualitative analysis of a song

QUANTITATIVE RESEARCH: GRAPHS AND MEASUREMENTS

PAGES 94–95

Quantitative data is measured – but there are many different ways to do this so a researcher has important decisions to make about the best method to use.

mini study Comparing quantitative and qualitative

END OF CHAPTER TREATS

PAGES 96–99

Multiple choice questions

Exam style questions 7 and 8

Model answers for exam style question

QUANT AND *Qual* APPROACHES

We have discussed quantitative and qualitative data previously in this book (see, for example, page 54). This chapter focuses on these types of data in more depth, beginning with a look at the qualitative approach in general and making some comparisons with the quantitative approach.

There's qualitative data, qualitative research, qualitative analysis and also the qualitative approach.

Painting in the style of *The Kiss* by Gustav Klimt.

Why qualitative?

The growth of the qualitative approach in psychology is due to a sense of dissatisfaction with some aspects of the quantitative approach.

The quantitative approach provides a narrow and contrived snapshot of behaviour

Traditional, quantitative methods try to separate the individual/participant from his or her social context – dealing with behaviour in isolation from where it usually occurs. It is just because of this that psychology students criticise lab experiments, saying for example:

- 'This study of eyewitness testimony lacked ecological validity because it was conducted in lab where people don't behave like they do in everyday life'.
- 'This study of memory lacked mundane realism because the task involved lists of numbers which is not an everyday memory task.

The qualitative approach conducts research within the natural context of people's lives and thus has greater real-world meaning.

The quantitative approach aims to be objective but it is inevitably subjective

Various problems arise when conducting research, such as experimenter effects and demand characteristics. Researchers try to control the effect that experimenters and the experimental situation have on participants' behaviour but such effects can never be fully removed.

Qualitative research acknowledges subjectivity by considering the effect that this has on the data collected (see 'reflexivity' on page 92).

Some qualitative research seeks to involve participants as equal partners in the research process, collaborating in the design of research.

The quantitative approach raises ethical issues

The collaborative nature of qualitative research may remove an additional problem found in quantitative research – the ethical issue of deception. In quantitative research participants often have to be deceived because otherwise their knowledge would predetermine their behaviour. In qualitative research, where participants are involved and the effects of their expectations are acknowledged, the need for deception is reduced.

The quantitative approach stifles discovery and theory generation

The quantitative approach focuses on hypotheses generated from previous research. This prevents researchers taking a fresh look at data and discovering new themes and theories. The quantitative approach is generally deductive – starting from an existing theory and then narrowing this down into a more specific hypothesis that we can test and finally ending with the data collected.

By contrast, the qualitative approach is more inductive, working from the bottom up rather than the top down. It starts with specific observations that then lead to the detection of patterns and ultimately theories. At the heart of qualitative analysis is the discovery of themes which emerge from the data.

Quantitative data	Qualitative data
Quantity	Quality
Deals with numbers	Deals with descriptions
Data that can be measured	Data that are not measured
Psychologists develop measures of psychological variables	Observing people through the messages they produce and the way they act
Looking at averages and differences between groups	Concerned with attitudes, beliefs, fears and emotions

The Kiss by Gustav Klimt

Painted between 1907 and 1908, when the artist was 45 years old	Representative of a style of art called *Art Nouveau*
Painting measures 180 × 180 cm	Shows a couple locked in a kiss
Bought for 25,000 crowns when it was first painted	Shows how bright, beautiful and golden everything is when you first kiss someone
33% of surface covered in gold leaf	Painted in oil and gold leaf on canvas
Listed as no. 12 on list of most popular paintings	Probably his most famous work

A psychology class

24 students	Very enthusiastic about psychology
18 girls, 6 boys	Mixture of boys and girls
72% gained Grade A on mock exam	Hardworking students
10 students plan to go on to study psychology at university	School located in an inner-city area
Most psychology teachers are female	Teacher's name is Mrs Jones

The qualitative approach is idiographic (drawing on unique experience) whereas the quantitative approach is nomothetic (making broad-ranging laws about likely behaviour). However, qualitative researchers often do try to make generalisations (draw conclusions) which is a nomothetic approach – as some of the examples on the next spread show.

key terms

- Deception
- Deductive
- Demand characteristics
- Ecological validity
- Experimenter effects
- Idiographic
- Inductive
- Mundane realism
- Nomothetic
- Operationalised
- Qualitative
- Quantitative
- Subjectivity

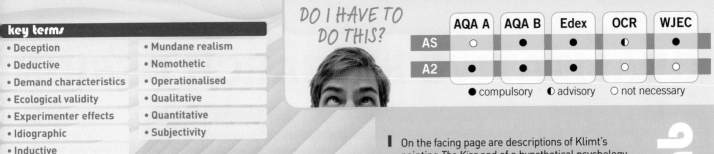

DO I HAVE TO DO THIS?

	AQA A	AQA B	Edex	OCR	WJEC
AS	○	●	●	◐	●
A2	●	●	●	○	○

● compulsory　◐ advisory　○ not necessary

Quant VERSUS qual

Discussions of the differences between the quantitative and qualitative approaches often make it sound as if it is a question of using one or the other – but is that the case? It might be better to view them on a continuum from extreme quantitative research to extreme qualitative research.

➤ Quantitative findings are amplified by qualitative data. For example, Stanley Milgram, in his obedience research (see page 36), found that 65% of participants were fully obedient (quantitative data) but he also reported the comments of observers (qualitative data), providing additional findings about the experience of participants:

> *'I observed a mature and initially poised businessman enter the laboratory smiling and confident. Within 20 minutes he was reduced to a twitching, stuttering wreck, who was rapidly approaching a point of nervous collapse. He constantly pulled on his earlobe and twisted his hands. At one point he pushed his fist into his forehead and muttered 'Oh God, let's stop it'. And yet he continued to respond to every word of the experimenter.' (page 377)*

➤ In quantitative research, the final conclusions may be qualitative in nature. For example, Milgram's conclusions were qualitative because he made judgements about the factors that lead to obedience.

➤ The dependent and/or independent variable in an experiment may be qualitative. For example, an experiment might investigate the effects of certain testing techniques on anxiety levels. To do this students are given two different types of tests and asked to report how they felt after taking the test. This would result in qualitative data. It would then be transformed to quantitative data in order to compare the effects of the different kinds of test.

What do we conclude?

One method is not better than the other, but each is more suitable than the other in particular circumstances. The qualitative approach may be a useful way to begin research in an area, and then quantitative methods might be used to test the emergent theories/hypotheses.

mini study

Looking for your own examples

A good way to begin your understanding of qualitative research is to look at some examples. Search the internet for summaries of such research by using the search phrase "qualitative study" (use double quotes so you search exactly for this phrase). Many studies that use the qualitative approach have the phrase 'a qualitative study' in their title.

Find three articles that interest you and note their:

- aims
- method
- findings
- conclusions.

1 On the facing page are descriptions of Klimt's painting *The Kiss* and of a hypothetical psychology class. Qualitative and quantitative descriptions are given of both. Try to do the same activity for the following:

  a A television series.

  b The town or city you live in.

  c A major world event such as the London Olympics or the 9/11 bombings in New York.

2 Based on your answers to question 1:

  a Outline the strengths and weaknesses of using quantitative data in the examples above.

  b Outline the strengths and weaknesses of using qualitative data in the examples above.

3 Think of a research study you know well (other than Milgram's obedience study). (If you are an OCR AS student you need to be able to do this activity for each of your core studies.)

  a Give examples of quantitative data collected in this study.

  b Outline **two** strengths and **two** weaknesses of the quantitative approach in this study.

  c Give examples of qualitative data collected in this study.

  d Outline **two** strengths and **two** weaknesses of the qualitative approach in this study.

4 Think of some examples for the items below.

  a A dependent variable that has been quantitatively operationalised.

  b A dependent variable that has been assessed qualitatively.

5 On page 57 a study by Gilligan and Attanucci is described. They asked people to report their own moral dilemmas and then classified each person's responses as a 'care' or 'justice' orientation or a mixture of the two. They found that men tended to have a justice orientation whereas women had a care orientation.

  a Identify the independent and dependent variables in this research.

  b What element of this research was qualitative?

  c What element of this research was quantitative?

  d Write an operationalised directional hypothesis for this study.

6 On page 73 a study by Solley and Haigh is described. They found that children drew more complex pictures of Santa before Christmas than afterwards.

  a Identify the independent and dependent variables in this research.

  b Describe the data that would have been collected in this study.

  c Explain in what way this data is qualitative.

  d In the final analysis quantitative data was used by counting instances – what could the researchers have counted?

QUALITATIVE RESEARCH DESIGN

In Chapters 1, 2 and 3 of this book we have considered the design of quantitative research. We did look at the collection of qualitative data when using open-ended questionnaires but there is more to qualitative research design than simply collecting qualitative data.

Successful qualitative research often depends on developing a sense of trust and understanding between researcher and participants.

1. Broad aims

The aims include an intention to view the phenomena as a whole, rather than trying to reduce them to smaller components. The aims may also be to record 'reality' from the perspective of participants or to understand the constructions that people make of the world.

2. Research question

It might seem like qualitative analysis involves just deciding to do research on a topic area, for example studying what people dream about or the kind of friendships people have. However, qualitative research should really begin with more focused research questions. For example:

- To explore dying cancer patients' own perspectives on euthanasia, especially in relation to autonomy (Karlsson *et al.*, 2012).
- To conduct an investigation of parents' descriptions of disruptive and coercive behaviours on the part of children and adolescents suffering from OCD (Lebowitz *et al.*, 2011).

In qualitative research questions are framed but hypotheses are generally avoided as these might bias observations.

3. Method

The researcher selects the method(s) to use in the collection of data. For example:

- *Interview* – the unstructured or **semi-structured interview** is probably the most commonly used method, but **structured** techniques (interviews or questionnaires) may also be used. These techniques are discussed in Chapter 3.
- *Direct observation* – observations would tend to be **naturalistic**, **participant** and **disclosed** (see pages 66–69). The method is referred to as ethnographic, the study of a group of people, such as a cultural group, in its natural context for a sustained time interval.
- *Indirect observation using artifacts*, i.e. the documents and records produced by humans, such as books, magazines, musical recordings, films, photographs, paintings, graffiti and so on.
- *Case study* – qualitative approaches tend not to study just one case but several individual cases (a single person, event, process, institution, organisation, social group or phenomenon).
- *Diaries* – asking participants and researchers to keep their own record of their thoughts over a period of time.
- *Focus groups* – groups of people with an interest or expertise in a particular area, for example a group of drug addicts or a group of health professionals dealing with addicts. Research might make use of a naturally occurring discussion group or might specially form one for the research study. The group may meet on one or more occasions and usually consists of less than a dozen members.

EXAMPLE 1

Aims: *The aim of a study by Inman et al. (2011) was to examine the 'lived experience' of Asian Indian–white couples in intercultural marriages.*

Method: *Ten highly educated Asian Indian–white professional couples were individually interviewed about their subjective experience of being in an interracial marriage, the challenges and strengths of this marriage, and the potential role of culture in their marriages.*

Results: *The couples' marital experiences were influenced by a complex intersection of ecosystemic factors with significant psychological impacts.*

Conclusion: *These findings highlight shortcomings in drawing simplistic conclusions regarding the success or failure of an interracial marriage.*

EXAMPLE 2

Aims: *Helweg-Larsen et al. (2010) explored the role that culture plays in smokers' description of their risk perceptions and experiences as targets of moralisation (i.e. the extent to which a culture makes smoking a 'bad thing').*

Method: *In-depth interviews were conducted with 15 smokers each from Denmark (a smoking-lenient culture) and the USA (a smoking-prohibitive culture).*

Results: *Smokers said they were well aware of the risks of smoking yet minimised the risks of active and passive smoking. Danes were particularly likely to minimise these risks and also more strongly rejected moralised opinions about smoking. Smokers described adjusting to moralisation by changing when and where but not how much they smoked.*

Conclusion: *It is important to consider cultural influences on moralisation and risk perception of smoking.*

EXAMPLE 3

Aims: *Löfgren-Mårtenson and Månsson (2010) acknowledged the widespread concern in Western society about the visibility of pornography in public places and on the internet. What are the consequences for young men and women, and how do they think about gender, sexuality and pornography?*

Method: *Data was collected, through 22 individual interviews and seven focus groups, from 51 participants (36 women and 37 men aged 14–20 years) in Sweden.*

Results: *Pornography was used as a form of social intercourse, a source of information, and a stimulus for sexual arousal. Pornography consumption was more common among the young men than among the women. For both the young men and women, the pornographic script functioned as a frame of reference in relation to bodily ideals and sexual performances.*

Conclusion: *Most of the participants had acquired the necessary skills of how to deal with the exposure to pornography in a sensible and reflective manner.*

key terms

- Disclosed observation
- Naturalistic observation
- Participant observation
- Purposive sample
- Sample
- Structured interview
- Semi-structured interview

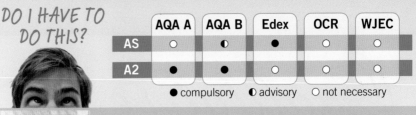

4. Sampling

Numbers

Usually qualitative research involves more than one person (or event). Typically the number of people is somewhere between 5 and 15.

Diversity

The researcher would seek diversity in the sample. For example, if he or she wished to investigate the experience of depression in teenagers, the study could involve teenagers experiencing clinical depression who came from different cultural and educational backgrounds.

When studying opinions the researcher may seek respondents at both ends of a spectrum (as well as some in the middle) to insure that all viewpoints are adequately represented.

Purposive

In order to obtain the kind of samples described above purposive sampling is used. This is the strategy of selecting participants based on who would be appropriate for the study. Such methods are used where there are a limited number of people suitable for the area being researched.

5. Recording the data

A full record is kept of all material and peripheral activity.

- Interviews or observations are recorded and fully transcribed.

- The record might also include paralinguistics (e.g. pauses, intonation) and non-linguistic elements (e.g. laughter, hand gestures), all of which convey meaning.

- A record is also kept of the researchers own thoughts, feelings and behaviors while data are collected. This is important for determining whether or not the researcher is himself or herself a source of bias.

EXAMPLE 4

Aims: Ownsworth et al. (2011) investigated the personal and social processes of adjustment at different stages of illness for individuals with a brain tumour.

Method: A purposive sample of 18 participants with mixed tumour types (9 benign and 9 malignant) and 15 family caregivers was recruited from a neurosurgical practice and a brain tumour support service. In-depth semi-structured interviews focused on participants' perceptions of their adjustment, including personal appraisals, coping and social support since their brain tumour diagnosis.

Results: The primary theme that emerged from the analysis entailed 'key sense making appraisals', which was closely related to the following secondary themes: (1) Interactions with those in the healthcare system, (2) reactions and support from the personal support network, and (3) a diversity of coping efforts.

Conclusion: Adjustment to having a brain tumour involved a series of appraisals about the illness that were influenced by interactions with those in the healthcare system, reactions and support.

1 Research questions are discussed on the facing page and two examples are provided. There are four further examples on this spread. For each example identify:

  a The general focus of the study.

  b The more specific focus of the study.

2 Imagine you are going to conduct research on the topic areas listed below. For each of them identify a more specific focus.

  a The content of dreams.

  b Graffiti.

  c Tattoos.

  d Children's drawings.

  e Smoking.

3 Four examples of qualitative research are described on the facing page and this page.

  a For each of them identify the method used.

  b For each them describe the sample.

  c (If you looked up your own examples for the study on the previous spread, you can answer these questions for your own studies.)

4 In the list of methods used in qualitative research, one method is described as 'indirect observation using artifacts'. Think of at least **three** other examples of artifacts.

5 In the study by Helweg-Larsen *et al.* (facing page) there is an independent variable.

  a Identify the independent variable.

  b How is this independent variable operationalised?

  c How did the Danes and Americans differ?

  d In what way is this difference a dependent variable?

A tattoo of The Blind Watchmaker – why the evidence of evolution reveals a universe without design.

Used with permission from Science Ink by Carl Zimmer © 2011.

mini study

Designing your own qualitative research study

On page 57, the suggested study was to design your own questionnaire. This time you might select the same topic but consider collecting qualitative data.

Alternatively you might select one of the topics suggested in question 2 above.

Once you have selected your topic you need to make the following important design decisions:

- Decide on a specific research question.
- Select a suitable method.
- Decide on your participants – who and how many? Where will you find them?
- Consider how to record the data ready for analysis.
- Work out the procedure that you will follow and test this using a pilot study.

Qualitative ANALYSIS

On the previous spread we considered how qualitative research is designed. The next step in the research process is the analysis of the qualitative data collected. The resulting outcome can be quantitative or qualitative.

Thematic analysis

Most qualitative analysis aims to be inductive or 'bottom-up' – the categories ('themes') that emerge are based or 'grounded' in the data. Subsequently, the categories/themes may lead to new theories/explanations (called 'emergent theory').

A less common approach to the analysis of qualitative data is a deductive or 'top-down' one, where the researcher starts with preset categories/themes. Such categories are likely to be generated by previous theories/research studies. The researcher would aim to see if the data are consistent with the previous theoretical viewpoint.

*Quant*itative outcomes

Results that have been obtained through qualitative methods can be 'reduced' to a quantitative form. For example, content analysis involves the study of qualitative data – words and meanings. However, a common way to deal with this is to select categories and count the frequency of events in each category (see page 72). Remember that the analysis can also be qualitative – in which case the meanings are retained.

The categories may emerge from the data or be derived from existing expectations (both are examples of thematic analysis).

For example, a number of studies have performed a qualitative analysis of graffiti, such as *latrinalia* (i.e. toilets). Comparisons can be made between men and women or between cultural groups. The first step is to study the data and decide on appropriate categories, such as graffiti related to relationships, sexual prowess, humour and so on. The instances can then be counted. This was the case in a review of latrinalia by Bruner and Kelso (1980). They concluded that women produced graffiti that was more interpersonal whereas men's graffiti was more likely to be competitive.

*Qual*itative outcomes

One problem with qualitative data is that it is difficult to summarise. *Quantitative* data can be readily summarised with **measures of central tendency** and **measures of dispersion**, and also with the use of graphs. None of these options is possible with purely descriptive findings. Instead, qualitative data is summarised by identifying repeated themes.

Qualitative analysis is a very lengthy process because it is painstaking and iterative – every item is carefully considered and the data is gone through repeatedly. The main intentions are:

➤ To impose some kind of order on the data.
➤ To ensure that the 'order' represents the participants' perspective.
➤ When using a bottom-up approach, to ensure that this 'order' emerges from the data themselves rather than any preconceptions.
➤ To summarise the data so that hundreds of pages of text or hours of videotapes can be reduced.
➤ To enable themes to be identified and general conclusions drawn.

There is no one method to use but the following table gives a general picture of what is done.

	General principles	*Applied to the analysis of graffiti*	*Applied to the analysis of videotaped play sessions with various children*
1	*Read and re-read the data transcript dispassionately, trying to understanding the meaning communicated and the perspective of the participants. No notes should be made.*	*Study a photographic or written record of a wide range of graffiti, using purposive sampling.*	*The play session can be transcribed to include details of what was said, and describe facial expressions and body movements.*
2	*Break the data into meaningful units – small bits of text that are independently able to convey meaning. This might be equivalent to sentences or phrases.*	*In the case of graffiti it would be each item of graffiti.*	*Each verbal and non-verbal movement would constitute a unit.*
3	*Assign a label or code to each unit. Such labels/ codes are the initial categories that you are using. You will have developed some ideas when initially reading through the data in step 1.* *When a top-down approach is used the categories will be provided by existing theories.* *Each unit may be given more than one code/label.*	*Each unit of graffiti is given a code to describe its meaning, such as 'humour' or 'advice', 'love' or 'power domination'.*	*Each unit is coded, for example 'playing with toy', 'sadness expressed', 'request made'.*
4	*Combine simple codes into larger categories/ themes.*	*Larger order categories are developed, such as 'interpersonal concerns'.*	*Larger categories are developed, such as 'negative emotion'.*
5	*A check can be made on the emergent categories by collecting a new set of data and applying the categories. They should fit the new data well if they represent the topic area investigated.*		
6	*The final report should discuss and use quotes or other material to illustrate these themes.*		
7	*Conclusions can be drawn, which may include new theories.*		

Using computer programs

Computer programs have been developed to help the process qualitative analysis.

Such programs can search for common words or phrases, or they allow the researcher to code text or pictures.

They can be used once the units have been coded, and pla items together with the same codes looking for patterns acros categories.

Examples include ATLAS.ti and code-a-text.

key terms
- Content analysis
- Measures of central tendency
- Measures of dispersion
- Thematic analysis

DO I HAVE TO DO THIS?

	AQA A	AQA B	Edex	OCR	WJEC
AS	○	◑	●	○	○
A2	●	●	○	○	○

● compulsory ◑ advisory ○ not necessary

Considering the interaction between quantitative and qualitative data and analysis

		Data	
		QUAL	QUANT
Analysis	QUAL	Grounded theory (or just emergent categories)	Draw conclusions in terms of what the quantitative data means
	QUANT	Identify themes/categories and then count instances	Use of descriptive and inferential statistics

mini study

Doing your own qualitative analysis

You may wish to analyse some of the data you collected on the previous spread, or you can use the data below. These are descriptions of the experience of having eating difficulties. Your tasks are:

1. Qualitative analysis: bottom-up (as described on the facing page).
2. Qualitative analysis: top-down – a list of well-known characteristics of eating disorders is given on the right. Use these categories to code the data below. Later you might combine categories into broader themes.
3. Quantitative analysis – use the categories on the right to perform a content analysis. Count occurrences of each category. You can then represent this data in a bar chart.

anxiety, abnormally low weight, distorted body image, restricting calorie intake, bingeing and purging, feelings of intense hunger or no hunger, interest in food, excessive exercise, low self-esteem

1 Describe how qualitative data can be turned into quantitative data.

2 Briefly describe (in about 100 words) how qualitative data can be analysed both in a bottom-up and a top-down fashion.

The Higher Education Academy has made a set of interviews available for students to use for qualitative analysis. A user guide is available to support the use of different kinds of qualitative analysis.

See http://www.heacademy. ac.uk/resources/detail/ subjects/psychology/ TQRMUL_Dataset_ Teaching_Resources

question 4.3

I have a very low self-esteem and body image problems. I do not have an eating disorder that I can pin point. I do not try and throw up and I do not stop eating. I do try diets. I do go to the gym at least 5 times a week. My problem is I was with a very abusive boyfriend who never liked the way that I looked. He told me every day that I needed to lose weight. I cannot look at myself in the mirror without clothes on. I have not been with this guy for two years and I can still hear what he has said in my head. Many many people tell me that I am beautiful and that I look great and that I am not fat but I do not believe them. I go to the bathroom when I am at work at least 20 times just so I can punish myself by looking in the mirror and calling myself fat.

I started off having anorexia ... living on 500 calories a day while keeping up a very strict fitness schedule. I have recently moved in with my boyfriend and we got married last year. I was doing very well but recent events have caused me to go back into those old comfy habits. I have begun to throw up everything I eat. I don't binge but I make myself sick after everything I eat.

My friend is 16. She sometimes goes without food all day at school and I can't be sure that she eats anything when she gets home. She makes excuses not to eat and always checks calories on packages. She seems obsessed with the idea that I'm thinner than she is. Any time I approach her about eating she edges around the subject or gets irritated.

I have had a eating disorder since I was 15 years old and am now 28. At present I weigh 100 pounds. When I was 18 years old I got down to 65 pounds and I had 4 cardiac arrests. I've also had 3 spontaneous pneumothorax because of dehydration. When things get bad and I feel out of control, I fall back into my eating disorder. I can't stop this disease and fear I am going to die.

My name is John and am in recovery from anorexia. I have been in and out of hospitals over two and a half years. It started when I weighed 265 pounds and decided to diet assisted by moderate exercise. I ended up eating only 300 calories a day and exercising for 8 hours a day. This involved getting up at 4 a.m. and going to bed at 1 a.m. Then I stopped eating totally and continued exercising. I wore baggy clothing and withdrew from family and friends.

Thoughts go through my head 'Don't eat anything all day, burn off 500 calories and then you are ahead of the game'. At night time I allow myself 300 calories at most, and if I feel I have gone too far I go off to the bathroom to get rid of it, which happens most times. I go through this cycle every day of my life, but it keeps me sane! Or at least I think it does. The fear of something going past my lips gives me nightmares. I wake up in the middle of the night with gut wrenching pains but I won't consume more calories. I am in control, or at least I think I am.

I am a 34-year-old mother of 2 who is in treatment for an eating disorder. I hate myself so much and feel so fat and ugly all the time. I desperately want to lose weight, but am forced to eat dinner every day so that my kids don't catch on that anything is wrong. However, I do purge both by vomiting and laxative abuse. My family is unaware of this.

When year 8 started I came back to school 12kg lighter. I've stopped the dieting and all ... but every time I see a picture of a beautiful girl in a magazine or Victoria Beckham (she is my idol) I start considering it and by that time I'm depressed about my looks.

My body is very weak, my face gets paler every day, but in the back of my mind I see beauty. I see that in a couple of months I will be the model my step mom never let me be. My waist is very small but when I look in the mirror I see fat. Pain is my game. Please tell me why my dad's girlfriend hit me? I chose this route to punish myself for what I'm not sure, maybe the attention.

I was badly abused as a child by my Grandmother and at the age of 17 developed anorexia. There then followed 13 nightmare years during which time my weight at one time dropped to an all time low of 4 stones 10 lbs and I was taken into intensive care. I have survived anorexia, I fought against the voice in my head that constantly demanded that I starved myself to death.

QUALITATIVE RESEARCH: RELIABILITY AND VALIDITY

Qualitative research aims to be scientific, therefore the concepts of reliability and validity and are important. Strategies to enhance and demonstrate both reliability and validity are a necessary part of the qualitative approach.

Reliability

Reliability is generally concerned with measurements, i.e. quantitative data. However, qualitative data can be converted to quantitative data to check reliability. For example, the record produced by one observer can be analysed by identifying categories and counting instances within each category (**content analysis**). This record can then be compared to another observer's record and **inter-rater reliability** can be calculated.

Methods should be developed for resolving disagreements among raters.

Validity

The definitions of **validity** we have looked at so far in this book are more appropriate for quantitative research. For example, 'testing what you intended to test' or 'the extent to which a research finding can be generalised beyond the research setting in which it was investigated'.

A more general definition of validity concerns the extent to which a research finding is 'true' or represents 'reality' – not 'the' reality but whatever reality is being investigated (see discussion on left).

● Internal validity

This concerns design integrity and the trustworthiness of a qualitative study. It is sometimes called *interpretative validity* because it is the degree to which data interpretation and conclusions are considered to reflect the participants' or phenomenon's reality.

It can be demonstrated through:

- *Contextual completeness* – the fullness and richness of the descriptions.
- *Reporting style* – the extent to which a qualitative report is perceived as genuine.
- *Coherence* – the extent to which the data and analysis hang together in a rational order.
- *Chain of evidence* – the extent to which later analyses can be traced back through the record.
- *Research positioning* – the quality of the record of direct and indirect effects is used to assess subjectivity.

What is reality?

Quantitative research assumes there is one reality and, when conducting research, this is what we are trying to discover. By contrast, qualitative researchers dispute that there is one single reality. They argue that 'reality' changes depending on whose perspective you are considering.

For example, when parents divorce, the events leading up to that divorce will be viewed differently depending on whether you hear the husband's story or the wife's story or that of their children or their friends. Each person will have seen and understood the events from their own perspective. What they see and understand is their reality.

The same would be true, for example, with understanding aggressive behaviour. The meaning of such behaviour is different depending on whether you are the aggressor or the person being aggressed against. Both realities are relevant to understand the meaning of the behaviour.

Qualitative researchers wish to understand human behaviour through these differing perspectives and therefore embrace the concept of no one single reality.

Validity is still an important concept because the researcher is seeking to achieve an accurate representation of the participants' or phenomenon's reality.

Subjectivity and reflexivity

Scientific research aims to be objective. However, qualitative research, by its very nature, is subjective – it aims to view the phenomena from the perspective of those who experience it and also the process of analysis depends on the researcher's perceptions. The term reflexivity is used to describe the extent to which the process of research reflects a researcher's values and thoughts.

In order to enhance the scientific nature of qualitative research this inevitable subjective bias must be recognised. Instead of trying to minimise or remove subjectivity, this is dealt with by acknowledging that the subjective nature is part of the research itself.

Therefore, the researcher enhances the validity of the research by including comments on how their influence has affected the research process. Researchers' attitudes should be fully discussed, including a consideration of how the research might have changed the researcher's perspective.

key terms

• Content analysis
• External validity
• Inter-rater reliability
• Internal validity
• Reflexivity
• Reliability
• Subjectivity
• Triangulation
• Validity

External validity

The qualitative researcher does not share the same level of concern about generalisability as does the quantitative researcher. However, that is not to say it is irrelevant and one of the common ways to consider external validity is making comparisons with findings from a variety of different sources. This is called triangulation, the process of looking at a number of different research findings (quantitative and qualitative) to see to what extent they all point in a similar direction.

For example, the effects of shift work on sleep disruption might be explored by interviewing a night worker, making detailed observations using equipment in a sleep laboratory and also asking them to keep a sleep record. If these all generate similar findings with regards to sleep disturbance, the external validity is high.

Similarly, triangulation may be used in an investigation of delay in a child's cognitive development by asking parents to complete a questionnaire at regular intervals, by observing the child's behaviour and by interviewing their class teacher.

Triangulation

In mathematics this term refers to a method of determining the exact location of a point (such as on a map) by taking measurements from various positions. In qualitative research one is not seeking a perfect fix but using multiple and diverse perspectives to provide a fuller picture of a phenomenon.

Observation of interactions

?

Analysis of children's work   Interview with children

mini study

Qualitative analysis of a song

You might not remember the song about Barbie and Ken, a hit in November 1997. It was called *Barbie Girl* – you can search online for the lyrics, or find it on YouTube to listen to.

Angie Burns (1998) heard the words and felt challenged to offer some deeper insights, using the qualitative tools she uses in her psychological research. She wondered whether the words are a send up of subordination and domination, or whether they display deeper attitudes about men and women in our culture.

Her analysis: Barbie is portrayed as a 'blonde bimbo' who will do anything if Ken says 'I'm always yours'. This equates love with ownership ('You're my doll') and sex ('You can touch'). Ken doesn't return Barbie's love declarations but orders her to service him ('Kiss me here touch me there').

Burns' analysis led her to conclude that the song represents the view that women want love and men want sex, and that women give sex to get love.

Try your own song analysis!

1 On the facing page the concept of reality is discussed. Two examples are provided (on divorce and aggression).

   a Think of your own example and list the different 'realities'.

   b How could you investigate each of these 'realities'? Identify more than one method.

   c Describe **one** way you could demonstrate the reliability of the data collected.

   d Describe **one** way you could demonstrate the validity of the data collected.

   e Explain how you could use triangulation to demonstrate the validity of your findings.

2 Explain the difference between subjectivity and objectivity.

3 Explain why science seeks to be objective.

4 Explain why subjectivity is a problem in qualitative research.

5 Explain why, in some ways, subjectivity is more of a problem in quantitative research.

6 What does 'reflexivity' mean?

7 Explain the concept of triangulation, using your own example.

8 Triangulation is used in research that is solely quantitative (researchers look for supporting evidence as a way of validating their research). Think of an example of triangulation from your own studies.

QUANTITATIVE RESEARCH: GRAPHS AND MEASUREMENT

Most of this chapter has focused on the qualitative approach in psychology. This final spread returns to the quantitative approach, which is concerned with measurement and the summary of data using, for example, graphs.

Psychometrics

Measurement is a distinctly quantitative activity. Psychologists seek to represent what people think, feel and do by using numbers.

For example, psychological tests are used to measure your intelligence or provide a score on various personality dimensions (see page 58).

Rating scales allow researchers to assign a value to participants' attitudes and feelings, such as asking participants to rate how happy they are on a scale of 1 to 5 where 5 is very happy (see page 54).

Research variables

In experiments the dependent variable (DV) is generally operationalised through measurement. For example, in Chapter 1 we considered an experiment to see how noise might affect concentration. The DV was the time taken to complete a concentration task. So we measured concentration in terms of time.

In this experiment the independent variable was noise – either no noise or some noise. We could have measured this too, for example, in terms of decibels.

In a study using correlational analysis the co-variables must be numerical.

In observational research data is often counted.

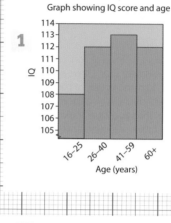

1 Graph showing IQ score and age

2 Content analysis of lonely hearts ads: people seeking resources (from Waynforth and Dunbar, 1995)

□ Women ■ Men

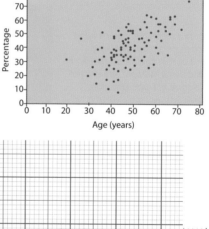

3 Driving under the influence of an illicit drug, reported by people of different ages

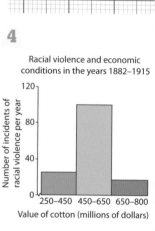

4 Racial violence and economic conditions in the years 1882–1915

Subjectivity and objectivity

There are nine million bicycles in Beijing,
That's a fact,
It's a thing we can't deny,
Like the fact that I will love you till I die.

We are 12 billion light years from the edge,
That's a guess,
No one can ever say it's true,
But I know that I will always be with you.

© Dramatico/Sony/ATV. Reproduced by permission.

The lyrics on the left come from a song sung by Katie Melua. Simon Singh (2005) complained: 'The role of the scientist is slowly being undermined with a growing belief that scientific results are merely subjective guesses that go in and out of fashion. In fact, scientific results are a careful attempt to objectively measure reality, and although they may be refined over time, they are always our best hope of getting at the truth.'

He suggested that Katie's lyrics should read:

We are 13.7 billion light-years from the edge of the observable universe,

That's a good estimate with well-defined error bars,

Scientists say it's true, but acknowledge that it may be refined.

Singh's observations were made in good humour, and Katie sportingly recorded the song using his lyrics. You can listen to this version on YouTube: www.youtube.com/watch?v=21iUUe-W8L4.

DO I HAVE TO DO THIS?

	AQA A	AQA B	Edex	OCR	WJEC
AS	●	●	●	●	●
A2	●	●	○	●	●

● compulsory   ◐ advisory   ○ not necessary

The relationship between final test mark and time spent on the test

Time taken (minutes)

6

Child's estimate of parent's IQ

Parental IQ

Child's age (years)

Levels of measurement are considered on page 104.

7

Religion important (%)

8

Reduction in anxiety: combined data from 99 studies

- Combined psychological and drug therapy
- Psychological therapy
- Drug therapy
- Placebo

1 There are eight graphs on this spread. For each graph:

a Identify what kind of graph it is (bar chart, histogram, line graph or scattergraph).

b Draw **two** conclusions from each graph (i.e. what does the graph show us about human behaviour?).

2 A psychologist investigated the relationship between sleep and exercise. Participants were asked to record the number of hours they slept the previous night. This was recorded as number of minutes of sleep. They were also asked to estimate how many minutes they had spent the previous day doing exercise (walking, running, doing any physical activity).

a Identify the co-variables in the study.

b Outline **one** strength and **one** weakness of the way that sleep has been measured in this study.

c Outline **one** strength and **one** weakness of the way that exercise has been measured in this study.

d Describe and evaluate **one** other way to measure exercise in this study.

e Suggest **two** examples of qualitative data that could have been collected in this study.

3 A psychologist designed a repeated measures study to investigate the effects of caffeine on how awake a person felt. In order to assess 'awakeness' the researcher measured participants' breathing rate before and after drinking coffee (assuming that a higher breathing rate would represent more 'awakeness').

a Identify the dependent variable (DV) in the study.

b Outline **one** strength and **one** weakness of the way that the DV has been measured in this study.

c Describe and evaluate **one** other way to measure the DV in this study.

d Identify the independent variable (IV) in this study.

e Explain how this IV could be operationalised.

mini study

Comparing quantitative and qualitative

Psychopathology is an important topic area in psychology. You will undoubtedly study one or more psychological disorders during your A level course, such as schizophrenia, depression, obsessive-compulsive disorder or autism. It might be best to choose a disorder you know nothing about.

Use the internet to collect quantitative and qualitative data about your selected disorder. You might work with a partner to produce a display of your findings.

- The quantitative data will be statistics – such as the frequency of the disorder, the ratio of male to female suffers, variations across cultural groups, etc. Present some of your findings in a graph (this is a form of data analysis).
- The qualitative data will be individuals' experiences of their disorder. There are many websites where people discuss such experiences. Produce a summary of what you read and make a display of this (this is a form of analysis).

You and your class should reflect on the usefulness of the two different kinds of data in understanding the disorder.

MULTIPLE-CHOICE QUESTIONS

1. Data related to how people think and feel are called:
   a. Quantitative.
   b. Questionnaire.
   c. Qualitative.
   d. Both a and c.

2. In a questionnaire, open questions tend to produce:
   a. Quantitative data.
   b. Unreliable data.
   c. Qualitative data.
   d. Both a and c.

3. Which kind of data is related to measurement?
   a. Quantitative data.
   b. Personal data.
   c. Qualitative data.
   d. Both a and b.

4. Which approach is concerned with subjective reality?
   a. Quantitative approach.
   b. Questionnaire approach.
   c. Qualitative approach.
   d. Both a and c.

5. Qualitative research raises fewer ethical problems because:
   a. It doesn't use people.
   b. It acknowledges that expectations will affect the data collected and therefore there is no need for deception.
   c. Qualitative researchers are more caring.
   d. Quantitative research is newer.

6. Which of the following statements is true?
   a. Quantitative research tends to be inductive.
   b. Quantitative research tends to be deductive.
   c. Qualitative research tends to be deductive.
   d. Inductive research is preferable to deductive research.

7. Induction is a:
   a. Bottom-up approach
   b. Top-down approach.
   c. Top-down and bottom-up approach.
   d. Middle approach.

8. The qualitative approach is a:
   a. Nomothetic approach.
   b. Idiographic approach.
   c. Can be a and b.
   d. Neither a nor b.

9. A focus group is:
   a. A study about perception.
   b. A technique used to ensure participants focus on what they have to do.
   c. A research method for finding out what people think and feel about a specific topic.
   d. All of the above.

10. Which of the following methods is not used in qualitative research?
    a. Experiment.
    b. Interview.
    c. Observation.
    d. Case study.

11. The term 'ethnographic' refers to:
    a. Prejudice about a cultural group.
    b. Studying groups of people in their own cultural setting.
    c. The realistic nature of qualitative research.
    d. A drawing style.

12. Purposive sampling is:
    a. Non-random.
    b. A method of selecting participants.
    c. Used when a limited number of people are suitable.
    d. All of the above.

13. Thematic analysis is a:
    a. Bottom-up approach
    b. Top-down approach.
    c. Top-down and bottom-up approach.
    d. Middle approach.

14. Thematic analysis is an iterative process. This means that the researcher:
    a. Has to be very careful.
    b. Cannot count instances.
    c. Cannot use abbreviations.
    d. Has to repeatedly go through the data.

15. Content analysis can produce:
    a. Quantitative data.
    b. Qualitative data.
    c. No data.
    d. Both a and b.

16. The scientific approach aims to be:
    a. Reflexive.
    b. Subjective
    c. Objective.
    d. Both b and c.

17. Reflexivity is the extent to which the research process:
    a. Is both objective and subjective.
    b. Is qualitative.
    c. Reflects the researcher's values and thoughts.
    d. Involves both participant and researcher.

18. Which of the following statements is true?
    a. Reliability and validity are both important in qualitative research.
    b. Only reliability is important in qualitative research.
    c. Only validity if important in qualitative research.
    d. Neither reliability and validity are both important in qualitative research.

19. Reliability can be checked in qualitative research by using:
    a. Test–retest reliability.
    b. Inter-rater reliability.
    c. Concurrent reliability.
    d. All of the above.

20. Triangulation:
    a. Only uses qualitative data.
    b. Only uses quantitative data.
    c. Can use either quantitative or qualitative data.
    d. Is not used in psychological research.

Answers on facing page

A cognitive psychologist specialises in the study of amnesia – individuals who have lost their ability to remember past events in their lives. The psychologist plans to undertake research by conducting a few case studies of individuals with amnesia.

Below are some quotes from one patient's diary.

Day 1:
I feel like I'm in the middle of a big crowd where I don't know anyone. I keep looking round hoping that I'll notice someone I recognise. During the day I forget what I'm doing, I boil the kettle to make a cup of tea but by the time I put the water in it's gone cold again.

Day 14:
This morning I turned the shower on but hadn't taken my towel into the bathroom. I went out to get it but must have got distracted and just dressed because when I went into the bathroom in the afternoon the shower was still running. In future I'm going to leave the light on to remind myself – I won't remember why I've done it but will have to go back in to turn the light off. I went out to the shops after that with a list – I always take a list now – but all I did for ages was look at the shop assistants in the hope that they would be familiar. It's so lonely.

Day 28:
I did really well today. I remembered you were coming to see me, well, I sort of did. I have a calendar where I write down everything that's going to happen. It's right by the kettle so I have to notice it even if I don't remember I put it there. I'm really glad you came here, I hate going to the hospital, everyone's unfamiliar, I just get lost among the people. I can use the map to find my way, that doesn't bother me, but it frightens me that everybody's faces look unfamiliar I feel like I'm on holiday in a foreign country all alone.

(a) Outline **one** strength and **one** weakness of using a case study. (2 marks + 2 marks)

(b) Suggest how the psychologist might select participants for the case studies. (3 marks)

(c) Use the study above to explain:

(i) What is meant by qualitative data. (3 marks)

(ii) What is meant by subjectivity. (3 marks)

(d) The psychologist plans to analyse the text to produce both qualitative and quantitative data. Use examples from the text above to support your explanation.

(i) Explain how the psychologist might produce a qualitative outcome. (6 marks)

(ii) Explain how the psychologist might produce a quantitative outcome. (2 marks)

(e) Explain how you might demonstrate whether the research is high in validity. (3 marks)

Examiner's tips for answering this question

(a) There is no requirement for context in this question but it never harms to include it anyway to provide more detail. Don't be lazy in your answer – try to explain your strength/weakness thoroughly.

(b) Take care to select a suitable answer – many sampling techniques wouldn't make sense in this context.

The question is worth 3 marks so requires a thoughtful, detailed answer.

(c) (i) The question guides you to do more than just define qualitative data – you need to use the stimulus material to provide examples.

(ii) The term 'subjectivity' is included in some specifications. Whenever a term is identified in the specification, this means you will need to be able to explain it. In this question your explanation must refer to the context above.

(d) (i) This question is worth a considerable number of marks which indicates the kind of length answer required. For 6 marks it might be a useful guide to write six sentences.

Note that the question says 'how' which means your focus should be on describing what it is the researcher would do, not explaining why.

It may be helpful, when describing what would be done, to use examples from the text itself.

(ii) There are considerably fewer marks for this part of the question, so limit the amount you write.

(e) This question is not asking for a definition of validity but again is asking *how* you would do it.

EXAM STYLE QUESTION 8

A school decides to conduct a study on the healthy habits of the students in the school using a questionnaire. They want to collect data about eating habits, exercise and smoking. It is important to know about (a) the students' habits and (b) their attitudes.

This is an extract from the questionnaire:

> 8. Do you smoke?
>
>   [ ] Never
>
>   [ ] Occasionally
>
>   [ ] Frequently
>
>   [ ] Excessively
>
> 9. If you do smoke, or have smoked, at what age did you start?
>
> 10. What do you think is the best reason not to smoke?

(a) Outline **one** strength and **one** weakness of using a questionnaire in this study. (2 marks + 2 marks)

(b) Explain **one** reason why a pilot study should have been carried out in the context of this study. (2 marks)

(c) (i) Identify **one** question in the extract above that would provide qualitative data. (1 mark)

(ii) With reference to the question you have identified in part (i), explain why this question would produce qualitative data. (3 marks)

(d) (i) Identify **one** sampling method that could have been used in this study. (1 mark)

(ii) In the context of this study, explain **one** reason for using the sampling method you have identified in (i). (2 marks)

(e) (i) The questions in the extract above can be criticised. Select **one** question and give one criticism of it. (2 marks)

(ii) Re-write the question you selected so that it overcomes the criticism you identified in (i). (2 marks)

(f) Describe **two** ways of making sure that this study would be carried out in an ethically acceptable way. (3 marks + 3 marks)

(g) (i) Explain what is meant by validity in the context of research. (3 marks)

(ii) Identify **one** threat to validity in this study. (2 marks)

(iii) Explain how you would deal with the threat to validity identified in (ii). (2 marks)

MODEL ANSWERS

A model answer is an answer that would get full marks. However, it isn't the only answer that would get full marks, it is simply one possible answer.

Exam style question 7

(a) Outline one strength and one weakness of using a case study. (2 marks + 2 marks)

One strength is that a case study provides the opportunity to collect rich, in-depth data. This means that information that may be overlooked using other research methods may be identified.

One weakness is that it is difficult to generalise from individual cases as each one has unique characteristics and/or because we can't make before and after comparisons.

(b) Suggest how the psychologist might select participants for the case studies. (3 marks)

The psychologist might contact hospitals to see if they have treated patients with amnesia and then ask such patients if they would be willing to take part in a study. If the psychologist ended up with too many patients then probably opportunity sampling would be used, just taking those most easily available.

(c) (i) What is meant by qualitative data? (3 marks)

Qualitative data is where meanings are expressed in words instead of numbers. In the data in the question, human behaviour is represented in terms of experiences.

(c) (ii) What is meant by subjectivity? (3 marks)

Subjectivity refers to being biased because of the expectations a researcher holds. This could affect the eventual analysis of this data because the psychologist might see patterns based on her previous knowledge about amnesia.

(d) (i) Explain how the psychologist might produce a qualitative outcome. (3 marks)

The psychologist would first of all read through the diary entries, making no notes.

Then he/she would divide the text into units. Each unit would then be coded in terms of its meaning. Later these codes can be combined into themes that exist in the data. For example, one theme might be loneliness and another theme might be strategies for coping.

Finally the themes can be used to summarise the data, providing some quotes from the text to illustrate the themes.

(d) (ii) Explain how the psychologist might produce a quantitative outcome. (3 marks)

The psychologist would use identify themes/categories as described above or might use pre-existing categories and use these categories to count up how often that kind of statement was made.

(e) Explain how you might demonstrate whether the research is high in validity. (3 marks)

In order to assess validity one way would be to look at other kinds of research on amnesia and see if the different studies all had results which supported each other. Such support confirms the 'trueness' of the data collected.

Exam style question 8

(a) Outline one strength and one weakness of using a questionnaire. (2 marks + 2 marks)

One strength is that once you have designed the questionnaire it would be relatively simple to give it out to everyone in the school, whereas interviewing everyone would take a lot of time.

One weakness is that the students may wish to present themselves in a good light and therefore might make it sound like they aimed to have more healthy habits than in fact they have.

(b) Explain one reason why a pilot study should have been carried out in the context of this study. (2 marks)

You would carry out a pilot study to check the design of the questionnaire, so you could see, for example, if some of the questions were confusing.

(c) (i) Identify one question in the extract above that would provide qualitative data. (1 mark)

Question 10.

(c) (ii) With reference to the question you have identified in part (i), explain why this question would produce qualitative data. (3 marks)

The answer would be in words and would tell you about what people think about smoking. There is a large range of possible answers as it is an open-ended question. This means that the answers couldn't be easily quantified (counted).

(d) (i) Identify one sampling method that could have been used in this study. (1 mark)

An opportunity sample.

(d) (ii) In the context of this study, explain one reason for using the sampling method you have identified in (i). (2 marks)

Doing an opportunity sample means that you can obtain the students easily because they are the first ones, rather than having to contact volunteers. This would mean it was quicker to complete the questionnaire.

(e) (i) The questions in the extract above can be criticised. Select one question and give one criticism of it. (2 marks)

Question 8, the terms used aren't explained so different people may interpret them differently. One person might think 10 a day was excessive whereas someone else would rate this as moderate.

(e) (ii) Re-write the question you selected so that it overcomes the criticism you identified in (i). (2 marks)

Instead of using the terms, moderate, excessive etc. I would use numbers e.g.0–5 a day, 6–10 a day, 11–20 a day, etc.

(f) Describe two ways of making sure that this study would be carried out in an ethically acceptable way. (3 marks + 3 marks)

1. Anonymity – I would ensure that people did not put their names on the questionnaires and would tell them about their rights of confidentialty as part of the informed consent.

2. Protection from psychological harm – I would make sure that there were no distressing questions, which could be checked during the pilot study.

(g) (i) Explain what is meant by validity in the context of research. (3 marks)

Validity refers to the legitimacy of a study. It concerns both internal validity (the extent to which a study has measured what was intended to be measured) and external validity (the extent to which the findings can be generalised).

(g) (ii) Identify one threat to validity in this study. (2 marks)

The questionnaire may not collect the 'right' sort of data, e.g. people may not be truthful about their smoking habits and lie to make themselves look better.

(g) (iii) Explain how you would deal with the threat to validity identified in (ii). (2 marks)

I would try to reduce dishonest answers by assuring them about confidentiality and that it was important to be honest so the healthy habits of school students could be properly assessed.

Inferential statistics

UNDERSTANDING INFERENTIAL STATISTICS PAGES 102–103

Inferential statistics are based on probability, so we start our chapter with a look at this as well as the null hypothesis and the concept of falsifiability.

mini study Probability misjudgement and paranormal belief

USING INFERENTIAL TESTS PAGES 104–105

Details of how to find an observed value and to determine whether it is significant, plus a look at levels of measurement.

MORE ON INFERENTIAL TESTS PAGES 106–107

Back to the null hypothesis and Type 1 and 2 errors, as well as a decision tree for selecting the right test to use.

mini study The Monty Hall problem

SPEARMAN'S CORRELATION TEST PAGES 108–109

Used to assess the significance of two co-variables measured at the ordinal or interval level.

mini study Finger length and exam performance
Also: Life events and illness, reaction time and hours of sleep, reaction time and time spent playing computers, working memory and IQ

CHI-SQUARED (χ^2) TEST PAGES 110–111

Used to assess difference or association with nominal data.

mini study Parental style and self-esteem
Also: Gender and conformity, sleep and age

WILCOXON T TEST PAGES 112–113

Used to assess the difference between two sets of related data that are ordinal or interval.

mini study The mere exposure effect
Also: Mere exposure again, smiling makes you happy, right brain left brain

MANN–WHITNEY *U* TEST PAGES 114–115

Used to assess the difference between two independent sets of data that are ordinal or interval.

mini study Falling in love
Also: Two-factor theory of love, digit ratio and gender, time of day, eyewitness testimony

THE SIGN TEST PAGES 116–117

Used to assess the difference between two sets of related data that are nominal.

mini study The availability heuristic
Also: Another test of the availability heuristic, evidence for extra sensory perception, inattentional blindness

PARAMETRIC STATISTICS PAGES 118–119

A special class of more powerful inferential tests, beginning with Pearson's product moment correlation.

mini study See page 109

t TESTS PAGES 120–121

Parametric tests of difference for related and independent samples.

mini study Testing the power of parametric statistics

END OF CHAPTER TREATS PAGES 122–125

Multiple choice questions
Exam style questions 9 and 10
Model answers for exam style question

UNDERSTANDING INFERENTIAL STATISTICS

You may have heard the phrase 'statistical test' – for example a newspaper might report that 'statistical tests show that women are better at reading maps than men'. If we wanted to know if women are better at reading maps than men we could not possibly test all the women and men in the world, so we just test a small group of women and a small group of men. If we find that the sample of women are indeed better with maps than the sample of men, then we infer that the same is true for all women and men. However, it isn't quite as simple as that because we can only make such inferences using statistical tests (called inferential tests). Such statistical tests are based on probabilities, so we will start the topic of inferential statistics by looking at probability.

Probability

Inferential tests allow psychologists to draw conclusions from their findings. These conclusions are based on the probability that a particular pattern of results could have arisen by chance or not. Consider the example above about gender differences in the ability to read maps. One study might test 20 women and 20 men to see who had a better understanding of maps, and find a difference favouring the women. The big question is – *is this difference due to chance*? Or is there a *real* effect (i.e. women are actually better than men). If the findings are not due to chance, then the pattern is described as **significant**, i.e. there is a real effect.

Samples and populations

Consider the following example from the psychologist and statistician Hugh Coolican (2004):

At my local chippy I am convinced that they save money by giving some people rather thin chips (because they then can get more chips from each potato). There are two chip bins under the counter – the owner of the chippy claims the two bins contain the same kind of chips but I suspect they are different. So I (sadly) tried an experiment. I asked for one bag of chips from each of the chip bins, and I measured the width of the chips in each bag.

Belief 1 is 'The two bins contain chips of an equal average width'. Belief 2 is 'One bin has thinner chips on average than the other'.

In fact I found a very small difference between the average width of the chips in each bag (as you can see in the bar chart on the below) but nothing to shout about.

We would expect small differences between samples (bags of chips) just because things do vary a little – this is simply random variation or 'chance'. What we are looking for is a sufficiently large difference between the samples to be sure that the bins (the total population) are actually different. Otherwise we assume the bins are the same, i.e. the samples are drawn from a single population rather than from two different populations.

- The *bins* contain the **populations** – in the earlier example about gender differences in map reading, the population is all the map reading abilities of all the men and women in the world.
- The *bags* of chips are **samples** – in our other example, the 20 women and 20 men comprise our samples.
- The belief that the two bins contain chips of the same width or the belief that there is no gender difference in map reading is called the **null hypothesis**. This is a statement of *no effect* – the samples are not different.
- The alternative belief is that one bin has thinner chips or that women are better than men – this is called the **alternative hypothesis**. This is a statement that something is going on, there is an effect – the samples are different.

Ultimately, we are interested in making a statement about the population(s) from which the samples are drawn.

The null hypothesis

The null hypothesis is a statement of no difference or no correlation. It is a statement that 'nothing is going on'. The null hypothesis isn't as strange as it sounds, as shown in the example on the facing page.

● Chance

In the example on the facing page about boyfriends and cheating you might have worked out the *likelihood* that the cheating was real (e.g. you might have felt 'fairly certain'). In research we need to be a bit more precise than that. In order to work out whether a difference is or is not significant we use inferential tests. Such tests permit you to work out, at a given probability, whether a pattern in the data from a study could have arisen by **chance** or whether the effect occurred because there is a real difference/correlation in the populations from which the samples were drawn.

But what do we mean by 'chance'? We simply decide on a probability that we will 'risk'. You can't be 100% certain that an observed effect was not due to chance but you can state *how* certain you are. In the kissing example you might say to your friend that you are 95% sure he is cheating. Which means you are fairly confident that you are right but nevertheless have a little bit of doubt.

In general, psychologists use a probability of 95%. This expresses the degree of uncertainty. It means that there is a 5% chance of the results occurring if the null hypothesis is true (there is nothing going on). In other words, a 5% probability that the results would occur even if there was no real difference/association between the populations from which the samples were drawn. This probability of 5% is recorded as $p=0.05$ (where p means probability).

In some studies psychologists want to be more certain – such as when they are conducting a replication of a previous study or considering the effects of a new drug on health. Then, researchers use a more stringent probability, such as $p=0.01$ or even $p=0.001$. This chosen value of 'p' is called the **significance level**, which we will discuss on the next spread.

key terms

- Alternative hypothesis (sometimes called the alternate hypothesis)
- Chance
- Inferential tests
- Null hypothesis
- Population
- Probability
- Sample
- Significant
- Significance level
- Statistical test

DO I HAVE TO DO THIS?

	AQA A	AQA B	Edex	OCR	WJEC
AS	○	○	●	○	○
A2	●	●	○	●	●

● compulsory ◐ advisory ○ not necessary

It's late at night and on your way home you happen to see you best friend's boyfriend with another girl, and he's doing more than talking. You think to yourself '*How likely is it that he would be kissing her if there is nothing going on between them?*'

➤ Null hypothesis – '*There is nothing going on, there is no relationship between them*'.

➤ Alternative hypothesis – '*There is something going on between them*'.

It isn't very likely that he would be kissing her if there was nothing going on, therefore you reject the null hypothesis and accept the alternative hypothesis – and tell your friend you are fairly certain that he is cheating on her.

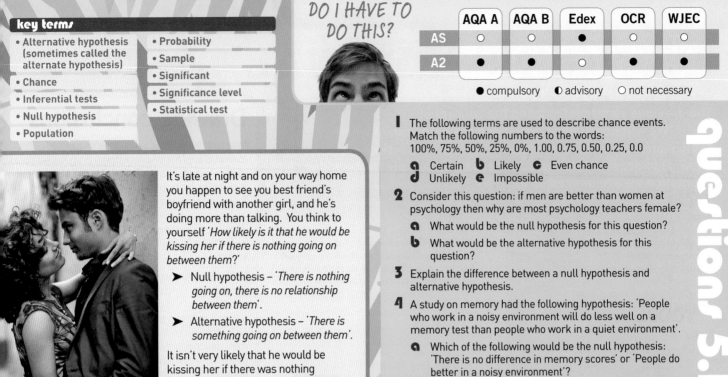

1 The following terms are used to describe chance events. Match the following numbers to the words:
100%, 75%, 50%, 25%, 0%, 1.00, 0.75, 0.50, 0.25, 0.0

a Certain **b** Likely **c** Even chance
d Unlikely **e** Impossible

2 Consider this question: if men are better than women at psychology then why are most psychology teachers female?

a What would be the null hypothesis for this question?

b What would be the alternative hypothesis for this question?

3 Explain the difference between a null hypothesis and alternative hypothesis.

4 A study on memory had the following hypothesis: 'People who work in a noisy environment will do less well on a memory test than people who work in a quiet environment'.

a Which of the following would be the null hypothesis: 'There is no difference in memory scores' or 'People do better in a noisy environment'?

b Is the alternative hypothesis above directional or non-directional?

5 Another study investigated the relationship between sleep and exercise, with the following hypothesis: 'The more exercise a person takes in a day, the more sleep they will have at night'.

Write an appropriate null hypothesis for this study.

6 What does the letter 'p' stand for in the statement '$p < 0.05$'?

7 Sometimes the statement $p \leq 0.05$ is used instead of $p = 0.05$. Explain the difference between the two of these.

8 Explain what is meant by the phrase 'significant at $p < 0.05$'. You must mention the null hypothesis in your answer.

9 Suggest why a researcher may choose to use $p < 0.01$ in preference to $p < 0.05$. (Try to give two reasons.)

Falsifiability

Inferential statistics require that we accept or reject the null hypothesis. The reason for doing this comes from Karl Popper's ideas about proof and disproof. Until the 1930s scientists believed that the their task was to find examples that would *confirm* their theories. Karl Popper, a philosopher of science, argued:

No matter how many instances of white swans we may have observed, this does not justify the conclusion that all swans are white (Popper, 1934).

No number of sightings of white swans can prove the theory that all swans are white, whereas the sighting of just one black one may disprove it. This led to the realisation that the only way to prove a theory correct was actually to seek *disproof* (falsification) – look for those black swans. Therefore, we start research with a null hypothesis: 'Not all swans in the world are white, i.e. there are black swans'.

We then go looking for swans and record many sightings but if there are no black swans this leads us to be reasonably certain (we can never be absolutely certain) that the null hypothesis is false.

We therefore can reject the null hypothesis (with reasonable certainty). If the null hypothesis isn't true this means that the alternative must be true, so now we can accept the alternative hypothesis ('All swans are white') with reasonable certainty!

This is, in the present state of knowledge, the best approximation to the truth.

mini study

Probability misjudgement and paranormal belief

One explanation given for why some people believe in paranormal phenomenon (such as extra sensory perception – ESP) is that such people underestimate the probability of coincidences. They therefore misinterpret normal events as paranormal. In order to test this possibility you need two items of information:

1. To know whether a person is a believer in the paranormal or not. A simple way to do this is just to ask people whether they believe in ESP (Blackmore, 1997).

2. To give the participant a probability task. Again a simple one involves asking people to imagine they are throwing a single 6-sided die 100 times. They should list the possible outcomes. People who are not good at probability will avoid repeats, such as 1, 2, 2, 4, 4, 4, 6. So you can score a person's sequence by counting up how often there are repeats in their 100 digits.

You should find that believers (sheep) have a lower score than non-believers (goats).

(You can find other probability tasks on the internet.)

USING INFERENTIAL TESTS

The previous spread introduced the concept of significance levels. We will now look at how these are determined when using statistical tests, also called inferential tests because they allow us to draw *inferences* from a research sample to the wider population we are interested in.

What is an 'inference'? The word 'infer' means to draw a conclusion on the basis of reasoning or evidence. For example 'The young girl inferred that her mother was angry from the sharp tone of her voice'.

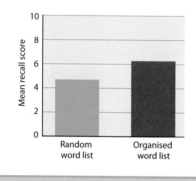

Bar chart showing the findings from a study on the effects of organisation on memory. We can draw conclusions about the samples from this graph but not about the population. We need an inferential test to be able to draw conclusions about the population.

Levels of measurement

One of the factors involved in deciding which inferential test to select is the level of measurement *used with the variables in the study – some statistical tests are restricted to certain levels of measurement (as you will see on the next spread).*

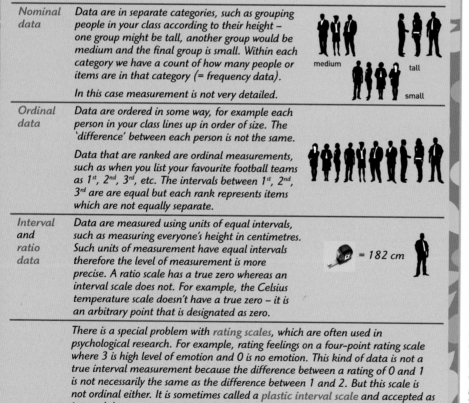

Nominal data	Data are in separate categories, such as grouping people in your class according to their height – one group might be tall, another group would be medium and the final group is small. Within each category we have a count of how many people or items are in that category (= frequency data). In this case measurement is not very detailed.
Ordinal data	Data are ordered in some way, for example each person in your class lines up in order of size. The 'difference' between each person is not the same. Data that are ranked are ordinal measurements, such as when you list your favourite football teams as 1st, 2nd, 3rd, etc. The intervals between 1st, 2nd, 3rd are are equal but each rank represents items which are not equally separate.
Interval and ratio data	Data are measured using units of equal intervals, such as measuring everyone's height in centimetres. Such units of measurement have equal intervals therefore the level of measurement is more precise. A ratio scale has a true zero whereas an interval scale does not. For example, the Celsius temperature scale doesn't have a true zero – it is an arbitrary point that is designated as zero.
	There is a special problem with rating scales, *which are often used in psychological research. For example, rating feelings on a four-point rating scale where 3 is high level of emotion and 0 is no emotion. This kind of data is not a true interval measurement because the difference between a rating of 0 and 1 is not necessarily the same as the difference between 1 and 2. But this scale is not ordinal either. It is sometimes called a* plastic interval scale *and accepted as interval data.*

NOIR *An acronym to help remember the four levels of measurement of data: nominal, ordinal, interval and ratio.*

Drawing conclusions

Inferential tests help us to draw inferences (conclusions) about **populations** from the **samples** of data tested. The main aim of any research study is to make some sense of the findings and use these to help explain human behaviour. This is what we mean when we 'draw conclusions'. What does the data show us about human behaviour in general (i.e. about the population rather than the sample)?

Descriptive statistics can be used when considering conclusions because they provide a *summary* of the data. They help us detect general patterns and trends. However, strictly speaking you cannot actually draw conclusions from descriptive statistics because you cannot go beyond the particular sample to draw *inferences* about people in general (the 'population').

For example, you *can* conclude from the bar chart on the left that the participants who studied an organised word list were able to remember more words compared with participants in a random word list condition. However you cannot conclude that *people* remember organised word lists better (i.e. organisation aids memory) because then you are assuming that people in the population will behave the same as the participants in your study.

In order to draw such inferences, we need inferential tests. These tests allow us to infer that a pattern in the data is likely (or not) to be due to chance. If it is not due to chance, we can conclude the pattern is 'real', i.e. **significant**.

Different inferential tests

Different inferential tests are used depending on (1) the research design and (2) the level of measurement (explained on the left). For example, if a study involves looking at the correlation between two variables measured at the ordinal level, then the inferential test to use would be a correlational test, such as Spearman's rank order correlation coefficient. On the next spread we will look at how to choose the right test.

Observed values

Each inferential test involves taking the data collected in a study and doing some calculations that produce a single number called the **test statistic**. In the case of Spearman's rank order correlation coefficient that test statistic is called *rho* whereas for the Mann–Whitney test it is *U*. The *rho* value calculated for any set of data is called the **observed value** (because it is based on the observations made). This is sometimes called the **calculated value** because it is the value you calculate.

key terms

- Calculated value
- Conclusions
- Critical value
- Degrees of freedom
- Descriptive statistics
- Directional hypothesis
- Inferential tests
- Interval data
- Level of measurement
- Nominal data
- Non-directional hypothesis
- Null hypothesis
- Observed value
- One-tailed test
- Ordinal data
- Plastic interval scale
- Population
- Rating scales
- Ratio data
- Sample
- Significant
- Significance level
- Table of critical values
- Test statistic
- Two-tailed test

DO I HAVE TO DO THIS?

	AQA A	AQA B	Edex	OCR	WJEC
AS	○	○	●	○	○
A2	●	●	○	●	●

● compulsory ◑ advisory ○ not necessary

Critical values

To decide if the observed value is significant this figure is compared to another number, found in a **table of critical values** (see example below). This is called the **critical value** and is the value that a test statistic must reach in order for the **null hypothesis** to be rejected.

To find the appropriate critical value in a table you need to know the following information:

1. **Degrees of freedom** (*df*) In most cases you get this value by looking at the number of participants in the study (*N*).
2. **One-tailed** or **two-tailed test** If the hypothesis was a **directional hypothesis**, then you use a one-tailed test, if it was **non-directional** you use a two-tailed test.
3. **Significance level** selected, usually $p \leq 0.05$ (5% level).
4. Whether the observed value needs to be greater than or less than the critical value for significance to be shown. You will find this information stated underneath each table.

Table of critical values

Below is an example of a table of critical values.

This table shows critical values for the Wilcoxon signed ranks test. Let's say you do a study and these are your four pieces of information:

1. Degrees of freedom = There were 20 people in your study, so $df/N = 20$.
2. You used a directional hypothesis so a two-tailed test is required.
3. You have selected a 5% significance level.
4. Your observed value is 53. For the Wilcoxon test the table of critical values says that the value of *T* must be equal to or less than the critical value for significance .

The final task is to make a statement, such as:

The observed value (53) is greater than the critical value (52) for $p \leq 0.05$, two-tailed test. Therefore, we cannot reject the null hypothesis.

Table1: Extract from table of critical values from the Wilcoxon signed ranks test

Level of significance for a one-tailed test	0.05	0.01
Level of significance for a two-tailed test	0.10	0.02
N	$T \leq$	
19	53	46
20	60	52
21	67	58
22	75	65

Calculated *T* must be EQUAL TO or LESS THAN the critical value in this table for significance at the level shown.

There are different tables of critical values for each different statistical test.

1. Explain what is meant by 'significance level'.

2. Give the general name for the value that is worked out using an inferential test.

3. What is the name of the test statistic for Spearman's test?

4. Give the general name given to the number, found in a significance table, that is used to judge the observed value produced by an inferential test.

5. Identify the four pieces of information used to find this value.

6. Explain when a one-tailed test is used instead of a two-tailed test.

7. Identify the level of measurement in the examples below:
   a. Rating how stressful certain experiences are.
   b. Counting the days a person has had off school.
   c. Asking people to indicate their reasons for days off school.
   d. Finding out the number of boys and girls doing A level Psychology, Maths and English.
   e. Putting IQ scores in rank order.
   f. Number of words correctly recalled on a test.

8. A race track presents information on the day's races. Suggest how this could be done using nominal, ordinal and interval data.

9. Identify the appropriate critical value in the table for the Wilcoxon test (on the left) and decide if significance would be shown in the following cases:
   a. Directional hypothesis, $N = 19$, 5% significance, observed value = 48
   b. Non-directional hypothesis, $N = 22$, 1% significance, observed value = 75
   c. Non-directional hypothesis, $N = 21$, 5% significance, observed value = 60

10. A research study tested the effect of alcohol on reaction time. Two groups of volunteers were obtained from a local university. They were then given a drink. One group received a drink containing a large measure of strong alcohol; the second group received an identical drink without alcohol, but with a strong alcoholic smell. Each participant's reaction time was measured by using a computer game.
    a. Identify the independent variable and the dependent variable in this study.
    b. Write a suitable null hypothesis for this study.
    c. Write an appropriate non-directional alternative hypothesis.
    d. Would a one-tailed or two-tailed test be suitable with this hypothesis?
    e. Describe the level of measurement used when measuring reaction time.
    f. Suggest an alternative level of measurement that could be used, and explain how it would be done.
    g. Outline **one** potential problem with validity in this study.
    h. The researchers will use a statistical test to assess the significance of their results. Explain why such tests are used.
    i. Identify a suitable level of significance that could be used in this study and explain your choice.

MORE ON INFERENTIAL STATISTICS

On this spread we are revisiting some concepts from the first two spreads in this chapter and meeting some new ones.

The null hypothesis and significance levels

On page 103 we gave an example of how much you understand about statistics without knowing it. Here is another example.

Making a good bet

The **null hypothesis** is an explanation that '*there is nothing going on*' whereas the **alternative hypothesis** represents the view that '*there is something going on, there is a detectable pattern*'.

Imagine that I am holding two packs of cards.

➤ One of these packs is shuffled so that the black and red cards are all jumbled up (i.e. there is nothing going on, there is no pattern). This pack represents the null hypothesis.

➤ The other pack has been arranged so all the red cards are first (i.e. there is something going on, a pattern). This pack represents the alternative hypothesis.

I choose one pack and turn over the first card – which turns out to be red. Would you bet £10 that this is the arranged pack? In other words, would you be pre pared to reject the null hypothesis after seeing just this one card? Probably not.

I turn over the second card, and it is red. And the third card is red, and the fourth card is red.

Would you now feel there was something going on? Does it seem pretty likely that this is the arranged pack. Would you bet £10 that it was? Probably. This means you are rejecting the null hypothesis that there is no effect after seeing four cards.

So what does this tell us about probability?

Probability

What is the **probability** of getting four red cards in a row *if there is nothing going on*. In other words, how likely is it that I get a pattern when the null hypothesis is actually true (there is nothing going on).

- The probability of turning over one red card in a random pack = 0.5
- The probability of turning over two red cards in a row is $0.5 \times 0.5^* = 0.25$ or 25%
- The probability of turning over three red cards in a row is $0.5 \times 0.5 \times 0.5^* = 0.125$ (12.5%)
- And finally, four cards is $0.5 \times 0.5 \times 0.5 \times 0.5^* = 0.0625$ (6%)

This shows that intuitively we are prepared to reject the null hypothesis around the 5% level.

*It isn't quite 0.5 because the cards aren't replaced, which means that the probability of drawing a red card is less than 0.5 after the first red card but not by much.

Thanks again to Hugh Coolican for this example.

Type 1 and Type 2 errors

In general psychologists use a 5% level of significance level. One reason for this is because it is a good compromise between being too lenient and too stringent. Consider the table on the right about a criminal. Which is worse – convict an innocent man (a **Type 1 error**) or to let a guilty man go free (a **Type 2 error**)?

The same question can be asked about accepting or rejecting the null hypothesis (H_0) (see bottom table) – is it worse to reject a null hypothesis which is in fact correct or to accept a null hypothesis which is wrong?

Consider this example – a research study is conducted with the following hypotheses:

- Alternative hypothesis (H_1) – women have better map reading abilities than men.
- Null hypothesis (H_0) – there is no difference between men and women in terms of map reading abilities.

The study tests 20 men and 20 women and finds a difference between these samples. This leads the researcher to reject H_0 and accept H_1 – but the real truth is that there is no difference in the **target population**. Our samples were biased. Therefore, we have committed a Type 1 error. We have concluded that there is something going on when in fact there is nothing going on. That's a false positive.

This is more likely to happen if the significance level is lenient (e.g. 10%) because a smaller difference between men and women would be sufficient to reject the null hypothesis.

		Truth	
		Guilty	*Not guilty*
Test result	**Guilty verdict**	True positive	*False positive (guilt reported)* TYPE 1 ERROR
	Not guilty verdict	*False negative (guilt not detected)* TYPE 2 ERROR	True negative

		Truth	
		H_1 is correct. There is something going on	*H_0 is correct. There is nothing going on*
Test result	**Reject H_0**	True positive	*False positive (likely when **p** too lenient, i.e. 10%)* TYPE 1 ERROR
	Accept H_0	*False negative (likely when **p** too stringent, i.e. 1%)* TYPE 2 ERROR	True negative

Choosing which statistical test to use

There are many statistical tests that are used by psychologists. These are divided into parametric and non-parametric tests. We will start with one kind – the non-parametric tests. For most students these are the only tests they have to study.

When deciding which non-parametric test is appropriate in any situation you can ask yourself the questions in the diagram below:

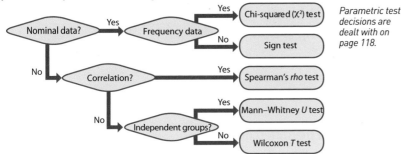

Parametric test decisions are dealt with on page 118.

Justifying your choice

Examination questions often involve the description of a research study and one of the questions that follows requires you to select an appropriate statistical test and explain why you would choose this test.

On each spread that follows we have provided information that will help you justify your choice of tests but *be warned that such justifications need to be adapted to suit particular circumstances*.

Essentially you should:

1. Identify the level of measurement with reference to the actual data. For example, you might write:
   - *'The data have been put into categories and are classified as nominal data.'*
   - *'The data have been measured on an rating scale which is the ordinal level of measurement (or better).'*

2. State whether a test of correlation or difference is required and justify this. For example, you might write:
   - *'The hypothesis states a correlation, i.e. states that two related variables co-vary systematically.'*
   - *'The hypothesis states that there is a difference between the two groups.'*

3. If a test of difference is required, state whether it is independent groups or repeated measures, and justify this statement. For example, you might write:
   - *'The design is independent groups as participants are allocated to one of two groups.'*
   - *'The design is repeated measures as each participant is tested twice.'*

key terms
- Alternative hypothesis
- Correlation
- Independent groups
- Null hypothesis
- Probability
- Repeated measures
- Target population
- Type 1 error
- Type 2 error

mini study

The Monty Hall problem

This probability puzzle is based on an American game show whose host was Monty Hall. Imagine you're on his show and given the choice of three doors: behind one door is a car but behind the others there are goats. You pick a door, say No.1. Monty Hall does not open that door but opens another, behind which is a goat. Monty Hall now says 'If you wish you can choose a different door'. Should you switch?

Try asking other people. Search for an explanation on YouTube.

questions 5.3

1. Considering the problem of a criminal trial on the facing page, do you think a Type 1 or Type 2 error would be worse?

2. Construct a similar grid for a case where a doctor is diagnosing a patient with cancer. The null hypothesis is that the patient is not diagnosed with cancer (nothing is going on). The alternative is that the patient is diagnosed with cancer. In reality the patient does or does not have cancer.

   In this case what would the Type 1 error be?

3. Explain the difference between a Type 1 error and Type 2 error.

4. A psychologist uses a 5% level of significance. What is the likelihood of making a Type 1 error in this study?

5. For each study outlined below state a suitable alternative and null hypothesis for the study. Briefly explain how you might conduct the study, invent a hypothetical set of data that might be produced and, finally, select an appropriate inferential test, justifying the reason for your choice.

   a. An experiment where reaction times are compared for each participant before and after drinking coffee.

   b. An investigation to see if reaction time is related to age.

   c. An experiment to compare stress levels in doctors and nurses, to see which group is more stressed.

   d. A study where two groups of participants were matched on memory ability. Each group used a different revision technique to learn a topic and then their performances were compared.

   e. A study to see whether more men or women own a pet.

6. A student designed an experiment that used a repeated measures design to investigate obedience to male and female teachers. The student decided to do this by observing how pupils behaved with different teachers. She asked various friends to record student behaviours in their classrooms.

   a. State a directional alternative hypothesis for this study.

   b. Suggest **three** behavioural categories that might be used to record the students' behaviours.

   c. Identify a sampling method that could be used in this study and explain why it would be chosen.

   d. Suggest some appropriate statistical measures that could be used when analysing the data (both descriptive and inferential). Justify your choice.

7. A psychologist designs a set of questions to collect data about smokers' and non-smokers' attitudes to smoking.

   a. Write **one** open and **one** closed question he might use.

   b. For each question the psychologist would like to summarise the answers that are given. Suggest **two** ways that data could be summarised.

   c. Suggest **one** strength and **one** weakness of presenting the questions in writing rather than conducting face-to-face interviews.

   d. What inferential test might be used in this study? Justify your choice.

SPEARMAN'S CORRELATION TEST

The first inferential test we will look at is a test of correlation – Spearman's rank order correlation coefficient. It is used to determine whether the correlation between two co-variables is significant or not.

Exam questions never require the calculation of inferential tests, but it will help your understanding of how to interpret the results to have a go. You can always avoid doing the actual calculations by using online calculators or a spreadsheet programme such as Microsoft Excel.

Spearman's rank order correlation test – a worked example (based on the mini study on the facing page)

STEP 1. State the alternative and null hypothesis

Alternative hypothesis: The digit ratio between index finger and ring finger is positively correlated to numeracy skills. (This is a directional hypothesis and therefore requires a one-tailed test.)

Null hypothesis: There is no correlation between digit ratio and numeracy skills.

STEP 2. Record the data and rank for each co-variable, calculate the difference

Rank A and B separately, from low to high (i.e. the lowest number receives the rank of 1).

If there are two or more of the same number (tied ranks), calculate the rank by working out the mean of the ranks that would have been given.

Participant number	Digit ratio	Numeracy score	Rank A	Rank B	Difference between rank A and rank B (d)	d²
1	1.026	8	10	2.5	7.5	56.25
2	1.000	16	5.5	9	−3.5	12.25
3	1.021	10	9	5	4.0	16.0
4	0.991	9	4	4	0	0
5	0.984	15	3	8	−5.0	25.0
6	0.975	14	1	7	−6.0	36.0
7	1.013	12	7	6	1	1.0
8	1.018	8	8	2.5	5.5	30.25
9	0.982	17	2	10	−8.0	64.0
10	1.000	5	5.5	1	4.5	20.25
N = 10					Σd² (sum of differences squared) = 261.0	

STEP 3. Find observed value of *rho* (the correlation coefficient)

$$rho = 1 - \frac{6\Sigma d^2}{N(N^2-1)} = 1 - \frac{6 \times 261.0}{10 \times (100-1)} = 1 - 1566/990 = 1 - 1.58 = -.58$$

STEP 4. Find the critical value of *rho*

N = 10, the hypothesis is directional therefore a one-tailed test is used.
Look up the critical value in the table of critical values (on the right).
For a one-tailed test where *N* = 10, the critical value of *rho* = 0.564 (p≤0.05).

Note that the observed value is negative – when comparing this figure to the critical value, only the value, not the sign, is important. The sign does, however, tell you whether the correlation is positive or negative. If the hypothesis is one-tailed and the sign (and therefore the correlation) is not as expected, then the null hypothesis must be retained.

STEP 5. State the conclusion

As the observed value (0.58) is greater than the critical value (0.564) it might appear that we should we reject the null hypothesis (at p≤0.05), however in this case the sign is in the wrong direction – the alternative hypothesis stated a positive correlation but a negative correlation was found. This means that we must accept the null hypothesis and conclude that there is no correlation between digit ratio and numeracy skills.

If the alternative hypothesis stated a negative correlation then we could reject the null hypothesis.

Example of a correlational analysis

One study of the relationship between stress and illness by Rahe et al. (1970) found a correlation of +.118 between the number of times a participant was ill and their stress score as measured by the SRRS (social readjustment rating scale). A figure of zero would be no correlation whereas a figure of +1.0 would be a perfect positive correlation. A correlation of +.118 may sound like a rather weak correlation but with over 2700 participants +.118 was significant. As the number of participants increases the value needed for significance decreases.

Incidentally, if the observed value had been −.118 this would still be significant; it would be a significant negative correlation.

Critical values of *rho*

Level of significance for a one-tailed test	0.05	0.01
Level of significance for a two-tailed test	0.10	0.02
N = 4	1.000	
5	.900	1.000
6	.829	.886
7	.714	.786
8	.643	.738
9	.600	.700
10	.564	.648
11	.536	.618
12	.503	.587
13	.484	.560
14	.464	.538
15	.443	.521
16	.429	.503
17	.414	.485
18	.401	.472
19	.391	.460
20	.380	.447
25	.337	.398
30	.306	.362

Observed value of *rho* must be EQUAL TO or GREATER THAN the critical value in this table for significance at the level shown.

Source: J.H. Zhar (1972) *Significance testing of the Spearman's Rank Correlation Coefficient. Journal of the American Statistical Association*, 67, 578–80. Reprinted with permission from the Journal of the American Statistical Association. Copyright 1972 by the American Statistical Association. All rights reserved.

Justifying the choice of Spearman's rank order correlation test

The hypothesis states a *correlation* between two co-variables.

The two sets of data are pairs of scores from one person or thing, i.e. they are *related*.

The data are at least *ordinal* (i.e. not nominal). See page 104 for an explanation.

DO I HAVE TO DO THIS?

	AQA A	AQA B	Edex	OCR	WJEC
AS	○	○	●	○	○
A2	●	●	○	●	●

● compulsory ◐ advisory ○ not necessary

HEALTH WARNING –

If you do conduct your own research studies, make sure no participants are younger than 16 and that you seek fully informed consent. If you are using sensitive information, such as tests of maths ability, then you must protect participants' confidentiality.

mini study

Finger length and exam performance

A number of studies have looked at the relationship between finger length and various abilities, such as numeracy or literacy. For example, a recent study by Brosnan (2008) examined finger length in 75 British children aged between six and seven (boys and girls), and found that children with a higher digit ratio between their index and ring fingers were more likely to have a talent in maths, while those with a shorter digit ratio were more likely to have a talent in literacy.

This relationship is thought to be due to biological factors, specifically the production of testosterone and oestrogen in the brain. Male babies are exposed to more testosterone (a male hormone) during prenatal development and this affects their finger length. Testosterone also promotes the development of the areas of the brain which are associated with spatial and mathematical skills, whereas oestrogen (a female hormone) is thought to promote the development of the areas of the brain which are associated with verbal ability.

In order to study the correlation between finger length and numeracy/literacy the researchers took photocopies of both the right and left hands of the children and measured the length of the index and ring fingers. They divided the length of the index finger by the length of the ring finger to calculate each child's 'digit ratio'.

The digit ratios were then correlated with the results from their *National Standard Assessment Tests* (SATs) for numeracy and literacy.

- You can repeat (replicate) this study using GCSE scores instead of SATs results, or you could use online tests of literacy and/or numeracy. In order to determine if your results are significant follow the worked example on the facing page.

Ring finger — Index finger

▲ **Literacy hand**
People with short ring fingers and long index fingers are better at literacy.

▼ **Numeracy hand**
Peeople with long ring fingers and short index fingers are more likely to excel in numeracy

More ideas using a correlational analysis

- **Life events and illness** The study by Rahe *et al.* (see facing page) can be replicated by calculating an illness score for participants over a period of time and giving them a life events or daily hassles assessment.
- **Reaction time and number of hours of sleep** Does lack of sleep have any effects? For example, it might be related to poor reaction time. You can measure reaction time using an online test.
- **Reaction time and time spent playing computer games** Perhaps playing computer games is related to reaction time – for example, people who play more computer games have a faster reaction time than people who don't.
- **Working memory and IQ** are expected to be positively correlated. You can find tests for both at www.bbc.co.uk.

1 A study on finger length and numeracy is described on the left.

a Identify the co-variables in this study.

b Identify a possible intervening variable in this study (a variable that links finger length to, for example, numeracy).

c Identify **two** ethical problems that might arise when conducting a study on finger length and numeracy, and state how these could be dealt with.

d Suggest problems that might occur when dealing with the ethical problems in the manner you suggested.

e Draw a scattergraph of the results on the facing page. This is a useful way of checking the outcome of the inferential test – does your graph show the same relationship as reported for the inferential test?

2 Researchers conducted a study to test the effect of mental factors on athletic performance using 30 university Sports and Exercise students as participant volunteers.

The students were matched in pairs according to their recorded maximum bench press (a measure of press-up strength), and they were also paired by gender. They were given a standard personality test that measured 'determination' as one co-variable in this study.

A competition was staged with the other participants as audience, where the paired students competed to see who could do the most press-ups before exhaustion. The reason for this part of the study was to push students to produce their best bench press scores.

A correlation test was completed, each student providing their 'determination' score and their maximum press-up score as the variables. 'Determination' was plotted against 'maximum press up' and Spearman's rank order correlation test used to calculate the correlation coefficient.

a Write a suitable non-directional hypothesis for this study.

b State a suitable null hypothesis for this study.

c Identify a suitable statistical (inferential) test to use for this study and explain why this test would be chosen.

d At $p \leq 0.05$ what is the critical value of *rho* required for significance to be shown in this study?

e The observed value calculated was +.32. Explain what +.32 indicates.

f Explain whether the null hypothesis would be accepted or rejected and why.

g If a one-tailed test had been required, would the observed value be significant?

h Give **one** strength and **one** weakness of a using a correlational analysis.

i The students were matched by bench press and gender. Explain why they were matched by gender.

j The researchers used a volunteer sample. Identify an alternative method of sampling and explain how it would be implemented in this study.

k Describe how the researchers could establish the validity and the reliability of the 'determination' score on the personality test.

CHI-SQUARED (χ^2) TEST

The second inferential test we will look at deals with nominal data, i.e. data that is in categories. We use this test when we have counted how many occurrences there are in each category – called 'frequency data'. For example, we might be interested to find out whether men and women do actually differ in terms of their finger length ratio (as discussed on the previous spread). Research has found that adult women usually have ratios of 1.0, i.e. their index and ring fingers are of equal length. The average for men is lower, at 0.98, since they tend to have longer ring finger than index finger, suggesting greater exposure to testosterone in the womb.

Chi-squared test – a worked example for a 2 × 2 contingency table (based on the mini study on the previous page)

STEP 1. State the alternative and null hypothesis

Alternative hypothesis: There is difference between men and women in terms of digit ratio (the ratio between the index and ring fingers). (This is a non-directional hypothesis and therefore requires a two-tailed test.)

Null hypothesis: There is no difference between men and women in terms of digit ratio.

There are online programmes that will calculate chi-squared for you (for example see http://math.hws.edu/javamath/ryan/ChiSquare.html and scroll about half way down the page).
You can also use Microsoft Excel.

STEP 2. Draw up a contingency table

	Male	Female	Totals
Digit ratio ≥ 1.00	5 (cell **A**)	12 (cell **B**)	17
Digit ratio < 1.00	10 (cell **C**)	9 (cell **D**)	19
Totals	15	21	36

This is a 2 × 2 contingency table as there are two rows and two columns. On the facing page there is a 3 × 2 contingency table as there are three rows and two columns. The first number is always rows and the second number is columns (rows then columns, RC as in Roman Catholic).

STEP 3. Compare observed and expected (*) frequencies for each cell

(*) Many students get confused about the term 'expected frequencies'. These are not what the researcher expects – they are the frequencies that would occur if the data were distributed evenly across the table in proportion to the row and column totals.

The expected frequencies are calculated by working out how the data would be distributed across all cells in the table if there were no differences, i.e. it was random.

	row × column/total = expected frequency (E)	Subtract expected value from observed value, ignoring signs. |(O–E)| (The straight lines mean 'ignore the sign)	Square previous value (O–E)^2	Divide previous value by expected value (O–E)^2 / E
Cell A	17 × 15 / 36 = 7.08	5 – 7.08 = 2.08	4.3264	0.6110
Cell B	17 × 21 / 36 = 9.92	12 – 9.92 = 2.08	4.3264	0.4361
Cell C	19 × 15 / 36 = 7.92	10 – 7.92 = 2.08	4.3264	0.5463
Cell D	19 × 21 / 36 = 11.08	9 – 11.08 = 2.08	4.3264	1.3905

In some books Yates's correction is recommended but Coolican (1996) says this is no longer modern practice.

STEP 4. Find the observed value of chi-squared (χ^2)

The chi-squared test can be used to investigate a difference (as in the worked example on this page) or an association (as on the facing page).

Add all the values in the final column in the table above.

This gives the observed value of chi-squared as 1.984.

STEP 5. Find the critical value of chi-squared (χ^2)

Calculate degrees of freedom (*df*) by multiplying (rows – 1) × (columns – 1) = 1.

Look up the value in table of the critical values (on the right).

For a two-tailed test, *df* = 1, the critical value of χ^2 = 3.84 ($p \leq 0.05$).

STEP 6. State the conclusion

As the observed value (1.984) is less than the critical value (3.84) we must accept the null hypothesis (at $p \leq 0.05$) and therefore we conclude that there is no difference between men and women in terms of digit ratio.

Critical values of χ^2

	Level of significance for a one-tailed test			
	0.10	0.05	0.025	0.01
	Level of significance for a two-tailed test			
df	0.20	0.10	0.05	0.02
1	1.64	2.71	3.84	5.41
2	3.22	4.60	5.99	7.82
3	4.64	6.25	7.82	9.84
4	5.99	7.78	9.49	11.67

Observed value of *rho* must be EQUAL TO or GREATER THAN the critical value in this table for significance at the level shown.

Source: abridged from R.A. Fisher and F. Yates (1974). *Statistical Tables for Biological, Agricultural and Medical Research* (6th Edition). London: Longman. Reproduced with permission by Pearson Education Limited.

The table shows one- and two-tailed values, though statisticians argue that you can only test one-tailed (directional) hypotheses with a chi-squared test.

Justifying the choice of the chi-squared (χ^2) test

The hypothesis states a *difference* between conditions or an *association* between variables.

The sets of data are *independent* (no individual has a score in more than one 'cell').

The data are in *frequencies* (i.e. *nominal*). Frequencies cannot be percentages.

Note: This test is unreliable when the *expected* (i.e. the ones you calculate) frequencies fall below 5 in any cell, i.e. you need at least 20 participants for a 2 × 2 contingency table.

DO I HAVE TO DO THIS?

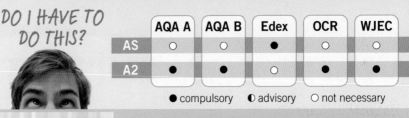

	AQA A	AQA B	Edex	OCR	WJEC
AS	○	○	●	○	○
A2	●	●	○	●	●

● compulsory ◐ advisory ○ not necessary

key terms
• Contingency table

A researcher investigated whether sleep patterns change as people get older. Data was collected by asking younger and older people how much sleep they usually had per night.

a Draw a contingency table to show the following data:

Old and young participants are asked whether they sleep more or less than eight hours per night on average. Of the old people 11 said they sleep more than eight hours and 25 said they sleep less. Of the younger participants 31 said they sleep more than eight hours and 33 said they sleep less.

b State an appropriate alternative hypothesis (directional) and null hypothesis for this investigation.

c The observed value of chi-squared for the data collected is 3.02 (one-tailed test). Is this value significant? Explain your decision.

d State whether this means you can reject the null hypothesis.

Chi-squared test – a worked example for a 3 × 2 contingency table (based on the mini study on the right)

STEP 1. State the alternative and null hypothesis

Alternative hypothesis: Certain parental styles are associated with higher self-esteem in adolescence. (This is a non-directional hypothesis and therefore requires a two-tailed test.)

Null hypothesis: There is no association between parental style and self-esteem in adolescence.

STEP 2. Draw up a contingency table

In this case it will be 3 × 2 (rows first then columns)

Parental style	Self-esteem High		Self-esteem Low		Totals
Authoritarian	10	(cell A)	4	(cell B)	14
Democratic	5	(cell C)	7	(cell D)	12
Laissez-faire	8	(cell E)	2	(cell F)	10
Totals	23		13		36

STEP 3. Compare observed and expected frequencies

	row × column / total = expected frequency (E)	Subtract expected value from observed value, ignoring signs |(O–E)|	Square the previous value (O–E)²	Divide previous value by the expected value (O–E)² / E
Cell A	14 × 23 / 36 = 8.94	10 – 8.94 = 1.06	1.1236	0.1257
Cell B	14 × 13 / 36 = 5.06	4 – 5.06 = 1.06	1.1236	0.2221
Cell C	12 × 23 / 36 = 7.67	5 – 7.67 = 2.67	7.1289	0.9294
Cell D	12 × 13 / 36 = 4.33	7 – 4.33 = 2.67	7.1289	1.6464
Cell E	10 × 23 / 36 = 6.39	8 – 6.39 = 1.61	2.5921	0.4056
Cell F	10 × 13 / 36 = 3.61	2 – 3.61 = 1.61	2.5921	0.7180

STEP 4. Find the observed value of chi-squared (χ^2)

Add all the values in the final column in the table above.

This gives the observed value of chi-squared (χ^2) = 4.0472

STEP 5. Find the the critical value of chi-squared (χ^2)

Calculate degrees of freedom (*df*) calculate (rows – 1) × (columns – 1) = 2

Look up the critical value in the table of critical values (on facing page).

For a two-tailed test, *df* = 2, the critical value of χ^2 = 5.99 ($p \leq 0.05$)

STEP 6. State the conclusion

As the observed value (4.0472) is less than the critical value (5.99) we must accept the null hypothesis (at $p \leq 0.05$) and therefore conclude that there is no association between parental style and self-esteem in adolescence.

mini study

Parental style and self-esteem

Psychological research has identified three different parenting styles: *authoritarian* (parents dictate how children should behave), *democratic* (parents discuss standards with their children) and *laissez-faire* (parents encourage children to set their own rules). Buri (1991) found that children who experienced authoritarian parenting were more likely to develop high self-esteem.

You can access the *Parental Authority Questionnaire* (PAQ) at http://faculty.sjcny.edu/~treboux/documents/parental%20authority%20questionnaire.pdf

There are various self-esteem questionnaires on the internet as well as one on page 61.

More ideas using a chi-squared test

* **Gender and conformity** Are women more conformist than men? Some studies have found this to be true but Eagly and Carli (1981) suggest this is only true on male-oriented tasks. Try different types of conformity tasks and see whether some have higher or lower levels of female conformity, for example ask general knowledge questions which are related to male or female interests. The answers from previous 'participants' should be shown so you can see if your real participant conforms to the majority answer.

* **Sleep and age** Research suggests that people sleep less as they get older. Compare older and younger participants in terms of whether they have more or less than eight hours of sleep.

WILCOXON *T* TEST

The Wilcoxon test is a '*test of difference*'. What does this mean? A test of difference enables us to consider whether two samples of data are different or not different from each other.

The 'proper' name for the T test is the Wilcoxon matched pairs signed ranks test – what a mouthful! The reason for this name is that Frank Wilcoxon produced another well-known statistical test, called the Wilcoxon rank sums test, which is a difference test. This test is a difference test for independent samples. For ease of reference we have called the test for repeated measures the Wilcoxon T test because the statistic that is calculated for the Wilcoxon matched pairs signed ranks test is called T.

The Wilcoxon T test is not to be confused with the t-test (on pages 120–121).

Frank Wilcoxon (1892–196 an American chemist a statistici

Tests of difference are generally used for experiments. For example, we might conduct an experiment to see if noisy conditions reduce the effectiveness of revision.

Case A – we could have two groups of participants:
- Group 1: participants revise in a silent room and are tested.
- Group 2: a different group of participants revise in a noisy room and are tested.

Case B – we might have two conditions:
- Condition 1: participants revise in a silent room and are tested.
- Condition 2: the same participants revise in a noisy room and are tested.

Case C – we might have two matched groups of participants:
- Group 1: participants revise in a silent room and are tested.
- Group 2: a different group of participants, each matched to the participants in Group 1 revise in a noisy room and are tested.

Case A is an independent groups design (we have two separate groups of participants). The Mann–Whitney U Test (on the next spread) is used for independent groups designs when data are ordinal or better. Chi-squared (see previous spread) is used for independent groups design with nominal data.

Case B (two conditions) is a repeated measures design as the same participants are tested twice. The Wilcoxon T test is used for related measures when data are ordinal or better. The sign test (see page 116) is used for nominal data in a related measures design.

Case C is a matched pairs design. Even though this involves two separate groups of participants, the participants are related to each other and therefore this kind of experimental design also uses a repeated measures test.

In some experiments there are more than two conditions or groups – for example, the study by Loftus and Palmer (1974) on leading questions had five different groups according to which verb was in the sentence (smashed, hit, etc). There are specific inferential tests that are used for designs with more than two conditions/groups.

The Wilcoxon *T* test – a worked example (based on the mini study on the facing page)

STEP 1. State the alternative and null hypothesis

Alternative hypothesis: Participants rate the more frequently seen face as more likeable than the less frequently seen face. (This is a directional hypothesis and therefore requires a one-tailed test.)

Null hypothesis: There is no difference in the likeability score for faces seen more or less often.

STEP 2. Record the data, calculate the difference between scores and rank

Once you have worked out the difference, rank from low to high, ignoring the signs (i.e. the lowest number receives the rank of 1).

If there are two or more of the same number (tied ranks) calculate the rank by working out the mean of the ranks that would have been given.

If the difference is zero, omit this from the ranking and reduce N accordingly.

Participant	Likeability for **more** frequently seen face	Likeability for **less** frequently seen face	Difference	Rank
1	5	2	3	9.5
2	4	3	1	3
3	3	3	omit	
4	6	4	2	6.5
5	2	3	–1	3
6	4	5	–1	3
7	5	2	3	9.5
8	3	4	–1	3
9	6	3	3	9.5
10	4	6	–2	6.5
11	5	2	3	9.5
12	3	4	–1	3

STEP 3. Find the observed value of *T*

T = the sum of the *ranks* of the less frequent sign.
In this case the less frequent sign is minus,
so $T = 3 + 3 + 3 + 6.5 + 3 = 18.5$.

STEP 4. Find the critical value of *T*

$N = 11$ (one score omitted). The hypothesis is directional therefore a one-tailed test is used.
Look up the critical value in the table of critical values (see right).
For a one-tailed test, $N = 11$, the critical value of $T = 13$ ($p \le 0.05$).

STEP 5. State the conclusion

As the observed value (18.5) is greater than the critical value (13) we must accept the null hypothesis (at $p \le 0.05$) and conclude that there is no difference in the likeability score for faces seen more or less often.

Critical values of *T*

	Level of significance for a one-tailed test	
	0.05	0.01
	Level of significance for a two-tailed test	
	0.10	0.02
N = 5	0	
6	2	0
7	3	2
8	5	3
9	8	5
10	11	8
11	13	10
12	17	13
13	21	17
14	25	21
15	30	25
16	35	29
17	41	34
18	47	40
19	53	46
20	60	52
25	100	89
30	151	137

Observed value of *T* must be EQUAL TO or LESS THAN the critical value in this table for significance at the level shown.

Source: R. Meddis (1975). *Statistical Handbook for Non-statisticians*. London: McGraw Hill.

Justifying the choice of the Wilcoxon *T* test

The hypothesis states a *difference* between two sets of data.

The two sets of data are pairs of scores from one person (or a matched pair) = *related*.

The data are at least *ordinal* (i.e. not nominal). See page 104 for an explanation.

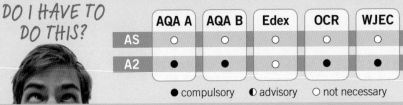

The mere exposure effect

There is a saying that 'familiarity breeds contempt', but psychological research has found that the opposite is generally true – we come to like things because of their familiarity. For example, people generally like a song more after they have heard it a few times, and advertisements often aim to increase our liking for a product through repeated exposure. Things that are familiar are less strange and threatening and thus become more likeable.

Robert Zajonc (pronounced 'zie-unts') conducted various experiments to demonstrate the *mere exposure effect*. For example, in one study Zajonc (1968) told participants that he was conducting a study on visual memory and showed them a set of photographs of 12 different men (face only). Each photograph was shown for two seconds. At the end participants were asked to rate how much they liked the 12 different men on a scale from 0 to 6. The key element of the study is that some photos were shown more often than others. One photo appeared 25 times whereas another only appeared once. Overall the frequencies were 0, 1, 2, 5, 10 and 25.

The same experiment was repeated with invented Chinese symbols and also with Turkish words. All the results are shown in the graph below.

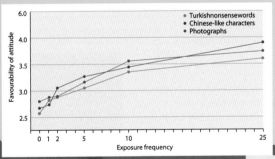

Who's face is nicest? According to the 'mere exposure effect' you should like the one you see most often.

I A psychologist designed a study to investigate whether short-term memory was better in the morning or the afternoon. The researcher decided to test participants in the morning and again in the afternoon. He used two different memory tests, one for the morning and one for the afternoon.

The participants were selected by placing an advertisement on a college noticeboard. The first 15 students who applied were selected.

The researcher expected the participants to do better in the morning.

(It may help you to understand the study if you invent some 'dummy' scores for the participants.)

a Write an appropriate alternative and null hypothesis for this study.

b Explain why the Wilcoxon *T* test would be the appropriate test to use with this data.

c For a one-tailed test and 5% level of significance, what is the maximum value of *T* that could be obtained and significance would still be shown?

d Identify the sampling method used in this study and explain **one** strength and **one** weakness of this sampling method.

e Two memory tests were used in this study. Explain why this was necessary.

f How could you establish whether the two memory tests were equivalent (i.e. that one test was not easier than the other).

g One problem with this study is that the students might do better in the afternoon because they had done a similar test in the morning. Therefore, the study was conducted again using a matched pairs design. Explain how this might be done (including the variables you would use for matching).

h Explain how counterbalancing could be used to deal with the order effects if a repeated measures design was used.

question 5.6

More ideas using a Wilcoxon *T* test

Mere exposure again The *mere exposure effect* can also be used to explain the fact that people prefer pictures of themselves that are reversed as in a mirror – because that is the way you usually see yourself and so it is more familiar (Mita *et al.*, 1977). You could take a few pictures of each participant with a digital camera and create a mirror image of the photograph. Show participants the photograph of themselves the right way and the mirror image, and record their ratings (on a scale of 1 to 5) for each photograph. Compare the ratings.

Smiling makes you happy You might think that you smile because you are feeling happy but psychological research shows it works the other way round too, i.e. you become happy because you are smiling. Laird (1974) told participants to contract certain facial muscles so he could measure facial muscular activity using electrodes. (You can also ask participants to bite on a pencil as a way of making them smile.) The instructions either resulted in something like a smile or like a frown. Participants who were made to 'smile' while rating cartoons for funniness, rated the cartoons as funnier than those who were made to produce a frown. You could replicate this by asking people to smile for some cartoons and frown for others, and rate each cartoon for humour.

Right brain left brain If you perform two tasks that involve the same brain hemisphere you should be slower on both tasks than if performing two tasks that involve the right and left hemispheres separately. For example, tap your right finger while reading a page from a book (both involve the left hemisphere). Then repeat the finger tapping without doing any reading. On each occasion count how many finger taps you manage in 30 seconds and compare these scores.

Graph (Favourability of attitude vs Exposure frequency)

Legend:
- Turkish nonsense words
- Chinese-like characters
- Photographs

Y-axis: Favourability of attitude (2.5 to 6.0)
X-axis: Exposure frequency (0, 1, 2, 5, 10, 25)

MANN–WHITNEY *U* TEST

This is a test of difference to be used when there are independent groups, i.e. where a study involves two groups of participants and each group is given a different level of the independent variable (IV). One group might work in a noisy condition whereas the other group works in silence (the IV is noise level), or one group might be tested in the morning and the other group tested in the afternoon (the IV is time of day).

The Mann–Whitney U test is named after the Austrian-born US mathematician Henry Berthold Mann and the US statistician Donald Ransom Whitney who published the test in 1947. They adapted a test designed by Frank Wilcoxon that was for equal sample sizes (called the Wilcoxon rank sum test – not the same as the one on the previous spread). The Mann–Whitney test can be used for groups of unequal size.

The Mann–Whitney *U* Test
– a worked example (based on the mini study on the facing page)

STEP 1. State the alternative and null hypothesis

Alternative hypothesis: Male participants interviewed on a high bridge give higher ratings of the attractiveness of a female interviewer than those interviewed on a low bridge. (This is a directional hypothesis and therefore requires a one-tailed test.)

Null hypothesis: There is no difference in the ratings of attractiveness given by those interviewed on a high or low bridge.

STEP 2. Record the data in a table and allocate points

To allocate points, consider each score one at a time.

Compare this score (the target) with all the scores in the other group.

Give 1 point for every score that is higher than the target score and 0.5 point for every equal score. Add these up to calculate the score for the target score.

Repeat for all scores.

STEP 3. Find the observed value of *U*

U is the lower total number of points. In this case it is 16.5.

STEP 4. Find the critical value of *U*

N_1 = number of participants in Group 1.

N_2 = number of participants in Group 2.

Look up the critical value in the table of critical values (below).

For a one-tailed test, $N_1 = 10$ and $N_2 = 14$, the critical value of $U = 41$ ($p \leq 0.05$).

NB When you have a directional hypothesis, remember to check whether the difference is in the direction that was stated in the alternative hypothesis.

Attractiveness ratings given by high bridge group	Points
7	1.5
10	0
8	1.0
6	3.5
5	7.0
8	1.0
9	0.5
7	1.5
10	0
9	0.5
N_1 = 10	16.5

Attractiveness ratings given by low bridge group	Points
4	10.0
6	8.5
2	10.0
5	9.5
3	10.0
5	9.5
6	8.5
4	10.0
5	9.5
7	7.0
9	3.0
3	10.0
5	9.5
6	8.5
N_2 = 14	123.5

STEP 5. State the conclusion

As the observed value (16.5) is less than the critical value (41) and the results are in the stated direction we can reject the null hypothesis (at $p \leq 0.05$) and therefore conclude that participants interviewed on a high bridge give higher ratings of attractiveness to a female interviewer than those interviewed on a low bridge, i.e. that physiological arousal leads to greater perceptions of attractiveness.

The two samples in the table above are unequal, which may happen when using an independent groups design.

Critical values of *U*

For a one-tailed test ($p \leq 0.05$)

N_2 \ N_1	2	3	4	5	6	7	8	9	10	11	12	13	14	15
2				0	0	0	1	1	1	1	2	2	2	3
3		0	0	1	2	2	3	3	4	5	5	6	7	7
4		0	1	2	3	4	5	6	7	8	9	10	11	12
5	0	1	2	4	5	6	8	9	11	12	13	15	16	18
6	0	2	3	5	7	8	10	12	14	16	17	19	21	23
7	0	2	4	6	8	11	13	15	17	19	21	24	26	28
8	1	3	5	8	10	13	15	18	20	23	26	28	31	33
9	1	3	6	9	12	15	18	21	24	27	30	33	36	39
10	1	4	7	11	14	17	20	24	27	31	34	37	41	44
11	1	5	8	12	16	19	23	27	31	34	38	42	46	50
12	2	5	9	13	17	21	26	30	34	38	42	47	51	55
13	2	6	10	15	19	24	28	33	37	42	47	51	56	61
14	2	7	11	16	21	26	31	36	41	46	51	56	61	66
15	3	7	12	18	23	28	33	39	44	50	55	61	66	72

For a two-tailed test ($p \leq 0.05$)

N_2 \ N_1	2	3	4	5	6	7	8	9	10	11	12	13	14	15
2							0	0	0	0	1	1	1	1
3			0	1	1	2	2	3	3	4	4	5	5
4		0	1	2	3	4	4	5	6	7	8	9	10
5	0	1	2	3	5	6	7	8	9	11	12	13	14
6	1	2	3	5	6	8	10	11	13	14	16	17	19
7	1	3	5	6	8	10	12	14	16	18	20	22	24
8	0	2	4	6	8	10	13	15	17	19	22	24	26	29
9	0	2	4	7	10	12	15	17	20	23	26	28	31	34
10	0	3	5	8	11	14	17	20	23	26	29	33	36	39
11	0	3	6	9	13	16	19	23	26	30	33	37	40	44
12	1	4	7	11	14	18	22	26	29	33	37	41	45	49
13	1	4	8	12	16	20	24	28	33	37	41	45	50	54
14	1	5	9	13	17	22	26	31	36	40	45	50	55	59
15	1	5	10	14	19	24	29	34	39	44	49	54	59	64

Observed value of *T* must be EQUAL TO or LESS THAN the critical value in this table for significance at the level shown.
Source: R. Meddis (1975). *Statistical Handbook for Non-statisticians*. London: McGraw Hill.

Justifying the choice of the Mann–Whitney *U* test

The hypothesis states a *difference* between two sets of data.

The two sets of data are from separate groups of participants = *independent groups*.

The data are at least *ordinal* (i.e. not nominal). See page 104 for an explanation.

DO I HAVE TO DO THIS?

	AQA A	AQA B	Edex	OCR	WJEC
AS	○	○	●	○	○
A2	●	●	◐	●	●

● compulsory ◐ advisory ○ not necessary

mini study

Falling in love

Psychologists have sought to explain the process of falling in love. One suggestion is that love is basically physiological arousal – arousal of your sympathetic nervous system which occurs when you are feeling scared or stressed or find someone physically attractive. Hatfield and Walster (1981) suggested that love is simply a label that we place on physiological arousal when it occurs in the presence of an appropriate object. A man or woman who meets a potential partner after an exciting football game is more likely to fall in love than he or she would be on a routine day. Likewise, a man or woman is more likely to fall in love when having experienced some bitter disappointment. The reason, in both cases, is to do with the two components of love: arousal and label.

This has been supported by various experiments, such as a memorable study by Dutton and Aron (1974). A female research assistant (unaware of the study's aims) interviewed males, explaining that she was doing a project for her psychology class on the effects of attractive scenery on creative expression. The interviews took place on a high suspension bridge (high arousal group) or a narrow bridge over a small stream (low arousal). When the interview was over, the research assistant gave the men her phone number and asked them to call her if they had any questions about the survey. Over 60% of the men in the high arousal condition did phone her compared with 30% from the low arousal group, suggesting that the men had mislabelled their fear-related arousal as sexual arousal.

The Capilano Suspension Bridge in Vancouver, Canada was used in the study by Dutton and Aron (see right). The bridge is narrow and long and has many arousal-inducing features: a tendency to tilt, sway and wobble, creating the impression that one is about to fall over the side; very low handrails of wire cable; and a 230-foot drop to rocks and shallow rapids below.

More ideas using a Mann–Whitney *U* test

Another study which investigated the two-factor theory of love was conducted by White *et al.* (1981). In this experiment high and low arousal was created by asking men to run on the spot for 2 minutes or 15 seconds respectively, and then showing a short video of a young woman. Those men who were more aroused (ran for 2 minutes) rated the woman as more attractive than those who were less aroused.

Digit ratio and gender (see page 109). You can collect data on the digit ratios of men and women and analyse it using the Mann–Whitney test by comparing the scores for men and women.

Time of day A number of studies have looked at how time of day affects our performance. For example, Gupta (1991) found that performance on IQ tests was best at 7pm as compared with 9am or 2pm, a factor which might be an important consideration when taking examinations.

Eyewitness testimony You could repeat the study by Loftus and Palmer (1974) using just two conditions (e.g. using the critical words 'hot' or 'smashed') and compare the speed estimates given by the two groups of participants.

1 Use descriptive statistics to summarise the results given in the worked example on the facing page, e.g. calculate measures of central tendency and dispersion, and also sketch an appropriate graph.

2 A psychology class decides to replicate the study by White *et al.* below.

  a Identify the independent and dependent variables in this study.

  b Write an appropriate alternative and null hypothesis for this study.

  c Is your alternative hypothesis directional or non-directional?

  d The students check the significance of their results using the Mann–Whitney test and find that $U = 40$ (there were 9 participants in one group and 13 in the other group). State what conclusion they could draw from their results at a 5% level of significance.

  e Explain how you might conduct this study, including how participants would be allocated to groups.

  f Explain why a video of a young woman was used to assess the dependent variable rather than a single photograph.

3 Another group of students decided to conduct an experiment looking at the effect of time of day on test performance, described below and on the previous spread. They used a matched pairs design.

  a Explain how this would be done. Include a description of at least two variables that would be used for matching. Explain why you choose these variables for matching.

  b What would be a suitable inferential test to use with this data? Justify your choice.

  c The students had 20 matched pairs and calculated an observed value of 60 for a two-tailed test (no tied scores). Would they accept or reject their null hypothesis at a 5% level of significance?

THE SIGN TEST

The sign test is anther 'test of difference'. This is used when analysing nominal data collected in a study with a repeated measures design.

The sign test – a worked example (based on the mini study on the facing page)

STEP 1. State the alternative and null hypothesis

Alternative hypothesis: People select the same gender as represented in their famous name category rather than selecting a different gender (the one actually most commonly represented). (This is a directional hypothesis and therefore requires a one-tailed test.)

Null hypothesis: There is no difference in the selection of gender.

STEP 2. Record the data and work out the sign

For each participant record the gender of the famous name category and the gender they select as the most common.

Then score a plus (+) if the two genders are the same or a minus (–) if genders selected are different.

Participant	Famous name category	Gender selected	Same?
1	male	female	–
2	male	female	–
3	male	male	+
4	male	female	–
5	male	male	+
6	male	male	+
7	female	female	+
8	female	female	+
9	female	male	–
10	female	female	+
11	female	male	–
12	female	female	+

STEP 3. Find the observed value of *S*

S = the number of times the less frequent value occurs.

In this case the less frequent sign is minus, so *S* = 5.

STEP 4. Find the critical value of *S*

N = the total number of scores (less any zero values).

In this case *N* = 12 (no scores omitted). The hypothesis is directional therefore a one-tailed test is used.

Look up the critical value in the table of critical values (see left).

For a one-tailed test, *N* = 12, the critical value of *S* = 2 ($p \leq 0.05$).

STEP 5. State the conclusion

As the observed value (5) is greater than the critical value (2) we must accept the null hypothesis (at $p \leq 0.05$) and conclude that there is no difference in the selection of gender.

Critical values of S

	0.05	0.01
Level of significance for a one-tailed test	0.05	0.01
Level of significance for a two-tailed test	0.10	0.02
N = 5	0	
6	0	0
7	0	0
8	1	0
9	1	1
10	1	1
11	2	1
12	2	2
13	3	2
14	3	2
15	3	3
16	4	3
17	4	4
18	5	4
19	5	4
20	5	5
25	7	7
30	10	9

Observed value of *S* must be EQUAL TO or LESS THAN the critical value in this table for significance to be shown.

Source: abridged from R.F. Clegg (1982). *Simple Statistics*. Cambridge: Cambridge University Press.

Justifying the choice of the sign test

The hypothesis states a *difference* between two sets of data.

The two sets of data are pairs of scores from one person (or a matched pair) = *related*.

The data are *nominal* (i.e. not ordinal or interval). See page 104 for an explanation.

mini study

The availability heuristic

Having said at the beginning of this chapter that people have quite a good intuitive sense of probability, it is important to point out that this is not always true. Psychologists have studied a number of cognitive biases that lead people to make inaccurate estimations of probability. One of these is the 'availability heuristic' – the likelihood of selecting something is related to its availability. This explains why people often overestimate the likelihood of dying in a car accident – it is because we read about such accidents often and therefore they are more available when making a probability judgement.

In one study Tversky and Kahneman (1973) read out male and female names to participants. Some of the names were famous names and some were not. Participants were then asked to estimate whether there were more male or female names in the list.

According to the availability heuristic participants should say 'male' if there were a lot of famous male names in the list because then 'male' is more available, and the same would apply if there were a lot of famous female names in the list.

One group of participants heard 19 famous male names and 20 less famous female names. A second group of participants heard 19 famous female names and 20 less famous male names (to counterbalance any gender effect). About 80% of participants' judgements were incorrect having been influenced by the famous names being more available and thus tipping the balance.

More ideas using a sign test

Another test of the availability heuristic Carroll (1978) conducted a study just before the US presidential election of 1979 between Gerald Ford and Jimmy Carter (Jimmy Carter eventually won). In this study one group of participants was asked to imagine Gerald Ford winning the election. A second group was told to imagine Jimmy Carter winning the election.

Later participants were asked who they thought would win. They tended to name the person they had been asked to imagine (i.e. who was most 'available' to them). You can adapt this study to something more current.

Evidence for extra sensory perception (ESP) In the early days of ESP testing, Zener cards (also called ESP cards) were used (shown on right). Each pack consisted of 25 cards, five each of each design. The cards were intended to be emotionally neutral to remove any response bias. A 'sender' (or agent) views each of the cards in the pack in turn and a 'receiver' guesses the symbol on that card. Before a trial begins the cards are placed in a random order. In order to demonstrate ESP a person must get more than five cards right – five is the level that would be expected by chance. Therefore, you score a plus if more than five cards are right, otherwise you score a minus.

Inattentional blindness refers to the fact people often fail to notice some stimulus that is in plain sight. Simons and Chabris (1999) memorably demonstrated this in a film of a basketball game where participants are asked to count the number of passes made by the white team. At the end they are asked if they saw anything unusual. Many people fail to notice a man dressed in a gorilla suit walking through the players. To get a film of this search YouTube for 'Gorilla Basketball'. The original is called 'selective attention test'.

1 If you decided to conduct a study on the availability heuristic (see left):

a Identify **one or more** problems that might arise when conducting the study.

b Suggest how you might deal with these problem(s).

c Explain why the sign test is a suitable test to use for this study.

d On the facing page there is a set of data from a study to test the availability heuristic. Decide on the best way to represent this data graphically and draw a suitable graph.

e With 12 participants and a one-tailed test, what value of S is required for significance to be shown?

2 A study on ESP is described below left.

a State a possible alternative and null hypothesis for this study.

b Is your alternative hypothesis directional or non-directional?

c Describe how you could obtain a volunteer sample for this study.

d Suggest an alternative sampling method and explain in what way this would be a better method than using a volunteer sample.

e Explain why the sign test would be the appropriate test to use with this data.

f A researcher conducted this study with 16 participants. The observed value of S was 4. For a one-tailed test at the 5% significance level, would we reject the null hypothesis? Explain your answer.

g If the value of S was 4, what would the data be for this set of results?

3 The data on page 112 could be analysed using the sign test. Try to do this and see what result you get.

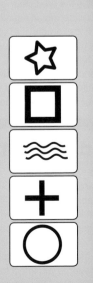

PARAMETRIC STATISTICS

Parametric statistics are preferred to non-parametric statistics because they are more powerful. However, they can only be used under certain circumstances.

Parametric assumptions

Some inferential tests can only be used if the data fit parametric assumptions. These assumptions are:

Assumption	Explanation	How to decide
The level of measurement is interval or ratio.	See an explanation of levels of measurement on page 104. **Plastic interval scales** are acceptable.	Are the intervals between the data truly equal interval?
The data are drawn from a population that has a normal distribution.	Note that it is not the sample that must be normally distributed but the **population**. A normal distribution is when most scores cluster around the mean with an equal number of scores above and below the mean, as illustrated below.	We expect many physical and psychological characteristics to be normally distributed, such as height, shoe sizes, IQ and friendliness. Therefore, you can justify the use of a parametric test by saying that the characteristic measured is assumed to be normal. You could also check scores to see if they are skewed or not (more scores on one side of the mean than the other side).
The **variances** of the two samples are not significantly different.	The variance is a measure of how spread out a set of data is around the mean. It is the square of the **standard deviation**.	This only matters when looking at **independent groups**. In the case of **repeated measures** (related samples) any difference in the variances should not distort the result (Coolican, 1996). For independent groups you can check the variances. The variance of one sample should not be more than four times the variance of the other.

However, parametric tests are quite robust – therefore they are reliable unless the parametric assumptions are met quite poorly.

What does 'powerful' mean?

Parametric statistical tests make calculations using the mean and standard deviation of a data set whereas non-parametric tests use ranked data, thus losing some of the detail.

The end result is that parametric tests can detect significance in some situations where non-parametric tests can't.

For example, imagine two sets of data collected from an independent group experiment. There is a small differences between the two data sets, and using the Mann–Whitney test the differences are found to be non-significant. However, if a parametric test is used it is possible that the increased power (like a magnifying glass) might actually be able to detect significance.

This means that, whenever possible, researchers prefer use parametric statistics.

Normal distribution

The normal distribution has the classic bell-shaped curve. It is the predicted distribution when considering an equally-likely set of results. For example, if a light bulb has a mean life time of 100 hours we would expect some light bulbs to last a little less than this and some to last a little more. If we plot the lifetime of 1000 light bulbs we would get a normal distribution.

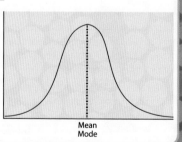
Mean
Mode

Skewed distribution

In some populations scores are not distributed equally around the mean. Consider a test of depression where 0–50 represents normal behaviour, and 50+ represents chronic depression. We would expect most scores to be towards the low end rather than the high end of this score range. The few high scores will affect the mean and produce a skewed distribution as illustrated (right). A data set like this would not be suitable for parametric statistics.

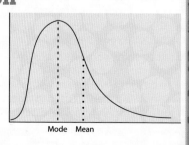
Mode   Mean

Choosing which parametric test to use

On page 107 there is a diagram guiding you in your choice of non-parametric tests. There are some additional choices to make when considering parametric tests.

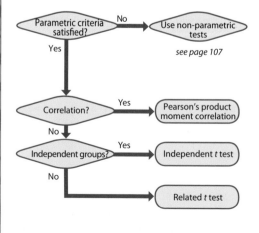

Parametric criteria satisfied? — No → Use non-parametric tests
see page 107

Yes ↓

Correlation? — Yes → Pearson's product moment correlation

No ↓

Independent groups? — Yes → Independent *t* test

No ↓

Related *t* test

key terms

- Independent groups
- Interval
- Normal distribution
- Plastic interval scale
- Population
- Ratio
- Repeated measures
- Standard deviation
- Variance

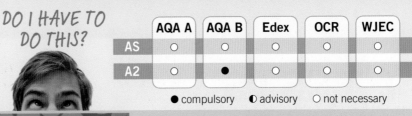

Justifying the choice of Pearson's product–moment correlation

The hypothesis states a *correlation* between two variables
The *two sets of data* are pairs of scores from one person or thing = *related*.
The data fit *parametric assumptions* (see facing page).

The Pearson's product–moment correlation – a worked example

STEP 1. State the alternative and null hypothesis

Alternative hypothesis: A person's age is positively correlated with the number of items they can remember on a memory test, an older person would have a high score on the memory test and a younger person would have a lower score on the memory test. (This is a directional hypothesis and therefore requires a one-tailed test.)

Null hypothesis: There is no correlation between age and recall on a memory test.

STEP 2. Record the data and calculations in a table

Calculate the mean for each data set.
Use the mean to calculate the figures in columns 3 and 6.
Calculate columns 4 and 7 by squaring the numbers in columns 3 and 6.
Calculate column 8 (multiple column 3 × column 7).

1	2	3	4	5	6	7	8
Participant	*x* Age (in years)	*x* − mean of *x*	Square this	*y* Score on test	*y* − mean of *y*	Square this	Multiply col 3 × col 7
1	12	−10.9	118.81	46	−6.1	37.21	66.49
2	27	4.1	16.81	64	11.9	141.61	48.79
3	20	−2.9	8.41	43	−9.1	82.81	26.39
4	18	−4.9	24.01	40	−12.1	146.41	59.29
5	33	10.1	102.01	35	−17.1	292.41	−172.71
6	36	13.1	171.61	68	15.9	252.81	208.29
7	16	−6.9	47.61	52	−0.1	0.01	0.69
8	13	−9.9	98.01	48	−4.1	16.81	40.59
9	15	−7.9	62.41	55	2.9	8.41	−22.91
10	39	16.1	259.21	70	17.9	320.41	288.19
N = 10	Mean x = 22.9		Sum of column 4 =908.9	Mean y = 52.1		Sum of column 7 = 1298.9	Sum of column 8 = 543.1

STEP 3. Find the observed value of *r*

$$r = \frac{\text{sum of column 8}}{\sqrt{(\text{sum of column 4} \times \text{sum of column 7})}}$$

$$= \frac{543.1}{\sqrt{(908.9 \times 1298.9)}} = .4998.$$

STEP 4. Find the critical value of *r*

Look up critical value in table of critical values (on the right).

$df = N - 2$

For a one-tailed test, $df = 8$, the critical value of $r = .549$ ($p \leq 0.05$).

See note on page 108 on negative correlations.

STEP 5. State the conclusion

As the observed value (.4998) is less than the critical value (.549) we must accept the null hypothesis (at $p \leq 0.05$) and conclude that there is no correlation between a person's age and recall on a memory test.

Critical values of *r*

	Level of significance for a one-tailed test	
	0.05	0.01
	Level of significance for a two-tailed test	
	0.10	0.02
df = (N − 2)		
2	.9000	.9500
3	.805	.878
4	.729	.811
5	.669	.754
6	.621	.707
7	.582	.666
8	.549	.632
9	.521	.602
10	.497	.576
11	.476	.553
12	.475	.532
13	.441	.514
14	.426	.497
15	.412	.482
16	.400	.468
17	.389	.456
18	.378	.444
19	.369	.433
20	.360	.423
25	.323	.381
30	.296	.349

Observed value of *r* must be EQUAL TO or GREATER THAN the critical value in this table for significance to be shown.

Source: J.F.C. Powell (1976). *Cambridge Mathematical and Statistical Tables.* Cambridge: Cambridge University Press.

question 5.9

1 With the following designs and data, which test should you use?

a Ordinal data on both measures in a study to see if two measures are associated.

b Interval data collected from an experiment with a matched pairs design.

c An experiment with an independent groups design in which the DV is measured on an interval scale.

d A study using a correlational technique in which one measure is ordinal and the other is ratio.

e A field experiment producing nominal data with an independent groups design.

f A study testing an association using a nominal level of measurement.

g A study using a correlational technique in which one measure is ratio and the other is ordinal.

2 Two studies are described below. For each study answer the questions a–g.

- A research study investigates the correlation between a person's scores on two personality tests, expecting to find a positive correlation. There were 20 participants involved in the study. The observed value that was calculated was +.433.

- Another study investigates the correlation between a person's reaction time and score on a memory test, expecting to find a negative correlation because reaction times are lower the faster you get. Fifteen participants were tested and the observed value that was calculated was −.521.

a Is this data suitable for a parametric or non-parametric test?

b What test would have been used to calculate the observed value? Explain your choice of test.

c If the hypothesis is non-directional, should you use a one-tailed or two-tailed test?

d Select an appropriate significance level and explain the reasons for your choice.

e Determine the appropriate critical value for this test.

f Should the null hypothesis be retained?

g Draw a sketch of what the scattergram for this data would look like.

t TESTS

t tests are tests of difference, used on data which fulfil the parametric assumptions described on the previous spread. The related t test is used for repeated measures designs as well as matched pairs. The independent t test is used for independent groups design.

The t test should not be confused with the T test (see page 112) which is a non-parametric test of difference for related measures.

Justifying the choice of the related t test

The hypothesis states a *difference* between two sets of data.

The two sets of data are pairs of scores from one person (or a matched pair) = *related*.

The data fit *parametric assumptions* (see explanation on page 118).

The related t test – a worked example
(based on the study described on page 129)

STEP 1. State the alternative and null hypothesis

Alternative hypothesis: People remember more words that are deeply processed (semantic condition) than words that are shallowly processed (rhyme condition). (This is a directional hypothesis and therefore requires a one-tailed test.)

Null hypothesis: There is no difference in the number of words remembered in the deeply processed or shallowly processed conditions.

STEP 2. Record the data and calculations in a table

Participant	Number of words recalled		Difference	d^2
	Semantic condition	Rhyme condition		
1	21	18	3	9
2	18	19	−1	1
3	25	22	3	9
4	12	16	−4	16
5	16	13	3	9
6	8	9	−1	1
7	18	16	2	4
8	24	20	4	16
9	21	14	7	49
10	16	17	−1	1
N = 10	Mean = 17.9	Mean = 16.4	15	171

STEP 3. Find the observed value of t

$$t = \frac{\sum d}{\sqrt{((N\sum d^2 - (\sum d)^2)/N - 1)}} = \frac{15}{\sqrt{(10 \times 171 - 15 \times 15)/9}} = 1.170$$

You will not be required to calculate any statistic in an exam – and can just use an online calculator such as www.graphpad.com/quickcalcs/ttest1.cfm (select 'paired t test').

STEP 4. Find the critical value of t

Look up critical value in table of critical values (on the right).

df = N – 1

For a one-tailed test, *df* = 9, the critical value of *t* = 1.833 ($p \leq 0.05$).

STEP 5. State the conclusion

As the observed value (1.170) is less than the critical value (1.833) we must accept the null hypothesis (at $p \leq 0.05$), and conclude that there is no difference in the number of words remembered in the deeply processed or shallowly processed conditions.

Critical values of t

Level of significance for a one-tailed test	0.05	0.01
Level of significance for a two-tailed test	0.10	0.02
df = (N – 2)		
1	6.314	12.706
2	2.920	4.303
3	2.353	3.182
4	2.132	2.776
5	2.015	2.571
6	1.943	2.447
7	1.895	2.365
8	1.860	2.306
9	1.833	2.262
10	1.812	2.228
11	1.796	2.201
12	1.782	2.179
13	1.771	2.160
14	1.761	2.145
15	1.753	2.131
16	1.746	2.120
17	1.740	2.110
18	1.734	2.101
19	1.729	2.093
20	1.725	2.086
25	1.708	2.060
30	1.697	2.042

Observed value of t must be EQUAL TO or GREATER THAN the critical value in this table for significance to be shown.

Source: abridged from R.A. Fisher and F. Yates (1982). *Statistical Tables for Biological, Agricultural and Medical Research*. (6th edition). London: Longman. Reproduced with permission by Pearson Education Limited.

When using the independent or related t-test, remember to check whether the sign of t is in the expected direction. If it is not, then you cannot reject the null hypothesis.

Why should you use a parametric test when non-parametric tests are easier to calculate?

Parametric tests are more powerful, which means that if a non-parametric test does not find a significant difference/correlation between samples a parametric test may do so because it is more sensitive.

DO I HAVE TO DO THIS?

	AQA A	AQA B	Edex	OCR	WJEC
AS	○	○	○	○	○
A2	○	●	○	○	○

● compulsory   ◑ advisory   ○ not necessary

Justifying the choice of the independent *t* test

The hypothesis states a *difference* between two sets of data.

The two sets of data are from separate groups of participants = *independent* samples.

The data fit *parametric assumptions* (see explanation on page 118).

The independent *t* test – a worked example (based on the study described on page 30)

STEP 1. State the alternative and null hypothesis

Alternative hypothesis: Female confederates receive help more quickly than male confederates. (This is a directional hypothesis and therefore requires a one-tailed test.)

Null hypothesis: There is no difference in the time taken to give help to female and male confederates.

STEP 2. Record the data in a table

Time (in seconds) for males to be helped	Time (in seconds) for females to be helped
56	74
34	96
49	83
74	80
61	40
30	22
52	97
83	121
110	92
43	73
	93
	85
$N_A = 10$	$N_B = 12$
Mean = 59.2	Mean = 86.75

STEP 3. Find the observed value of *t*

The data in the table are used to calculate the observed value of *t*. The formula for the independent *t* test is lengthy so this time an online calculator was used.

The observed value of *t* = 1.882

STEP 4. Find the critical value of *t*

Look up critical value in table of critical values (on the left).
Calculating $df = N_A + N_B - 2 = 10 + 12 - 2 = 20$
For a one-tailed test, $df = 20$, the critical value of $t = 1.725$ ($p \leq 0.05$)

STEP 5. State the conclusion

As the observed value (1.882) is greater than the critical value (1.725) it would appear that we could reject the null hypothesis. However, a check of the mean values shows that the direction of difference is not in the predicted direction. Therefore, we cannot reject the null hypothesis and we can conclude that there is no difference in the time taken to give help to female and male confederates.

1 In a study on memory, participants are given two word lists to learn. One list is organised into categories and the other is unorganised. The researcher expects to find a difference in the recall of the two lists.

  a Is the hypothesis directional or non-directional?

  b What would be a suitable inferential test to use with this data? Explain your answer.

  c If there were 12 participants and the significance level was set at $p \leq 0.05$, what is the lowest observed value that would be significant?

2 The same study is repeated but this time two groups of participants are used – one group is given the organised list and the other group is given the disorganised list. In the first study it was found that participants remembered more from the organised list.

  a Is the hypothesis directional or non-directional?

  b Give **two** reasons why you could use a parametric test with this data.

  c There were ten participants in each group. Calculate *df* for this number of participants.

  d If the significance level was set at $p \leq 0.05$, would the results be significant if the observed value of the statistic was 1.931?

3 Some students investigate whether students have faster reaction times in the morning or in the afternoon. They expected that reactions times will be faster in the morning. The observed value of *t* for 20 students is calculated to be –1.92.

  a Is the hypothesis directional or non-directional?

  b What would be a suitable inferential test to use with this data? Explain your answer.

  c If the significance level was set at $p \leq 0.05$, would the observed value be significant?

  d Would you reject or retain the null hypothesis?

mini study

Testing the power of parametric statistics

For this 'study' create a set of dummy data for, example ten pairs of scores. Use an online calculator (see below) to work out the observed value for the following statistics:

- The Wilcoxon matched pairs signed ranks *T* test (for related data).
- The Mann-Whitney *U* test (or Wilcoxon rank sum test) for independent groups).
- The related *t* test.
- The independent *t* test.

Change the data and see how it affects the significance levels. You should find some data sets where the observed statistic is not significant when using a non-parametric statistic but is significant using a parametric one.

Online statistics calculators:

http://www.socr.ucla.edu/htmls/SOCR_Analyses.html
http://easycalculation.com/statistics/statistics.php
For *U* test: http://elegans.som.vcu.edu/~leon/stats/utest.html

1. The null hypothesis is a statement of:
   a. No findings.
   b. No difference.
   c. No significance.
   d. No trouble.

2. The abbreviation *p* stands for:
   a. Primary.
   b. Prediction.
   c. Promise.
   d. Probability.

3. $p < 0.01$ means:
   a. There is less than a 10% chance that results occurred by chance.
   b. There is more than a 1% chance that results occurred by chance.
   c. There is less than a 1% chance that results occurred by chance.
   d. There is less than a 99% chance that results occurred by chance.

4. The term falsifiability refers to the fact that:
   a. Most hypotheses are false.
   b. A hypothesis cannot be proved, it can only be disproved.
   c. The intention is to disprove a null hypothesis.
   d. All swans are white.

5. Inferential tests draw inferences from:
   a. A research sample to the population.
   b. A research sample to another research sample.
   c. The population to the research sample.
   d. All of the above.

6. Data that are in categories are called:
   a. Nominal data.
   b. Ordinal data.
   c. Interval data.
   d. Ratio data.

7. Strictly speaking, data from a rating scale are:
   a. Nominal data.
   b. Ordinal data.
   c. Interval data.
   d. Ratio data.

8. Data that is measured using units of equal measurement are:
   a. Nominal data.
   b. Ordinal data.
   c. Interval data.
   d. Intelligent data.

9. The test statistic calculated for Wilcoxon's test is:
   a. *T*
   b. *t*
   c. *rho*
   d. *U*

10. The actual value that is calculated for a test statistic is called the:
    a. Observed value.
    b. Calculated value.
    c. Critical value.
    d. Both a and b.

11. The abbreviation *df* stands for:
    a. Degrees of figure.
    b. Degraded figure.
    c. Degrees of freedom.
    d. Degree of fun.

12. Generally *df* is equivalent to the:
    a. Number of participants in a study.
    b. Highest data number collected.
    c. Importance of the study.
    d. Probability.

13. The significance level most commonly used in psychology is:
    a. 10%
    b. 5%
    c. 2%
    d. 1%

14. Which of the following is another way to write 5%?
    a. 0.5
    b. 0.05%
    c. 0.5
    d. 0.05

15. If an experiment has a directional hypothesis, the type of test used is called a:
    a. One-tailed test.
    b. Two-tailed test.
    c. Three-tailed test.
    d. 5% test.

16. A Type 1 error is a:
    a. false positive.
    b. false negative.
    c. true positive.
    d. true negative.

17. A Type 2 error occurs when:
    a. The null hypothesis is wrongly rejected.
    b. The alternative hypothesis is wrongly rejected.
    c. The alternative hypothesis is wrong.
    d. The alternative hypothesis is wrongly accepted.

18. A Type 2 error is more likely to happen when the required significance level is:
    a. Not reached.
    b. Too high (e.g. 1%).
    c. Not set.
    d. Too low (e.g. 10%).

19. What would be the appropriate test to select if you conducted an experiment with a repeated measures design and ordinal level data?
    a. Spearman's rank order correlation test.
    b. Chi-squared test.
    c. Wilcoxon *T* test.
    d. Mann–Whitney *U* test.

20. What would be the appropriate test to select if you conducted a study with ordinal data and requiring a correlational analysis?
    a. Spearman's rank order correlation test.
    b. Chi-squared test.
    c. Wilcoxon *T* test.
    d. Mann–Whitney *U* test.

Answers on facing page

EXAM STYLE QUESTION 9

An experiment was conducted to test context effects on memory. Past research has found that people remember more if they are tested in the same room as where original learning took place.

A group of psychology students replicated this study using a class of students in their school. The class were all taught maths in the same room. For the psychology experiment the students were divided into two groups. Group A did a maths test in their usual classroom and Group B did the maths test in a different classroom.

The table below shows the results of the study. A statistical test was carried out and was significant at $p \leq 0.01$.

Group A		Group B	
Student number	Score on maths test	Student number	Score on maths test
1	15	16	10
2	18	17	7
3	20	18	14
4	15	19	8
5	16	20	10
6	11	21	7
7	25	22	9
8	21	23	11
9	24	24	15
10	18	25	9
11	19	26	4
12	19	27	8
13	23	28	12
14	21	29	10
15	15	30	10
Mean	18.67	Mean	9.6
Median	18	Median	10
Mode	15	Mode	10
Standard deviation	3.84	Standard deviation	2.77

(a) (i) Write down a suitable alternative hypothesis for the above study. *(2 marks)*

(ii) For the hypothesis you have written, explain whether a one-tailed or two-tailed statistical test would be appropriate. *(2 marks)*

(iii) What does 'one- or two-tailed' mean? *(2 marks)*

(b) (i) Identify the experimental design used in this study. *(1 mark)*

(ii) Explain **one** strength and **one** weakness of this design in this study. *(2 marks + 2 marks)*

(c) Identify a suitable statistical test for this study. Give reasons for your choice. *(1 mark + 3 marks)*

(d) (i) What does the expression 'a statistical test ... was significant at $p \leq 0.01$' mean? *(2 marks)*

(ii) Explain why a researcher might use a 0.01 level of significance instead of 0.10. *(2 marks)*

(iii) Explain why a Type 2 error is more likely when using a 0.01 level of significance. *(2 marks)*

(e) Explain what the standard deviation tells us about the two groups of data. *(3 marks)*

(f) (i) Sketch a suitable graph for the data in the table above. *(4 marks)*

(ii) What conclusions about the effect of context on memory can you draw from your graph? *(2 marks)*

(g) The mean, median and mode were calculated for each data set. Explain which measure would be the most useful. *(2 marks)*

Examiner's tips for answering this question

(a) (i) Always include both levels of the independent variable in a hypothesis and operationalise as far as possible.

(a) (ii) The question says 'explain' and there are 2 marks available. Both of these are clues that you need to do more than just say 'one-tailed' or 'two-tailed'.

(b) (i) This time only a simple 1-mark answer.

(b) (ii) The question states 'in this study' which means that, for full marks, you must contextualise your answer. In order to do this you must be careful to select a strength/weakness that is appropriate.

(c) You must state the appropriate test (some students forget this bit!) and then must make three relevant points to get full marks.

(d) (i) Take care to avoid the mistake of thinking that 0.01 is 10% or even 0.01%.

(d) (ii) The term 'explain' means you are required to give more than a simple answer. For full marks there must be some elaboration in your answer.

(d) (iii) For full marks you must mention the null hypothesis in your answer.

(e) Again 'explain' means going further than a simple statement, e.g. just saying one is bigger than the other. What does this size difference mean?

(f) (i) There is no need to draw a precise graph as only a sketch is required. However, you will need to make sure the graph is carefully labelled and appropriate for the data. A graph showing every participant's score will gain no marks.

(f) (ii) Any question asking for conclusions requires more than simply stating the findings. Conclusions should be linked to the original aims of the study.

(g) Yet another question with the word 'explain' requiring more than a simple statement as an answer. Use your knowledge of relative strengths/weaknesses of the measures of central tendency to provide an elaborated answer.

EXAM STYLE QUESTION 10

There is a saying that 'hunger is the best cook'. A psychologist decided to test the relationship between hungriness and the tastiness of food. He prepared a dish of scrambled eggs and toast for 20 participants. Before each participant started to eat, he asked them how long it was since they had last eaten. After they had the meal he asked them to rate the tastiness of the meal on a scale of 1 to 10 where 10 was very tasty.

The alternative hypothesis for this study was 'Time since participants last ate (in hours) is positively correlated with the tastiness rating of food'.

The psychologist plotted his findings as shown below.

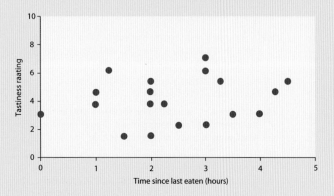

Graph showing the relationship between hungriness and tastiness

(a) Describe the aims of this study. *(2 marks)*

(b) How were hungriness and tastiness operationalised? *(2 marks + 2 marks)*

(c) This study uses a correlational analysis. Describe **one** strength and **one** weakness of a study using this method of analysis. *(2 marks + 2 marks)*

(d) Write a suitable null hypothesis for this study. *(2 marks)*

(e) (i) The correlation coefficient calculated was +.15. What is meant by the term 'correlation coefficient'? *(2 marks)*

(ii) Using the table of critical values on the right, state whether the correlation coefficient is significant at the $p \leq 0.05$ level. Explain your answer. *(3 marks)*

(iii) Using the correlation coefficient and/or the scattergraph, describe the relationship between the two variables in this study. *(2 marks)*

(f) (i) Explain what is meant by reliability. *(2 marks)*

(ii) Tastiness is measured using a rating scale. How could you check the reliability of this scale? *(2 marks)*

(g) The psychologist decides to conduct another study to research the relationship between hunger and food. This time he decides to conduct an experiment with two independent groups of participants. One group will be hungry and the other will not be hungry. He intends to see which group will rate photographs of food as being more attractive.

Describe how you would conduct this study, include all important design details, such as selection of participants, allocation to groups and details of the procedure. Ethical issues could also be included. *(8 marks)*

Critical values of *rho*

Level of significance for a one-tailed test	0.05	0.01
Level of significance for a two-tailed test	0.10	0.02
N = 10	.564	.648
11	.536	.618
12	.503	.587
13	.484	.560
14	.464	.538
15	.443	.521
16	.429	.503
17	.414	.485
18	.401	.472
19	.391	.460
20	.380	.447
25	.337	.398
30	.306	.362

Observed value of *rho* must be EQUAL TO or GREATER THAN the critical value in this table for significance to be shown.

MODEL ANSWERS

A model answer is an answer that would get full marks. However, it isn't the only answer that would get full marks, it is simply one possible answer.

Exam style question 9

(a) (i) Write down a suitable alternative hypothesis for the above study. *(2 marks)*
There is a difference between the memory test results of students tested in the classroom where they were taught and students tested in a different classroom.

(ii) For the hypothesis you have written, explain whether a one-tailed or two-tailed statistical test would be appropriate. *(2 marks)*
A two-tailed test would be appropriate because it is a non-directional hypothesis.

(iii) What does 'one- or two-tailed' mean? *(2 marks)*
One-tailed means are stating the direction of an effect, e.g. whether scores will be better or worse on one condition than the other.
Two-tailed means you are not stating the direction of the difference.

(b) (i) Identify the experimental design used in this study. *(1 mark)*
Independent groups.

(ii) Explain one strength and one weakness of this design in this study. *(2 marks + 2 marks)*
One strength is that participants won't do better the second time around because they have already done the test once.
A weakness is that one group may do better than the other because there are better students in that group. In other words, participant variables are not controlled.

(c) Identify a suitable statistical test for this study. Give reasons for your choice. *(1 mark + 3 marks)*
The Mann–Whitney test would be suitable because (1) a test of difference is required because we are comparing two sets of data, (2) a test for independent groups is required because the data is from two independent groups (Group A tested in their classroom and Group B tested elsewhere), and (3) the data is ordinal because a rating scale was used.

(d) (i) What does the expression 'a statistical test ... was significant at $p \leq 0.01$' mean? *(2 marks)*
It means that there is a less than 1% probability that the results obtained are due to chance.

(ii) Explain why a researcher might use a 0.01 level of significance instead of 0.10. *(2 marks)*
The 0.01 level is used when psychologists want to be more certain – such as when they are conducting a replication of a previous study or considering the effects of a new drug on health.

(iii) Explain why a Type 2 error is more likely when using a 0.01 level of significance. *(2 marks)*
Using a more stringent level of significance (0.01) means that you are less likely to reject the null hypothesis and therefore may accept one that is in fact false.

(e) Explain what the standard deviation tells us about the two groups of data. *(3 marks)*
The standard deviation of Group B is smaller than for Group A which shows us that the data are closer to the mean. This suggests that the students in Group B were of more similar ability.

(f) (i) Sketch a suitable graph for the data in the table above. *(4 marks)*
A graph must be clearly labelled and could display the mean, median, mode and/ or standard deviation for both groups but NOT the individual scores of participants.

(ii) What conclusions about the effect of context on memory can you draw from your graph? *(2 marks)*
The graph shows that students who were tested in the same classroom did better on the memory test, which suggests that contextual cues do improve memory.

(g) The mean, median and mode were calculated for each data set. Explain which measure would be the most useful. *(2 marks)*
The mean would be most useful because it reflects the values of each score in the final analysis. As there are no outliers it is not necessary to use the median.

Exam style question 10

(a) Describe the aims of this study. *(2 marks)*
The aims of this study are to find out if being hungry affects a person's judgement about how good food tastes.

(b) How were hungriness and tastiness operationalised? *(2 marks + 2 marks)*
Hungriness was operationalised in terms of the length of time (in hours) since a person last ate.
Tastiness was operationalised by asking people to rate how tasty they thought the food was.

(c) This study uses a correlational analysis. Describe one strength and one weakness of a study using this method of analysis. *(2 marks + 2 marks)*
One strength is that you can make use of existing data.
One weakness is that a causal relationship is not shown though people often mistakenly assume that it has been shown.

(d) Write a suitable null hypothesis for this study. *(2 marks)*
This is no relationship between how hungry a person is and the tastiness rating they give for food.

(e) (i) What is meant by the term 'correlation coefficient'? *(2 marks)*
It refers to a number that represents the extent to which two variables are related.

(ii) Using the table of critical values on the right, state whether the correlation coefficient is significant at the $p \leq 0.05$ level. Explain your answer. *(2 marks)*
The hypothesis is directional so a one-tailed test is required for 20 participants. The critical value is .380. As the observed value (+.15) is lower this means the result is not significant.

(iii) Using the correlation coefficient and/or the scattergraph, describe the relationship between the two variables in this study. *(2 marks)*
The relationship is a weak positive correlation.

(f) (i) Explain what is meant by reliability. *(2 marks)*
Reliability refers to consistency, that you would expect to get the same result again if you did the exact same measurement (same person with same test).

(ii) Tastiness is measured using a rating scale. How could you check the reliability of this scale? *(2 marks)*
You could use the scale with a sample group of people and get them to rate some food once, and then ask them to rate the same food on another occasion to see if both scores were the same (test–retest).

(g) Describe how you would conduct this study. *(8 marks)*
I would obtain 20 participants using opportunity sampling (e.g. just asking any students I saw in the common room).
The first 10 students would be placed in the 'hunger group'. This group would be deprived of food for 6 hours before the test. To ensure they did this, they would have to report to the lab 6 hours before testing.
The other group would also report at this time but they would be given two meals in the 6 hours.
It would be important for participants to be given full details before agreeing to take part – telling the students in the hunger group that they would have no food for 6 hours.
After 6 hours both groups of participants would be shown 10 pictures of food and asked to rate each picture.

6

Designing and reporting your own research

DESIGNING YOUR OWN STUDY

PAGES 128–129

Design decisions to be made when conducting an experiment or a study using a correlational analysis.

mini study Levels of processing

DESIGNING YOUR OWN STUDY CONTINUED

PAGES 130–131

Our look at designing research continues with questionnaires, interviews, observations and content analysis.

mini study Content analysis of magazine or newspaper article

REPORTING A RESEARCH STUDY

PAGES 132–133

All the research studies that form part of your A level psychology course were published in a psychological journal. The report follows certain conventions of presentation.

mini study Coursework

VALIDATING KNOWLEDGE

PAGES 134–135

Looking at the role of peer review in verifying the validity of published research.

mini study Saved the best to last

DESIGNING YOUR OWN STUDY

A good way to assess a student's understanding of research methods is to ask the student to design a research study. Therefore 'design a study' questions are a popular form of exam assessment. The questions on the facing page are examples of such 'design a study' questions.

These questions tend to be quite challenging for students – probably because students lack the experience to think on their feet about research design, especially under the stress of exam conditions.

Throughout this book there have been many suggested activities to help you practise the skills of research design and to help you improve your understanding.

On this spread (and the next one) there are opportunities to further develop these design skills.

In an exam question you may just be asked to write about one part of the design, such as the procedures or just the informed consent form.

The term 'procedures' is somewhat undefined and can include sampling techniques, ethical issues and problems with to validity, because that is part of what you would actually do, but it would not include treatment of results.

'Procedures' means a set of actions or operations. It is defined as a fixed, step-by-step sequence of activities or course of action (with definite start and end points) that must be followed in the same order to perform a specific objective.

Sometimes the word 'method' is used instead of 'procedure'.

Replication is the key to providing procedural detail. In the OCR Unit 4 exam the questions say 'Describe the method you would use to conduct your practical project. 13 marks are awarded for replicability and appropriateness and 6 for the quality of the design and its feasibility'. Note that 'replication' is a key criterion.

Designing an experiment or a study using a correlational analysis

When answering an exam question and, when identifying design decisions to be made, explain the reasons for your choices.

Preliminary decisions

1. Formulate research question/aims	The research question/aims are likely to be given to you in the exam question.
	Decide on target population.
2. Identify the independent and dependent variables (IV and DV) or the co-variables	Decide on the levels of the IV (pages 8–9).
	For both an experiment and a study using a correlational analysis, make decisions about how you will operationalise both variables (pages 18–19).
	This may include considering what **materials** you will be using. For example, if you plan to measure concentration using a test of concentration you need to construct or find a suitable test.
	Such a test is a form of questionnaire – so there are further design issues that can be considered (see next spread).
	The operationalisation of the variables may also involve using observational techniques, which are also discussed on the next spread.
3. Experiment only: decide on the kind of experiment and the experimental design	Lab, field or natural? (pages 38–39, summary table of strengths and weaknesses).
	Repeated measures, independent groups or matched pairs? (pages 14–15).
	Experimental and control groups/conditions (pages 44–45).
4. Write a hypothesis	Directional or non-directional? (pages 10–11).
	Make sure it is operationalised (pages 18–19).

Secondary

5. Selection of participants	Identify a suitable technique and explain how it would be used.
	Consider size and composition of the sample (with reference to the target population) (pages 16–17) .
	If using independent groups, explain how to assign participants to groups (pages 16–17).
6. Ethical issues	Identify and consider how ethical issues will be dealt with (pages 12–13, 40–41, 42–43).
7. Problems with validity	Identify and consider how problems with validity will be dealt with (pages 20–21, 32–33, 34–35, 36–37).

Procedures – what you will actually do

8. Standardised procedures	This is the part that is like writing the recipe for a cake (pages 20–21).
	The main criterion for assessment is replicability – to what extent could someone else follow these instructions and repeat exactly what the researcher did?
	Outline standardised instructions given to each participant. This includes informed consent. Explain when and what materials will be given, where the participants are tested, how long they will have, etc.
9. Pilot study	Before conducting the full-scale study, a pilot study might be conducted with a few people similar to the target population (page 12).

Treatment of results

10. Consider statistics to use	Descriptive statistics (pages 22–23).
	Select appropriate inferential tests, including the level of significance to be used (pages 102, 107 and118).

key terms
- Materials
- Procedures
- Replication

DO I HAVE TO DO THIS?

	AQA A	AQA B	Edex	OCR	WJEC
AS	◑	◑	●	●	○
A2	●	●	●	●	○

● compulsory　◑ advisory　○ not necessary

mini study
Levels of processing

One very popular student activity has always been the levels of prcessing experiment by Craik and Lockhart (1972). They proposed that the reason we remember things over time (i.e. long-term memory) is that we have processed some things more deeply. Processing refers to what you do with information. The more complex the thing you do with the to-be-remembered information, the more memorable the information becomes.

They gave participants a list of common nouns (see below) and asked a question about the word. There were three types of question:

1. *An analysis of the physical structure (shallow processing), a participant might be asked 'Is the word printed in capital letters?'*
2. *An analysis of sound (phonemic processing), for example 'Does the word rhyme with 'train'?'*
3. *An analysis of meaning (deeper processing), such as 'Is the word a type of fruit?'*

There were 60 words in the original study. Afterwards the participants were shown 180 words and asked to identify any of the original words. Participants remembered most words from question type 3 and least from question type 1. This suggests that deeper processing leads to enhanced memory.

You can replicate this study using the materials below. In order to do this you will need to make many of the design decisions on the left, or justify ones that have already been made.

List of nouns and questions asked

1.	SPEECH	Is the word in capital letters? YES/NO
2.	brush	Is the word something used for cleaning? YES/NO
3.	cheek	Does the word rhyme with 'teak'? YES/NO
4.	FENCE	Is the word in small letters? YES/NO
5.	FLAME	Does the word mean something hot? YES/NO
6.	FLOUR	Is the word in capital letters? YES/NO
7.	honey	Is the word in small letters? YES/NO
8.	KNIFE	Does the word mean a type of furniture? YES/NO
9.	SHEEP	Is the word a type of farm animal? YES/NO
10.	copper	Is the word in capital letters? YES/NO
11.	GLOVE	Does the word rhyme with 'shove'? YES/NO
12.	MONK	Is the word in small letters? YES/NO
13.	daisy	Does the word rhyme with 'teak'? YES/NO
14.	miner	Is the word in small letters? YES/NO
15.	cart	Does the word rhyme with 'start'? YES/NO
16.	CLOVE	Is the word in capital letters? YES/NO
17.	ROBBER	Does the word mean a type of flower? YES/NO
18.	mast	Does the word rhyme with 'rove'? YES/NO
19.	fiddle	Is the word in small letters? YES/NO
20.	CHAPEL	Does the word rhyme with 'grapple'? YES/NO
21.	SONNET	Does the word mean something to wear? YES/NO
22.	WITCH	Does the word rhyme with 'rich'? YES/NO
23.	sleet	Is the word a type of weather? YES/NO
24.	brake	Is the word in small letters? YES/NO
25.	twig	Does the word rhyme with 'coach'? YES/NO
26.	grin	Does the word rhyme with 'school'? YES/NO
27.	DRILL	Does the word mean a kind of fish? YES/NO
28.	moan	Does the word mean a mode of travel? YES/NO
29.	CLAW	Is the word a part of an animal? YES/NO
30.	singer	Does the word rhyme with 'ringer'? YES/NO

Exam questions can give clues about what to include. Make sure you do use these helpful hints!

1. Write a consent form which would be suitable for the levels of processing experiment on the left. Make sure there is sufficient information about the study for the participants to make an informed decision about whether to participate.

2. A psychologist conducts an experiment to see if a particular drug enhances memory. The study uses an independent groups design where one group of participants will receive the new drug and the other group a placebo.

   Write a suitable consent form. Make sure there is sufficient information about the study for the participants to make an informed decision about whether to participate.

3. A research study discovers a positive correlation between exercise and happiness. The research team decide to conduct a further study to see if exercise actually *causes* happiness.

   Describe how they might design an experiment to investigate this causal relationship. Include in your answer sufficient detail to enable someone to carry out this study in the future.

   It is useful to refer to the following:

   - Fully operationalised independent and dependent variables.
   - Details of how you would control extraneous variables.
   - The procedure that you would use. You should provide sufficient detail for the study to be carried out.

4. Your task is to answer questions about how a piece of research related to the passage below could be conducted.

   Psychologists often investigate behaviour by conducting an experiment. For example, they investigate why people are more helpful than at other times.

   You must choose one of the options A–C:

A	Are people more helpful after watching a pro-social film?
B	Do people remember more in the morning or the afternoon?
C	Do relaxation exercises reduce stress?

   You must use a repeated measures design experiment and plan to collect at least ordinal level data. It must be a practical project that could be conducted.

   a State the null hypothesis for your practical project.

   b Describe the method you would use to conduct your practical project. Ensure that the study you describe can be replicated and that your design is feasible.

   13 marks are awarded for replicability and appropriateness and 6 for the quality of the design and its feasibility.

   c Give **one** strength of using an alternative experimental design in this practical project.

   d Assess the validity of your investigation in measuring the dependent variable.

   e Suggest **one** idea for possible future research related to your practical project.

DESIGNING YOUR OWN STUDY
CONTINUED

On the previous spread we looked at the design of experiments and studies using a correlational analysis. This spread will consider design decisions related to other research methods.

Designing a questionnaire or interview

Preliminary decisions

1. Formulate research question/aims	The research question/aims are likely to be given to you in the exam question.
	If you are just designing a questionnaire/survey a hypothesis is unlikely to be necessary. However you may be using a questionnaire as a means of measuring the IV or DV in an experiment or a study using a correlational analysis, in which case you will have a hypothesis.
	Decide on target population.
2. Design of questionnaire/ interview	Structured or semi-structured?
	Types of questions – open or closed?
	Length of questionnaire, use of lie scale, etc. (pages 54–55, 56–57).
3. Pilot study	Before conducting the full-scale study, a pilot study might be conducted with a few people similar to the target population (page 12).

Secondary decisions

4. Selection of participants	Identify a suitable technique and explain how it would be used.
	Consider size and composition (with reference to the target population) (pages 16–17).
5. Ethical issues	Identify and consider how ethical issues will be dealt with (pages 12–13, 40–41, 42–43).
6. Problems with validity	Identify and consider how problems with validity will be dealt with (pages 32–33, 34–35, 36–37).
7. Problems with reliability	The reliability of a questionnaire should be checked and if found to be unreliable, techniques should be used to improve it (pages 60–61).

Procedures – what you will actually do

8. Standardised procedures	This is the part that is like writing the recipe for a cake (pages 20–21).
	The main criterion for assessment is replicability – to what extent could someone else follow these instructions and repeat exactly what the researcher did.
	Outline standardised instructions given to each participant. This includes informed consent. Explain when and what materials will be given, where the participants are tested, how long they will have, etc.

Treatment of results

9. Consider statistics to use	Analysis is likely to focus on individual questions.
	Qualitative or quantitative methods are used with open questions (pages 90–91).
	Descriptive statistics (pages 22–23).
	Select appropriate inferential tests, including the level of significance to be used (pages 102, 107 and 118).

Designing an observation or content analysis

Preliminary decisions

1. Formulate research question/aims	This is likely to be given to you in the exam question.
	If you are just designing an observation a hypothesis is unlikely to be necessary. However, observation can be used as a means of measuring the IV or DV in an experiment or study using a correlational analysis, in which case you will have a hypothesis.
	Decide on target population.
2. Kinds of observation	Naturalistic or controlled?
	Direct or indirect (content analysis)?
	Structured or unstructured techniques?
	Overt or covert observation?
	Participant or non-participant observation? (pages 66–67, 68–69, 72–73).
3. Materials	Development of behaviour checklist. Identify target behaviours (may require qualitative analysis) (pages 68–69, 90–91).
	Design of data collection sheet.
4. Pilot study	Before conducting the full scale study, a pilot study might be conducted with a few people similar to the target population (page 12).

Secondary decisions

5. Selection of participants/ observations	Identify a suitable technique and explain how it would be used.
	Consider size and composition (with reference to the target population) (pages 16–17).
	Sampling also applies to how often observations are recorded (time or event sampling) (pages 68–69)
	Will observations be recorded real-time or afterwards (method of recording audio or video)?
	Time of day, number of observers.
6. Ethical issues	Identify and consider how ethical issues will be dealt with (pages 12–13, 40–41, 42–43).
7. Problems with validity	Identify and consider how problems with validity will be dealt with (pages 70–71).
8. Problems with reliability	The reliability of observations should be checked and if found to be unreliable, techniques should be used to improve it (pages 70–71).

Procedures – what you will actually do

8. Standardised procedures	Same issues apply as on left – but apply to observers as well as participants.

Treatment of results

10. Consider statistics to use	Descriptive statistics (pages 22–23).
	Select appropriate inferential tests, including the level of significance to be used (pages 102 , 107 and 118).

WORLD SPORT NEWS

mini study

Content analysis of magazine or newspaper article

Select an article related to your studies (A2 Edexcel students should select something related to criminology, child psychology, health psychology or sports psychology – see specification on page 142).

Qualitative analysis to produce categories

The initial analysis will be qualitative (see page 90).

1. Read your article several times without making any notes.
2. Decide on a top-down or bottom-up approach:

   • Top-down – use pre-existing categories. For example, if the article you are reading is related to motivation in sport use categories from the theories you have studied.

   • Bottom-up – let the categories develop from the text itself. In order to do this you need to break the data into meaningful units – this might be equivalent to sentences or phrases. Next, code each unit (what does it represent/mean?). Finally, combine codes into larger themes/categories.

Representation of results

Use your categories to represent the text.

This may involve a quantitative analysis:
• Count up instances of each category.
• The frequencies can then be represented graphically and/or with inferential statistics.

You can also do a qualitative analysis:
• Use examples or direct quotes to illustrate each category.

Conclusions

Discuss possible conclusions with reference to existing theories and/or research studies.

You may propose new insights.

Exam questions may specify that you discuss certain aspects of design, such as the procedures only or just the consent form. Read the question carefully to ensure you answer what is required.

1 A psychologist was researching how children's attitudes towards their family changes as they move from early adolescence (aged 12) to late adolescence (aged 18). Describe how you would collect data for this study using a questionnaire.

In your description it will be useful to refer to the following:

• The kind of questions you would use.
• The sample to be used.
• A description of the procedure that you would use. You should provide sufficient detail for the study to be carried out.

2 People believe that football fans are very aggressive. Design an observational study to investigate the aggressiveness of spectators at a football match.

In your answer, refer to an appropriate method of investigation and materials/apparatus and procedure. Justify your design decisions and provide sufficient detail to allow for reasonable replication of the study.

3 TV programmes before 9pm are supposed to contain less sex and violence. Design a study that could test this by comparing programmes shown on TV from 8–9pm and 9–10pm. Your design brief should include:

• A suitable hypothesis.
• Categories that might be used in this content analysis.
• A sampling method.
• A description of the procedure that you would use. You should provide sufficient detail for the study to be carried out.

4 Your task is to answer questions about how a piece of research related to the passage below could be conducted.

One way of finding out about human behaviour is to ask people about what they think and feel. Psychologists sometimes use interviews to do this.

You must choose one of the options A–C:

> A Attitudes to eating.
> B Experience of stress in daily life.
> C Successful revision techniques.

You must design a study that uses an interview to collect data by volunteer sampling. It must be a practical project that could be conducted.

Answer all the questions below in relation to your project.

a Construct a research question for your project.

b Describe the method you would use to conduct your practical project. 13 marks are awarded for replicability and appropriateness and 6 for the quality of the design and its feasibility.

c Outline **one** weakness of using an interview in your project.

d Explain **one** strength and **one** weakness of using closed questions in your project.

e How could you improve the reliability of your interview?

f Suggest a more appropriate sampling method you could have used to obtain participants for your project. Explain your answer.

REPORTING A RESEARCH STUD

Your study of psychology has involved hundreds of research studies, such as Loftus and Palmer (1974) and Milgram (1963). These names and dates refer to articles that have been published in a psychology journal. Such articles form the bedrock of psychology, or indeed any science. The way they are presented follows a fairly standard format.

JOURNAL OF VERBAL LEARNING AND VERBAL BEHAVIOR 13, 585–589 (1974)

**Reconstruction of Automobile Destruction:
An Example of the Interaction Between Language and Memory[1]**

ELIZABETH F. LOFTUS AND JOHN C. PALMER

University of Washington

Two experiments are reported in which subjects viewed films of automobile accidents and then answered questions about events occurring in the films. The question, "About how fast were the cars going when they smashed into each other?" elicited higher estimates of speed than questions which used the verbs *collided, bumped, contacted,* or *hit* in place of *smashed.* On a retest one week later, those subjects who received the verb *smashed* were more likely to say "yes" to the question, "Did you see any broken glass?", even though broken glass was not present in the film. These results are consistent with the view that the questions asked subsequent to an event can cause a reconstruction in one's memory of that event.

How accurately do we remember the details of a complex event, like a traffic accident, that has happened in our presence? More specifically, how well do we do when asked to estimate some numerical quantity such as how long the accident took, how fast the cars were traveling, or how much time elapsed between the sounding of a horn and the moment of collision?

It is well documented that most people are markedly inaccurate in reporting such numerical details as time, speed, and distance (Bird, 1927; Whipple, 1909). For example, most people have difficulty estimating the duration of an event, with some research indicating that the tendency is to overestimate the duration of events which are complex (Block, 1974; Marshall, 1969; Ornstein, 1969). The judgment of speed is especially difficult, and practically every automobile accident results in huge variations from one witness to another

as to how fast a vehicle was actually traveling (Gardner, 1933). In one test administered to Air Force personnel who knew in advance that they would be questioned about the speed of a moving automobile, estimates ranged from 10 to 50 mph. The car they watched was actually going only 12 mph (Marshall, 1969, p. 23).

Given the inaccuracies in estimates of speed, it seems likely that there are variables which are potentially powerful in terms of influencing these estimates. The present research was conducted to investigate one such variable, namely, the phrasing of the question used to elicit the speed judgment. Some questions are clearly more suggestive than others. This fact of life has resulted in the legal concept of a leading question and in legal rules indicating when leading questions are allowed (*Supreme Court Reporter*, 1973). A leading question is simply one that, either by its form or content, suggests to the witness what answer is desired or leads him to the desired answer.

In the present study, subjects were shown films of traffic accidents and then they answered questions about the accident. The subjects were interrogated about the speed of

[1] This research was supported by the Urban Mass Transportation Administration, Department of Transportation, Grant No. WA-11-0004. Thanks go to Geoffrey Loftus, Edward E. Smith, and Stephen Woods for many important and helpful comments. Reprint requests should be sent to Elizabeth F. Loftus, Department of Psychology, University of Washington, Seattle, Washington 98195.

585

This is the first page of the journal article reporting the study by Loftus and Palmer (1974) on the effect of leading questions. It was published in the Journal of Verbal Learning and Verbal Behaviour.

Have a look at some journal articles on the internet – just type the name of a study into Google and you may find the original article.

Conventions for reporting psychologica

Scientific journals contain research reports that are usually organised into the following sections:

Abstract

A summary of the study covering the aims, hypothesis, the method (procedures), results and conclusions. The conclusions usually include implications of the current study.

Introduction and aims/hypothesis

This outlines what a researcher intends to investigate. It begins with a review of previous research (theories and studies), which provides the background to the study to be conducted. The focus of this research review should lead logically to the study to be conducted so the reader is convinced of the reasons for this particular research. It is like a funnel starting broadly and narrowing down to the particular research hypothesis

The researcher(s) may state their **research prediction**(s) and/or a **hypothesis**/es.

Method

A detailed description of what the researcher(s) did, providing enough information for **replication** of the study.

The method section is often subdivided into:

- *Design* – state the design, e.g. repeated measures or covert observation.
- *Participants* – containing information about how many participants took part, and details of age, gender and any other important characteristics. The method of selection is also explained.
- *Apparatus/materials* – descriptions of any **psychological tests** or **questionnaires** or other **materials** used. The full details are not usually included but examples may be provided.
- *Procedures* – this may include the **standardised instructions** to participants, the testing environment, the order of events and so on.
- *Ethics* – significant **ethical issues** may be mentioned, as well as how they were dealt with, such as issues related to privacy in an observational study.

Psychology journals

There are thousands of scholarly journals publishing over one million research papers each year. They differ from 'popular' magazines because they contain in–depth reports of research. The articles are written by academics and are peer reviewed.

Several hundred such journals specifically relate to psychology, such as The Psychologist, Archives of Sexual Behaviour, Journal of Early Adolescence and British Journal of Psychology.

These journals may be published quarterly. Academic textbooks are based on such articles and link research claims to scholarly reports, as you can see by looking in the references at the back of this book.

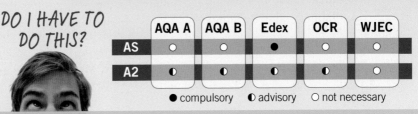
key terms

- Descriptive statistics
- Ethical issues
- Graphs
- Hypothesis
- Inferential statistics
- Materials
- Measures of central tendency
- Measures of dispersion
- Observed value
- Psychological test
- Qualitative research
- Questionnaire
- Replication
- Research prediction
- Significance level
- Standardised instructions
- Test statistic

Investigations

Results

This section contains what the researcher(s) found, which includes:

- **Descriptive statistics** – tables and **graphs** showing frequencies and **measures of central tendency** and **measures of dispersion**.

- **Inferential statistics** – the use of statistical tests to determine the significance of the results. Any test used is identified and the **observed value** of the **test statistic** reported. The **significance level** for the observed value is given, e.g. $p < 0.05$.

(The *British Psychological Society* now recommend that the exact value of p should be given (e.g. $p = 0.013$). This is because most researchers use a software programme to calculate their observed value and this gives them the exact critical value.)

In the case of **qualitative research** categories and themes are described along with examples within these categories.

Discussion

The researcher aims to interpret the results and consider their implications for future research as well as suggesting real-world applications. This section may include:

- *Summary of the results* – the results are reported in brief and some explanation may be offered about what these results show.

- *Relationship to previous research* – the results of the study are discussed in relation to the research reported in the introduction and possibly other research not previously mentioned.

- *Consideration of methodology* – criticisms may be made of the methods used in the study and improvements suggested. This list of criticisms should be brief – it doesn't make sense to raise a lot of criticisms at the end of the study because it begs the question about why they weren't dealt with before conducting the study.

- *Implications* for psychological theory and possible real-world applications.

- *Suggestions* for future research.

References

The full details of any journal articles or books that are mentioned.

mini study
Coursework

In the old days, Psychology A level involved producing a file of coursework that was marked and counted towards your final grade. Students had to design, conduct and report their own studies. The reporting part required using the conventions described on this spread.

Select one of the studies you have conducted and present it in the form of a journal article, following the conventions outlined on this spread.

question 6.3

1. Select a research study that you know well and write the abstract for the study. Your abstract should be about 150 words in length.

2. Select another research study from an area of your course that you know well. Construct an appropriate introduction section by using other research you know.

3. A group of students decide to conduct some research to find out how homosexuality is presented in the media. They collect a range of different newspapers and magazines by picking them up on the train to and from university. They identify some key words and phrases to look for. They decide to group these into positive, negative and neutral statements and count how many of each they find per newspaper or magazine.

   a. Identify the research method being used in this study.

   b. Explain **one** strength and **one** weakness of this method in the context of this study.

   c. Explain what is meant by quantitative and qualitative data.

   d. Will the students' method produce quantitative or qualitative data?

   e. Imagine that you are the psychologist and are writing up the report of the study. Write an appropriate methods section which includes reasonable detail of design, participants, materials and procedure. Make sure that there is enough detail to allow another researcher to carry out this study in the future.

4. A research study investigated the effects of isolation in 40 sheep by placing each individual sheep on a hillside on its own. The sheep's heart rate was measured after 15 minutes of isolation and again 15 minutes after the sheep had been shown pictures of other sheep projected onto a wall. The hypothesis is 'A sheep in isolation has a different heart rate to sheep who are not isolated'.

   The results of the study were that the mean heart rate per minute after isolation was 102.5 beats per minute, and after exposure to the pictures it was 78.3 beats per minute.

   Imagine that you are the psychologist and are writing up the report of the study. Write an appropriate results section. You should include the following:

   a. A table showing the results of the study.

   b. A sketch of an appropriately labelled bar chart.

   c. Identification of the appropriate statistical test with justification for its use.

   d. The level of significance that might be used and why.

   e. Whether the psychologist would use a one-tailed or a two-tailed test.

   f. How the psychologist could use the results of the statistical test to determine whether or not the null hypothesis should be rejected.

   g. Based on the bar chart draw a suitable conclusion in relation to the hypothesis.

   h. Suggest **one or more** implications that could be drawn from this study.

5. Look at the back of this book and find one reference to a journal article. Identify the researcher's names, the title of the article, the name of the journal, the issue number of the journal and the page numbers of the article.

VALIDATING KNOWLEDGE

Psychology, in common with all scientific subjects, develops its knowledge base through conducting research and sharing the findings of such research with other scientists. But how do we know that what we read is true? Peer review is an essential part of the process whereby quality is judged. It is in the interest of all scientists that their work is held up for scrutiny and any work that is flawed or downright fraudulent is detected and the results of such research ignored. But this is actually quite difficult to achieve.

Fraudulent research

The Cyril Burt affair

In the early 1950s, the eminent psychologist Sir Cyril Burt published results from studies of identical twins that was used as evidence to show that intelligence is inherited. Burt (1955) started with 21 pairs of twins, later increasing this to 42 pairs of twins reared apart. In a subsequent study Burt (1966) increased his sample to 53 pairs of identical twins raised apart, reporting an identical correlation to the earlier twin study of .771. The suspicious consistency of these correlation coefficients led Kamin (1974) to accuse Burt of inventing data. When a reporter, Oliver Gillie (1976), tried but failed to find two of Burt's research assistants this appeared to confirm the underlying fraud and Burt was publicly discredited. These accusations have been challenged (e.g. Joynson, 1989) but the most recent view is that Burt was astonishingly dishonest in his research (Mackintosh, 1995).

The Burt affair is particularly worrying because we trust psychologists to be honest, and also because his research was used to shape social policy. Burt helped to establish the 11-plus examination used in the UK to identify which children should go to grammar school rather than secondary moderns. He argued that since IQ was largely genetic then it was appropriate to test and segregate children into schools suitable for their abilities.

Some more recent cases of fraud

In 2010 Professor Marc Hauser of Harvard University was found responsible for scientific misconduct related to a number of published scientific papers. His main area of research concerned cotton-top tamarin monkeys and their cognitive abilities. He appears to have drawn conclusions for which he has been unable to provide evidence.

In 2011 Professor Diederik Stapel of Tilburg University in the Netherlands admitted inventing data in over 30 different publications. His admissions came after colleagues realised that some of his data were 'too good to be true' and they spent months observing his work, eventually blowing the whistle on him.

In the light of such prominent cases of professional misconduct Leslie John and colleagues (2012) surveyed over 2,000 psychologists asking them to anonymously report their involvement in questionable research practices. They found that 70% said they cut corners in reporting data and 1% admitted to falsifying data. They concluded that questionable practices may constitute the prevailing research norm.

Aftermath

Such practices raise two key issues. First, there is the issue of lack of trust. In the future people are likely to be less trusting of scientific data.

Second is the problem that the data from such fraudulent studies remains published. Despite the fact the journals involved usually publish retractions (stating that the evidence is flawed or fraudulent), there are people who will continue to use the faulty data not knowing that it is discredited.

The role of peer review

Peer review (also called 'refereeing') is the assessment of scientific work by others who are experts in the same field (i.e. 'peers'). The intention of peer review is to ensure that any research that is conducted and published is of high quality.

Peer reviewers are largely unpaid. Usually there are a number of reviewers for each application/article/assessment. Their task is to report on the quality of the research and then their views may be considered by a peer review panel.

The Parliamentary Office of Science and Technology (2002) suggests that peer review serves three main purposes:

- *Allocation of research funding* – Research is paid for by various government and charitable bodies. For example, the government-run *Medical Research Council* is one of the leading UK sources of funding for research. In 2008–9 they had £605 million to spend (Hansard, 2007) and obviously a duty to spend this responsibly. Public bodies such as this require reviews to enable them to decide which research is likely to be worthwhile.

- *Publication of research in scientific journals and books* – Scientific or scholarly journals provide scientists with the opportunity to share the results of their research. The peer review process has only been used in such journals since the middle of the 20th century as a means of preventing incorrect or faulty data entering the public domain. Prior to peer review, research was simply published and it was assumed that the burden of proof lay with opponents of any new ideas.

- *Assessing the research rating of university departments* – All university science departments are expected to conduct research and this is assessed in terms of quality (Research Excellence Framework, REF). Future funding for the department depends on receiving good ratings from a peer review.

Peer review and the internet

The sheer volume and pace of information available on the internet means that new solutions are needed in order to maintain the quality of information. Scientific information is available in numerous online blogs, online journals and, of course, Wikipedia (an online encyclopedia). To a large extent such sources of information are policed by the 'wisdom of crowds' approach – readers decide whether it is valid or not, and post comments and/or edit entries accordingly. Several online journals (such as *ArXiv* and *Philica*) ask readers to rate articles. On *Philica* papers are ranked on the basis of peer reviews. On the internet 'peer' is coming to mean 'everyone' – perhaps a more egalitarian system.

WIKIPEDIA

Wikipedia deals with the issue of peer review by having various levels of editors to check information posted. However they recognise that, while it may be simple to detect incorrect information, it is more difficult to recognise 'subtle viewpoint promotion' than in a typical reference work. On the other hand, they point out, that bias that would be unchallenged in a traditional reference work is more likely to be considered on Wikipedia. In addition, the online form of Wikipedia permits instant revision when mistakes are spotted.

key terms
- Extraneous variable
- Objectivity
- Peer review

DO I HAVE TO DO THIS?

	AQA A	AQA B	Edex	OCR	WJEC
AS	○	○	○	○	○
A2	●	○	○	○	◐

● compulsory ◐ advisory ○ not necessary

Evaluation

It is clear why peer review is essential – without it we don't know what is mere opinion and speculation as distinct from real fact.

However, whilst the benefit of peer review is beyond question, certain features of the process can be criticised.

Finding an expert

It isn't always possible to find an appropriate expert to review a research proposal or report. This means that poor research may be passed because the reviewer didn't really understand it.

Anonymity

Anonymity is usually practised so that reviewers can be honest and objective. However, it may have the opposite effect if reviewers use the veil of anonymity to settle old scores or bury rival research. Research is conducted in a social world where people compete for research grants and jobs, and make friends and enemies. Social relationships inevitably affect objectivity. Some journals now favour open reviewing (both author and reviewer know each other's identity).

Publication bias

Journals tend to prefer to publish positive results, possibly because editors want research that has important implications in order to increase the standing of their journal. This results in a bias in published research which in turn leads to a misperception of the true facts.

Furthermore, it appears that journals also avoid publishing straight replications of a study, a fundamental part of research validation. Chris French (2011) submitted a replication of a study of paranormal phenomena and found that it was not even considered for peer review. He suggests that journals are as bad as newspapers for seeking eye-catching stories.

Preserving the status quo

Peer review results in a preference for research that goes with existing theory rather than dissenting or unconventional work. The former editor of the medical journal *The Lancet*, Richard Horton (2000) made the following comment, 'The mistake, of course, is to have thought that peer review was any more than a crude means of discovering the acceptability – not the validity – of a new finding.'

Science is generally resistant to large shifts in opinion. Change takes a long time and requires a 'revolution' in the way people think. Peer review may be one of the elements that slow change down.

Cannot deal with already published research

We noted on the facing page the problem that, once a research study has been published, the results remain in the public view even if they have subsequently been shown to be fraudulent or simply the result of poor research practices. For example, Brooks (2010) points to peer-reviewed research that was subsequently debunked but nevertheless continued to be used in a debate in parliament.

'Editors and scientists alike insist on the pivotal importance of peer review. We portray peer review to the public as a quasi-sacred process that helps to make science our most objective truth teller. But we know that the system of peer review is biased, unjust, unaccountable, incomplete, easily fixed, often insulting, usually ignorant, occasionally foolish, and frequently wrong.'
(Richard Horton, 2000)

questions 6.4

1 Explain what is meant by 'peer review'.

2 Explain why peer review is essential to the process of producing valid scientific data.

3 Outline **three** criticisms of peer review.

4 Consider a radio programme that you listen to or a magazine that you read.
  a Do you think these are peer reviewed?
  b How do you think that could be done?
  c Do you think it should be done? Explain your answer.

5 Do your own research on peer review by searching the internet for current views on best practice.

mini study
Saved the best to last

This is one of my favourite studies. Students often say that noise is a potential extraneous variable in a study. Read on …

H.B. Hovey set out to demonstrate the willingness of participants to help an experimenter. He gave college students an intelligence test and told them that there would be distractions and that they were to do their best regardless.

The distractions were:

'7 bells, 5 buzzers; a 5500-watt spotlight; a 90,000 volt rotary spark gap; two adjustable organ pipes and three metal whistles, 14, 24 and 26 in. long; a 55-pound circular saw (36 in. in diameter) mounted on a wooden frame; a mounted camera operated by a well known photographer; and … four students performing stunts.' (Hovey, 1928, pages 586–587)

Hovey found that participants did not differ in their distractability and that performance on the mental test was not affected when compared with a matched control group who did the test without any distractions.

AQA A AS

Remember that specifications change – this specification is correct at time of publication, but do check.

The numbers represent the left hand page number for the spread where the topic is covered. The use of brackets indicates 'of some relevance'.

Unit 1 There are also research methods questions on the Unit 2 exam but less detailed knowledge is required.		(52), (128, 130)
Methods and techniques	Experimental method, including laboratory, field and natural experiments.	8, 30, 38
	Studies using a correlational analysis.	64
	Observational techniques.	66
	Self-report techniques, including questionnaire and interview.	54, 56
	Case studies.	74
Investigative design	Aims.	8
	Hypotheses, including directional and non-directional.	10
	Experimental design (independent groups, repeated measures and matched pairs).	14
	Design of naturalistic observations, including the development and use of behavioural categories.	68, 70
	Design of questionnaires and interviews.	58, 60, 62
	Operationalisation of variables, including independent and dependent variables.	8, 18
	Pilot studies.	12
	Control of extraneous variables.	20, 32, 34
	Reliability and validity.	32, 34, 36, 44, 58, 60, 70
	Awareness of the British Psychological Society (BPS) Code of Ethics.	40
	Ethical issues and ways in which psychologists deal with them.	12, 40, 42
	Selection of participants and sampling techniques, including random, opportunity and volunteer sampling.	16
	Demand characteristics and investigator effects.	32, 34
Data analysis and presentation	Presentation and interpretation of quantitative data, including graphs, scattergrams and tables.	22, 94
	Analysis and interpretation of quantitative data. Measures of central tendency, including median, mean, mode. Measures of dispersion, including ranges and standard deviation.	22
	Analysis and interpretation of correlational data. Positive and negative correlations and the interpretation of correlation coefficients.	64
	Presentation of qualitative data.	54
	Processes involved in content analysis.	74

AQA A A2

Unit 4		
Candidates will be expected to:	• Extend their knowledge, understanding and skills of research design, data analysis, and data interpretation and reporting gained at AS.	52
	• Develop an understanding of the nature of science and scientific method.	
	• Understand the application of scientific method in psychology.	128, 130, 132
	• Design investigations.	
	• Understand how to analyse and interpret data arising from such investigations.	
	• Report on practical investigations.	
	• Gain sufficient understanding of the design and conduct of scientific research in psychology. Candidates will need to practise these skills by carrying out, analysing and reporting small-scale investigation.	
The application of scientific method in psychology	The major features of science, including replicability, objectivity, theory construction, hypothesis testing, the use of empirical methods.	52
	Validating new knowledge and the role of peer review.	134
Designing psychological investigations	Selection and application of appropriate research methods.	Chapters 1, 2 and 3
	Implications of sampling strategies, for example bias and generalising.	16, 36
	Issues of reliability, including types of reliability, assessment of reliability, improving reliability.	60, 70, 92
	Assessing and improving validity, including internal and external.	32, 34, 36
	Ethical considerations in design and conduct of psychological research.	12, 40, 42, (78)
Data analysis and reporting on investigations	Appropriate selection of graphical representations.	22, 94
	Probability and significance, including the interpretation of significance and Type 1/Type 2 errors.	102, 106
	Factors affecting choice of statistical test, including levels of measurement.	104
	The use of inferential analysis, including Spearman's rho, Mann–Whitney, Wilcoxon, chi-squared.	108, 110, 112, 114
	Analysis and interpretation of qualitative data.	86, 88, 90, 92
	Conventions of reporting on psychological investigations.	132

Examples of AQA A AS exam questions

January 2011 Unit 1

Psychologists carried out a laboratory experiment to investigate the effectiveness of cognitive interviews. All participants watched the same film of a robbery. They were randomly allocated to Group One or Group Two. Participants were then asked to recall the robbery. The investigators used a cognitive interview to access recall of participants in Group One and a standard interview to access recall of participants in Group Two.

The results of this experiment are summarised in Figure 1 on the right.

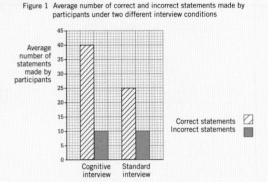

Figure 1 Average number of correct and incorrect statements made by participants under two different interview conditions

(a) What experimental design was used in this experiment? *(1 mark)*

(b) Explain **one** limitation of the design that was used in this experiment. *(2 marks)*

(c) Explain what the results suggest about the effectiveness of the cognitive interview. *(2 marks)*

(d) Participants in the standard interview were simply asked to describe what happened in the film.

Suggest **one** way in which participants in the cognitive interview condition could have been asked to recall what happened. *(2 marks)*

(e) What is meant by the term investigator effects? Explain possible investigator effects in this study. *(4 marks)*

January 2011 Unit 2

Some research into obedience has been carried out in laboratories. Other studies into obedience have been carried out in the real world, including field experiments and observations.

(a) Outline **one** advantage of conducting obedience research outside a laboratory setting. *(2 marks)*

(b) Outline **one** limitation of conducting obedience research outside a laboratory setting. *(2 marks)*

Examples of AQA A A2 exam questions

January 2011 Unit 4

A teacher has worked in the same primary school for two years. While chatting to the children, she is concerned to find that the majority of them come to school without having eaten a healthy breakfast. In her opinion, children who eat 'a decent breakfast' learn to read more quickly and are better behaved than children who do not. She now wants to set up a pre-school breakfast club for the children so that they can all have this beneficial start to the day. The local authority is not willing to spend money on this project purely on the basis of the teacher's opinion and insists on having scientific evidence for the claimed benefits of eating a healthy breakfast.

(a) Explain why the teacher's personal opinion cannot be accepted as scientific evidence. Refer to some of the major features of science in your answer. *(6 marks)*

A psychologist at the local university agrees to carry out a study to investigate the claim that eating a healthy breakfast improves reading skills. He has access to 400 five-year-old children from 10 local schools, and decides to use 100 children (50 in the experimental group and 50 in the control group). Since the children are so young, he needs to obtain parental consent for them to take part in his study.

(b) The psychologist used a random sampling method. Explain how he could have obtained his sample using this method. *(3 marks)*

(c) Explain limitations of using random sampling in this study. *(3 marks)*

(d) Explain why it is important to operationalise the independent variable and the dependent variable in this study and suggest how the psychologist might do this. *(5 marks)*

(e) The psychologist used a Mann–Whitney test to analyse the data. Give **two** reasons why he chose this test. *(2 marks)*

(f) He could have used a matched pairs design. Explain why this design would have been more difficult to use in this study. *(2 marks)*

(g) Other than parental consent, identify **one** ethical issue raised in this study and explain how the psychologist might address it. *(2 marks)*

(h) The psychologist asks some of his students to conduct a separate observational study at the same time on the same group of children. The aim of this observational study is to test the idea that eating a healthy breakfast affects playground behaviour.

Design an observational study to investigate the effects of a healthy breakfast on playground behaviour. Include in your answer sufficient detail to allow for reasonable replication of the study. You should state the hypothesis you are setting out to test.

In your answer, refer to an appropriate method of investigation and materials/apparatus and procedure. Justify your design decisions. *(12 marks)*

AQA B AS

Remember that specifications change – this specification is correct at time of publication, but do check.

The numbers represent the left hand page number for the spread where the topic is covered. The use of brackets indicates 'of some relevance'.

Unit 1 There are also research methods questions on the Unit 2 exam but less detailed knowledge is required.		**(128, 130)**
Aims	• To promote a critical understanding of quantitative and qualitative methods employed in psychological research. • To promote an understanding of the use of descriptive statistics. • To demonstrate how data can be represented. • To develop an awareness of ethical issues in psychological research. • To develop an appreciation of how science works in psychological research.	52
Planning research	Qualitative and quantitative research: the distinction between qualitative and quantitative data collection techniques; strengths and limitations of quantitative and qualitative data.	8, 10, 22, 54, 86
	Formulating research questions. Stating aims. Formulating hypotheses (experimental/alternative/research).	8, 10, (18)
	Populations and sampling. Sampling techniques, including opportunity, random, stratified and systematic.	16
Experimental methods	Experiments: field, laboratory and quasi-experiments.	8, 30, 38
	Issue of ecological validity.	36
	Independent and dependent variables. Manipulation and control of variables in experiments. Extraneous and confounding variables.	8, 20, 32, 34
	Experimental designs: repeated or related measures, matched pairs, independent groups and appropriate use of each.	14, (44)
	Controls associated with different designs, including counterbalancing and random allocation. Strengths and limitations of different experimental designs.	14
	Strengths and limitations of experimental methods.	38
Non-experimental methods	Self-report methods: questionnaire construction, including open and closed questions, types of interviews: structured and unstructured.	54, 56, 62
	Pilot studies and their value.	12
	Correlation studies. The difference between an experiment and a correlation study.	64
	Observational studies: natural and laboratory settings; covert and overt; participant and non-participant observation.	66, 68
	The process of content analysis.	72
	Case studies. The role of case studies in psychology. Strengths and limitations of these methods.	74
Representing data	Appropriate use of the following tabular and graphical displays: bar charts, graphs, scattergrams and tables.	22, 94
Descriptive statistics	Use of measures of central tendency (mean, median, mode) and measures of dispersion (range and standard deviation).	22
	Calculation of mean, median, mode and range.	22
	Correlation as a description of the relationship between two variables. Positive, negative and zero correlations.	64
Ethics	An awareness of the code of ethics in psychology as specified by the British Psychological Society. The application of the code of ethics in psychological research.	12, 40, 42

AQA B A2

Unit 4		**(52)**
Aims	• To build on knowledge of research methods and statistics acquired in previous units. • To enable understanding of the concepts of hypothesis testing and significance. • To promote an understanding of significance testing using inferential statistics. • To inform decision making about the appropriateness of different inferential tests in different circumstances. • To enable the development of a critical understanding of research issues in psychology. • To develop an appreciation of how science works in psychological research.	128, 130, (132)
Inferential statistics	Statistical inference: the concepts of probability and levels of significance; use of critical values in testing for significance. Hypothesis testing. One- and two-tailed tests. Type I and Type II errors.	102, 104, 106
	Positive, negative and zero correlation.	64
	Limitations of sampling techniques and generalisation of results.	16, 36
	Statistical tests: use of non-parametric and parametric tests.	118
	Statistical tests of difference: the sign test; Wilcoxon signed ranks test; Mann–Whitney; related t-test (repeated measures) and independent t-test.	112, 114, 116, 120
	Statistical tests of association: Spearman's rank order correlation; Pearson's product moment correlation; the chi-squared test.	108, 110, 118
	Factors affecting the choice of statistical test, including levels of measurement, type of experimental design. Criteria for parametric testing: interval data; normal distribution; homogeneity of variance.	104, 118
Issues in research	Strengths and limitations of different methods of research.	Chapters 1, 2 and 3
	Strengths and limitations of qualitative and quantitative data.	22, 86, 88, 90
	Reliability and validity applied generally across all methods of investigation. Ways of assessing reliability including test–retest and inter-observer.	20, 32, 34, 36, 60, 70
	Ways of assessing validity, including face validity and concurrent validity.	58
	Critical understanding of the importance of ethical considerations within the social and cultural environment. Ethical considerations in the design and conduct of psychological studies and within psychology as a whole.	12, 40, 42, (78)

Examples of AQA B AS exam questions

June 2011 Unit 1

A psychologist wanted to test the effectiveness of a relaxation technique designed to help children to overcome their phobias.

The participants were 20 children aged eight years who were terrified of the dark.

The psychologist trained the children's parents to use a relaxation technique with their children before bedtime. Before starting to use the relaxation technique, the parents rated their child's anxiety at bedtime using a five-point scale. A rating of one on the anxiety scale indicated that the child was relaxed. A rating of five indicated that the child was extremely anxious and upset.

The psychologist asked each parent to apply the relaxation technique every night for two weeks. At the end of each week, they rated their child's anxiety using the same scale.

After two weeks, the psychologist collected the anxiety ratings from the parents and analysed the data.

The results are shown in **Table 1** below.

Table 1: The median anxiety ratings at weekly interviews

	Before relaxation technique	At the end of week one	At the end of week two
Median anxiety ratings at weekly intervals	4.5	3.5	2.0

(a) What might the psychologist conclude from the median anxiety ratings shown in **Table 1**? Justify your answer. *(2 marks)*

(b) Sketch an appropriate graphical display of the data shown in **Table 1**. *(3 marks)*

(c) (i) The median is a measure of central tendency. Name **one** other measure of central tendency. *(1 mark)*

   (ii) Give **one** limitation of the measure of central tendency that you have named in your answer to (c)(i). *(1 mark)*

(d) Name **one** ethical issue that the psychologist should have taken into account in this study. Explain how the psychologist could have addressed this issue. *(3 marks)*

(e) The psychologist asked the parents to rate their own child's anxiety.

   Briefly discuss at least **one** methodological problem involved in parents rating their own child's anxiety. *(3 marks)*

(f) In this study, the psychologist used a repeated measures design, testing the same children on more than one occasion.

   Explain how the psychologist could have studied the effectiveness of the relaxation technique using an independent groups design. *(3 marks)*

(g) Three months later, the psychologist decided to carry out interviews with each of the parents.

   (i) Outline what further information might be gained by carrying out the follow-up interviews that could not have been gained in the original study. *(3 marks)*

   (ii) Write **one** suitable open question that the psychologist could ask the parents in the interview. *(1 mark)*

Examples of AQA B A2 exam questions

June 2011 Unit 4

A health visitor reported that parents frequently made comments that their baby boys were keen to explore their surroundings. Such comments were rarely made about baby girls.

A psychologist decided to investigate this further. She interviewed the parents of twenty baby boys and twenty baby girls. All babies were aged between twelve and eighteen months. Each parent was interviewed individually for approximately half an hour. The interview contained a set of specific questions about exploratory behaviour. Examples of specific questions were:

'How does your baby react to a new toy?'
'Imagine you are visiting someone with your baby. Describe how your baby behaves if given the freedom to move around the room.'

The interviews were recorded. Afterwards, the psychologist listened to the recordings. Based on the content of each interview, the psychologist rated each baby's exploratory behaviour on a scale of 1–10. A high score on the scale indicated a lot of exploratory behaviour, and a low score indicated little exploratory behaviour.

The median ratings of exploratory behaviour for the twenty baby boys and twenty baby girls were calculated. The data obtained are shown in **Table 1** below.

Table 1: The median ratings for exploratory behaviour in baby boys and girls

	Baby boys	Baby girls
Median	7.5	3.5

(a) Write a suitable hypothesis for this study. *(2 marks)*

(b) Explain what is meant by qualitative **and** quantitative data collection. Refer to this study in your answer. *(3 marks)*

(c) The psychologist used an inferential statistical test to see whether there was a significant difference between the ratings for exploratory behaviour in baby boys and baby girls.

   Name an appropriate statistical test that the psychologist could have used to compare the scores in baby boys and baby girls. Give **one** reason for your answer. *(2 marks)*

   A difference was found at the 10% level ($p = 0.10$).

(d) What conclusion could the psychologist draw from the results of the statistical analysis? Explain your answer. *(2 marks)*

(e) In this study, the psychologist carried out the rating on her own. Explain why it might have been better to have two psychologists rating the recordings. *(2 marks)*

(f) The psychologist used the same set of twenty questions with all the parents. Briefly outline **two** advantages of carrying out the interview in this way. *(2 marks)*

(g) Design an observational study to investigate differences in the exploratory behaviour of baby boys and baby girls in an unfamiliar room. Include in your answer sufficient detail to enable someone to carry out this study in the future.

   It is useful to refer to the following:
   • the variables to be considered
   • the sample to be used
   • materials
   • an outline of the proposed procedure. *(7 marks)*

EDEXCEL AS

Remember that specifications change – this specification is correct at time of publication, but do check.

The numbers represent the left hand page number for the spread where the topic is covered. The use of brackets indicates 'of some relevance'.

Unit 1 (52)

Social psychology	Describe the survey as a research method in psychology, including the questionnaire and interview. Identify, describe and apply unstructured, structured and semi-structured interviews, open and closed questions, alternative hypotheses and issues around designing surveys. Evaluate the survey as a research method, including strengths and weaknesses, and the issues of reliability, validity and subjectivity.	54, 56, 58, 60, 62
	Describe and compare, including strengths and weaknesses, the difference between qualitative and quantitative data. Ways of analysing qualitative data, e.g. use of themes.	54, 86, 88, 90, 92
	Describe, assess and apply guidelines, such as British Psychological Society (BPS) guidelines, about the use of humans in psychological research, including guidelines about what not to do and what to do to protect human participants. Guidelines to include consent, deception, right to withdraw, debriefing of participants and competence.	12, 40, 42
	Identify, describe and apply different sampling techniques, including random sampling, stratified sampling, volunteer and self-selected sampling, and opportunity sampling, including advantages and disadvantages of each technique.	16
	Devise and conduct **one** practical to gather data relevant to topics covered in the Social Approach, which must be a survey (questionnaire or interview) to gather relevant data. The survey should gather both qualitative and quantitative data. Make design decisions in devising an interview schedule/questionnaire, including sampling decisions.	54, 56, 58, 60, 128
	Collect data and present an analysis of both the qualitative and quantitative data and draw brief conclusions about the topic from the analyses.	
	For example: gender differences in obedience, prejudicial attitudes towards age, in/outgroup attitudes.	
Cognitive psychology	Natural, laboratory and field experiment, independent variable (IV) and dependent variable (DV).	8, 30, 38
	Experimental hypothesis, directional (one-tailed) and non-directional (two-tailed), operationalisation of variables.	10, 18
	Repeated measures, matched pairs and independent groups design, counterbalancing, randomisation, order effects.	14
	Describe and evaluate, including strengths and weaknesses, the experimental method (laboratory, natural, field) in terms of: experimental control (including the effects of situational and participant variables), objectivity, reliability, validity, experimenter effects, demand characteristics.	20, 32, 34, 36, 60
	Measures of central tendency, measures of dispersion (at least range), bar graph, histogram and frequency graph as ways to present data collected.	22, 94
	Devise and conduct **one** practical, which must be an experiment, to gather data relevant to a topic covered in the Cognitive Approach for this course. Comment on the research design decisions. Collect, present and comment on data gathered, including using measures of central tendency (mean, median, mode), measures of dispersion (at least range), bar graph, histogram, frequency graph as relevant.	Chapters 1 and 2
	For example: interference in STM, levels of processing task, state or context dependency task.	59, 129

Unit 2

Psychodynamic approach	Describe and evaluate the case study as a research method used in psychology and as used in the psychodynamic approach.	74
	Describe, assess and apply issues of reliability, validity, subjectivity, objectivity and generalisability in the analysis of qualitative data.	86, 92
	Describe, assess and apply the terms 'cross-sectional' and 'longitudinal' as applied to research methods.	78
	Describe, assess and apply issues of ethics and issues of credibility with regard to using personal data from methods such as case studies (e.g. should such data be in the public domain?).	74
	Describe and evaluate the correlational method/design. Identify, describe and apply a positive and a negative correlation, and a strength (e.g. +.87) of correlation.	64
	Identify, describe and apply different sampling techniques, including random sampling, stratified sampling, volunteer and self-selected sampling, and opportunity sampling, including advantages and disadvantages of each technique.	16
	Devise and conduct one practical, which must be use a correlational design, using two rating scales and self-report data. Class data collection is acceptable. Draw a scattergram of the results. Carry out a Spearman's test on the data and interpret the finding (e.g. +.87 is a strong correlation). **Note:** with regards to inferential tests, no calculations will have to be carried out in the examinations and formulae do not have to be learnt. Write a short report of the procedure, sample, apparatus and results. Assess the correlation as a research tool in terms of advantages and limitations.	54, 56, 58, 60, 64, 108, 128, 130, 132
	For example: self reports of own tidiness and parent strictness, self-report on e.g. obstinacy, orderliness, parsimony.	63, 111
Biological approach	Describe and evaluate twin and adoption studies as research methods.	150, 157
	Alternative, experimental and null hypothesis, dependent variable (DV) and independent variable (IV) in experiments.	10, 102
	One- or two-tailed with regards to tests, levels of significance (e.g. $p \leq 0.01$, 0.05), critical and observed values.	104
	Mann–Whitney U, critical value and observed value.	114
	The use of control groups, experimental procedures, including allocating groups to conditions (e.g. randomising) and sampling.	16, 44
	Levels of measurement.	104
	Describe and evaluate the laboratory experiment method as it is used in general with human and with animal participants (including details specified for the Cognitive and Biological Approaches). Describe and evaluate, including strengths and weaknesses, the use of animals in laboratory experiments in the biological approach.	78
	Evaluate the use of animals in experiments in terms of credibility, ethical and practical issues.	
	Evaluate the use of laboratory experiments in terms of validity, reliability and generalisability.	8, 20, 32, 34, 36
	Devise and conduct one practical, which must be a test of difference collecting ordinal or interval/ratio data using an independent groups design. Carry out a Mann–Whitney test and interpret the findings. Write up the hypothesis, results and analysis of the study using an appropriate graph and a table of the results. Draw brief conclusions, considering issues of validity, reliability, credibility and generalisability.	10, 54, 56, 58, 60, 114, 128, 130, 132
	For example: compare male/female verbal ability/spatial ability, right- and left-handed people on different abilities.	
Learning approach	Describe and evaluate observation as a research method in psychology.	66, 68, 70
	Identify, describe and apply the terms participant, non-participant, overt, covert, naturalistic observations.	
	With regards to inferential statistics, identify, describe and apply (i) levels of measurement (ii) reasons for choosing a chi-squared (χ^2) test, Spearman and Mann–Whitney (iii) how to compare the observed and critical value(s) to judge significance. **Note:** with regard to inferential tests, no calculations will have to be carried out in the examinations and formulae do not have to be learnt.	104, 108, 110
	Describe, assess and apply guidelines, such as British Psychological Society (BPS) guidelines, about the use of humans in psychological research including guidelines about what not to do and what to do to protect human participants. Guidelines to include consent, deception, right to withdraw, debriefing of participants and competence.	12, 40, 42
	Carry out an observation using participants either from real life or using another medium, such as television. This practical must be designed and conducted according to ethical principles. The observation must focus on some aspect of learning theory (such as modelling or reinforcement). Analyse the findings to produce results, including using the chi-squared (χ^2) test. Apply issues of validity, reliability, generalisability and credibility to their results.	66, 68, 70, 72, 110, 128, 130, 132
	For example: nursery observation of toy choice, observation of TV – to see if positive reinforcement leads to desired response more than if no reward.	

Examples of Edexcel AS exam questions

June 2011 Unit 1

Questions 1–4 relate to the investigation below.

Mr Swain decides to investigate whether giving feedback via e-mail to his students about their work will improve their performance on future tests. He selects two of his classes and decides to give class **A** feedback and class **B** no feedback.

For questions 1 and 2 choose ONE answer from A, B, C or D

1. Which type of design is being used in this study? *(1 mark)*

    A Repeated measures

    B Independent groups

    C Matched pairs

    D Correlation

2. The students in class B are told that neither class will get feedback. Which ethical guideline is being broken here? *(1 mark)*

    A Right to withdraw

    B Consent

    C Deception

    D Confidentiality

For question 3 choose ONE answer from A, B or C.

3. Mr Swain devises the following hypothesis for his study: 'Students who receive feedback about their work will do better on future tests than those who receive no feedback.'

    Which of the following types of hypothesis is this an example of? *(1 mark)*

    A Directional (one-tailed)

    B Non-directional (two-tailed)

    C Null

For questions 4–6 choose ONE answer from A, B, C or D.

4. Class B, which receives no feedback, is also known as the ... *(1 mark)*

    A experimental group

    B control group

    C independent group

    D laboratory group

5. Qualitative data is normally gathered in the form of ... *(1 mark)*

    A percentages

    B numbers

    C words

    D graphs

6. Which of the following may be seen as an advantage of the matched pairs design? *(1 mark)*

    A Full control of variables

    B No order effects

    C High in ecological validity

    D Needs fewer participants than other designs

Unit 2 questions are similar to those on Unit 1.

15. Mrs Smith took over Mrs Jones's psychology class in January because Mrs Jones went on maternity leave. Mr Brown's class was not affected by staff change. Researchers decided to use this as a natural experiment to discover whether the students' level of attendance is affected by staff change part way through the year.

Figure 1: Table of results to show class attendance throughout the year

	Mrs Smith's & Mrs Jones's class	Mr Brown's class
Class attendance (%) before January	80%	95%
Class attendance (%) from January onwards	92%	93%

(a) Define what is meant by natural experiment. *(2)*

(b) Identify both the independent variable (IV) and the dependent variable (DV) in this experiment. *(2)*

(c) Write a suitable null hypothesis for this experiment. *(2)*

(d) Using the table in Figure 1, describe the results of this experiment. *(3)*

(e) Identify **one** participant or situational (extraneous) variable in this experiment and suggest how it may have affected the results. *(2)*

January 2011 Unit 1

16. As part of the course requirements for cognitive psychology you will have conducted a practical using an experiment.

    Evaluate your experiment. You may wish to look at:
    - Your sample
    - How you controlled variables
    - Your research design decisions
    - Any ethical issues.

Edexcel-type question

An animal behaviour unit conducted research on rats' learning behaviour in mazes. They measured how many trials each rat took to learn the maze as a measure of learning ability. The correlated the scores between parent rats and their offspring to see if there was any genetic link.

The results are shown in the scattergraph below.

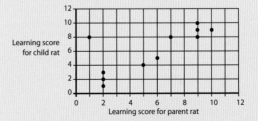

(a) Put a circle around the anomaly (outlier) on the scattergraph above. (1)

(b) Interpret the results of the correlation as shown in the scattergraph. (2)

(c) This correlational study involved the use of non-human animals, but non-human aimals are also used in experiments. Outline **one** strength of the use of non-human animals in experiments in terms of practical issues. (2)

EDEXCEL A2

Remember that specifications change – this specification is correct at time of publication, but do check.

The numbers represent the left hand page numbe for the spread where the topic is covered. The use of brackets indicates 'of some relevance'.

Unit 3		(52)
Criminology	Describe research methods used to assess witness effectiveness, including the laboratory experiment and the field experiment.	8, 10, (14), 30, 32, 34, 36, 38, (44)
	Evaluate, including the relative strengths and weaknesses, the research methods listed above, including their use in criminological psychology and reliability, validity and ethical issues.	
	Conduct a content analysis of magazine or newspaper articles or summarise two magazine or newspaper articles.	72, 90, 130
Child psychology	Describe the observational research method (including both naturalistic observations and structured observations, such as the strange situation) and the case study research method.	66, 70, 74
	Evaluate, including the relative strengths and weaknesses, the research methods above including their use in child psychology and reliability, validity and ethical issues.	
	Describe and evaluate cross-cultural and longitudinal ways of studying children in psychology.	76
	Conduct a content analysis of magazine or newspaper articles or summarise two magazine or newspaper articles.	72, 90, 130
Health psychology	Describe and evaluate the use of animals in laboratory studies when researching into drugs. Describe and evaluate two research methods using humans to study the effects of drugs.	8, 30, 54, 58, 60, 62, 78
	Evaluate, including relative strengths and weaknesses, research methods using animals (including both practical and ethical strengths and weaknesses) and humans (including issues of reliability and validity).	
	Conduct a content analysis of magazine or newspaper articles or summarise two magazine or newspaper articles.	72, 90, 130
Sport psychology	Describe and evaluate the use of questionnaires and correlations as a research method in sport psychology.	54, 58, 60, 62, 64
	Evaluate, including the relative strengths and weaknesses, the research methods listed above, including their use in sport psychology and reliability, validity and ethical issues.	
	Outline what is meant by qualitative and quantitative data and compare in terms of strengths and weaknesses.	54, 86
	Conduct a content analysis of magazine or newspaper articles or summarise two magazine or newspaper articles.	72, 90, 130

Unit 4		
Clinical psychology	Describe what is meant by primary and secondary data in doing research. Evaluate the use of primary and secondary data in doing research.	155, 157
	Describe and evaluate two research methods used in the study of schizophrenia, including one study for each of the two research methods to illustrate the use of the relevant method. Suitable examples: twin studies, case studies, animal experiments.	74, 78, 157
Psychology involves ethical issues in the treatment of participants (both humans and animals)	Describe five ethical guidelines (such as British Psychological Society (BPS) ethical guidelines) in psychological research, which relate to human participants.	12, 40, 42
	Describe five ethical principles that relate to the use of animals (non-human) in research in psychology.	78
	Describe and evaluate ethical issues in research in psychology, both regarding humans and regarding animals (non-human).	78
	Describe and evaluate (including strengths and weaknesses) two studies in terms of ethical considerations.	40

Psychology involves using different research methods	Describe and evaluate the following research methods and describe and evaluate one published study for each research method:
	  i) laboratory, field and natural experiments
	  ii) observations
	  iii) questionnaires
	  iv) interviews
	  v) content analyses
	  vi) correlations as designs
	  vii) case studies.
		8, 30, 38
		66, 68
		54
		56
		72
		64
		74

	Plan a study of your own when given a context, giving aim, hypotheses, design, procedure, ethical considerations, and how results would be analysed (including choice of statistical test as appropriate), and be able to evaluate the study.	128, 130
	Evaluate psychological studies with reference to the research methods used, including making suggestions for improvements (e.g. improving controls, changing the chosen method, improving reliability or validity). Note: a study may be given as stimulus material for evaluation.	10, 16, 18, 20, 32, 34, 36, 58, 60

Examples of Edexcel A2 exam questions

June 2011 Unit 3

Section A: Criminological psychology

A2 Psychologists often use laboratory experiments to investigate whether violence in the media causes anti-social behaviour.

Describe **one** feature of the laboratory experiment as a research method used in criminological psychology. *(2)*

A3 Describe **one** field study you have learned about in criminological psychology. Evaluate the field experiment as a research method. *(12)*

Section B: Child psychology

B1 It is rare for children to suffer extreme privation. Often psychologists use the case study as a research method in such situations.

(a) Describe the case study as a research method as it is used in child psychology. *(4)*

(b) Case studies are known to be useful in studying rare cases. Explain **one** other strength of using the case study as a research method. *(2)*

(c) Describe the weaknesses of using the case study as a research method. *(3)*

Section C: Health psychology

C2 (a) During your course you will have conducted a practical investigation on a topic in health psychology using either a content analysis or a summary of two article sources.

(i) Identify the area of health psychology you investigated for your practical. *(1)*

(ii) Describe how you carried out your content analysis or summary. *(3)*

(b) Explain the findings (results and/or conclusions) of your practical investigation using research, theories and/or concepts you have learned about in health psychology. *(4)*

Section D: Sport psychology

D2 Luanne conducted a questionnaire to investigate how sprinters felt after a big race. She collected both quantitative and qualitative data.

(a) Explain what is meant by quantitative data. *(2)*

(b) Explain what is meant by qualitative data. *(2)*

June 2011 Unit 4

6 (a) Describe the main features of observations as a research method. *(4)*

(b) (i) Explain **one** weakness of observations as a research method. *(2)*

(ii) Explain how the weakness you have explained in (b)(i) could be put right. *(2)*

7 (a) Read the information below about a psychological study.

A study was conducted into sleep deprivation in rats. The aim of the study was to see what happened if a rat was not allowed to sleep.

Each experimental rat was paired with a control rat. Every time an experimental rat fell asleep they were woken up by being pushed into water. At the same time the control rat was pushed into water whether it was asleep or awake.

The experimental rats that had been deprived of sleep suffered from many health problems and all died within a few weeks. The control rats however remained healthy.

The researchers concluded that lack of sleep caused the health problems and death of the experimental rats, and this suggests that humans would suffer if they did not get enough sleep.

Evaluate this study in terms of reliability, validity and generalisability. *(6)*

(b) Describe ethical issues that researchers should take into account when undertaking psychological research using animals. *(4)*

Edexcel-type question – Unit 3

Section A: Criminological psychology

(a) During your course you will have conducted a practical investigation on a topic in criminological psychology using either a content analysis or a summary of two article sources.

(i) Identify the area of criminological psychology you investigated for your practical. *(1)*

(ii) Describe how you carried out your content analysis or summary. *(3)*

(b) You will have gathered qualitative and/or quantitative data (information) for your practical investigation.

(i) Describe how you analysed the data (information) you gathered. *(3)*

(ii) Outline the conclusion(s) you drew from your practical investigation. *(2)*

Section B: Child psychology

Research on children often involves the use of structured observations.

(a) Describe the use of structured observations as a research method in child psychology. *(4)*

(b) Evaluate the structured observational research method in terms of **one** strength and **one** weakness. *(4)*

(c) A research intends to use the structured observational method in a study with children. Explain **one** ethical and **one** methodological issue that Kelly would need to be considered. *(4)*

Section C: Health psychology

Research on drugs often involves the use of non-human animals.

(a) Describe **one** research method using non-human participants that is used to investigate the effects of drugs. *(3)*

(b) Explain **one** strength of using non-human participants to study the effects of drugs. *(2)*

(c) Explain why researchers may choose to use humans instead of animals to research the effects of drugs. *(3)*

Section D: Sport psychology

(a) Describe the correlational research method as it is used in sport psychology. *(3)*

(b) Explain **one** strength and **one** weakness of the correlational method. *(4)*

(c) Interviews are also used in research on sport psychology. Explain why a research might choose to use an interview rather than a questionnaire to collect data in sports psychology. *(4)*

OCR AS

Remember that specifications change – this specification is correct at time of publication, but do check.

The numbers represent the left hand page number for the spread where the topic is covered. The use of brackets indicates 'of some relevance'.

Unit 1		(52)
Methods	Candidates will need to be familiar with four techniques for collecting/analysing data, and be able to identify strengths and weaknesses of the four techniques, both in general terms and in relation to source material. These are: • self-report • experiment (repeated measures and independent measures, matched subjects design) • observation • correlation.	
	For self-report this should include a knowledge and understanding of rating scales and open and closed questions and the strengths and weaknesses of each.	54, 56, 58, 60, 62
	For experiment this should include a knowledge and understanding of experimental design (independent measures and repeated measures) and the strengths and weaknesses of each.	8, 14, 30, 38, (44)
	For observation this should include a knowledge and understanding of participant and structured observation, time sampling and event sampling and the strengths and weaknesses of each.	66, 68, 70
	For correlation this should include a knowledge and understanding of positive and negative correlations and the interpretation of scattergraphs.	64
Investigative design	Frame hypotheses (null and alternate, one- and two-tailed).	10
	Identify variables (for experiment – identify and explain the difference between independent and dependent variables).	8
	Suggest how variables might be operationalised/measured.	18
	Suggest (in relation to source material) strengths and weaknesses of measurement and alternative forms of measurement.	60, 94
	Comment on the reliability and validity of measurement.	20, 32, 36, 58, 60
	Describe opportunity sampling, random sampling and self-selected sampling techniques.	16
	Identify strengths and weaknesses of opportunity, random and self-selected sampling techniques. Identify strengths and weaknesses of sampling techniques described in source material.	
	Suggest appropriate samples/sampling techniques in relation to source material.	
	Identify ethical issues in source material and suggest ways of dealing with ethical issues.	12, 40, 42
	Describe ethical issues relating to psychological research with human participants.	
	Suggest appropriate procedures in relation to source material.	Chapters 1, 2 and 3
Data analysis and presentation	Identify and describe the differences between qualitative and quantitative data.	54, (86)
	Identify strengths and weaknesses of qualitative and quantitative data.	
	Suggest appropriate descriptive statistics for data in source material (mean, median, mode).	22
	Sketch appropriate summary tables/graphs from data in source material (bar charts, scattergraphs).	22, 94
	Draw conclusions from data/graphs.	22, 94
Practical work	It will benefit candidates to have been involved in the design and conduct of small-scale research activities throughout the teaching of this unit. Candidates may keep a written record of their activities if desired but this will NOT be taken into the examination. The examination will require candidates to respond to source material of the following types.	128, 130
	A brief outline of a piece of research Candidates could be asked to: • identify strengths and weaknesses of the research method in general. • identify strengths and weaknesses of the specific research described in the source material. • suggest improvements to the research and their likely effects. • consider issues such as reliability and validity of measurements. • consider ethical issues raised by the source material. **The data produced by a piece of a research** Candidates could be asked to: • suggest appropriate descriptive statistics/graphical representations of data (Note: no inferential statistics are required for this unit). • draw conclusions from data/graphs. • sketch summary tables/graphs. **An outline of a proposed piece of research** Candidates could be asked to: • suggest appropriate hypotheses (null/alternate, one-tailed/two-tailed). • suggest how variables might be operationalised/measured. • suggest appropriate samples/sampling methods. • outline possible procedures. • evaluate the suggestions they have made.	
Core studies	Candidates will be assessed on issues and methods in relation to the core studies:	Covered above
	Issues: ethics, ecological validity, longitudinal and snapshot, qualitative and quantitative.	74, 76
	Methods: experimental (laboratory and field), case study, self-report, observation, methodological issues such as reliability and validity.	

Examples of marked student answers (with examiner's comments) are provided on the OCR website.
See www.ocr.org.uk/qualifications/type/gce/hss/psychology/documents/ and select 'support materials'.
This gives you useful insight into to how to maximise your marks.

Examples of OCR AS exam questions

June 2010 Unit 1

Section A

Researchers conducted a study investigating the correlation between amount of sleep and concentration. First, participants were asked how long they had slept the previous night in hours and minutes. This was then recorded as 'total minutes slept'. Concentration was then assessed using a letter cancellation task in which subjects had two minutes to read an extract from a book, counting the number of times that the letter 'f' appeared. The data is presented in the table below.

Participant (initials)	Total minutes slept the night before	Number of times the letter 'f' was identified
MM	480	14
MJ	270	12
JW	420	24
CC	390	20
EP	450	25
HA	180	8
MH	300	16
JD	360	18

1. Identify **one** strength and **one** weakness of the correlational method. *[4]*

2. Suggest an appropriate alternate hypothesis for this study. *[4]*

3. Identify **two** findings from the data in this study. *[3]*

4. Outline **one** strength and **one** weakness with the way that concentration was measured in this study. *[6]*

5. Explain what is meant by a positive correlation. *[2]*

Section B

Researchers conducted an independent measures design experiment in a local coffee bar, investigating whether receiving physical contact from someone increases their rating of friendliness.

The experiment took place between 11am and 2pm on a Wednesday. As members of the public left the coffee bar after paying, some were touched lightly on the upper arm by the cashier, whereas others were not. Outside the coffee bar, members of the public were asked how friendly they thought the staff were on a scale of 1 ('not very friendly') to 10 ('extremely friendly').

6. Identify the sampling technique used to obtain participants for this study and suggest **one** weakness with it. *[4]*

7. What is an 'independent measures design'? *[2]*

8. Identify **two** controls that could have been used in this study and explain why they would have been needed. *[6]*

9. (a) Identify the dependent variable (DV) in this study. *[2]*

   (b) Outline **one** strength and **one** weakness of the way that the dependent variable (DV) has been measured in this study. *[6]*

Section C

A researcher has become interested in studying stress associated with driving and wishes to conduct an investigation to assess stress levels of motorists in England using the self-report method.

10. Identify **one** strength and **one** weakness of using the self-report method in this study. *[4]*

11. Describe and evaluate an appropriate sampling technique for this study. *[10]*

12. Suggest an appropriate question using a rating scale, which could be used in this study. *[2]*

13. Evaluate the validity of using this question in this study. *[4]*

January 2011 Unit 1

Section A

Psychologists wanted to investigate why we don't laugh when we tickle ourselves. One idea is that it is a social act that is out of our control and must be done to us by another person. To investigate this, participants had the sole of their feet tickled by another person at any time during a 30-second period. Later on the same participants had to tickle themselves. They put their feet on a tickling machine (a feather on a rotating turntable) at any time they chose during a 30-second period. The volume of laughter was recorded in decibels.

1. (a) Identify the experimental design used in this study. *[2]*

   (b) Outline **one** strength and **one** weakness of using this experimental design in this study. *[6]*

2. Identify the independent variable (IV) and dependent variable (DV) in this study. *[2]*

3. Describe and evaluate **one** other way to measure the dependent variable (DV) in this study. *[10]*

Section B

A psychologist conducted a correlation study to investigate the relationship between the number of friends people claim to have on internet social networking sites and the number of times they go out socialising each month. The data was obtained from students in a psychology class who left the classroom one at a time to provide details to a researcher sitting outside.

The findings from the study are presented in the scattergraph below.

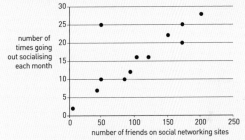

4. (a) How many participants was data collected from in this study and how do you know this? *[2]*

   (b) Name and briefly describe the sampling method in this study. *[2]*

   (c) Identify **one** strength and **one** weakness of using this sampling method for this study. *[4]*

5. (a) From the scattergraph presented above, what is the mode for 'the number of times going out socialising each month' and how do you know this? *[2]*

   (b) Outline **two** other findings from the scattergraph. *[4]*

6. (a) What is qualitative data? *[2]*

   (b) Suggest **two** examples of qualitative data that could have been collected in this study. *[4]*

Section C

Look at me! A group of psychologists are interested in conducting an observation study of people's behaviour as they walk past a shop window. The psychologists want to see if people pay any attention to their own reflection and, if so, what they do.

7. (a) Describe an appropriate procedure that could be used in this study. *[6]*

   (b) Evaluate the reliability and validity of carrying out the study in this way. *[6]*

8. (a) What is time sampling? *[2]*

   (b) Describe **one** strength and **one** weakness of time sampling if it were to be used in this study. *[4]*

9. Identify **one** ethical issue in this study. *[2]*

OCR A2

Remember that specifications change – this specification is correct at time of publication, but do check.

The numbers represent the left hand page numbe for the spread where the topic is covered. The use of brackets indicates 'of some relevance'.

Unit 4		[52]
Section A Research methods: the design of a practical project	The question paper will contain a short passage setting the scene and provide the focus for a set of research questions.	128, 130
	The assessment task will require the design of a specific practical project that could be carried out by candidates, for example a repeated measures design for an experiment involving two conditions and collecting at least ordinal data.	
	It is recommended that the process of designing, conducting and evaluating be practised within a classroom setting in preparation as candidates may be asked about practical difficulties or problems and how they could be overcome.	
Research methodology	A range of techniques, such as experiment, self-report, questionnaire and correlation.	8, 30, 38, 54, 56, 62, 64, 66, 68, 70, 74, 76
	The selection of a research question, the framing of operationalised hypotheses including null and research hypotheses; one- and two-tailed.	10, 18, 104
	The description and justification of the design – independent samples, repeated measures, matched pairs.	14, 40, 42
	Populations, a suitable sample and sampling method/technique.	16
	Materials.	
	The procedure, including the measurement of variables.	60, 94
	Using observations, self-reports or tests that generate nominal or at least ordinal data.	
	Control of extraneous variables (participant, experimenter and situational).	10, 32, 34, 58
	Counterbalancing of conditions and allocation of participants to groups.	14, (44)
	Ethical issues.	12, 40, 42 (78)
	The levels of measurement of the data.	104
	Collection and recording of data.	Chapters 1, 2 3 and 4
	Presentation of the data, including descriptive statistics, measures of central tendency and dispersion, data tables and graphs.	22
	Analysis of data: non-parametric tests (sign test, chi-squared, Wilcoxon, Mann–Whitney, Spearman) and levels of significance (probability, Type 1 and Type 2 errors).	102, 104, 106, 108, 110, 112, 114, 116
Evaluation of methodology	The strengths and weaknesses of different research methods.	38, 62,64, 66, 74, 76
	The strengths and weaknesses of any aspect of the design, the validity and reliability of the measurements.	14, 20, 32, 34, 36, 44, 58, 60, 70
	The ethics of the procedure.	12, 40, 42
Consideration of	Possible future research.	[52]
	Alternative designs and samples.	Chapters 1, 2, 3 and 4
Section B Approaches, perspectives, methods, issues and debates	Candidates will be assessed on issues and methods arising throughout the whole AS and A2 course.	As above
	Issues: ethics, ecological validity, longitudinal and snapshot, qualitative and quantitative.	
	Methods: experimental (laboratory and field), case study, self-report, observation, methodological issues such as reliability and validity.	
	E.g. Specimen paper	
	(a) Using your knowledge of psychology, outline the design of a basic experiment.	
	(b) Describe how the experimental method was used in any two pieces of psychological research that you have studied. [8]	
	(c) Using examples, compare the use of experiments with any one other method used in psychology. [12]	
	(d) Explain the advantages of using the experimental method. [8]	
	(e) Discuss how laboratory-based research can be useful in our understanding of everyday life. [8]	

Examples of marked student answers (with examiner's comments) are provided on the OCR website.
See www.ocr.org.uk/qualifications/type/gce/hss/psychology/documents/ and select 'support materials'.
This gives you useful insight into to how to maximise your marks.

Examples of OCR A2 exam questions

June 2010 Unit 4

Your task is to answer questions about how a piece of research related to the task below could be conducted.

Psychologists use correlational designs to investigate relationships between variables that are difficult to investigate experimentally. Correlational designs are often used to investigate the relationship between environmental variables and human behaviour. For example, research has examined environmental variables, such as heat, sunshine, pollution and social density (crowding) and their relationships with happiness, aggression, helping behaviours and performance on cognitive tasks.

You must choose **one** of the options (a)–(g):

(a) The relationship between levels of exposure to sunlight and happiness.

(b) The relationship between social density (crowding) and aggressive behaviours.

(c) The relationship between social density (crowding) and helping behaviours.

(d) The relationship between social density (crowding) and performance on cognitive tasks.

(e) The relationship between pollution levels and aggressive behaviours.

(f) The relationship between temperature and aggressive behaviours.

(g) The relationship between noise and performance on cognitive tasks.

You must use a correlational design and plan to collect at least ordinal level data. It must be a practical project that could be conducted.

Answer all the questions below in relation to your correlational design.

1. State an alternate hypothesis for your practical project. *[3]*

2. Describe the method you would use to conduct your practical project.

   13 marks are awarded for replicability and appropriateness and 6 for the quality of the design and its feasibility. *[13 + 6]*

3. Which inferential (non-parametric) test would you use to analyse the data? Give reasons for your choice. *[3]*

4. (a) Sketch a graph to present the data that could be collected. *[3]*

   (b) Explain **one** weakness of conducting this practical project as a correlation. *[3]*

5. What could this graph tell you about the relationship between the two variables? *[3]*

6. How would you address any **one** ethical issue in the conduct of this project? *[3]*

7. Outline **one** other way your research question could be investigated. *[3]*

Jan 2011 Unit 4

Your task is to answer questions about how a piece of research related to the passage below could be conducted.

Psychologists are interested in helping people overcome their fears, anxieties and phobias. One way of finding out about these is to ask people to fill out a questionnaire. In this way they can write about their fears, anxieties or phobias and how they can be overcome without having to talk about them.

You must choose **one** of the options (a)–(g):

(a) Fear of crime

(b) Anxiety in sport

(c) School phobia

(d) Phobia of open spaces

(e) Fear of horses

(f) Social phobia

(g) Examination anxiety

You must design a study that uses a questionnaire to collect data by opportunity sampling. It must be a practical project that could be conducted.

Answer all the questions below in relation to your practical project.

1. Construct a research question for your practical project. *[3]*

2. Describe the method you would use to conduct your practical project.

   13 marks are awarded for replicability and appropriateness and 6 for the quality of the design and its feasibility. *[13 + 6]*

3. Outline **one** advantage of using a questionnaire in your project. *[3]*

4. (a) Explain **one** strength of using closed questions in your project. *[3]*

   (b) Explain **one** weakness of using closed questions in your project. *[3]*

5. Explain how using leading questions could influence the results of your practical project. *[3]*

6. How could you ensure that your questionnaire would not cause too much distress to the participants?

7. Suggest a more appropriate sampling method you could have used to obtain participants for your practical project. Explain your answer. *[3]*

WJEC AS

Remember that specifications change – this specification is correct at time of publication, but do check.

The numbers represent the left hand page numbe[r] for the spread where the topic is covered. The use of brackets indicates 'of some relevance'.

Unit 2		(52)
Focus on applying to a novel situation	Define and offer advantages and disadvantages of qualitative and quantitative.	54, 86
	Research methods, including laboratory experiments, field experiments, natural experiments, correlations, observations, questionnaires, interviews and case studies.	8, 30, 38, (44), 54, 56, 62, 64, 66, 70, 74
	Issues of reliability and ways of ensuring reliability (split-half, test–retest, inter-rater).	60, 153
	Issues of validity (experimental and ecological) and ways of ensuring validity (content, concurrent, construct).	20 32, 24, 36, 58
	Ethical issues relating to research, including a lack of informed consent, the use of deception, a lack of the right to withdraw from the investigation, a lack of confidentiality, a failure to protect participants from physical and psychological harm.	12, 40, 42
	Define and offer advantages and disadvantages of different sampling methods, including opportunity, quota, random, self-selected (volunteer), stratified and systematic.	16
	Define and offer advantages and disadvantages, and draw conclusions from the following ways of describing data, including: - Development of a coding system – content analysis - Categorisation - Mean - Median - Mode - Range - Scattergraphs - Bar charts - Histograms.	22, 64, 72, 94

WJEC A2

Unit 3		
Research methods	Aims and hypotheses (directional, non-directional and null hypotheses).	10, 102
	Design issues relating to specific research methods and their relative strengths and weaknesses.	8, 14, 30, 38, (44), 54, 56, 62, 64, 66, 70, 72, 74, (76)
	Operationalisation of independent variables, dependent variables and co- variables.	18
	Ways of overcoming confounding variables.	20, 32, 34
	Ethical issues and ways of overcoming these issues.	12, 40, 42
	Procedures, including sampling and choice of apparatus.	16
	Appropriate selection of descriptive and inferential statistics for analysis of data.	22, 94, 102, 104 (106)
	Levels of significance.	102, 104
	Levels of measurement including nominal level, ordinal level, interval and ratio level.	104
	Statistical tests including chi-squared test, sign test, Mann–Whitney U test, Wilcoxon matched pairs, signed ranks test, and Spearman's rank order correlation coefficient.	108, 110, 112, 114, 116
Issues in research (examined with mini essays)	Issues relating to findings and conclusion, including reliability and validity.	34, 36, 38, 58, 60
	The advantages of the use of the scientific method in psychology.	52
	The disadvantages of the use of the scientific method in psychology.	52
	Ethical issues in the use of human participants in research in psychology.	12, 40
	Ways of dealing with ethical issues when using human participants in research in psychology.	42
	Ethical issues in the use of non-human animals in research in psychology.	78
	Ethical issues arising from two applications of psychology in the real world (e.g. advertising, military).	78

Guidance on how these questions are marked can be found on the WJEC website, see www.wjec.co.uk/index.php?level=21&subject=97

Select 'Examiner's reports'.

Examples of WJEC AS exam questions

January 2010 Unit 2

A psychologist is conducting an observation. Following four therapy sessions, 50 people with an animal phobia were observed to see how close they would go to the animal of which they have a phobia. The psychologist measures the distance between the caged animal and participant in metres. The psychologist decides to use a quota sample of participants with spider, snake or rat phobias. The psychologist then displays the results in a histogram (see right).

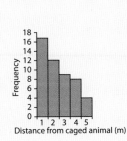

(a) Outline **one** advantage and **one** disadvantage of using an observation in this research. *[3]*

(b) Identify **one** issue of reliability in this research and describe how you could deal with this issue of reliability. *[3]*

(c) Identify **one** issue of validity in this research and describe how you could deal with this issue of validity. *[3]*

(d) Outline **one** advantage and **one** disadvantage of quota sampling in this research. *[3]*

(e) Discuss **one** ethical issue that might arise in this research. *[3]*

(f) State **one** conclusion that can be drawn from the histogram in this research. *[3]*

June 2011 Unit 2

A psychologist is conducting a natural experiment to investigate the effects of debt on the examination results of university students. The examination results of students who have low levels of debt (less than £5,000) and students who have high levels of debt (more than £12,000) were investigated. The psychologist is using a self-selected (volunteer) sample of students. The psychologist calculated the median examination results which were then put into a table (see below).

	Median examination results (maximum mark = 100)
Students with low levels of debt	78
Students with high levels of debt	71

(a) Outline **one** advantage and **one** disadvantage of using a natural experiment in this research. *[3]*

(b) Identify **one** issue of reliability in this research and describe how you could deal with this issue of reliability. *[3]*

(c) Identify **one** issue of validity in this research and describe how you could deal with this issue of validity. *[3]*

(d) Outline **one** advantage and **one** disadvantage of self-selected (volunteer) sampling in this research. *[3]*

(e) Discuss **one** ethical issue that might arise in this research. *[3]*

(f) State **one** conclusion that can be drawn from the median scores in this research. *[3]*

Examples of WJEC A2 exam questions

June 2011 Unit 3

Read the following material and answer ALL the questions that follow. You are advised to spend at least 5 minutes reading the information provided.

A natural experiment was carried out in a factory to test if 'weather affects people's mood'. Twenty employees were chosen by systematic sampling. They were asked to fill in a questionnaire. A scale was used to measure mood. A high score (5) indicated a 'happy' mood and a low score (1) indicated an 'unhappy' mood.

The same participants filled the questionnaire in twice: once when the sun was shining brightly and once when it was raining heavily.

1	2	3	4	5
Unhappy	Slightly unhappy	Neither happy nor unhappy	Slightly happy	Happy

(a) Define what is meant by the term 'natural experiment'. *[2]*

(b) Explain **one** advantage and **one** disadvantage of a natural experiment. *[4]*

(c) Identify the independent variable (IV) and the dependent variable (DV) in the above study. *[2]*

(d) (i) Define what is meant by the term 'systematic sample'. *[2]*
   (ii) Explain how a systematic sample could have been used to select participants in this research. *[2]*

(e) (i) Describe what is meant by the term 'confounding variable'. *[2]*
   (ii) Explain **two** confounding variables that may have affected the above study. *[4]*

(f) (i) Define what is meant by the term 'non-directional hypothesis'. *[2]*
   (ii) State **one** appropriate directional hypothesis for the above study. *[2]*

(g) (i) Define what is meant by the term 'nominal level data'. *[2]*
   (ii) Explain **one** advantage of this type of data. *[2]*

January 2010 Unit 4

An investigation was carried out to see if there is a correlation between mathematical ability and self-esteem. Ninety pupils sat a mathematical test which was scored out of 100. They then completed a self-esteem questionnaire. Self-esteem was rated between 10 and 100 (a high score equalled high self-esteem). A Spearman's rank order correlation coefficient of +0.87 was found.

An educational psychologist warned the investigator that self-esteem research involving children may produce the ethical issues of lack of informed consent and the failure to protect participants from psychological harm.

(a) (i) Define what is meant by the term 'correlation coefficient'. *[2]*
   (ii) What is meant by 'correlation coefficient of +0.87' (line 6) in this study? *[2]*

(b) (i) Define what is meant by the term 'co-variables'. *[2]*
   (ii) Identify the **two** co-variables in this study. *[2]*

(c) Define what is meant by the term 'operationalised'. *[2]*

(d) Explain **one** advantage and **one** disadvantage of using a correlation. *[4]*

(e) Explain **one** sampling method that could have been used in this study to select participants. *[2]*

(f) Define what is meant by the term 'reliability'. *[2]*

(g) Explain how either content or concurrent validity could be used to ensure validity in this study. *[2]*

(h) Describe what is meant by:
   (i) 'a lack of informed consent' (lines 8–9) *[2]*
   (ii) 'failure to protect participants from psychological harm' (lines 9–10). *[2]*

GLOSSARY

ABBA A form of *counterbalancing* to deal with *order effects* in which participants do condition A then B, then B and finally A. 14

absolutist The view is that some things are simply right or wrong, there is no relative position. For example, murder may be seen as wrong no matter what the circumstances. See *utilitarian*. 78

adoption studies offer a means of investigating the relative contributions of genes and environment by comparing a characteristic (such as IQ or smoking) in an adopted child with its biological parents/siblings (genetic link) and adopted parents/siblings (environmental link). See *twin studies* and *concordance rate*.

aims A statement of what the researcher(s) intend to find out in a research study. 10, 18

alternative hypothesis (or **alternate hypothesis**) A testable statement about the relationship between two variables. See *hypothesis* and *research prediction*. 11, 102, 106

anonymity A means of dealing with the *ethical issue* of *privacy*. Participants should not be identifiable. 41, 43, 75

attrition The loss of participants from a study over time. Those participants who are less interested or who have done less well may not be available for re-assessment in a *longitudinal study* or in the second condition of a *repeated measures design*, which means that the remaining sample is biased in favour of those who are more interested, more motivated, more successful, etc. 77

availability sample See *opportunity sample*. 16

bar chart A graph used to represent the frequency of data; the categories on the *x*-axis have no fixed order and there is no true zero. See *histogram*. 23

behaviour checklist A list of the behaviours to be recorded during an observational study. Similar to a *coding system*. 68, 70

behavioural categories Dividing a target behaviour (such as stress or aggression) into a subset of behaviours. 68, 72

bias A systematic distortion. It is a problem in research studies (e.g. *experimenter bias*, *interviewer bias*, *observer bias*, *social desirability bias*, *volunteer bias*). 16

boredom effect A kind of *order effect*. In a *repeated measures design*, participants may do less well on a later condition because they have lost interest. 14

briefing Giving instructions or preparatory information to someone. Provided at the beginning of a study, whereas *debriefing* is at the end. 12

calculated value See *observed value*. 104

case study A research investigation that involves a detailed study of a single individual, group of people, institution or event. Case studies provide a rich record of human experience but are hard to generalise from. 74, 76

ceiling effect occurs when test items are too easy for a group of individuals. Therefore, too many people do very well, i.e. 'hit the ceiling'. 58

chance An event that happens with no cause. 102

clinical interview A form of *semi-structured* or *unstructured interview* similar to the kind of interview used by a GP when determining a medical diagnosis. 56

closed questions In a questionnaire, questions that have a predetermined range of answers from which respondents select one. Produces *quantitative data*. Answers are easier to analyse than those for *open questions*. 54, 56

code of ethics A set of principles designed to help professionals behave honestly and with integrity. 42

coding system A systematic method for recording observations in which individual behaviours are given a code for ease of recording. Similar to a *behaviour checklist*. 68, 70, 72

cohort effect An effect caused because one group of participants has unique characteristics due to time-specific experiences during their development, such as growing up during the Second World War. This can affect both *cross-sectional* or *snapshot studies* (because one group is not comparable with another) and *longitudinal studies* (because the group studied is not typical). 77

conclusions The implications drawn from the *findings* (results) of a study; what the findings tell us about people in general rather than about the particular participants in a study. 11, 22, 104

concordance rate A measure of similarity (usually expressed as a percentage) between two individuals or sets of individuals on a given trait. There are two ways to calculate this. Pairwise concordance is defined as C/(C+D), where C is the number of concordant pairs and D is the number of discordant pairs. In probandwise concordance a proband is used, for example where one member of a set of twins is diagnosed with schizophrenia, the other member of the twin pair is the proband. Probandwise concordance is a measure of the proportion of twins who have the illness who have an affected twin and can be calculated with the formula of 2C/(2C+D), in which C is the number of concordant pairs and D is the number of discordant pairs.

concurrent validity A form of *external validity* related to questionnaires and interviews. A means of establishing *validity* by comparing an existing test or questionnaire with the one you are interested in. If the tests show a significant *positive correlation* this establishes the *concurrent validity* of the new test/questionnaire. 59

confederate An individual in an *experiment* who is not a real participant and has been instructed how to behave by the investigator/experimenter. 12, 19, 30

confidentiality An *ethical issue* concerned with a participant's right to have personal information protected. 41, 43, 75

confounding variable A variable that is not the *independent variable* (IV) under study but which varies systematically with the IV. Changes in the *dependent variable* may be due to the confounding variable rather than the IV, and therefore the outcome is meaningless. To 'confound' means to cause confusion. See *extraneous variable*. 20, 30, 32, 34

construct validity A means of assessing the *internal validity* of a *psychological test* by demonstrating the extent to which performance on the test measures an identified underlying construct. 59

content analysis A kind of *observational study* in which behaviour is observed indirectly in written or verbal material. A detailed analysis is made of, for example, books, diaries or TV programmes. May involve an initial *qualitative analysis* to produce categories, which then can be represented with *qualitative data* (examples from each category) or *quantitative data* analysis (counting the frequency of particular behaviours in each categories). 72, 90, 92

content validity A means of assessing the *internal validity* of a *psychological test* or measurement. It aims to demonstrate that the content (e.g. questions) of the test/measurement represents the area of interest. 58

contingency table A grid used to display the relationship between two or more items of frequency data. 110

continuous observation See *unstructured observation*.

control refers to the extent to which any *variable* is either held constant or regulated by a researcher. Both are examples of exercising influence or control. See *experimental control*. 20, 44

control condition In an *experiment* with a *repeated measures design*, the condition that provides a baseline measure of behaviour without the experimental treatment, so that the effect of the experimental treatment may be assessed. See *experimental condition*. 44

control group In an *experiment* with an *independent groups design*, a group of participants who receive no treatment. Their behaviour acts as a baseline against which the effect of the *independent variable* may be measured. See *experimental group*. 39, 44

controlled observation A form of investigation in which behaviour is observed but under conditions where certain *variables* have been organised by the researcher, in contrast with a *naturalistic observation*. 66

correlation (correlational analysis) Determining the extent of a relationship between two *variables*; *co-variables* may not be linked at all (*zero correlation*), they may both increase together (*positive correlation*), or as one co-variable increases, the other decreases (*negative correlation*). Usually a *linear correlation* is predicted, but the relationship can be *curvilinear*. 64, 107

correlation coefficient A number between –1 and +1 that tells us how closely the *co-variables* in a correlational analysis are related. 64

counterbalancing An *experimental* technique designed to overcome *order effects*. Counterbalancing ensures that each condition is tested first or second in equal amounts. 14, 21

co-variables The two measured variables in a *correlational analysis*. The variables must be continuous (*ordinal* or *interval data*). 64

covert observations See *undisclosed observations*. 69

critical value In an inferential test the value of the *test statistic* that must be reached to show significance, i.e. for the *null hypothesis* to be rejected. 105

cross-cultural study A kind of *natural experiment* in which the *independent variable* is different cultural practices and the *dependent variable* is a behaviour, such as aggression. This enables researchers to investigate the effects of culture/socialisation. 76

cross-sectional study One group of participants representing one section of society (e.g. young people or working class people) are compared with participants from another group (e.g. old people or middle class people). See *longitudinal study* and *snapshot study*. 77

curvilinear correlation A non-linear relationship between *co-variables*. For example, arousal and performance do not have a *linear* (straight line) relationship. Performance on many tasks is depressed when arousal is too high or too low, but it is high when arousal is moderate. 64

debriefing A post-research interview designed to inform the participants of the true nature of the study and to restore them to the state they were in at the start of the study. It can also be used to gain useful feedback about the *procedures* in the study. Debriefing is usually <u>not</u> seen as an *ethical issue*; it is a means of dealing with ethical issues. 12, 40, 42

deception An *ethical issue*, most usually where a participant is not told the true aims of a study (e.g. what participation will involve) and thus cannot give truly *informed consent*. Very occasionally deception actually involves the provision of false information, i.e. lying. 40, 43, 71, 86

deductive A form of reasoning from the general to the particular, e.g. developing a theory first and then generating a hypothesis from this. 53, 86

degrees of freedom (*df*) The number of values which are free to vary given that the overall total values are known. 105

demand characteristics A cue that makes participants unconsciously aware of the aims of a study or helps participants work out what the researcher expects to find. These may act as a *confounding variable*. 32, 34, 78, 86

dependent variable (DV) A measurable outcome of the action of the *independent variable* in an *experiment*. 8, 18

descriptive statistics Methods of summarising a data set, such as *measures of central tendency* and dispersion, and the use of *graphs*. 22–23, 104, 133

difference studies A form of *quasi-experiment*. Studies in which two groups of participants are compared in terms of a *dependent variable* (such as males versus females, or extraverts versus introverts). This is not a true *experiment* because the apparent *independent variable* (gender or personality) has not been altered. Often misnamed a *natural experiment*. 39

directional hypothesis States the kind of difference (e.g. more or less) or relationship (positive or negative) between two groups of participants or between different conditions. See *non-directional hypothesis*. 10, 19, 105

disclosed observations See *undisclosed observations*. 88

double blind design A research design in which neither the participant nor the researcher is aware of the condition that an individual participant is receiving. 20, 21, 32

DV See *dependent variable*.

ecological validity A form of *external validity*, concerning the ability to generalise a research effect beyond the particular setting in which it is demonstrated to other settings. Ecological validity is established by representativeness (*mundane realism*) and *generalisability* (to other settings). 36, 38, 70, 73, 86

effect size A measure of the strength of the relationship between two *variables*. 76

empirical data Information generated by direct observation or testing. 52

ethical committee A group of people within a research institution that must approve a study before it begins. 42, 45, 71

ethical guidelines See *code of ethics*. 42

ethnographic A method of qualitative research focused on the everyday lives of individual (cultural) groups as reported by members of those groups. It involves immersion in the group in order to report the perspective of group members. 88

ethical issues arise in research where there are conflicts between research goals and participant's rights. 12, 31, 40, 42, 45, 132

event sampling An observational technique in which a count is kept of the number of times a certain behaviour (event) occurs. See *time sampling*. 68, 72

experiment A *research method* that involves the direct manipulation of an *independent variable* in order to test its possible causal relationship with a *dependent variable*. See *laboratory experiment*, *field experiment*, *natural experiment*, *quasi-experiment*. 8, 14, 20, 30, 38

experimental condition In an *experiment* with a *repeated measures design*, the condition containing the *independent variable*. See *control condition*. 9, 11, 44

experimental control The use of techniques designed to eliminate the effects of *extraneous variables* in an *experiment*. See *control*. 20–21

experimental design A set of procedures used to control the influence of *participant variables* in an *experiment*, namely *repeated measures design*, *independent groups design* or *matched pairs design* (can be remembered using *RIM*). 14, 19

experimental group In an *experiment* with an *independent groups design*, a group of participants who receive the experimental treatment (the *independent variable*). See *control group*. 44

experimental hypothesis The *alternative hypothesis* in an *experiment*. 11

experimental realism The extent to which participants take an *experiment* seriously. If the simulated task environment is sufficiently engaging, the participants pay attention to the task and not to the fact that they are being observed, thus reducing *demand characteristics*. 32

experimental validity concerns both *internal* and *external validity* of an *experiment*. However, some exam boards regard it as just the *internal validity* of an experiment. 33

experimenter The person who directly interacts with participants when an *experiment* is carried out. The study may be designed by someone else, called the *investigator*. 20, 33

experimenter bias The effect that an experimenter's expectations have on the participants and thus on the results of the experiment – a kind of *experimenter effect*. 33

experimenter effects Anything the *experimenter* does which has an effect on a participant's performance in a study, other than what was intended. This includes *experimenter bias*. 86

external reliability A calculation of the extent to which a measure varies from another measure of the same thing over time. This can be assessed using the *test–retest method*. See also *reliability*. 60

external validity The degree to which a research effect can be generalised to, for example, other settings (*ecological validity*), other people (*population validity*) and over time (*historical validity*). 36, 38, 65, 70, 92, 93

extraneous variable In an *experiment*, any variable other than the *independent variable* that might potentially affect the *dependent variable* and thereby confound the results. There is some disagreement about the use of the terms *extraneous variable* and *confounding variable*. Strictly speaking extraneous variables do not vary systematically with the *independent variable (IV)* and therefore do not act as an alternative IV. They are simply nuisance variables that muddy the waters and make it more difficult to detect a significant effect. However, in practice, both terms are used somewhat interchangeably and most exam boards only mention one or the other! 14, 20, 30, 31, 32, 34, 38, 45, 52, 71, 135

face validity A form *of external validity* related to *questionnaires* and *interviews*. The extent to which the items look like what a test claims to measure. 59

fatigue effect A kind of *order effect*. In a *repeated measures design* participants may do less well on one condition rather than another because they have become tired or bored. 14

field experiment This is a controlled *experiment* that is conducted outside a lab. The key features are that the *independent variable* is still manipulated by the experimenter and, therefore, causal relationships can be demonstrated; it is conducted in a more natural setting than a *lab experiment* and may therefore have greater *ecological validity*; and participants are usually unaware that they are participating in an experiment, thus reducing *demand characteristics*. 30, 38

field study Any study that takes place away from the lab and within the context in which the behaviour normally occurs. 30

findings The factual data produced in a study, *quantitative* or *qualitative data*. *Conclusions* may be drawn from findings if the study was *valid* and *reliable*. The same as the *results* of a study.

floor effect occurs when test items are too difficult for a group of individuals. Therefore, too many people do poorly, i.e. 'hit the floor'. 58

forced choice question The participant must choose one item or alternative from (usually) the two offered. 54

Forer effect The observation that individuals will give high accuracy ratings to descriptions of their personality that supposedly are tailored specifically for them, but are in fact vague and general enough to apply to a wide range of people. 53

generalisability The degree to which the *findings* of a particular study can be applied to the *target population*. 16, 37

graph A pictorial representation of the relationship between *variables*. 23, 94, 133

Hawthorne effect The tendency for participants to alter their behaviour merely as a result of knowing that they are being observed. It acts as an *extraneous variable*. 30, 32

histogram A type of frequency distribution in which the number of scores in each category of continuous data are represented by vertical columns. In contrast to a bar chart, the data in a histogram have a true zero and a logical sequence. There are also no spaces between the bars. 23

historical validity A form of *external validity*, concerning the ability to *generalise* a research effect beyond the particular time period of the study. 36

holistic approach Perceiving the whole display rather than the individual features and/or the relations between them. 74

hypothesis A precise and testable statement about the world, specifically of the relationship between data to be measured. It is a statement about *populations* and not *samples*. Usually derived from a theoretical explanation. 10, 18, 19, 64

idiographic An approach to research that focuses more on the individual case as a means of understanding behaviour rather than a way of formulating general laws of behaviour (the *nomothetic* approach). 86

imposed etic A technique or theory developed in one culture and then used to study the behaviour of people in a different culture with different norms, values, experiences, etc. 76

independent groups design An *experimental design* in which participants are allocated to two (or more) groups representing different conditions. Allocation is usually achieved using *random techniques*. Contrast with *repeated measures design* and *matched pairs design* (RIM). 14, 35, 44, 77, 107, 118

independent variable (IV) Some event that is directly manipulated by an *experimenter* in order to test its effect on another variable (the *dependent variable*). 8, 18, 30

inductive A form of reasoning from the particular to the general, e.g. conducting a series of observations or research studies and using them to form a theory. See *deductive*. 53, 86

inferential statistics/tests Procedures for drawing logical conclusions (inferences) about the population from which samples are drawn. 22, 102, 104, 106–107, 106–121, 133

informed consent An *ethical issue* and an *ethical guideline* in psychological research whereby participants must be given comprehensive information concerning the nature and purpose of the research and their role in it, in order that they can make an informed decision about whether to participate. 12, 40, 43, 71

internal reliability A measure of the extent to which something is consistent within itself. For a *psychological test* to have high internal reliability, all test items should be measuring the same thing. This can be assessed using the *split-half* method. See also *reliability*. 60

internal validity The extent to which a procedure is measuring what it was intended to measure (rather than some other behaviour). In an *experiment* internal *validity* concerns whether an observed effect can be attributed to the experimental manipulation rather than some other factor. 32, 34, 35, 36, 38, 65, 70, 92

inter-interviewer reliability The extent to which two interviewers produce the same outcome from an *interview*. 60, 62

inter-observer reliability The extent to which there is agreement between two or more observers involved in observations of a behaviour. This is measured by *correlating* the observations of two or more observers. A general rule is that if (total number of agreements) / (total number of observations) > +.80, the data have high inter-observer reliability. 70, 72

inter-rater reliability *Correlating* the judgements of two or more ratings of behaviour, as when using a rating scale. Can happen in a *questionnaire* or *interview* when behaviour has been rated or in an *observation* when behaviour has been rated. 70, 92

interval data Data is measured using units of equal intervals, such as when counting correct answers or using any 'public' unit of measurement. See *plastic interval scales*. Remember *NOIR*. 104, 118

intervening variable A *variable* that comes between two other variables and can be used to explain the relationship between two variables. For example, if a *positive correlation* is found between ice cream sales and violence this may be explained by an intervening variable – heat – which causes both the increase in ice cream sales and the increase in violence. 65

interview A *research method* that involves a face-to-face, 'real-time' interaction with another individual and results in the collection of data. See *semi-structured interview*, *structured interview* and *unstructured interview*. 52, 54, 56, 58

interviewer bias The effect of an interviewer's expectations, communicated unconsciously, on a respondent's behaviour. 56, 58, 62

investigator The person who designs a research study and <u>might</u> conduct it. In some cases someone else (sometimes referred to as the *experimenter*) is the one who directly interacts with participants. See *investigator effects*. 21, 33

investigator bias The effect that the investigator's expectations have on the participants and thus on the results of an *experiment* or any study. See *experimenter bias*. 33

investigator effects Anything that the *investigator* (*experimenter*) does which has an effect on a participant's performance in a study other than what was intended. This includes direct effects (as a consequence of the investigator interacting with the participant) and indirect effects (as a consequence of the investigator designing the study). Some people only include direct effects in their definition of an investigator effect – the unconscious cues from the investigator/experimenter. Investigator effects may act as a *confounding* or *extraneous variable*. Investigator effects are not the same as *participant effects*. 20, 33, 34, 38, 71

IV See *independent variable*.

John Henry effect A *control group* might try extra hard to show that the old way is just as good or better than a new approach. This is a form of *participant effect* and a threat to *internal validity*. 45

lab Any setting (room or other environment) specially fitted out for conducting research. A lab (laboratory) is not the only place where scientific *experiments* can be conducted. It is, however, the ideal place for well-controlled scientific research because it permits maximum control. Labs are not used exclusively for experimental research, e.g. *controlled observations* are also conducted in labs. 30, 67

lab experiment An *experiment* carried out in the controlled setting of a *lab*. The lab environment enables the *experimenter* to control *extraneous variables* and therefore more reliable causal conclusions can be drawn about the relationship between the *independent* and *dependent variable*. Not all lab experiments have low *ecological validity* though there is usually a balance to be struck between *control* and *generalisability*. 30, 38

leading question A question that is phrased in such a way (e.g. 'Don't you agree that...?') that it makes one response more likely than another. The form or content of the question suggests what answer is desired. 34, 54, 56, 58, 62

level of measurement refers to the different ways of measuring items or psychological variables; the lower levels are less precise.

levels of the IV In an *experiment* the *independent variable (IV)* is usually in two (or more) forms, such as using the verb hit or smashed. Sometimes one of these forms (levels) can be considered a neutral condition. It is called the *control condition* in a *repeated measures design*. In an *independent groups design* the group experiencing that neutral condition is called the *control group*. 8, 14

lie scale A set of items included in a psychological questionnaire to indicate whether or not the respondent has been truthful in other parts of the test. 59

Likert scale Respondents can indicate the extent to which they agree or disagree with a statement. There are usually five levels ranging from 'strongly agree' through 'neutral' to 'strongly disagree'. 54

linear correlation A systematic relationship between *co-variables* that is defined by a straight line. See *curvilinear correlation*. 64

longitudinal study A study conducted over a long period of time. Often a form of *repeated measures design* in which participants are assessed on two or more occasions as they get older: the *independent variable* is age. See *cross-sectional study*. 77

matched pairs design An *experimental design* in which pairs of participants are matched in terms of *variables* relevant to the study, such as age, IQ, perceptual ability and so on. One member of each pair receives one *level of the IV* and the second pair member receives the other level of the IV. This means that *participant variables* are better controlled than is usually the case in an *independent groups design* experiment. 15

matched subjects design Same as *matched pairs design*.

materials refers to any equipment, tests, questionnaires and so on that are used in a research study. 128, 132

mean A *measure of central tendency*. The arithmetic average of a group of scores, calculated by dividing the sum of the scores by the number of scores. Takes the values of all the data into account in the final calculation (whereas the *mode* and *median* do not use the data values and make no final calculation). 22

measures of central tendency A descriptive statistic that provides information about a 'typical' or average response for a set of scores. See *mean*, *median*, *mode*. 22, 90, 133

measures of dispersion A *descriptive statistic* that provides information about how spread out a set of scores are. See *range*, *standard deviation*. 22, 90, 133

median A *measure of central tendency*. The middle value in a set of scores when they are placed in rank order. 22

meta-analysis A researcher looks at the *findings* from a number of different studies in order to reach a general conclusion about a particular hypothesis. 76

mode A *measure of central tendency*. The most frequently occurring score in a set of data. 22

mundane realism Refers to how a research study mirrors the real everyday world. The simulated task environment is realistic to the extent to which experiences encountered in the environment will occur in the real world. 31, 37, 38, 86

natural experiment A *research method* in which the *experimenter* has not manipulated the *independent variable (IV)* directly, but where it the IV has varied as a consequence of some other action, such as comparing children who have spent time in hospital with children who haven't. The experimenter makes use of such 'naturally' occurring *variables* and observes their effect on a *dependent variable*. Strictly speaking, an *experiment* involves the deliberate manipulation of an IV by the experimenter, so causal conclusions usually should not be drawn from a natural experiment. In addition, participants are not *randomly allocated* to conditions in a natural experiment, which may reduce *external validity*. See also *quasi-experiment*. 38

naturalistic observation A *research method* carried out in a unaltered setting, in which the *investigator* does not interfere in any way but merely observes the behaviour(s) in question. 66, 68, 71, 76, 88

negative correlation A relationship between two *co-variables* such that as the value of one co-variable increases, that of the other decreases. A perfect negative correlation is –1.0. 64

NOIR An acronym to help remember the four levels of measurement of data: *nominal*, *ordinal*, *interval* and *ratio*.

nominal data Data that are in separate categories, such as grouping people according to their favourite football team (e.g. Liverpool, Inverness Caledonian Thistle, etc.). Remember *NOIR*. 104

nomothetic An approach to research that focuses more on general laws of behaviour than on the individual, possibly unique, case (the *idiographic* approach). 86

non-directional hypothesis A form of hypothesis that states a difference, *correlation* or association between two *variables* but does not specify the direction (e.g. more or less, positive or negative) of such a relationship. 10, 19, 104

non-participant observation Observations made by someone who is not participating in the activity being observed. See *participant observation*. 69

normal distribution A symmetrical bell-shaped frequency distribution. This distribution occurs when certain *variables* are measured, such as IQ or the life of a light bulb. Such 'events' are distributed in such a way that most of the scores are clustered close to the *mean*. 118

null hypothesis An assumption that there is no relationship (difference, association, etc.) in the population from which a sample is taken with respect to the *variables* being studied. There is nothing going on. See *alternative hypothesis*. 11, 102, 105, 106

objectivity Being uninfluenced by personal opinions or past experiences, being free of *bias*. As distinct from *subjectivity*. 52, 75, 135

observation (observational study) A research technique where a researcher watches or listens to participants engaging in whatever behaviour is being studied. The observations are recorded. There are *naturalistic observations* and *controlled observations*. Observational methods may also be used in an *experiment* – in which case 'observation' is a *research technique* instead of a *research method*. 52, 66–71, 72, 76

observed value The value of a *test statistic* calculated for a particular data set. Also called the *calculated value*. 104, 133

observer bias In observational studies there is a danger that observers' expectations affect what they see or hear. This reduces the *external validity* of the observations. 70, 73, 76

one-tailed hypothesis Another name for a *directional hypothesis*. 10

one-tailed test Form of test used with a *directional hypothesis*. 105

one-way mirror A mirror that is reflective on one side but transparent on the other. This allows observers to watch *participants* without them being aware of the observers' presence. Participants may be told that they are being observed but this makes the observations less intrusive. 67, 71

open questions In an *interview* or *questionnaire*, questions that invite respondents to provide their own answers rather than select one of those provided. Tend to produce *qualitative data*, in which case answers are more difficult to analyse than those for *closed questions*. 54, 56

operationalise Ensuring that *variables* are in a form that can be easily tested. It means that the definition of a variable or construct is provided in the measurement of it. A concept such as 'educational attainment' or 'sociability' needs to be specified more exactly if we are going to investigate it in an *experiment* or *observational* study. The researcher identifies something more 'concrete' that can be measured, for example 'sociability' can be measured in terms of the number of friends a person has, or the extent to which a person seeks the company of others. 18, 33, 54, 68, 73, 87

opportunity sample A *sample* of *participants* produced by selecting people who are most easily available at the time of the study. Sometimes called *availability sampling*. 16

order effect In a *repeated measures design*, a *confounding variable* arising from the order in which conditions are presented, e.g. a *practice effect* or *fatigue effect*. Counteracted by using *counterbalancing*. 14, 20, 34

ordinal data Data are ordered in some way, e.g. asking people to put a list of football teams in order of liking. Liverpool might be first, followed by Inverness, etc. The 'difference' between each item is not the same; i.e. the individual may like the first item a lot more than the second, but there might only be a small difference between the items ranked second and third. Remember *NOIR*. 104

overt observation An *observational* technique where observations are 'open', i.e. the *participants* are aware that they are being observed. 68, 69

p See *probability*.

participant An individual who takes part in a research study and provides data for analysis. The term '*participant*' has come into use as a replacement for '*subject*' because the former reflects more accurately the active nature of participation. 8, 40

participant effects A general term used to acknowledge the fact that *participants* react to cues in an *experimental* situation and that this may affect the *validity* of any conclusions drawn from an investigation. For example, *demand characteristics*. Participant effects are not the same as *investigator effects*. 32, 34, 38, 58

participant observation Observations made by someone who is also participating in the activity being observed, which may affect their *objectivity*. See *non-participant observation*. 69, 88

participant variables Characteristics of individual *participants* (such as age, intelligence, etc.) that might influence the outcome of a study. This is not the same as *participant effects*. 14, 20, 32, 34, 35, 77

peer review The practice of using independent experts to assess the quality and validity of scientific research and scholarly articles. 134

pilot study A trial run of a research study, involving only a few participants who are representative of the *target population*. It is conducted to test any aspects of the research design, with a view to making improvements before conducting the full research study. 12, 15

piloting Similar to a pilot study but it just involves testing a part of an eventual study, such as testing a *questionnaire*. 55

placebo A condition that should have no effect on the behaviour being studied, it contains no active ingredient. Therefore, it can be used to separate out the effects of the *independent variable* from effects caused merely by receiving <u>any</u> treatment. 45

plastic interval scale The intervals are arbitrarily determined so we cannot actually know for certain that there are equal intervals between the numbers, as when using a rating scale. However, for the purposes of analysis, such data may be accepted as *interval data*. 104, 118

population All the people in the world. In any study, the sample of participants is drawn from a *target population*. 70, 102, 104, 118

population validity A form of *external validity*, concerning the extent to which the *findings* of a study can be *generalised* to other groups of people besides those who took part in the study. 36, 70

positive correlation A relationship between two *co-variables* such that as the value of one co-variable increases, this is accompanied by a corresponding increase in the other co-variable. A perfect positive correlation is +1.0. 64

practice effect A kind of *order effect*. In a *repeated measures design*, participants may do better on one condition rather than another because they have completed it first and therefore may have improved their ability to perform the task. 14

predictive validity A means of assessing the *validity* or trueness of a *psychological test* by correlating the results of the test with some later example of the behaviour that is being tested. If the test result is *positively correlated* with the later behaviour this confirms the validity of the test. 59

presumptive consent A method of dealing with lack of *informed consent* or *deception*, by asking a group of people who are similar to the *participants* whether they would agree to take part in a study. If this group of people consent to the *procedures* in the proposed study, it is presumed that the real participants would agree as well. 41, 42

primary data Information observed or collected directly from first-hand eperience. See *secondary data*.

privacy An *ethical issue* that refers to a zone of inaccessibility of mind or body and the trust that this will not be 'invaded'. Contrast with *confidentiality*. Can be dealt with in some situations by providing *anonymity*. 41, 43, 69, 71

probability (*p*) A numerical measure of the likelihood or *chance* that certain events will occur. 102, 106

procedures The steps taken when a research study is conducted. Sometimes the 'procedures' are taken to include design decisions as well. See *standardised procedures*. 128

protection from harm An *ethical issue*. During a research study, *participants* should not experience negative psychological effects, such as lowered self-esteem or embarrassment. 40, 43

psychological test The measurement of any psychological ability, such as personality or intelligence or emotional type. 58, 132

purposive sample is a *sample* selected in a deliberate and non-random fashion to achieve a certain goal. 16, 88, 89

qualitative (research) Dealing with descriptions rather than things that can be counted (*quantitative*). 86, 88–89, 133

qualitative analysis Any form of means of extracting meaning from data that focuses more on words (i.e. what participants say) than on forms of numerical data. Qualitative analyses interpret the meaning of an experience to the individual(s) concerned. See *thematic analysis*. 72, 131

qualitative data Information in words that cannot be counted or quantified. Qualitative data can be turned into *quantitative data* by placing them in categories and counting frequency. 54–55, 57, 74

quantitative Dealing with numerical data (how much, how often, etc). 86

quantitative analysis Any form of means of extracting meaning from data that uses numerical data as the basis for investigation and interpretation (e.g. *descriptive* or *inferential statistics*). 72, 131

quantitative data Information that represents how much or how long, or how many, etc. there are of something; i.e. a behaviour is measured in numbers or quantities. 54–55, 57, 74

quasi-experiment Research designs that are 'almost' experiments but lack one or more features of a true experiment. This includes *natural experiments* and *difference studies*. 39

questionnaire A *research method* in which data is collected through the use of written questions, which may be *open* or *closed questions*. Also called a *survey*. 52, 54, 56, 62, 132

questionnaire fallacy The erroneous belief that a *questionnaire* actually produces a true picture of what people do and think. 58

quota sample Similar to a *stratified sample* except participants are not selected from strata using a *random sampling* technique. 17

random Happening without any pattern. 16

random allocation Allocating participants to *experimental groups* or conditions using *random* techniques. 14, 38

random sample A *sample* of *participants* produced by using a *random* technique such that every member of the *target population* being tested has an equal chance of being selected. 16, 19

range A *measure of dispersion* that measures the difference between the highest and lowest score in a set of data. 22

rating scale A means of assessing attitudes or experiences by asking a respondent to rate statements on a scale of 1 to 3 or 1 to 8, etc. Produces *ordinal data*. 54, 68, 104

ratio data The same as *interval data* except ratio data has a true zero point, as in most measures of physical quantities. Remember *NOIR*. 104, 118

reflexivity In *qualitative research*, a researcher reflects or thinks critically during the research process about the factors that affect the behaviour of both researchers and *participants*. This reflective process recognises the social dynamics of the research process and how this affects data collected. Reflections can be used when interpreting the results. 92

reliability A measure of consistency both within a set of scores or items (*internal reliability*) and also over time such that it is possible to obtain the same results on subsequent occasions when the measure is used (*external reliability*). 60, 62, 70, 92

repeated measures design A type of *experimental design* in which each participant takes part in every condition under test. Contrast with *independent groups design* and *matched pairs design* (*RIM*). 14, 35, 44, 107, 118

replication The opportunity to repeat an investigation under the same conditions in order to test the *validity* and *reliability* of its *findings*. 36, 38, 53, 73, 128, 132

representative sample A *sample* selected so that it accurately stands for or represents the *population* being studied. 16

research hypothesis See *hypothesis*. 11

research method A way of conducting research (such as an *experiment* or a *questionnaire*) as distinct from the *research design* of the investigation. 55

research prediction A forecast of the outcome of a study based on the *hypothesis*. The research prediction is about *samples*, whereas the hypothesis is about *populations*. 19, 132

research technique The specific *procedures* used in a variety of research methods, such as *control* of *variables*, *sampling* methods and *coding systems*. 55

response set A tendency for respondents to answer all questions in the same way, regardless of context. This would *bias* their answers.

results See *findings*.

right to withdraw An *ethical issue*. Participants should have the right to withdraw from participating in an *experiment* if they are uncomfortable with the study. 40, 43

RIM An acronym to help remember the three *experimental designs* (*repeated measures*, *independent groups* and *matched pairs*).

role play A controlled observation in which participants are asked to imagine how they would behave in certain situations, and act out the part. This method has the advantage of permitting one to study behaviours that might be unethical or difficult to study in an *experiment* or other *research method*. 76

sample A selection of participants taken from the *target population* being studied and intended to be *representative* of that population. 16, 89, 102, 104

sampling The process of obtaining a *sample*. 68

sampling technique/procedure The method used to *sample* participants, such as *random*, *opportunity* and *volunteer sampling*, or to sample behaviours in an observation such as *event* or *time sampling*. 16

scattergram or **scattergraph** A graphical representation of the relationship (i.e. the *correlation*) between two sets of scores. 23, 64

science A systematic approach to gaining and verifying knowledge. 18, 52

scientific method An objective means of testing *hypotheses* in order to develop *empirically*-based explanations/theories. 53

secondary data Information used in a research study that was collected by someone else or for a purpose other than the current one. For example, published data or data collected in the past. See *primary data*. 142

self-report method Any *research method* where *participants* are asked to report their own attitudes, abilities and/or feelings, such as a *questionnaire*, *interview* or some *psychological tests* (if a test measures an ability then it is not a self-report method). 52

self-selected sample A *sample* of *participants* produced by participants themselves determining whether they will take part in a study. This is generally taken to be equivalent to *volunteer sample* but strictly speaking can include situations where, for example, a participant crosses the road and their behaviour is recorded as part of an observational study. 16

semi-structured interview An interview that combines some pre-determined questions (as in a *structured interview*) and some questions developed in response to answers given (as in an *unstructured interview*). 56, 62, 72, 88

significance A statistical term indicating that the research *findings* are sufficiently strong to enable a researcher to reject the *null hypothesis* under test and accept the *research hypothesis*. 64, 102, 104

significance level The level of *probability* (*p*) at which it has been agreed to reject the *null hypothesis*. 102, 104, 105, 133

single blind design A type of *research design* in which the *participant* is not aware of the research aims and/or of which condition of the *experiment* they are receiving. 14, 32

situational variables Factors in the environment that could act as an *extraneous variable*, such as noise, time of day or the behaviour of an *investigator*. 20, 34

snapshot study A study carried out over a very short period of time, such as hours and days, in comparison to a *longitudinal study*. May be used to specifically refer to studies looking at the effects of age. See *cross-sectional study*. 77

social desirability bias A tendency for respondents to answer questions in such a way that presents themselves in a better light. 54, 56, 58, 62

speciesism The assumption that some individuals are superior based solely on the grounds that they are members of the species *Homo Sapiens*. Speciesim is similar to sexism or racism – where superiority is defined by sex or race. 78

split-half reliability A method of determining the *internal reliability* of a *questionnaire* or *psychological test*. Test items are split into two halves and the scores on both halves compared. Scores should be similar if the test is reliable. 60

standard deviation A *measure of dispersion* that shows the amount of variation in a set of scores. It assesses the spread of data around the *mean*. 22, 118

standardised instructions A set of instructions that are the same for all participants so as to avoid *investigator effects* caused by different instructions. 21, 33, 132

standardised procedures A set of *procedures* that are the same for all participants so as to enable *replication* of the study to take place. 21, 33

statistical test See *inferential test*. 102

stratified sample A *sampling technique* in which groups of *participants* are selected in proportion to their frequency in the *population* in order to obtain a *representative sample*. The aim is to identify sections of the population, or strata, that need to be represented in the study. Individuals from those strata are then selected for the study using a *random* technique. If the sample is not randomly selected from the stratum, it is then a *quota sample*. 17

structured interview Any *interview* in which the questions are decided in advance. 56, 62, 88

structured observation The researcher uses various 'systems' to organise observations, such as a *sampling technique* and *behavioural categories*. 66

studies using correlational analysis Any study that uses *correlational analysis* to determine the meaning of the data. 64

subject See *participant*.

subjectivity refers to an individual's personal view, affected by beliefs and emotions. As contrasted with *objectivity*. 86, 92

survey The general name for *questionnaires* and *interviews*.

systematic sample A method of obtaining a representative *sample* by selecting every 5th, 7th, 10th person, etc. This can be *random* if the first person is selected using a random method; then you select every 5th, 7th, 10th person after this. 16

table of critical values A table that contains the numbers used to judge significance (whether the *null hypothesis* can be rejected). The *observed* (*calculated*) value of the *test statistic* is compared to the number in the table (called the *critical value*) to see if the observed value is significant. 105

target population The group of people that the researcher is interested in. The group of people from whom a *sample* is drawn. The group of people about whom *generalisations* can be made. See *population*. 16, 19, 20, 106

test statistic An *inferential test* is used to calculate a numerical value. For each test this value has a specific name, such as *T* for the Wilcoxon test. 104, 133

test–retest method A method used to check *reliability*. The same *questionnaire*, *interview* or *psychological test* is given to the same *participants* on two occasions to see if the same results are obtained. 60

thematic analysis A technique used when analysng *qualitative data*. Themes or categories are identified before starting a piece of research; then responses from an *interview* or *questionnaire* or *observation* are organised according to these themes. 90

time sampling An *observational technique* in which the observer records behaviours in a given time frame, e.g. noting what a target individual is doing every 15 or 20 seconds or 1 minute. The observer may select one or more categories from a *behaviour checklist*. Contrast with *event sampling*. 68, 72

triangulation Comparing the results of two or more studies of the same thing to see if they are in agreement. This demonstrates the *validity* of the individual results. 93

twin studies Research conducted using twins. If nature (genetics) is a more important influence than nurture (environment) then we would expect monozygotic (MZ) twins to be more similar than dizygotic (DZ) twins in terms of a target behaviour, such as intelligence or personality. (MZ twins are identical genetically whereas DZ twins on average share only 50% of the same genes.) Such studies may look at twins reared apart to reduce the *confounding variable* of a shared environment. See *adoption studies* and *concordance rate*.

two-tailed hypothesis See *non-directional hypothesis*. 10

two-tailed test Form of test used with a *non-directional hypothesis*. 105

Type 1 error Rejecting a *null hypothesis* that is true. This is a false positive and is more likely to happen if the *significance level* selected is too high (lenient, e.g. 10%). 106

Type 2 error Accepting a *null hypothesis* that is in fact not true. This is a false negative and is more likely to happen if the *significance level* selected is too low (stringent, e.g. 1%). 106

undisclosed observations (covert observations) Observing people without their knowledge, e.g. using *one-way mirrors*. Knowing that behaviour is being observed is likely to alter a participant's behaviour. 69

unstructured interview An interview that starts out with some general aims and possibly some questions, and lets the interviewee's answers guide subsequent questions. 56, 62

unstructured observation Every instance of a behaviour is recorded in as much detail as possible. This is useful if the behaviours you are interested in do not occur very often. 66, 68

utilitarian A type of morality where decisions about what is right or wrong are based on the principle of what is useful or practical for the majority of people. Established by weighing costs and benefits for individuals and society. See *absolutist*. 78

validity Refers to whether an observed effect is a genuine one. This includes the extent to which a researcher has measured what he/she intended to measure (*internal validity*) and the extent to which the *findings* can be applied beyond the research setting (*external validity*). 32, 36, 52, 54, 58, 62, 92

variables Anything of relevance in a study that can vary or change. See *independent variable* and *co-variable*, *dependent variable*, *extraneous variable* and *confounding variable*. 8

variance A *measure of dispersion*, describing the spread of data around the mean. It is the square of the *standard deviation*. 118

volunteer An individual who, acting on their own volition, applies to take part in an investigation. 16

volunteer bias A form of *sampling bias* because *volunteer* participants are usually more highly motivated than *randomly* selected *participants*. 16

volunteer sample A *sample* of *participants* produced by a *sampling technique* that relies solely on inviting people to take part. 16

x axis The horizontal axis on a graph, going across the page. Usually is the *independent variable*. 23, 64

y axis The vertical axis on a graph, going up vertically. Usually is the *dependent variable* or 'frequency'. 23, 64

zero correlation No relationship (*correlation*) between *co-variables*. 64

REFERENCES

Abernethy, E.M. (1940). The effect of changed environmental conditions upon the results of college examinations. *Journal of Psychology, 10,* 293–301.

Baddeley, A.D. and Longman, D.J.A. (1978). The influence of length and frequency on training sessions on the rate of learning type. *Ergonomics, 21,* 627–635.

Bandura, A., Ross, D. and Ross, S.A. (1961). Transmission of aggression through imitation of aggressive models. *Journal of Abnormal and Social Psychology, 63,* 575–582.

Bateson, P. (1986). When to experiment on animals. *New Scientist, 109,* 30–32.

BEO (2004). Behavioural observation, University of Bern. http://www.psy.unibe.ch/beob/proj_ex.htm and http://www.psy.unibe.ch/beob/home_e.htm (accessed September 2004).

Bickman, L. (1974). Clothes make the person. *Psychology Today, 8 (4),* 48–51.

Blackmore, S.J. (1997). Probability misjudgement and belief in the paranormal A newspaper survey. *British Journal of Psychology, 88,* 683–689.

Brooks, M. (2010). We need to fix peer review now. New Scientist blog. http://www.newscientist.com/blogs/thesword/2010/06/we-need-to-fix-peer-review-now.html (accessed February 2012).

Brosnan, M. (2008). Digit ratio as an indicator of numeracy relative to literacy in 7-year-old British school children. *British Journal of Psychology, 99,* 75–85.

Browning, C. (1992). *Ordinary Men: Reserve Police Battalion 101 and the Final Solution in Poland.* New York: HarperCollins.

Bruner, E.M. and Kelso, J.P. (1980). Gender differences in graffiti: A semiotic perspective. *Women's Studies International Quarterly, 3,* 239–252.

Buri, J.R. (1991). Parental authority questionnaire. *Journal of Personality Assessment, 57 (1),* 110–119.

Burns, A. (1998). 'Pop' psychology or Ken behaving badly. *The Psychologist, 11 (7),* 360.

Burt, C.L. (1955). The evidence for the concept of intelligence. *British Journal of Psychology, 25,* 158–177.

Burt, C.L. (1966). The genetic determination of differences in intelligence: a study of monozygotic twins reared together or apart. *British Journal of Psychology, 57,* 137–153.

Buss, D. (1989). Sex differences in human mate preferences. *Behavioural and Brain Sciences, 12,* 1–49.

Carmichael, L., Hogan, P. and Walter, A. (1932). An experimental study of the effect of language on the reproduction of visually perceived forms. *Journal of Experimental Psychology, 15,* 73–86.

Carroll, J.S. (1978). The effect of imagining an event on expectations for the event: An interpretation in terms of the availability heuristic. *Journal of Experimental Social Psychology, 14(1),* 88–96.

Charlton, T., Gunter, B. and Hannan, A. (eds) (2000). *Broadcast Television Effects in a Remote Community.* Hillsdale, NJ: Lawrence Erlbaum.

Colapinto, J. (2000). *As Nature Made Him: The Boy who was Raised as a Girl.* New York: Quartet Books.

Coolican, H. (1996). *Introduction to Research Methods and Statistics in Psychology.* London: Hodder and Stoughton.

Coolican, H. (2004). Personal communication.

Crabb, P.B. and Bielawski, D. (1994). The social representation of material culture and gender in children's books. *Sex Roles, 30 (1/2),* 69–79.

Craik, F.I.M. and Lockhart, R.S. (1972). Levels of processing: A framework for memory research. *Journal of Verbal Learning and Verbal Behaviour, 11,* 671–684.

Craik, F.I.M. and Tulving, E. (1972). Depth of processing and the retention of words in episodic memory. *Journal of Experimental Psychology, 104,* 268–294.

Dunayer, J. (2002). Animal equality. http://www.upc-online.org/thinking/animal_equality.html (accessed January 2012).

Dutton, D.G., and Aron, A.P. (1974). Some evidence for heightened sexual attraction under conditions of high anxiety. *Journal of Personality and Social Psychology, 30,* 510–517.

Eagly, A.H. (1978). Sex differences in influenceability. *Psychological Bulletin, 85,* 86–116.

Eagly, A.H. and Carli, L. (1981). Sex of researchers and sex-typed communications as determinants of sex differences in influenceability: A meta-analysis of social influence studies. *Psychological Bulletin, 90,* 1–20.

Ekman, P. and Friesen, W.V. (1978). *Manual for the Facial Action Coding System.* Palo Alto, CA: Consulting Psychology Press.

Epstein, R., Lanza, R.P. and Skinner, B.F. (1981). 'Self-awareness' in the pigeon. *Science, 212,* 695–696.

Festinger, L., Riecken, H.W. and Schachter, S. (1956). *When Prophecy Fails.* Minneapolis: University of Minnesota Press.

Fick, K. (1993). The influence of an animal on social interactions of nursing home residents in a group setting. *American Journal of Occupational Therapy, 47,* 529–534.

Forer, B.R. (1949). The fallacy of personal validation: A classroom demonstration of gullibility. *Journal of Abnormal and Social Psychology, 44,* 118–123.

French, C. (2011). Failing the future? *The Skeptic, 22 (4)/23 (1),* 13.

Freud, S. (1909). 'Analysis of phobia in a five-year-old boy'. In J. Strachey (ed. and trans.) *The Complete Psychological Works: The Standard Edition* (vol. 10). New York: Norton, 1976.

Furlong, C. (2011). A fresh look at the London riots. http://www.thesaint-online.com/2011/12/a-fresh-look-at-the-london-riots/ (accessed January 2012).

Gillie, O. (1976). Crucial data faked by eminent psychologist, *Sunday Times,* October 24, 1976, London.

Gilligan, C. and Attanucci, J. (1988). Two moral orientations: gender differences and similarities. *Merrill-Palmer Quarterly, 34,* 223–237.

Gray, J.A. (1991). On the morality of speciesism. *The Psychologist, 14,* 196–198.

Griffiths, M.D. (1993). Fruit machine addiction in adolescence: A case study. *Journal of Gambling Studies, 9,* 387–399.

Gupta, S. (1991). Effects of time of day and personality on intelligence test scores. *Personality and Individual Differences, 12 (11),* 1227–1231.

Hansard (2007). http://www.publications.parliament.uk/pa/cm200607/cmhansrd/cm071024/text/71024w0028.htm (accessed December 2008).

Hatfield, E. and Walster, G.W. (1981). *A new look at love.* Reading, MA: Addison-Wesley.

Helweg-Larsen, M., Tobias, M.R. and Cerban, B.M. (2010). Risk perception and moralisation among smokers in the USA and Denmark: A qualitative approach. *British Journal of Health Psychology, 15,* 871–886.

Hilts, P. (1995). *Memory's Ghost: The Strange Tale of Mr. M. and the Nature of Memory.* New York: Simon and Schuster.

Hodges, J. and Tizard, B. (1989). Social and family relationships of ex-institutional adolescents. *Journal of Child Psychology and Psychiatry, 30(1)*, 77–97.

Hofling, K.C., Brontzman, E., Dalrymple, S., Graves, N. and Pierce, C.M. (1966). An experimental study in the nurse–physician relationship. *Journal of Mental and Nervous Disorders, 43*, 171–178.

Horton, R. (2000). Genetically modified food: consternation, confusion and crack up. *Medical Journal of Australia, 172*, 148–149.

House of Lords Select Committee on Animals in Scientific Procedures Report, The Stationery Office, 16 July 2002, retrieved December 6, 2006.

Hovey, H.B. (1928). Effects of general distraction on the higher thought processes. *American Journal of Psychology, 40,* 585–591.

Inman, A.G, Altman, A., Kaduvettoor-Davidson, A., Carr, A. and Walke, J.A. (2011). Cultural intersections: A qualitative inquiry into the experience of Asian–White interracial couples. *Family Process, 50,* 248–266.

Intons-Peterson, M.J. (1983). Imagery paradigms: How vulnerable are they to experimenters' expectations? *Journal of Experimental Psychology – Human Perception and Performance, 9,* 394–412.

Jarvis, M. and Chandler, E. (2001). *Angles on Child Psychology*. Cheltenham: Nelson Thornes.

John, L.K., Loewenstein, G. and Prelec, D. (2012). Measuring the prevalence of questionable research practices with incentives for truth-telling. *Psychological Science* (in press).

Jordan, R.H. and Burghardt, G. (1986). Employing an ethogram to detect reactivity of black bears (*Ursus americanus)* to the presence of humans. *Ethology, 73,* 89–155.

Joronen, K. and Åstedt-Kurki, P. (2005). Familial contribution to adolescent subjective well-being. *International Journal of Nursing Practice, 11 (3),* 125–133.

Jost, A. (1897). Die assoziationsfestigkeit in iher Abhängigheit von der Verteilung der Wiederholungen. *Zeitschrift für Psychologie, 14,* 436–472.

Joynson, R.B. (1989). *The Burt Affair*. London: Routledge.

Kamin, L.J. (1977). *The Science and Politics of IQ*. Harmondsworth: Penguin.

Karlsson, M., Milberg, A. and Strang, P. (2012). Dying cancer patients' own opinions on euthanasia: An expression of autonomy? A qualitative study. *Palliative Medicine, 26 (1),* 34–42.

Kilkenny, C., Parsons, N., Kadyszewski, E., Festing, F.W., Cuthill, I.C., Fry, D., Hutton, J. and Altman, D.G. (2009). Survey of the quality of experimental design, statistical analysis and reporting of research using animals. *PLoS ONE, 4 (11)*. Can be accessed at www.plosone.org/article/info:doi/10.1371/journal.pone.0007824 (accessed January 2012).

Kohlberg, L. (1978). Revisions in the theory and practice of moral development. *Directions for Child Development, 2, 83–88.*

Köhnken, G., Milne, R., Memon, A. and Bull, R. (1999). A meta-analysis on the effects of the cognitive interview. *Special Issue of Psychology, Crime and Law, 5,* 3–27.

Laird, J.D. (1974). Self-attribution of emotion: The effects of facial expression on the quality of emotional experience. *Journal of Personality and Social Psychology, 29,* 475–486.

Lamb, M.E. and Roopnarine, J.L. (1979). Peer influences on sex-role development in preschoolers. *Child Development, 50,* 1219–1222.

Lebowitz, E.R., Vitulano, L.A. and Omer, H. (2011). Coercive and disruptive behaviours in pediatric Obsessive Compulsive Disorder: A qualitative analysis. *Psychiatry, 74 (4),* 362–371.

Löfgren-Mårtenson, L. and Månsson, S.-A. (2010). Lust, love and life: A qualitative study of Swedish adolescents' perceptions and experiences with pornography. *Journal of Sex Research, 47 (6),* 568–579.

Loftus, E.F. and Palmer, J.C. (1974). Reconstruction of automobile destruction: An example of the interaction between language and memory. *Journal of Verbal Learning and Verbal Behavior, 13,* 585–589.

Mackintosh, J. (ed.) (1995). *Cyril Burt: Fraud or Framed?* Oxford: Oxford University Press.

Manstead, A.R. and McCulloch, C. (1981). Sex-role stereotyping in British television advertisements. *British Journal of Social Psychology, 20,* 171–180.

Middlemist, D.R., Knowles, E.S. and Matter, C.F. (1976). Personal space invasions in the lavatory: suggestive evidence for arousal. *Journal of Personality and Social Psychology, 33,* 541–546.

Milgram, S. (1963). Behavioural study of obedience. *Journal of Abnormal and Social Psychology, 67,* 371–378.

Mita, T.H., Dermer, M. and Knight, J. (1977). Reversed facial images and the mere-exposure hypothesis. *Journal of Personality and Social Psychology, 35,* 597–601.

Orne, M.T. (1962). On the social psychology of the psychology experiment – with particular reference to demand characteristics and their implications. *American Psychologist, 17 (11),* 776–783.

Orne, M.T. and Scheibe, K.E. (1964). The contribution of nondeprivation factors in the production of sensory deprivation effects: The psychology of the 'panic button'. *Journal of Abnormal and Social Psychology, 68,* 3–12.

Ownsworth, T., Chambers, S., Hawkes, A., Walker, D.G. and Shum, D. (2011). Making sense of brain tumour: A qualitative investigation of personal and social processes of adjustment. *Neuropsychological Rehabilitation, 21 (1),* 117–137.

Parliamentary Office of Science and Technology (2002). Postnote: Peer Review. *September 2002, no 182*. http://www.parliament.uk/post/pn182.pdf (accessed December 2008).

Peterson, L.R. and Peterson, M.J. (1959). Short-term retention of individual verbal items. *Journal of Experimental Psychology, 58,* 193–198.

Piliavin, I.M., Rodin, J. and Piliavin, J.A. (1969). Good Samaritanism: an underground phenomenon. *Journal of Personality and Social Psychology, 13,* 1200–1213.

Popper, K.R. (1934). *The Logic of Scientific Discovery.* English translation, 1959. London: Hutchinson.

Rahe, R.H., Mahan, J. and Arthur, R. (1970). Prediction of near-future health-change from subjects' preceding life changes. *Journal of Psychosomatic Research, 14,* 401–406.

Rank, S.G. and Jacobsen, C.K. (1977). Hospital nurses' compliance with medication overdose orders: a failure to replicate. *Journal of Health and Social Behaviour, 18,* 188–193.

Reicher, S. and Stott, C. (2011). *Mad Mobs and Englishmen? Myths and Realities of the 2011 Riots.* Kindle edition: Robinson.

Regan, T. (1984). *The Case for Animal Rights.* New York: Routledge.

Roediger, H.L. and Karpicke, J.D. (2006). The power of testing memory: Basic research and implications for educational practice. *Perspectives on Psychological Science, 1,* 181–210.

Roethlisberger, F.J. and Dickson, W.J. (1939). *Management and the Worker: An Account of a Research Program Conducted by the Western Electric Company, Chicago.* Cambridge, MA: Harvard University Press.

Rosenberg, M. (1989). *Society and the Adolescent Self-Image.* Revised edition. Middletown, CT: Wesleyan University Press.

Rosenthal, R. (1966). *Experimenter effects in behaviour research.* New York: Appleton.

Rosenthal, R. and Fode, K.L. (1963). The effect of experimenter bias on the performance of the albino rat. *Behavioural Science, 8 (3),* 183–189.

Ryback, R.S. (1969). The use of the goldfish as a model for alcohol amnesia in man. *Quarterly Journal of Studies on Alcohol, 30,* 877–882.

Rymer, R. (1994). *Genie: Escape from a Silent Childhood*. London: Michael Joseph.

Samuel, J. and Bryant, P. (1984). Asking only one question in the conservation experiment. *Journal of Child Psychology and Psychiatry*, 25 (2), 315–318.

Schaffer, H.R. and Emerson, P.E. (1964). The development of social attachments in infancy. *Monographs of the Society for Research in Child Development*, 29(3 Serial No. 94), 1–77.

Schellenberg, E.G. (2004). Music lessons enhance IQ. *Psychological Science*, 15, 511–514.

Schultheiss, O.C., Wirth, M.M. and Stanton, S.J. (2004). Effects of affiliation and power motivation arousal on salivary progesterone and testosterone. *Hormones and Behaviour*, 46 (5), 592–599.

Schultz, N.R., Kaye, D.B. and Hoyer, W.J. (1980). Intelligence and spontaneous flexibility in adulthood and old age. *Intelligence*, 4, 219–231.

Schunk, D.H. (1983). Reward contingencies and the development of children's skills and self-efficacy. *Journal of Educational Psychology*, 75, 511–518.

Simons, D.J. and Chabris, C.F. (1999). Gorillas in our midst: sustained inattentional blindness for dynamic events. *Perception*, 28(9), 1059–1074.

Singer, P. (1990). *Animal Liberation*, 2nd edition. New York: Avon Books.

Singh, S. (2005). Katie Melua's bad science. http://www.guardian.co.uk/education/2005/sep/30/highereducation.uk (accessed February 2012).

Sneddon, L.U., Braithwaite, V.A., Gentle, M.J., Broughton, B. and Knight, P. (2003). Trout trauma puts anglers on the hook. *Proceedings from the Royal Society*, April 30.

Solley, C.M. and Haigh, G. (1957). A note to Santa Claus. *The Menninger Foundation*, 18, 4–5. [Cited in Stotland, S. and Zuroff, D.C. (1990). A new measure of weight locus of control: The Dieting Beliefs Scale. *Journal of Personality Assessment*, 54, 191–203].

Stroop, J.R. (1935). Studies of interference in serial verbal reactions. *Journal of Experimental Psychology*, 18, 643–662.

Treaty of Lisbon (2009). http://eur-lex.europa.eu/JOHtml.do?uri=OJ:C:2007:306:SOM:EN:HTML (accessed January 2012).

Tversky, A. and Kahneman, D. (1973). Availability: A heuristic for judging frequency and probability. *Cognitive Psychology*, 4, 207–232.

Veitch, R. and Griffitt, W. (1976). Good news, bad news: affective and interpersonal effects. *Journal of Applied Social Psychology*, 6, 69–75.

Watson, J.B. and Rayner, R. (1920). Conditioned emotional reactions. *Journal of Experimental Psychology*, 3, 1–14.

Waynforth, D. and Dunbar, R.I.M. (1995). Conditional mate choice strategies in humans – evidence from lonely-hearts advertisements. *Behaviour*, 132, 755–779.

Wearing, D. (2005). *Forever Today: A Memoir of Love and Amnesia*. London: Corgi.

Weick, K.E., Gilfillian, D.P. and Keith, T.A. (1973). The effect of composer credibility on orchestra performance. *Sociometry*, 36, 435–462.

White, G.L., Fishbein, S. and Rutstein, J. (1981). Passionate love and the misattribution of arousal. *Journal of Personality and Social Psychology*, 41, 56–62.

Widdowson, E.M. (1951). Mental contentment and physical growth. *Lancet*, 1, 1316–1318.

Zajonc, R.B. (1968). Attitudinal effects of mere exposure, *Journal of Personality and Social Psychology (Monograph)*, 9, 1–29.

Zimbardo, P.G., Banks, P.G., Haney, C. and Jaffe, D. (1973). Pirandellian prison: the mind is a formidable jailor. *New York Times Magazine*, 8 April, 38–60.

Useful websites

Psychological tests

Queendom (http://www.queendom.com/)
Claims to be the world's largest testing centre, tests and questionnaires on everything.

York University, Toronto (http://www.yorku.ca/rokada/psyctest/)
Site providing access to copywrited psychological tests that can be downloaded and used by student researchers.

Teacher resource sharing sites

Psychexchange (http://www.psychexchange.co.uk/blog/)

Psychlotron (http://www.psychlotron.org.uk)

Audio-visual

Mindchangers programme (BBC) on Hawthorne effect, excellent series on key psychological studies. Can find copy of programme at http://www.psychblog.co.uk/mind-changers-938.html

TED (http://www.ted.com/talks)
Talks by remarkable people, e.g. Robin Ince (Science Versus Wonder), Eric Mead (Power of the Placebo), Ben Goldacre (Bad Science).

Other things

Bad science blog (http://www.badscience.net/)
Ben Goldacre's blog (and book) about issues in science.

Dream analysis (http://psych.ucsc.edu/dreams/Coding/index.html)
Coding rules for the Hall/Van de Castle System of Quantitative Dream Content Analysis.

Observational studies (http://www.umchs.org/umchsresources/administration/forms/umchsforms.html#education)
Checklists, observations forms, etc.

Sense about science (http://www.senseaboutscience.org.uk/index.php/site/project/132/)
Auditing celebrities who produce bad science.

Statistical test calculation (http://www.dkstatisticalconsulting.com/statistics-resources/)
Provides Microsoft Excel templates for various statistical tests.

Take part in research (http://psych.hanover.edu/Research/exponnet.html)
Site full of links to a vast array of psychology experiments to take part in.

Teaching research and statistics (http://www.teachpsychscience.org/resource.asp?tier2=15)
Resources for teaching research and statistics in psychology.

The Complete Companions for A Level Psychology

Written by an expert team of experienced authors and editors led by **Mike Cardwell** and **Cara Flanagan**

For AQA A

The Student Books

978 019 912981 2

978 019 912984 3

The Exam Companions

978 019 912982 9

978 019 912985 0

The Mini Companions

978 019 912983 6

978 019 912986 7

The AS Visual Companion

978 185 008548 5

The Teacher's Companions

978 185 008295 8

978 185 008396 2

The AS Digital Companion

978 185 008394 8

The AS Audio Companion
CD-ROM with printable activity sheets and site licence

978 019 912972 0

For WJEC

The Student Books

978 185 008440 2

978 185 008571 3

The AS Revision Companion

978 019 913617 9

For all A Level courses

Research Methods Companion

978 019 912962 1

Order your copies now

tel 01536 452620   **email** schools.enquiries.uk@oup.com
fax 01865 313472   **web** www.oxfordsecondary.co.uk/psychology

OXFORD UNIVERSITY PRESS